HISTORY DAILY
365 FASCINATING HAPPENINGS: VOL. 1

FRANCIS CHAPPELL BLACK

History Daily: 365 Fascinating Happenings Vol. 1

First Edition Published in 2023 by Yesterday Today Publishing

Copyright (c) Francis Chappell Black

The right of Francis Chappell Black to be identified as the author of the work has been asserted by him in accordance with the Copyright, Designs, and Patents Act 1988.

All Rights Reserved. No part of this publication may be reproduced or transmitted in any form or by any means without prior permission of the copyright owner. Any person who does any unauthorized act in relation to this publication may be liable to criminal prosecution and civil claims for damages.

ISBNs:

978-0-9918558-8-9 (eBook)

978-0-9918558-6-5 (Paperback)

Contact the Author: francischappellblack@gmail.com

PREFACE

History is the exploration of the human past, as explained in written documents left behind by people. The past, with its complex choices and events, participants dead, and history recounted, is what the public understands as the permanent foundation on which historians stand.

Whether or not you like history, there's no rejecting its impact on us. But as provisioners of the past, historians comprehend that the foundation is quicksand, that pieces of each story are untold, and that what has been communicated is biased by today's conditions. While not incorrect to say that history is the study of the past, history is also the systematic study of human behavior.

History Daily: 365 Fascinating Happenings is a daily account of events that shape our world on a particular date. Our journey will include the stories that have enriched the human condition throughout all recorded history. Many of our stories will deal with unhappy events starring some of history's most unfortunate, infamous, and hopeless characters and events.

The entries included in this book encompass a full calendar year of historical stories written to inform and entertain you. I hope you will enjoy them, and if you do, please tell a friend. Or better yet, buy them

PREFACE

a copy of their own. Stay tuned as Volume 2, plus other versions of this book will be coming soon.

Unfortunately, we were required by the massive word count of this endeavor to split the publication into two volumes. In its complete form, it was simply too large for Amazon KDP or Ingram Spark to print. We decided to publish Volumes 1 and 2, each covering half of the year. We hope that you will find the results satisfactory.

Cheers,

Francis Chappell Black

HISTORY DAILY
365 FASCINATING HAPPENINGS

VOL. 1

(January 1 — June 30)

JANUARY 1
1863

On this day in history, as the third year of the civil war approached, and the carnage on the battlefield continued, American President Abraham Lincoln issued the Emancipation Proclamation. The Proclamation pronounced "that all persons held as slaves" within the rebellious states "are, and henceforward shall be free." The Proclamation also permitted formerly enslaved people to "be received into the armed service of the United States." The Proclamation affected the status of the 4 million enslaved African Americans in the secessionist Confederate states, thus freeing them.

By the close of 1862, the situation was not looking suitable for the Union. The Confederate Army had overwhelmed Union forces in major battles, and Britain and France were close to officially recognizing the Confederacy as an independent nation. In a letter to *New York Tribune* editor Horace Greeley in August 1862, Lincoln admitted, "my paramount object in this struggle is to save the Union, and it is not either to save or to destroy slavery." Lincoln's wish was that declaring a national policy of emancipation would create an urgency for the South's enslaved people to rush into the ranks of the Union army, thus depleting the Confederacy's labor pool, on which the Southern states depended to wage war against the North.

Lincoln needed a Union military success before he could unveil the proclamation. On September 22, 1862, after the Battle of Antietam, he issued a preliminary Emancipation Proclamation declaring all enslaved people free in the rebel states as of January 1, 1863. Lincoln limited the proclamation's language to slavery in states not in federal control as of 1862, failing to address the contentious issue of slavery within the nation's border states. In his attempt to appease all parties, Lincoln left many ambiguities that civil rights advocates would be forced to face in the future.

Republican abolitionists in the North were happy that Lincoln had finally pushed for the issue for which they had elected him. Though enslaved people in the South declined to rebel en masse with the proclamation's signing, they slowly began to free themselves as Union forces entered Confederate territory. By the war's end, enslaved people were leaving their former masters in droves. They fought and grew crops for the Union Army, performed other military jobs, and worked in the North's mills. Though the proclamation was not celebrated by all northerners, particularly Caucasian workers, and troops afraid of job competition from a flood of formerly enslaved people, it did have the separate benefit of convincing Britain and France to keep a wide berth from official diplomatic relations with the Confederacy.

The sweeping wording of the Emancipation Proclamation was restrictive in many ways. Freedom for enslaved people only applied to those in the secessionist Confederate states, leaving slavery untouched in loyal border states like Missouri, Kentucky, Maryland, and Delaware. Also, the promised emancipation was conditional upon a Union victory in the civil war. In addition, the Proclamation also explicitly exempted parts of the Confederate states that had already come under Union control.

President Lincoln stated that he aimed to save the Union as best he could – by preserving slavery, destroying it, or eliminating and protecting part. As president, Lincoln could not proclaim any such declaration; as commander in chief of the army and navy of the United States, he could only issue directions to the territory within his lines. Yet the Emancipation Proclamation applied only to territory outside his lines. It was asked at the time if the Proclamation had any teeth. But what ended up happening was that as the Union lines progressed into the South, the number of enslaved people freed grew with the advancement.

President Lincoln demonstrated his executive war powers by proclaiming the Emancipation Proclamation. The secessionist Confederate states employed enslaved people in all facets of their war machine except fighting. This allowed the Confederacy to commit more men to the battlefield. In a demonstration of his political genius, Lincoln masterfully justified the Emancipation Proclamation as a "Fit and necessary war measure" to nullify the effectiveness of the Confederacy's use of enslaved people in the war effort. Lincoln declared that the Proclamation would be implemented under his power as Commander-in-Chief and that the enslaved person's freedom would be maintained by the "Executive government of the United States."

The Proclamation infuriated white Southerners, who saw it as the beginning of a race war. It invigorated abolitionists and dashed the hopes of Europeans hoping to cash in by helping the Confederacy. Both free and enslaved African Americans were "over the moon" about the prospects of freedom. Many enslaved souls would run from their enslavers and get to the nearest Union line to obtain independence and join the Union Army. The Emancipation Proclamation would lead to the passing of the 13th Amendment in December of 1865, thus making slavery and involuntary servitude unconstitutional, "except as a punishment for crime."

Though the signing of the Emancipation Proclamation showed Lincoln's growing determination to conserve the Union no matter what, he still delighted in the ethical rightness of his choice. Lincoln stated on New Year's Day in 1863 that he never "felt more certain that I was doing right than I do in signing this paper." Although he dithered about slavery in the early years of his presidency, he would be remembered as "The Great Emancipator." To Confederate sympathizers, however, Lincoln's signing of the Emancipation Proclamation reinforced their view of him as a despised tyrant and ultimately motivated his assassination by John Wilkes Booth on April 14, 1865.

FRANCIS CHAPPELL BLACK

In February 1865, Lincoln told portrait painter Francis B. Carpenter that the Emancipation Proclamation was "the central act of my administration and the greatest event of the nineteenth century." It would go down in history as one of the most important documents in human freedom.

JANUARY 2
1865

On this day in history, in Virginia City, Montana, welterweight Con Orem and heavyweight Hugh O'Neill brawled for 185 rounds in a highly contested bare-knuckle boxing match. By far one of the most prolonged bouts ever to have taken place in boxing history, the fighters, with hometown hero and Ohio-born native Con Orem, the declared underdog from the onset, battled the taller and heavier O'Neill for $1000 in purse money.

Five days later, the Montana Post dedicated its entire front page to the great fight between Orem and O'Neill. The article was written by the Post's editor Thomas Dimsdale, who was friends with John Condle Orem, or, as he is generally termed, Con Orem, who was born in 1835 in Carroll County, Ohio, and was a blacksmith by trade. Dimsdale was effusive in his praise of Orem. He told the reader that Orem had spent much time in the Rocky Mountains, buffalo hunting and shooting game. As a result, he became quite proficient with a rifle and bowie knife and had many hand-to-hand encounters with "Old Bruin."

Having begun his fighting career in 1861, he had become a veteran of many fights, including a loss to pugilist Owen Geohegan, though Dimsdale felt that the result of the fight was more than crooked. Dimsdale relates, "After 19 rounds, in 23 minutes, the mob broke up the fight on the pretense of a foul, the referee, with a revolver looking into his ear, deciding against Orem."

Dimsdale tells us far less about the challenger, an Irish miner named Hugh O'Neill. He says that O'Neill "more than once settled the pretensions of some tough customers in the outside world in a style which boded no good easy times for any future opponent." It seems that Dimsdale liked rooting for the underdog. Hugh O'Neill had 53 pounds and 2 inches on Con Orem.

O'Neill, the Irishman, wore green shorts with the old Harp and stars with his name embroidered in full. Orem wore the stars and stripes with an eagle on his trunks and bore the motto "May the best man win." Orem stood 5'6 ½" and weighed in at 137 lbs. O'Neill stood 5'9" and weighed 190 pounds.

"At 20 minutes to 2 o'clock, time was called, and quickly, each man toed the scratch and began." The first round was short and lively. Both fighters took rights to the ribcages and struggled for a while, then both fell.

Under London Prize Fight Rules, the round ended when somebody was on the ground. And because no one seemed to mind if a fighter went down to rest, a round might end in seconds or go on indefinitely. The fight would end when one man – or both – could no longer continue.

Things started to get going in the third round. O'Neill knocked Orem down. Loud cheers from O'Neill's friends and offers of three to one, in the hundreds against Orem. By the seventeenth round, both fighters were quite bloodied as they traded punches, gouges, and headbutts. O'Neill knocked Orem down a lot, but the latter always got up. Throughout the fight, Con would utilize going down quite a bit to maintain his stamina and prolong the fight, much to O'Neill's growing agitation.

By the 126th round, O'Neill's left eye was closing, "nothing but misses registered; Orem slipped down." By the 137th round, O'Neill was "failing." By the 168th, Orem was "getting faint." But neither man would concede.

Finally, after O'Neill dominated the 180th through the 185th rounds but didn't have enough left in the tank to put Orem down, the men attending to the fighters had enough. The referee ordered the backers of both fighters to sort things out. From all that, Dimsdale tells us, the fight had lasted for 185 minutes without ceasing.

Happily, for all involved, it was decided to call the match a draw. All Bets were off, and wagers were returned. Purse money for the fighters was divided. The brass band hired to entertain the crowd struck up a lively tune. Everyone was happy except the two men who had endured 185 rounds without a winner.

Con Orem seems to have come out of the match ok. An ad in the following week's Montana Post reminded residents of Virginia City that Orem, owner of the Champion Saloon, was offering "private lessons in boxing and sparring once a week." Hugh O'Neill was not as fortunate. A notice in the same issue announced that his friends were planning a benefit in his honor. They were determined to make up for him a sum sufficient to leave him on the sunny side of "square" instead of in debt.

Montana Post editor Thomas Dimsdale took the time and effort to report on each round of the fight, but he should have reported on the one detail that matters most to history: the time the contest ended. Bare-knuckle fights were ranked not by the number of rounds but by duration. Dimsdale wrote that Con Orem withstood 185 rounds in 185 minutes. This is a stretch of the imagination on the editor's part. In the decades after the match, the legend grew as these things are bound to do. Some observers stated that the fight never ended until after midnight. Some have observed that the best guess is that the fight did not last 3 hours and 5 minutes, but more likely, it lasted around 5 hours and 30 minutes. If this was the case, Hugh O'Neill and Con Orem set the American record for a fight duration – unless that record belongs to J. Fitzpatrick and James O'Neil, who fought for 4 hours and 20 minutes in Berwick, Maine, in 1860.

JANUARY 3
1920

On this day in history, Boston Red Sox owner and theatrical Producer Harry Frazee made the most regrettable decision to sell pitcher, slugger, and future Hall of Famer Babe Ruth to the New York Yankees for the sum of $125,000 in cash and a $350,000 loan. This would begin the 86-year championship drought for Major League Baseball's (MLB) Red Sox emanating from what would popularly be called the "Curse of the Bambino."

Preceding the beginning of the drought after the World Series won in 1918, the Red Sox were the most successful professional baseball team. Until then, the Red Sox had won five of the first 15 World Series titles in Major League baseball history. Babe Ruth was a member of three of those winning championship teams. Primarily a pitcher at the time, Ruth was the winning pitcher in two of the six games in the 1918 World Series, giving him the self-assurance to report late to Spring Training in 1919, demanding a huge pay raise from owner Harry Frazee and the Red Sox.

Ruth was the beneficiary of a new three-year contract worth $27,000. In the 1919 MLB season, Boston only managed a sixth-place finish in the standings. Despite the results, Ruth, knowing that he was the most popular player in baseball, demanded that his salary be doubled, contract notwithstanding.

Frazee, the theatrical producer, and director who had purchased the Red Sox and Fenway Park, the Red Sox's famed stadium in 1916 using copious amounts of credit, also needed money to produce a proposed Broadway musical called No, No, Nanette. With all those financial strains, Frazee agreed to sell the rights to Ruth to the Yankees, who had never played in the World Series by that point.

Ruth was not in Boston when the deal was reached – he was in California. As Yankees owners Jacob Ruppert and Tillinghast Huston discussed terms with Frazee, they sent manager Miller Huggins to Los Angeles to speak to Ruth. After some initial obstacles, Huggins finally found the slugger on a golf course. Ruth originally wanted an extraordinary $20,000 salary and a part of Ruppert's cash payment to Frazee. Huggins ultimately talked Ruth into $10,000 and $21,000 more in bonuses for the 1920 and 1921 seasons.

When the sale of Babe Ruth was finally announced to the press on January 5, 1920 – 11 days after it was first negotiated – the reaction was a mix of depression in Boston and enthusiasm in New York. But it also prompted early clues of the public's fascination toward sharply climbing player salaries – an issue that would characterize labor negotiations in baseball for many decades. In a January 7 editorial, The New York Times wrote:

"Neither club can be blamed for its part in this affair; but it marks another long step toward the concentration of baseball-playing talent in the largest cities, which can afford to pay the highest prices for it. That is a bad thing for the game; and it is still worse to give a valuable player stranded on a weak club the idea that if he holds out for an imposing salary, he can get somebody in New York or Chicago to pay for his services."

Frazee did his best to tone down the effects of the sale, labeling Ruth as "selfish" to the press and saying the Yankees were "taking a gamble." But while the Yankees ended up paying nearly half a million dollars for the slugger (considering the sum of the original sale, the money loan to Frazee, Ruth's yearly salary, and his ensuing bonuses), the imminent World Series championships and prestige to come makes it reasonable to say in retrospection that the "gamble" paid off.

With Ruth, who now was a position player with immense batting capabilities, the Yankees would win four World Series titles. Over the course of the 20th century, the Yankees would win the World Series 22 times, while the Red Sox, in the 86 years after Ruth was dealt to the Yankees, only managed to get to the World Series four times, losing all in the seventh games. With the unfortunate loss to the New York Mets in the 1986 finale, the Red Sox were branded with the official "Curse of the Bambino" stamp.

Red Sox fans tried everything to put an end to the curse. They spray-painted a "Reverse Curve" street sign to read "Reverse the Curse. They tried to find a piano. Ruth was said to have thrown it in a pond in 1918. They even, incredibly enough, staged an exorcism outside Fenway Park in a bid to have the curse overturned.

But only in 2004 would the Red Sox go on to defeat the Yankees in the AL Championship Series after falling behind three games to nil and ultimately win a berth in the World Series. In the World Series, the Red Sox would defeat the St. Louis Cardinals in 4 straight games to win their first World Series in 86 years, thus ending the "Curse of the Bambino."

JANUARY 4
1969

On this day in history, conjoined twins Daisy and Violet Hilton died in Charlotte, North Carolina, due to the Hong Kong flu. Born on February 5, 1908, in Brighton, England, to an unmarried barmaid named Kate Skinner, the twins were born joined at the hips and buttocks; they shared blood circulation and were connected at the pelvis, but they shared no major organs. It was feared by the doctor who delivered them that they would not survive a month. The doctor also believed separating the twins would cause one or both to die.

Daisy and Violet's mother felt that her children's condition was payback for her having had premarital sex. At the time, children with congenital disabilities in England were referred to as "monsters." The twin's mother, Kate Skinner, felt overwhelmed by the situation and could not see a path forward with disabled children. Her employer, Mary Hilton, who assisted with the childbirth, saw an opportunity to make money, so she purchased the children from their mother.

So began a life of exploitation at the girl's expense. First, they were put on display at the Queen's Arm pub in Brighton where, for a fee, patrons could view one of nature's oddities. In their memoir, the sisters wrote, "Our earliest and only recollections are the penetrating smell of brown ale, cigars, and pipes and the movements of the visitors' hands which were forever lifting our baby clothes to see just how we were attached to each other." By the age of three, they toured throughout England in 1911. Then Mary Hilton. With her husband and daughter, they then took the girls to Germany and Australia. By 1916 they were all touring in the United States. In 1926, Bob Hope formed an act with the twins called the Dancemedians, who performed a tap-dancing routine. They became so successful in the 1920s that, at one point, they were making $5000 per week.

Made to call Mary Hilton "Auntie" and her husband (or any other man she was with) "Sir," the children's sole purpose was to make money for their handlers. They were struck and beaten if they did not do as they were told. In their memoirs in the 1950s, they stated, "When we displeased her, she whipped our backs and shoulders with the buckle end of a belt." When Mary Hilton died in Alabama, the girls were bequeathed to Mary's daughter Edith Meyers and her husband, Myer Meyers.

The Meyers were harsher than Mary Hilton. The girls were never given proper schooling and were taught to become proficient at the saxophone and violin. The Meyers threatened to institutionalize the sisters if they failed to comply or tried to leave. Despite their significant earnings, the girls never saw a penny of it.

The famed illusionist, Harry Houdini, took an interest in the sisters and advised them to research how popular they had become. The girls had never known about their celebrity, so they hired a lawyer, Martin Arnold, who helped unshackle the 21-year-old sisters from the Meyer's. Daisy and Violet received emancipation in 1931 and were awarded $100,000 in damages.

Emancipation opened a whole new world for Daisy and Violet. This included the possibility of romance and sex. And if one sister took a lover to bed, the other sister was right by her side. How was this situation handled? Violet stated, "Why, I just turn over and read a book and eat an apple."

The sisters went into vaudeville as "The Hilton Sisters' Revue." Daisy would dye her hair blond and wear different clothes to stand out from her sister Violet. In 1932 they appeared in Todd Browning's movie Freaks. Afterward, as their popularity faded, it became more and more challenging to make a living. In the late 1930s, the sisters each married gay men, most likely as a publicity stunt. Daisy even gave birth to a child, but the infant was given up for adoption. In 1952 they starred in an exploitation movie based on their lives. In conjunction with this movie, Daisy and Violet undertook personal appearances at screenings of both their films.

The sisters gave their last public appearance at a drive-in in 1961 in Charlotte, North Carolina. Their manager deserted them there, and with no means of transportation or money, the sisters were forced to work at a nearby grocery store, where they would world for the rest of their lives. The store manager even redesigned one of the counters so they could work together.

On January 4, 1969, after they did not show up for work, their worried boss called the police. Daisy and Violet were found dead in their home, victims of the Hong Kong Flu. Autopsies were performed, and it was stated that Daisy was the first to die and Violet a few days later. Authorities believe Violet had been too ill to call for help. The women were 60 years old.

JANUARY 5
1930

On this date in history, one of crime's most prolific duos met for the first time in Dallas, Texas. Bonnie Parker and Clyde Barrow would form a partnership that would wreak havoc over the central and southern United States for 21 months from 1932 to 1934 during what was known as the "public enemy era."

Clyde Barrow led a gang of criminals, better known as the Barrow gang, on an intense crime spree between 1932 and 1934, while Bonnie Parker was his girlfriend. Barrow and Parker's lives came to a sudden, if not expected end in a hail of police bullets on May 23, 1934, in Bienville Parish, Louisiana, after a large posse of Texas law enforcement officers and FBI ambushed the couple on the side of the road.

When Bonnie met Clyde on January 5, 1930, she was a 19-year-old Dallas waitress who was recently unemployed. Clyde Barrow was 20 years old and recently paroled from prison for several offenses related to robbery, safe-cracking, and car theft. He escaped from the prison shortly after his reincarceration using a weapon Bonnie had smuggled into him. He was recaptured soon after that and sent back to prison.

Associates and immediate family members stated that prison had profoundly affected the young budding criminal. He had been bullied and raped mercilessly by a fellow inmate. So terrible was the torture he endured that Barrow killed the perpetrator with a metal pipe to the head. A fellow inmate serving a life sentence took the wrap for Barrow, thus saving him from a life sentence. The whole experience turned Barrow, in the words of fellow inmate Ralph Fults, "from a schoolboy to a rattlesnake."

When they met that fateful January day in 1930, Parker was still married to an imprisoned murderer whom she had married when she was 16 years old in 1926. They met at the home of their mutual friend Clarence Clay at 105 Herbert Street in Dallas. Bonnie was in the kitchen making hot chocolate for a female friend who had recently broken her arm. When Clyde and Barrow met, it was "love at first sight."

And the rest, as they say, is history. The love between the two was unwavering and would last to their dying day. They would begin a felonious crime spree that would see Clyde commit 13 murders, robberies, and burglaries. Many newspapers portrayed Bonnie Parker as a "gun-toting cigar-smoking moll," but nothing could be further from the truth. She often stayed in the car during heists and never used a gun. She constantly encouraged Barrow to "kidnap and release" people instead of killing them. Those photos with her holding a gun on Clyde with a cigar in her mouth were staged. She went on the run with Clyde Barrow because she loved him, not because she was inclined to be a hard-hearted criminal like her mate.

In the end, their story gripped a nation, and they became romantic heroes rather than villains, with thousands of people watching their every move. Their deaths would ultimately mark the end of the "public enemy era" in the United States.

(Photo: With a shotgun, Bonnie reaches for a pistol in Clyde's waistband. May 1934, Wikimedia Commons.)

JANUARY 6
1941

On January 6, 1941, American President Franklin Delano Roosevelt delivered his celebrated "Four Freedoms" speech to Congress on this day. With time it came to be deemed so significant that a plaque commemorating it hangs inside the Statue of Liberty, and murals showing the Four Freedoms appear in public buildings across the U.S.

Technically, it was the 1941 State of the Union address, but it is now remembered as the Four Freedoms speech. Roosevelt stated that:

> "In the future days, which we seek to make secure, we look forward to a world founded upon four essential human freedoms.
>
> The first is freedom of speech and expression – everywhere in the world.
>
> The second is the freedom of every person to worship God in his own way – everywhere in the world.
>
> The third is the freedom from want – which, translated into world terms, means economic.
>
> Understandings that will secure to every nation a healthy peacetime life for its inhabitants – everywhere in the world.
>
> The fourth is freedom from fear – which, translated into world terms, means a world-wide reduction of armaments to such a point

and ins such a thorough fashion that no nation will be able to commit an act of physical aggression against any neighbor – anywhere in the world.

That is no vision of a distant millennium. It is a definite basis for a kind of world attainable in our own time and generation. That kind of world is the very antithesis of the so-called new order of tyranny which the dictators seek to create with the crash of a bomb.

— *Franklin D. Roosevelt, excerpted from the State of the Union Address to the Congress, January 6, 1941*

The declaration of the Four Freedoms as a defense for war would resonate throughout the rest of the war. The Freedoms became the core of America's war aims and the center of all efforts to unite public support for the war. With the formation of the Office of War Information (1942), the Freedoms were marketed as values essential to American life and examples of American exceptionalism.

The Four Freedoms Speech was admired, and the aspirations were significant in postwar politics. However, in 1941 the speech received intense condemnation from anti-war factions. Opponents reasoned that the Four Freedoms were merely a covenant for Roosevelt's New Deal, social reforms that had already generated deep partitions within Congress. Conservatives who resisted social programs and added government interference fought against Roosevelt's effort to defend and portray the war as crucial for protecting grandiose goals.

While the Freedoms did become a potent quality of American thinking on the war, they were never the absolute validation for the war. Polls and inquiries conducted by the United States Office of War Information (OWI) revealed that self-preservation and retribution for the attack on Pearl Harbor were still the most prevailing reasons for war.

Roosevelt hoped to provide a rationale for why America should abandon the isolationist policies that emerged from World War 1. Of isolationism, Roosevelt stated: "No realistic American can expect from a dictator's peace international generosity, or return of true independence, or world disarmament, or freedom of expression, or freedom of religion – or even good business. Such a peace would bring no security for us or our neighbors. Those, who would give up essential liberty to purchase a little temporary safety, deserve neither liberty nor safety."

The President was speaking as Hitler was attempting to overtake the world and at a time when America was deeply committed to isolationism, as most citizens of the U.S. were quite anxious to avoid becoming entangled in another war. But the President warned, "The future and safety of our country and of our democracy are overwhelmingly involved in events far beyond our borders."

The "Four Freedoms" speech also coincided with the beginnings of the Lend-Lease Act, which promoted Roosevelt's plan to become the "arsenal of democracy" and support the Allied cause with as many supplies and war materials as possible. It should also be noted that the speech also created the ideological basis for America's involvement in World War 2, "all framed in terms of individual rights and liberties that are the hallmark of American politics."

Franklin Roosevelt died on April 12, 1945, never having seen the defeat of Nazi Germany or the realization of his "Four Freedoms" dream. Yet later that same year, the United Nations was created, and with it, a Commission on Human Rights headed up by Eleanor Roosevelt, the President's widow.

On December 10, 1948, the United Nations created the Universal Declaration of Human Rights. The Declaration and the subsequent system that grew out of it were deeply impacted by Roosevelt's "Four Freedoms."

JANUARY 7
1970

On this date in history, a farmer in Bethel, New York, sued fellow farmer Max Yasgur, who rented out his farm for the Woodstock Music and Art Festival, for $35,000 for damage to their properties caused by the 500,000 hippies who attended the festival.

Woodstock's organizers were having great difficulties finding a location in Wallkill, N.Y., about 30 miles from the town of Woodstock, to hold their music festival. Place after place was turning them down. Eventually, their search led them to nearby Bethel, where a local real estate agent put them in touch with a local dairy farmer named Max Yasgur.

Yasgur and the organizers agreed to lease a 600-acre field for $75,000. Yasgur was a pro-Vietnam political conservative who supported free speech and expression, even if it differed from his own. Yasgur once told the New York Times, "If the generation gap is to be closed, we older people have to do more than we have done." Yasgur addressed the town council and told them that despite agreeing with them that the hippie lifestyle, which included heavy drug use and anti-war slogans, was not ideal, he stated that "Tens of thousands of Americans in uniform gave their lives in war after war just so these kids would have the freedom to do exactly what they are doing. That's what this country is all about, and I am not going to let you throw them out of our town just because you don't like their dress or their hair or the way they live or what they believe. This is America, and they are going to have their festival."

So, on August 15, 1969, the festival billed as "An Aquarian Exposition: 3 Days of Peace and Music" kicked off.

Yasgur's decision to lease land for a gathering of long-haired hippies was not popular in Bethel. He was given the cold shoulder, threatened with arson, had his dairy products boycotted, and threatened with physical harm. This only worked to steel the farmers' resolve.

During the festival, Yasgur, who by that time had become a folk hero to those assembled, told the audience, "You've proven to the world that a half a million kids – and I call you kids because I have children that are older than you – a half million young people can get together and have three days of fun and music and have nothing but fun and music, and God bless you for it!"

Yasgur's neighbors turned against him soon after the festival. One neighbor would sue him on January 7, 1970, for $35,000, stating that concertgoers "used their property as a site of shelter and defecation and left their property strewn with refuse." Yasgur suffered severe property damage and a loss of resources when the farmer gave away water, milk, and milk products after some people in Bethel had started charging concertgoers for water.

Yasgur always maintained that he never regretted letting the festival happen, and he later received $50,000 from the concert organizers to help mitigate the damage to his property. The farmer refused any further attempts for a Woodstock revival, and he finally sold the farm in 1971 and moved to Florida. In 1973 Max Yasgur died of a heart attack and was buried in New York State. *Rolling Stone* magazine paid tribute to Yasgur with a full-page obituary – something quite remarkable for a non-musician.

(Photo: An advertisement poster for the Woodstock Festival, 1969. Wikimedia Commons.)

JANUARY 8
1790

On this day in history, United States President George Washington conveyed to Congress the first State of the Union address in American history. The speech was given in the Senate Chamber of Federal Hall in New York City. His address touched upon defense, foreign policy, economics, education, and immigration-related topics to those gathered. Everything from his choice of clothing, who was standing beside him, to the very way he delivered his speech was scrutinized. Despite the apparent importance placed on this speech, it was the shortest State of the Union Address given up to this day, at only 1,089 words.

Part of the U.S. Constitution, Article II, Section 3, Clause 1, states that the president "shall from time to time give to the Congress Information of the State of the Union and recommend to their Consideration such Measures as he shall judge necessary and expedient."

While the State of the Union address is a routine and expected part of presidencies today, they were a big deal at the time. The Constitution was still relatively new, and the government and citizens were still learning how to live by it. So, by delivering this speech, President Washington was satisfying one of the requirements of his job and setting an example for Americans and future presidents alike.

Washington did not go into a great deal of detail. He told those gathered that there would be challenges that the new country would face, and he spoke of what he expected of the future. He stated, with regards to security, that "To be prepared for war is one of the most effectual means of preserving peace." This was Washington's way of telling his country that they needed to create an army and gather the resources to maintain it. He felt that creating an army should be done immediately.

He went on to say that the President should deal with foreign policy. Immigration and the need to bring in new citizens was discussed. He also stated that citizens would be needed to participate in the country's government. Washington then began to speak of the everyday lives of the citizens. He said that "the advancement of agriculture, commerce, manufactures…the promotion of science and literature. Knowledge is in every country the surest basis of public happiness," in hopes of motivating the citizens to seize upon these "fields of knowledge in order to better the country." He told everyone that attaining knowledge was needed to "know and to value their own right; to discern and provide against invasions of them etc.…" Finally, he also spoke of the duty the Houses owed the country and the cooperation needed for the future. Washington stated there was a "great satisfaction from a cooperation with you in the pleasing though arduous task of ensuring to our fellow citizens the blessings which they have a right to expect from a free, efficient, and equal government."

JANUARY 9
1570

On this day in history, Czar Ivan IV (The Terrible) ordered his personal army, the *oprichniki*, to massacre the inhabitants of the Russian city of Novgorod. Once a robust and independent city-state, the city was now part of Ivan the Terrible's Russia. Although initially an act of retribution against the imagined betrayal of the local Orthodox church, the massacre of Novgorod soon became the most brutal and heinous act in the history of the *oprichniki*, with victims numbering between 2000 and 20,000, not to mention countless acts of highly extreme, violent cruelty.

Ivan The Terrible was a brutal autocrat, likely paranoid and mentally unstable. He had been suspicious of Novgorod since he killed his cousin, Prince Vladimir Andreyevich, and his family claiming treason and betrayal. It was no coincidence that Novgorod still contained several of his late cousin Vladimir's supporters and retainers.

It was also wrongly feared that the once powerful city-state was looking to ally itself with and defect to Poland. This was something Ivan could not allow. Czar Ivan IV feared the Polish King, who had ruled most of Eastern Europe by this time. At one point in the past, a town had rebelled against Ivan's rule and had allowed the Poles to take possession. Ivan was able to retake the city but never forgot the deception of the inhabitants. He may have feared that the same was going to happen with Novgorod.

Ivan and his army of *oprichniki* advanced upon the city during winter. Having survived several famines over the previous few years, Novgorod put up little struggle when Ivan and his forces attacked the city. For over a month, the *oprichniki* murdered, raped, raped, tortured, and robbed the city's citizens. Even the religious orders and their churches were pillaged. Monks and priests were killed in their churches and monasteries with abandon.

Nothing seemed off limits for the Czar's army to destroy and kill. Merchants and traders were killed for their goods. Ivan had many alleged conspirators tried and brutally executed. A common punishment was to throw citizens into an icy river under the ice, and if anybody made it to shore, they were promptly killed. Cold, hunger, and disease also killed hundreds of families, evicted, and exiled from the city and surrounding villages.

Ivan's attack on Novgorod contributed significantly to the decline of the once-great city. After the attack, most citizens fled further persecution at the hands of their ruler, or died from increasingly damning conditions exacerbated by high taxes and food shortages (and of the epidemics that tend to accompany poor living conditions) that followed the departure of the *oprichniki*.

As part of his attack on the city, Ivan burned the fields, laying waste to roughly 90 percent of the arable land around Novgorod. Coupled with the previous years' crop failures, this would create a massive food shortage. With the loss of most of its production capacity and with the economy in tatters, Novgorod, a city that, until Ivan IV, rivaled Moscow as the seat of power in Russia, lost its political standing, and the Novgorod Republic officially became a thing of the past.

(Photo: Portrait of Ivan IV by Viktor Vasnetsov, 1897. Wikimedia Commons)

JANUARY 10
49 BCE

On this day in history, Julius Caesar crossed the Rubicon River in Northern Italy and set off a civil war in the Roman Republic. There had been many civil wars over the previous century in the Roman Republic, yet the one begun by Julius Caesar would alter Roman history forever. On January 10, 49 BCE, Caesar led a single legion, Legio XIII, south over the Rubicon River from Cisalpine Gaul to Italy to venture to Rome. In doing so, he automatically broke the law on *imperium* (roughly "right to command"), thus making him no longer legally allowed to command his troops, making armed conflict with Rome inevitable. This action would ultimately lead to Caesar becoming dictator for life (dictator perpetuo).

Bringing an army into Italy past the Rubicon River was illegal. Crossing the river amounted to insurrection, treason, and a declaration of war on the state. Caesar had gone against the Roman Senate and conquered Gaul. He would enamor himself to his troops even further by paying them directly and sharing in the booty. This was now Caesar's army, not Rome's.

According to Roman historian Suetonius, Julius Caesar was undecided when he approached the Rubicon and attributed the crossing to a "supernatural apparition." Upon crossing the Rubicon, Caesar, according to Suetonius, apparently quoted the Athenian playwright Meander, in Greek, "*alea iacta esto,*" let the die be cast. It was stated that Caesar dined with Sallust, Hirtius, Oppious, Lucius Balbus, and Sulpicus Rufus the night after his famous crossing into Italy.

When word reached the Roman Senate that Caesar had crossed the Rubicon, they were beside themselves with anger and fear. The Senate had no army with which to defend itself in Rome, and within weeks Caesar had occupied the city and Italy. Under the leadership of Pompey the Great, the senators gathered an army in the Balkans. Caesar went into the Balkans and decimated Pompey's army. Yet the civil war was far from over. Soon there were anti-Caesarian revolts all over the Empire. Even with the assassination of Pompey, the uprisings continued. After a moderate amount of time, Caesar quelled the rebellions and Caesar went on to make himself dictator of Rome.

Despite having the love and admiration of the public, the elites had grown to hate their new leader. In 44 BCE, a group of Senators conspired, and Caesar was assassinated as he entered the Roman Senate House. Once again, a civil war started between Mark Antony and Octavian (grand nephew of Caesar), with the latter being victorious. Later Octavian became Augustus, the de-facto first Emperor of Rome. When Caesar crossed the Rubicon River, he started a chain of events that led to the fall of the Roman Republic and the creation of an Imperial system in Rome.

The phrase "crossing the Rubicon" has survived to this day and refers to anyone or group which commits itself irrevocably to a difficult or extreme course of action, like the modern phrase "passing the point of no return." Caesar's decision for swift action forced changes in the very fabric of Roman society, changes which altered the course of world history.

JANUARY 11
1569

On this day in history, England's first national state lottery took place. The lottery was a way to raise funds for government use and has existed since the Chinese Han Dynasty used lotteries (keno) between 205 and 187 BC to raise funds for the construction of the Great Wall. During the reign of Augustus, the Roman Empire was responsible for repairs to the City of Rome. Even the Bible mentions a form of lottery system used by Moses in Numbers 26. Lotteries became more popular in medieval Europe, where they were sometimes used to raise funds for public welfare projects.

England's ports in the 1560s were in dire need of refreshment and refurbishment. The only way to pay for the many repairs needed to England's numerous ports was to raise taxes, a move Parliament refused to consider. Loans on the Antwerp money market were costly, and any surplus funds from Queen Elizabeth's personal income were nonexistent as she routinely overspent. So, the Queen's principal secretary of state, Sir William Cecil, a master manipulator, managed to get Elizabeth to agree to a lottery scheme which, if all went well (and it didn't), the needed funds for the ports would be raised.

In August 1567, a Royal Proclamation was published, heralded as "A VERY RICH LOTTERIE GENERALL WITHOUT ANY BLANCK-

ES." The proceeds were for "the reparation of the havens (harbors) and the strength of the realme and towards such other publique good works." Posters advertising the lottery were five feet high and twenty inches wide, showing the ticket prices and the prizes. The signs were prominently displayed on walls and doors throughout the City of London.

Yet the lottery was unpopular; the public simply did not trust it. Cecil had hoped to sell 400,000 tickets at 10 shillings a piece to yield a net profit of £100,000 for harbor repairs. Cecil planned to give nearly 30,000 prizes of a total value of about £55,000, returning to each of the 370,000 unlucky players half a crown, or twenty-five percent of their original bet. The first prize was £5,000 (a tidy £100,000 in today's money) split £3,000 in cash, £700 in gold and silver plate, and the remainder in good tapestry and the highest quality linen. The second prize was £3500 (£70,000 today) divided into £2,000 in money, £600 in plate, and the rest in tapestry and linen. There were eleven more exclusive prizes in declining value to £140 and then various from £100 to 14 shillings.

Another incentive offered was freedom from arrest for a seven-day period for criminals coming into the larger towns to purchase tickets. However, those charged with major crimes such as murder, treason, or piracy were not eligible. Guaranteed safe conduct may have been the theory, but it did not work in practice. A State official called I. Aldaye wrote to Cecil on April 30, 1569, stating, "A prisoner in the Counter (one of five prisons in Southwark) for debt. Thought he should have been protected under the Proclamation of the Lottery, but it was made jest of."

Tickets went on sale in August 1567, with the original date being June 25, 1568. Several times the draw had to be postponed due to low sales. In the end, fewer than 34,000 tickets were sold, so the prizes given had to be reduced to one-twelfth of the original total. The first prize winner could now expect to take home only £416, 13s, and 4d (being a twelfth of the £5000 top prize). History does not record who held the winning ticket in this lottery debacle. The only one to have benefitted from the lottery was the Queen herself. She is said to have taken much of the prize money for her own use shortly before the draw. As she always found it difficult to live within her means, people tended to believe this story.

As for rebuilding the nation's ports, an emergency twelve-month loan had to be raised from London merchants via the Privy Council. Future repairs had to be financed through different modes of taxation, such as the charging of two shillings and sixpence for all new licenses for the nation's taverns.

For the remainder of Queen Elizabeth's reign, lotteries remained out of fashion.

JANUARY 12
1956

On this day in history, the FBI arrested six Great Brink's robbery gang members six days before the statute of limitations on the crime expired. One criminal gang member felt that he was being stiffed out of his share of the loot and turned State's evidence for a reduced sentence. Thus 10 of the 11 original robbers would end up behind bars. The armed robbery occurred on January 17, 1950, at the Brink's building at the corner of Prince St. and Commercial St. in the North End of Boston, Massachusetts.

Dubbed the "Crime of the Century," it was the largest heist up to that date, with $1.2 million in cash and $1.5 million in checks, money orders, and securities taken by the criminals. Donning masks and chauffeur hats, they held up 5 Brink's employees at gunpoint and perfectly executed their well-rehearsed plan.

Their planning had been meticulous. They had staked out the Brink's building for a year to observe the employee's daily routine from a building across the street. They also managed to remove and make copies of the keys by a locksmith from the lock cylinders in the many doors necessary to access the building and its rooms. Members of the gang (of which there were 11) went into the building several times after hours to get a sense of the layout and practice their planned entrance and escape. The gang even broke into the alarm company in Boston to look over the plans for the security system inside the Brinks building.

Just after 7:00 p.m., on January 17, 1950, well-known security firm Brinks, Inc., in Boston, Massachusetts, were shutting down operations for the day, returning bags of undelivered cash, checks, and other stuff to the company safe on the second floor of the Brink's building at the corner of Prince St. and Commercial St. in the North End of Boston, Massachusetts.

Shortly before 7:30 p.m., they were shocked by five men—heavily disguised, hushed, wearing gloves to prevent leaving fingerprints and soft shoes to mute noise. The thieves quickly tied up the employees and began transporting away the money.

Within minutes, they'd stolen more than $1.2 million in cash and another $1.5 million in checks and other securities, making it the biggest heist in America at the time.

As the robbers left the scene, a Brink's worker called the Boston Police Department. Moments later, police arrived at the Brink's building, and special agents of the FBI rapidly entered the investigation.

From the beginning, there was little to go on for the investigators. Police learned that between five and seven robbers had entered the building. All of them wore Navy-type peacoats, gloves, and chauffeur's caps. Each robber's face was hidden behind a mask. Some gang members wore crepe-soled shoes to quiet their footsteps, while others wore rubbers.

The robbers talked very little. They moved with precision which suggested the crime had been thoroughly planned. The criminals managed to open at least four locked doors to gain entry to the second floor, where the five employees were securing the money collected from Brink's customers that day.

All five employees had been required to lie face down on the floor at gunpoint. Their hands were tied behind their backs, and adhesive tape was placed over their mouths.

A buzzer sounded as the money was being put in bags and piled between the second and third doors leading to the Prince Street entrance. The robbers removed the adhesive tape from the mouth of one employee and learned that the buzzer meant that someone wanted to enter the vault area. The person ringing the buzzer was a garage attendant. Two gang members moved toward the door to seize him; seeing the garage attendant walk away, apparently unaware that a robbery was being committed, they did not follow him.

The FBI and the Boston police had very little evidence to go on – a piece of rope and a chauffeur's hat, and a witness who observed the getaway vehicle. The truck that the robbers had used was chopped up in pieces in Stoughton, Massachusetts, near one of the gang member's homes, Joseph O'Keefe. By June 1950, various gang members began getting arrested for other crimes. Joseph O'Keefe and Staley Gusciora were arrested in Pennsylvania for a burglary. O'Keefe was sentenced to 3 years and Gusciora to 5-to-20 at Western State Penitentiary in Pittsburgh. Police had heard through their informants that the two were pressuring other gang members for money to fight their convictions. It was later maintained that the bulk of O'Keefe's share went to his legal defense.

FBI agents tried to turn O'Keefe and Gusciora on the rest of the gang, but they were unsuccessful. The Federal force, by this time, knew who the players were in the robbery but just lacked the evidence to make any arrests. After O'Keefe was released from prison, he was again arrested for burglary. He was released on a $17,000 bail. O'Keefe stated that he never saw his share of the robbery after he gave it to another gang member to hold, so since he needed money, he kidnapped a different gang member and demanded his portion of the loot for ransom.

A small ransom was paid, but it was decided that O'Keefe needed to be eliminated. An underworld hitman, Elmer "Trigger" Burke, was hired to kill O'Keefe. Burke traveled to Boston and shot O'Keefe but failed to kill him. While he was in the hospital, O'Keefe was again approached by the FBI, and this time, on January 6, 1956, he decided to spill the beans on his co-conspirators.

Ten of the eleven gang members were arrested and charged. The eleventh was already dead. Eight of the men received life sentences and would be paroled by 1971, except for the leader of the gang, "Big Joe" McGinnis, who died in prison. O'Keefe was sentenced to four years and was paroled in 1960. Only $58,000 of the $2,7 million stolen was ever recovered.

JANUARY 13
2022

On this day in history, California Governor Gavin Newsom denied the release of Robert F. Kennedy's assassin Sirhan Sirhan after 53 years in prison. This was Sirhan's 16th attempt at parole for the June 5, 1968, assassination of the presidential hopeful at the Ambassador Hotel in Los Angeles. That evening, Kennedy had secured the critical Democratic presidential nomination by winning the state of California in the primary. Sirhan was initially sentenced to death on May 22, 1969, yet that sentence was commuted to life when the California Supreme Court paused capital punishment in 1971.

Governor Newsom would explain in a nine-page decision why he disagreed with the state parole board who had recommended that Sirhan be released. The Governor stated that even though Sirhan was 77 years old, he felt he still posed a significant risk to the public primarily because he refused to accept full responsibility for killing Kennedy.

"Mr. Sirhan's implausible and unsupported denials of responsibility and lack of credibility elevate his current risk level," the Governor stated in his decision. "They indicate that Mr. Sirhan, despite decades of incarceration and purported efforts in rehabilitation, has failed to address the deficiencies that led him to assassinate Senator

Kennedy. The record further demonstrates that Mr. Sirhan has not meaningfully disclaimed political violence – committed by him or in his name – nor shown that he appreciates the unique risks created by his commission of a political assassination. These gaps in Mr. Sirhan's insight have a close nexus to his current risk of inciting further political violence."

Sirhan expressed remorse at his August parole hearing and said he had entrusted his life to peace. He said, "Senator Kennedy was the hope of the world, and I injured, and I harmed all of them, and it pains me to experience that, the knowledge of such a horrible deed if I did, in fact, do that.... I'm still responsible for being there and probably causing the whole incident through my gun or other guns."

Two of Kennedy's children, Douglas Kennedy, and Robert F. Kennedy Jr., submitted letters on Sirhan's behalf. Robert Jr. stated that he believed his father would have shown Sirhan mercy.

For Governor Newsom, who referred to Robert Kennedy as his "political hero," his decision was personal. He told reporters that along with a photo of his father and appellate court Judge William Newsom, he also keeps a picture of Kennedy on his desk.

In his decision, Newsom stated that Sirhan's actions deprived the Kennedy family of a husband and a father and the nation of a "promising young leader" during a time of great turmoil for the country. Kennedy's assassination was just nine weeks after Martin Luther King Jr.'s killing and four years after Kennedy's older brother, President John F. Kennedy, was murdered in Dallas.

Newsom wrote in his decision that "Mr. Sirhan's crimes also caused great harm to the American people.... The gravity of Mr. Sirhan's crimes alone counsels against his release."

Shortly after midnight on June 5, 1968, Senator Robert Kennedy was shot at the Ambassador Hotel in Los Angeles after being declared the winner of the California presidential primary. Directly after he proclaimed to his shouting supporters that the country was ready to stop with its disagreeable divisions, Kennedy was shot numerous times by 24-year-old Palestinian Sirhan Sirhan. He died a day later, on June 6, 1968.

The summer of 1968 was a turbulent time in the United States. Both the Vietnam War and the anti-war movement were still raging. Martin Luther King Jr. had been assassinated earlier that year, stirring riots across the country. On top of this unrest, President Lyndon B. Johnson decided not to run for a second term as president. Robert Kennedy, JFK's younger brother, and former U.S. Attorney General, decided to run for president and experienced overwhelming support.

Many recognized Kennedy as the only person in American politics competent enough to unite the people. He was adored by the minority community for his honesty and loyalty to the civil rights cause. After winning California's primary, Kennedy was able to obtain the Democratic nomination and go head-to-head against Richard Nixon in the general election.

As star athletes Rafer Johnson and Roosevelt Grier accompanied Kennedy out a rear area of the Ambassador Hotel. Sirhan Sirhan moved forward with a rolled-up campaign poster, hiding his .22 revolver. He was just a foot away when he fired numerous shots at Kennedy. Grier and Johnson grappled Sirhan to the ground, but not before five bystanders had been shot. Grier was distressed afterward and blamed himself for allowing Kennedy to be shot.

Sirhan, who was born in Palestine, confessed to the offense at his trial and received a death sentence on March 3, 1969. However, because California overturned all death penalty sentences in 1972, Sirhan has spent the remainder of his life behind bars. The *New York Times* stated that Sirhan felt Kennedy was "instrumental" in persecuting Palestinians. Hubert Humphrey ran for the Democrats in 1968 but lost to Nixon.

JANUARY 14
1948

On this day in history, Dutch Jewish Nazi collaborator Anna "Ans" van Dijk was executed by firing squad at the age of 42 at Fort Bijlmer in Amsterdam. Ans van Dijk betrayed Jews to the Nazis during World War II. She was the only Dutch woman to be executed for her wartime undertakings.

Ans van Dijk was born in Amsterdam on December 24, 1905. She was the daughter of Jewish parents, and by 1927 she had married a man named Bram Querido. After the marriage ended in 1935, she became involved in a lesbian relationship with a woman named Miep Stodel, and she set up a millinery shop called Maison Evany in Amsterdam. The two women would live in a flat above the store. The shop would eventually be shut down by the Nazi occupiers in 1941 as part of their mass seizure of Jewish property. Jews were prohibited from owning businesses or working in retail shops, amongst other draconian restrictions. With that, Stodel had seen enough and fled to Switzerland in 1942.

As the Nazis started to deport Jews from Amsterdam, van Dijk initially helped the resistance by supplying her fellow Jews with hiding places, identity papers, and necessities. In the process of doing this, she decided to go into hiding herself. On Easter Sunday in 1943, however, she was betrayed and was arrested along with other Jews by the *Sicherheitsdienst* (SD; the Nazi Intelligence service) detective Peter Schaap of the Office of Jewish Affairs of the Amsterdam police. Schaap was a "handler" of people who hunted for Jews in Nazi-occupied Amsterdam.

Fortunately for van Dijk's survival, she was captured by Schaap, a man who recognized something in van Dijk's manner. Schaap offered her release in exchange for her assistance in capturing other Jews in hiding. She accepted the offer, which in addition to saving her life, included cash incentives for each person turned in to the SD.

"(She) was the best of the ten who worked for me at the time," said Schaap of van Dijk after the war. During her initial few weeks on the job, she betrayed nine Jews, including her brother, his wife, and their three children. Going by a fake name, the sly van Dijk convinced dozens of Jews that she sought to help them. Instead, she betrayed their hiding places to Schaap, who in turn had the Jews arrested. Among her many strategies, van Dijk maintained a "trap house" close to Anne Frank's childhood home in the River Quarter to ensnare unsuspecting Jews. She may have been accountable for the deaths of as many as 700 Jewish people.

A vehicle pulled up in front of a narrow brick building in central Amsterdam around 10 a.m. on August 4, 1944. Up on the top floor of the Annex at 263 Prinsengracht, eight Jews had been hiding there since 1942. Members of the Gestapo appeared from the car and went inside the building, where they apprehended Anne Frank, along with her family and their four friends. Within a year, all but one of the eight people were dead. It has also been stated that Ans van Dijk may have betrayed Anne Frank and her family. Despite independent and police studies, there has not been any way to prove or disprove van Dijk's complicity in Anne Frank's capture.

By the war's end, more than 100,000 Dutch Jews had been deported to Nazi death camps and murdered.

At the war's end, van Dijk moved to The Hague, where she was subsequently arrested at a friend's home on June 20, 1945, and she was charged with 23 counts of treason. On February 24, 1947, she was brought before a Special Court in Amsterdam. She pleaded guilty to all

23 charges before her, stating that she had only acted out of self-preservation. She was ultimately found guilty and sentenced to death. The prosecutor notably accused van Dijk of having "a satanic hunting instinct," and an ex-lover called her "a devil in human form." She appealed her conviction, but in September 1947, the Special Court of Appeals denied her request and confirmed the sentence. She also requested a royal pardon, but that, too, was rejected.

On January 14, 1948, van Dijk was executed by a firing squad of 12 soldiers at Fort Bijlmer in Amsterdam. The day before, she had been baptized and joined the Roman Catholic Church in a final, desperate bid to save her life. The 42-year-old Ans van Dijk was given an anonymous burial.

JANUARY 15
1934

On this day in history, while robbing the First National Bank in East Chicago, Indiana, John Dillinger of the Dillinger Gang is shot several times by Detective William O'Malley but survives because he is wearing a bulletproof vest. O'Malley was not so lucky; Dillinger shot and killed him with a Thompson submachine gun. Dillinger would be charged with the policeman's murder but would never live to stand trial.

At 2:50 pm on a Monday afternoon, 10 minutes before closing time, three members of the Dillinger Gang, John Dillinger, John "Red" Hamilton, and a driver for the getaway car whose identity has not been established, double-park outside the bank. Hamilton stays inside the door, and Dillinger goes inside and pulls his submachine gun out of a case and yells, "This is a stickup!" startling the dozen or so patrons in the bank. "Put your hands up, everybody."

Realizing the gravity of the situation, bank vice-president Walter Spencer hits the silent-alarm button under his desk; a block away, it rang at police headquarters. As the customers raised their hands and got up against the wall, one forgot his cash on the teller's counter. "You go ahead and take your money," Dillinger stated. "We don't want your money. Just the banks."

At this point, Hamilton cleared the cash from the teller's counters into a leather satchel. Soon afterward, a police officer named Hobart Wilgus entered the bank, unaware that a hold-up was in progress. Dillinger disarmed the startled cop and emptied his gun and gave it back to him. He noticed Wilgus eyeing the submachine gun and stated, "Oh, don't be afraid of this. I'm not even sure it'll shoot."

A few moments later, Hamilton finished gathering up the cash. By this time, many police officers had gathered outside, but this did not bother the unflappable Dillinger. He had told Hamilton to "Take your time and be sure you get all the dough. We'll take care of them birds on the outside when we get there."

Dillinger then proceeded to use V.P. Spencer and Officer Wigus as human shields as they moved to exit the bank for the getaway car, which for some reason, the police had not taken notice of. As the four shuffled across the sidewalk towards the vehicle, a 43-year-old detective named Patrick O'Malley shouted, "Wilgus!" Officer Wilgus turned, giving O'Malley a clear shot at Dillinger. O'Malley fired his pistol four times, hitting Dillinger in his bulletproof vest. At this point, Dillinger aimed and fired at O'Malley, a father of three little girls, dropping him to the pavement with eight bullet holes across his chest.

At this point, the six remaining police officers opened fire on the two bank robbers. Hamilton was hit several times, but Dillinger got him in the car, along with the pouch. As the bullets pounded the getaway car, the driver careened off down Chicago Avenue, eluding police pursuit. In minutes they were gone.

The killing of Detective O'Malley did much to sully the "Robin Hood" image that John Dillinger had cultivated for himself. He would tell anyone who would listen that he had not shot the police officer, but too many eyewitnesses had stated otherwise. He would officially be charged with O'Malley's murder, despite not living long enough to stand trial. After leaving Hamilton in a safe house in Chicago to heal from his wounds, Dillinger and his girlfriend, Billie Frechette, would escape to Arizona.

In April, the Dillinger gang hid at a resort in Wisconsin, but the FBI was tipped off. On April 22, the FBI raided the resort. In a disastrous operation, three civilians were mistakenly shot, one of whom died.

Baby Face Nelson murdered one agent, hit another, and seriously wounded a police officer; the whole Dillinger gang absconded.

With two associates from the gang, Dillinger traveled to Chicago, surviving a shoot-out with Minnesota police along the way. On June 30, he took part in his last robbery in South Bend, Indiana. They escaped with $30,000 while killing one officer and wounding four civilians.

In July, Anna Sage, a Romanian-born brothel madam in Chicago and a friend of Dillinger's, agreed to work with the FBI in exchange for clemency in an upcoming extradition hearing. She also hoped to claim the $10,000 bounty for Dillinger's capture. On July 22, Sage and Dillinger went together to watch the gangster movie *Manhattan Melodrama* at the Biograph Theatre near her house. Twenty FBI agents and police officers staked out the theatre and waited for him to leave with Sage, who indicated she would wear an orange dress to identify herself.

At 10:40 pm on July 22, 1934, outside the Biograph Theater in Chicago, John Dillinger was gunned down by the FBI task force. Two bystanders were wounded in the gunfire. Public Enemy No. 1, as FBI Director J. Edgar Hoover had deemed him, was dead. Dillinger's death happened only two months after the deaths of notorious criminals Bonnie Parker and Clyde Barrow. Some newspapers also claimed that people dipped their handkerchiefs and dresses into the pool of blood that had formed as Dillinger lay dead in an alley.

Some historians have claimed that another man, not Dillinger, was killed outside the Biograph, citing autopsy findings on the corpse that allegedly contradict Dillinger's known medical record.

JANUARY 16
1936

On this day in history, Albert Fish is executed at Sing Sing prison in New York. Dubbed the "Moon Maniac," Fish was one of America's most infamous and deranged killers. He was a suspect in at least five murders during his life. He admitted to three murders that police could trace to an acknowledged homicide, and he acknowledged stabbing at least two additional individuals. Fish once bragged that he "had children in every state," and once he declared that his number of victims was about 100. However, whether he was discussing rapes or cannibalization is unknown, nor is it sure if the assertion was factual.

Known for being one of the evilest pedophiles, serial child killers, and cannibals of all time, Albert Fish was arrested on December 13, 1934, and prosecuted for the kidnapping and murder of Grace Budd. He was found guilty and executed by an electric chair on January 16, 1936, at 65.

Fish was born to Randall and Ellen Fish on May 19, 1870, in Washington, D.C. His family had long suffered from mental illness. His uncle was diagnosed with mania, his brother was held in a mental institution, and his sister was diagnosed with a "mental affliction." His mother experienced visual hallucinations. Three other family members were diagnosed with mental illness.

His parents abandoned him when he was young, sending him to an orphanage. There he was subject to regular beatings and violent acts of brutality. It was said that he began to enjoy the abuse because it gave him pleasure. When asked about the orphanage, Fish stated, "I was there 'til I was nearly nine, and that's where I got started wrong. We were unmercifully whipped. I saw boys doing many things they should not have done."

By 1880 Ellen Fish, now a widow working for the government, soon took Albert from the orphanage. He had little formal education and grew up learning to work more with his hands. Before long, after Fish returned to live with his mother, he began an association with another boy who initiated him to drink urine and eat feces.

According to Fish, in 1890, he moved to New York City and began his crimes against children. He made money working as a prostitute and started to molest boys. He enticed children from their homes, tortured them in different ways—his favorite was using a paddle spiked with nails—and then raped them. As time passed, his sexual fantasies with children grew more malicious and stranger, often resulting in the murdering and cannibalizing of them.

In 1898 he married and fathered six children. The kids led average lives until 1917 when Fish's wife left for another man. At that time, the children remembered Fish sometimes asking them to participate in his sadomasochistic games.

After his marriage ended, Fish wrote to women listed in the personal columns of newspapers, describing in explicit detail the sexual acts he would like to have with them. The depictions were so nasty and disgustful that they were never made freely available, although they later were used as evidence in court.

According to Fish, no women ever replied to his letters.

Fish developed house painting skills and often traveled to states primarily populated with African Americans because he felt police would spend less time looking for the killer of African American children than Caucasian children. Therefore, he chose Black children to endure torture using his "instruments of hell," which included the paddle, knives, and a meat cleaver.

In 1928, Fish answered an ad from 18-year-old Edward Budd, who wanted part-time work to help with the family finances. Fish, who introduced himself as Mr. Frank Howard, met with Edward and his family to discuss the job. Fish told the family that he was a Long Island farmer looking to pay a strong young man $15 weekly. The job seemed perfect, and the Budd family, excited by Edward's luck finding the job, instantly trusted the mild, polite Mr. Howard.

Fish told the Budd family that he would return in a week to take Edward and a friend of Edward's to his farm to start working. Fish did not show up on the promised day but sent a telegram apologizing and said he would return soon. When Fish arrived on June 4, he came bearing gifts for all the Budd children. To the Budds, Mr. Howard seemed like a loving grandfather.

After lunch, Fish stated that he had to go to a children's birthday party at his sister's home and would return later to get Eddie and his friend. He then suggested that the Budds allow him to take their oldest daughter, 10-year-old Grace, to the party. The unsuspecting parents agreed. Grace, excited about going to a party, left the house and was never seen alive again.

The investigation into Grace's disappearance labored on for six years before detectives received a big break in the case. On November 11, 1934, Mrs. Budd received an anonymous letter giving monstrous details of the murder and cannibalism of her daughter.

The writer informed Mrs. Budd about the empty house her daughter was taken to in Worcester, New York, and how she was strangled, cut into pieces, and eaten. As if to comfort Mrs. Budd, the writer stated emphatically that Grace had not been sexually molested.

Tracking the paper, the written letter led police to a boarding house where Fish was residing. Fish was arrested and instantly admitted to killing Grace and the other children. Fish, smiling as he described the gruesome details of the tortures and murders, the detectives felt they were looking at the devil incarnate.

On March 11, 1935, Fish's trial began, and he pleaded innocent because of insanity. He said voices told him to kill children and commit other terrible crimes. Despite the psychiatrists describing Fish as insane, the jury found him sane and guilty after a 10-day trial. He was condemned to die by electrocution.

On January 16, 1936, Fish was electrocuted at Sing Sing prison in Ossining, New York, reportedly something Fish considered "the ultimate sexual thrill," though later that assessment was dismissed as a rumor.

JANUARY 17
1706

On this day in history, Benjamin Franklin, polymath, inventor, scientist, printer, politician, freemason, diplomat, the first United States Postmaster General, Founding Father of the United States, and a drafter and signer of the American Declaration of Independence, was born.

As a child, he received little formal education. The 15th of 17 children born to Josiah Franklin in Boston, Massachusetts, young Benjamin left school at ten after two years to work in his father's candle and soap shop. Even though his father could not afford to send him to school, Benjamin became a prodigious reader with an unquenchable thirst for knowledge and educated himself. He could also speak four languages: English, French, Spanish, and Italian. He could also read and write Latin.

This was just the beginning of many significant achievements during the lifetime of the brilliant Benjamin Franklin. As a scientist, he would become a primary figure in the American Enlightenment and the history of physics through his studies of electricity. He also became known for charting and naming the current, still known as the Gulf Stream. His work with the latter was able to shave two weeks off the return trip by ships from Europe to North America. He is an inventor known for the lightning rod, bifocal glasses, the Franklin stove, rocking chairs, flexible catheters, and the American penny. He founded many civic organizations, including Philadelphia's first fire department, the Library Company, and the University of Pennsylvania. Franklin was named "The First American" for his early campaigning for colonial unity and as author and spokesman in London for several colonies. He has been called "the most accomplished American of his age and the most influential in inventing the type of society America would become."

He was widely admired in America when, as an agent for several American states, he persuaded the Parliament of Great Britain to repeal the very unpopular Stamp Act. Franklin was also the first United States Ambassador to France. As a very skilled diplomat, he was greatly looked upon by the French as America's agent in Paris and was instrumental in developing positive Franco-American relations. His efforts would prove extremely important for the American Revolution in securing French aid.

Throughout the years, he was active in community affairs, colonial and state politics, and national and international affairs. From 1785 to 1788, he served as President of the Supreme Executive Council of the state of Pennsylvania, an office like that of governor today. In 1787 he hosted the Constitutional Convention, which took place in Philadelphia. At one point, he owned and dealt with enslaved people, but by the late 1750s, he began arguing against slavery. He became an abolitionist and promoted education and the integration of African Americans into United States society.

In 1790 Benjamin Franklin died of respiratory disease at the age of 84.

(Photo: A painting of Benjamin Franklin from 1778. Wikimedia Commons)

JANUARY 18
1778

On this day in history, Captain James Cook, a British explorer, navigator, and cartographer in the British Navy, while aboard HMS *Resolution*, was the first European to "discover" the Hawaiian Islands while on a mission to find the western Pacific Northwest Passage.

Cook had been sailing for many years, undertaking expeditionary journeys to Tahiti, New Zealand, Australia, the South Pacific, and the Antarctic region to map, chart, and explore the globe for Britain. In passing the Hawaiian Islands, they made initial landfall at Waimea harbor, Kauai, and Cook named the archipelago the Sandwich Islands in honor of John Montague, the 4th Earl of Sandwich and one of Cook's patrons as well as the acting First Lord of the Admiralty. It was determined that the inhabitants spoke a version of the Polynesian language they had already been familiar with from their previous travels in the South Pacific.

Cook and his crew only stayed briefly on the islands. By February 2, they were off again searching for the Northwest Passage, which was unsuccessful due to ice conditions. By late November 1778, Cook's two ships, HMS *Resolution* and HMS *Discovery*, were back at the Hawaiian Archipelago, where they sailed around for eight weeks looking for a suitable place to lay anchor. They eventually landed at Kealakekua Bay, on "Hawaii Island," the largest of the islands, on January 17, 1779. During their circumnavigation of the islands, the two ships were accompanied by large numbers of canoes filled with gifts whose occupants fearlessly came on board the vessels. Eventually, Cook was escorted to one of the islands by a chief and a priest and subjected to a strange ritual before allowing to return to the HMS *Resolution*. Unbeknownst to Cook, his arrival corresponded with the Makahiki, a Hawaiian harvest festival of worship for the Polynesian god Lono. Cook and his crew were welcomed as gods and, for the next entire month, exploited the Hawaiians' goodwill.

Cook brought with him a large amount of metal and metal objects to the island. Foreign to the islanders, as there is no metal on the island, Cook and his crew soon began trading with the islanders, thus increasing their importance. Such was the value of iron that the islanders began selling anything they could for it – even sex. Venereal disease and others like measles and chicken pox began to spread among the population, which had no immunity to these foreign illnesses. As a lousy house guest often outstays their welcome, so too did the British explorers. When one of the crew members died, the veil of European immortality was lifted, thus straining relations.

On February 4, 1779, Cook and Company left the island again in search of the Northwest Passage. However, after a week at sea, a storm damaged the foremast of HMS *Resolution*, and they were forced to return to Hawaii to repair the ship. Upon their arrival, they were greeted by islanders throwing rocks at them. No longer seen as gods, they stole a small cutter from HMS *Discovery*. Cook began negotiations with King Kalaniopuu for the return of the cutter. Talks broke down on the beach when a lesser chief was shot and killed, and a mass of Hawaiians descended upon the British shore party. During the skirmish, Cook himself was clubbed on the head and stabbed several times. Cook and four British Marines died on the beach while a few crew members returned to *Resolution*. In retaliation, the British fired at the Hawaiians from their ships, killing about thirty islanders.

In keeping with their practice at the time, the Hawaiians removed Cook's body from the beach, and they proceeded with funerary rituals like those reserved for chiefs and esteemed elders of their society. Firstly, the body was disemboweled, then baked to allow the removal of the flesh, and the bones were meticulously cleaned for preservation. Some of Cook's remains were finally restored to the British for a burial at sea after an appeal by the crew.

JANUARY 19
1807

On this day in history, Confederate General Robert E. Lee, commander of the Confederate States of America's land forces during the American Civil War, was born in Stratford Hall, Virginia. At the beginning of the Civil War, Lee resigned from the U.S. Army and rose to control the Army of Northern Virginia, the Confederate's largest and most powerful army.

Robert E. Lee was the fifth child of Revolutionary War hero and governor of Virginia, Henry "Light-Horse Harry" Lee. Henry Lee, being fiscally irresponsible, left for the West Indies when Robert was six, and he never returned. Robert's mother, Ann Carter Lee, was left to raise all her children independently.

Robert secured an appointment to West Point in 1825 and was a top student graduating second in his class with no demerits, and he entered the prestigious Engineer Corps. Throughout the peace of the 1830s and early 1840s, he was assigned to various posts throughout the country and rose from second lieutenant to captain. In 1831 he married Mary Anna Custis, the great-granddaughter of George Washington's wife Martha and her first husband, Daniel P. Custis. Because of his marriage to Mary, Lee improved his financial position, and his name became associated, however distantly, with the Revolutionary War commander and first president, a thing which added to his prestige during and after the Civil War.

He showed great poise and leadership during his time in the Mexican American War and served as Superintendent of the United States Military Academy. Lee opposed slavery from a logical perspective. However, he did support its legality and even used slave labor on his plantation. When Virginia seceded from the Union, Lee chose to follow his home state, despite his longing for the country to remain together and despite an offer of a high command in the U.S. Army. During the first year of the Civil War, he served in minor military operations and was a senior advisor to Confederate President Jefferson Davis.

After the wounding of General Joseph E. Johnston during the Peninsula Campaign in June 1862, Lee assumed control of the Army of Northern Virginia. He defeated George McClellan's Army of the Potomac at the Seven Days Battle but failed to destroy them. Lee was victorious at the Second Battle of Bull Run in August. His invasion of Maryland that September ended with the inconclusive Battle of Antietam, after which he retreated to Virginia. Lee would then win battles at Fredericksburg and Chancellorsville before losing mightily at the Battle of Gettysburg in July 1863. By the spring of 1864, General Ulysses S. Grant assumed command of the Union armies. Grant and Lee's armies met and fought inconclusive battles at Wilderness and Spotsylvania and then settled into the Siege of Petersburg, followed in April 1865 by the acquiring of Richmond and the devastation of most of Lee's army. Lee finally ceded to Grant at Appomattox Court House on April 9, 1865.

Saved from being hanged as a traitor by a very forgiving Lincoln and Grant, Lee returned to his family after the cessation of hostilities. He accepted a job as president of Washington College (later Washington and Lee University) and devoted his efforts to reviving the fortunes of that institution. On September 28, 1870, Lee suffered a massive stroke. He died at his home, surrounded by his family, on October 12.

In the aftermath of the war, Lee had accepted "the extinction of slavery" as laid out in the Thirteenth Amendment, yet conversely, he opposed racial equality for African Americans. After his death, Lee became a cultural icon in the South and is, to this day, largely seen as one of the Civil War's greatest generals. In an 1874 speech before the Southern Historical Society in Atlanta, Georgia, Benjamin Harvey Hill described Lee as follows:

"He was a foe without hate; a friend without treachery; a soldier without cruelty; a victor without oppression, and a victim without murmuring. He was a public officer without vices; a private citizen without wrong; a neighbor without reproach; a Christian without hypocrisy, and a man without guile. He was a Caesar, without his ambition; Frederick, without his tyranny; Napoleon, without his selfishness; and Washington, without his reward."

JANUARY 20
1942

On this day in history, the Wannsee Conference, where 15 high-ranking Nazi Party and German government officials gathered at a villa in a Berlin suburb to discuss and coordinate the implementation of the "Final Solution of the Jewish Question."

The "Final Solution" was the code name for the deliberate, systematic, physical annihilation of the European Jews. At some time during the summer of 1941, it is believed that Adolf Hitler gave the go-ahead for this European-wide strategy for mass murder. On July 31, 1941, just after the German conquering of the Soviet Union, Nazi Reichsmarschall Herman Goring ordered the director of the Reich Security Main Office (RSHA), SS Obergruppenfuhrer Reinhard Heydrich, to ensure that all the various government and military departments worked together in the implementation of the "Final Solution to the Jewish Question."

Initially, the mass murder of Jews happened after the invasion of the Soviet Union. Groups like the mobile killing units of the SS, the Einsatzgruppen, and Order Police Battalions, were dispatched to the occupied Soviet Union for the express purpose of murdering all Jews. The extermination of roughly one million Jews happened before the plan of action for the Final Solution was fully implemented.

Heydrich's mission was to create a plan for a "total solution of the Jewish question" in regions under German control and to coordinate the participation of all involved government and military organizations. The result was the *General Plan Ost* (General Plan for the East) called for the deportation of populations in occupied Eastern Europe and the Soviet Union for use as slave labor or to be slaughtered. The attendees of the Wannsee Conference determined that the Jewish population of the Soviet Union to be about five million, including nearly three million in Ukraine. The initial plan was to implement *General Plan Ost* after the conquest of the Soviet Union. European Jews were to be deported to the occupied parts of the Soviet Union, where they would be worked to death in road-building projects.

When it became apparent that the Soviet Union was not to be subdued so quickly, it became the goal of the Wannsee Conference to come up with an alternative. The new plan called for the rounding up of all Jews throughout Europe, transporting them eastward, and organizing them into labor gangs. The work and living conditions would be sufficiently hard to kill large numbers by "natural diminution"; those who survived would be "treated accordingly."

The men participating in the conference were among the elite of the Reich. Eight of them held doctorates from German universities. They all understood the policy regarding Jews. They all knew that the cooperation of their various departments was vital if they were going to make such an ambitious plan to succeed.

Among the agencies represented at the conference were the Department of Justice, the Gestapo, the Race and Resettlement Office, the Foreign Ministry, the SS, and the office in charge of allocating Jewish property. Also attending the meeting was the Polish occupation administration, whose regions included more than two million Jews a representative of the General Government, the head of Heydrich's office for Jewish affairs, Adolph Eichmann, prepared the conference notes.

Heydrich stated, "Another possible solution of the (Jewish) problem has now taken the place of emigration – the evacuation of the Jews to the east.... Such activities are, however, to be considered as provisional actions, but practical experience is already being collected, which is of great importance in relation to the future final solution of the Jewish problem."

Those gathered needed little explanation. They knew that "evacuation to the east" was another phrase for concentration camps and that the "final solution" was to be the systematic murder of Europe's Jews, which is now referred to as the Holocaust. The final statement of the Wannsee Conference never directly stated extermination. However, within a few months of the meeting, the Nazis had created the first concentration camps installed with poison-gas chambers in Poland. The final responsibility for the entire project was given to Heinrich Himmler and his SS and Gestapo.

One copy of the Wannsee Conference Protocol with circulated minutes survived the war. It was found in March 1947 among various files at the German Foreign Office. It was used as evidence in the Nuremberg Trials. The Wannsee House, the site of the conference, is now a Holocaust memorial.

JANUARY 21
1994

On this day in history, Lorena Bobbitt was found temporarily insane after cutting off her husband's penis the year before. Lorena had testified that she was the victim of domestic violence throughout her marriage to John Wayne Bobbitt and that her husband had raped her just before her castrating him. Since then, she has become an advocate for survivors of domestic violence and has worked tirelessly for their benefit.

Lorena and John Bobbitt met at a club near the Quantico, Virginia, Marine Corps base where he was a lance corporal. She was 19 years old, and he was 21. When they met, she was Ecuadorian, born and raised in Venezuela, Lorena was a manicurist in Manassas, Virginia. She was thin, 5'2", beautiful, with long brown hair. She held a U.S. immigration Visa that was soon to expire. The pair would marry on June 18, 1989.

Trouble in the marriage soon began. John turned out not to be the man with whom she had dated. He drank, spent money with little regard for tomorrow, and he struck her repeatedly. Over their four-year marriage, the police were called many times to intervene in various disputes between the couple. In mid-June 1993, Lorena requested a restraining order against her husband. Two days later, at 3 a.m., he came home drunk on June 23, 1993. Then he raped her. After the attack, she went to the kitchen and saw a knife. She went back to the bedroom and proceeded to cut off her sleeping husband's penis.

Lorena, still clutching the knife and the severed penis, then drove away from their apartment building. On her way to a friend's house, she discarded the severed penis in a field by a convenience store. On her friend's recommendation, she called the police and told them where she had dumped the penis. Police were able to locate it, and reattachment surgery was successful. As well, Lorena had a rape kit examination at the same hospital.

In November 1993, John went on trial for marital sexual assault. (Though his wife had accused him of rape, at the time, Virginia law required couples either be living apart or for serious physical injury to have occurred to trigger a charge of marital rape.) He was found not guilty.

In January 1994, Lorena was put on trial for malicious wounding. Were she to be found guilty, she faced a sentence of 20 years in prison and deportation from the United States. Lorena would testify that she had endured many rapes at the hands of her husband throughout their marriage. Her lawyer argued that she had been subjected to years of spousal abuse and driven temporarily insane. In slicing off her husband's penis, she had been subjected to an "irresistible impulse."

The prosecution's case revolved around the statement Lorena gave police that "He (John) always have an orgasm, and he doesn't wait for me to have an orgasm (sic)." She later stated that this quote was inaccurate because she could not access a translator. John testified that at no time during their marriage did he commit acts of violence against her. However, other witnesses corroborated that Lorena had appeared with bruises and that John was seen striking and pushing Lorena. Friends of John's stated under oath that they heard him state that he liked forced sex.

Lorena was declared not guilty by reason of temporary insanity and was thus spared a prison sentence. However, she had to submit to a 45-day psychiatric examination, as required by Virginia law, after which she was to be released.

Lorena remained in the Manassas area after the trial. She became a

U.S. citizen in the summer of 1994. Her divorce from John was finalized in 1995. She made some paid appearances in South America but refused a 1 million dollar offer to appear nude in Playboy magazine. She would support herself by working as a real estate agent, a cosmetologist, and an administrative assistant.

She created the Lorena Gallo Foundation in 2007, which helped victims of domestic violence and their children to help raise awareness of the issue. She stated that she never knew that she had the option to seek refuge in a shelter during her marriage. She said that "As an immigrant woman, I was too often too scared to call the police for help. My abusive husband always threatened that he could have the police detain me and have me deported back to my country."

JANUARY 22
1908

On this day in history, a police officer ran furiously toward Kate Mulcahey, doing everything he could to gain her attention. "Madam, you mustn't," he urged. "What would Alderman Sullivan say?" Then he proceeded to arrest her. She was ordered to pay a 5 dollar fine, and when she refused, she was placed in jail. When she came before the judge the next day, she stated that "I've got as much right to smoke as you have. I never heard of this new law, and I don't want to hear about it. No man shall dictate to me."

Mulcahey's crime was breaking the 1-day old Sullivan Ordinance prohibiting women from smoking in public places. The ordinance did not prohibit women from smoking in general, nor did the ordinance bar women from smoking in public, only in public places. Kate Mulcahey, it should be pointed out, was not in a public place; she was in the great outdoors of New York City.

New York City Alderman Timothy Sullivan, better known as "Little Tim," to distinguish him from his cousin, "Big Tim" Sullivan, a Lower East Side political boss, vehemently felt that any woman who smoked in public was immoral and suffering from a loose character. He readily admitted that he had never actually seen a woman smoke in public, but he was sure that he would lose all respect for a woman should he see her do so.

Alderman Sullivan was also getting pressure from Christian lobbyists who were stating that public smoking was sinful and wicked behavior that respectable women should not engage in. The Women's Christian Temperance Union, which was chiefly known for its fight against alcohol, also joined the fight against women smoking in public. Giving into public pressure was when "Little Tim" proposed his ordinance that banned women, not men, from lighting cigarettes in a public place. He humbly named it the Sullivan Ordinance, and it passed unanimously in a very short time.

The spirit of the Sullivan Ordinance not only prohibited females from smoking in parks and public places but also in privately run businesses as well. For the owner of one restaurant, the Café Martin, this law did not sit well with him at all. James B. Martin, the owner of Café Martin, catered to New York's elite, as well as visitors from Europe. When he saw the wife of an ambassador light up a cigarette, he prevented his waiter from intervening. He told the New York Times that "Personally, I think New York is ready to allow ladies to smoke in good restaurants." It was not long before other establishments followed suit and began to defy the Sullivan Ordinance.

The newspapers reported the arrest of Katie Mulcahey, and except for the Christian Temperance groups, the public was solidly behind her. The city's lawyers reviewed the wording of the Sullivan Ordinance, and nowhere contained within was their mention of a fine or punishment for public smoking. Katie was promptly released from custody without nary a blemish on her record. Katie was the first and only person charged with breaking Sullivan's Ordinance. Two weeks later, the mayor of New York, George B. McClellan Jr., vetoed the law, which was struck off the books.

The same thing would be tried three years later by the board of Aldermen, who wanted to ban smoking by women. They were quickly defeated when the city's chief legal officer declared it against the law. In his ruling, he stated that women could smoke "at will on the city streets, be it cigarette, cigar or pipe." By trying to crack down on women smoking, the aldermen inadvertently opened the door to further freedoms for women.

Throughout the remainder of the decade and the next, women activists fought for more gender equality. Their most significant rallying point, women's suffrage, was finally achieved in 1920.

JANUARY 23
1897

On this day in history, Elva Zona Heaster Shue, a young housewife in Greenbrier County, West Virginia, is found dead in her home by an 11-year-old boy. At first, it is ruled a death by natural causes, but later it is determined that murder was the reason when the mother of the decedent, Mary Jane Heaster, claimed that her dead daughter's spirit visited her four times and told her the real cause of her death. The resulting murder trial is perhaps the only case in American history where the alleged testimony of a ghost helped to secure a conviction.

Upon finding the body of Elva Shue, the young boy, who had been sent by her husband to find out if she required anything from the market, ran to tell his mother and then on to the husband, Edward Shue, with the grim news. Appearing distraught, Edward hurried home to his wife. The local doctor and coroner arrived to examine Elva, whose head was being cradled by Edward. After a brief examination, Dr. Knapp declared that Elva "died of an everlasting faint," i.e., a heart attack. He would later claim that she was pregnant.

The body was prepared for burial, with Edward taking complete control of the situation. He placed her in the casket, always handling the head. He put a folded sheet on one side of her head with an article of clothing on the other. Then he tied a large scarf around her neck and explained that it was Elva's favorite. She was buried the next day.

A month later, the dead woman's mother began telling people that Elva's spirit had visited her four nights in a row accusing Edward of Elva's violent death. The mother stated that Elva said to her that Edward had attacked her in a fit of rage, violently breaking her neck. Elva's mother, Mary Jane Heaster, now fully believed that Edward Shue had killed her daughter.

Mary Jane Heaster went to the local prosecutor in Lewisburg and retold her tale. At first, the prosecutor, John A. Preston, was not inclined to believe the story he was being told. Still, after several hours of questioning Mary Jane, he became convinced that there was a basis for an investigation.

Dr. Knapp was contacted and admitted that he had only conducted a cursory view of Elva's body. Edward Shue's background was investigated, and it was found that he was a convicted felon who had previously had two other wives who had died under mysterious circumstances. An exhumation was ordered, and an inquest jury was created. Edward complained about these two events and was told he would be forced to attend the inquest if he did not voluntarily attend. He stated that he knew he would be arrested, "but they will not be able to prove I did it." This very careless statement showed that he had at least had knowledge that his wife had been murdered.

The autopsy results did not come out in Shue's favor. It was stated at the inquest that "the discovery was made that the neck was broken, and the windpipe mashed. On the throat were the marks of fingers indicating that she had been choken (sic).... The neck was dislocated between the first and second vertebrae. The ligaments were torn and ruptured. The windpipe had been crushed at a point in front of the neck."

The findings were immediately made public. Shue was arrested, jailed, and held for trial.

On June 22, 1897, Shue was found guilty after the jury had only deliberated for one hour and ten minutes. He was sentenced to life in prison. The local newspaper declared that Shue was convicted with circumstantial evidence and not because of a "ghost's testimony." After a failed lynching a few days later, Shue was taken to the state prison in Moundsville, where he died during an epidemic in March 1900.

JANUARY 24
41 BCE

On this date in history, Roman Emperor Caligula was assassinated because of a conspiracy by officers of the Praetorian Guard, senators, and courtiers. Caligula was described as an insane emperor who was very self-absorbed, short-tempered, who was a capricious killer, and one who indulged in too much spending and sex. He was accused of sleeping with other men's wives and bragging about openly in front of the husbands. He killed for mere amusement, deliberately wasted money on an abundance of foolish things, which caused starvation amongst his people, and he desired a statue of himself in the Temple of Jerusalem for his devotion. He was accused of throwing a whole section of spectators at a games event into the arena during the intermission to be eaten by the animals because there were no prisoners available, and he was bored. Overall, he was not a nice man.

Gaius Julius Caesar Germanicus was born in 12 C.E. to the famous Roman general Germanicus and his wife, Agrippina, the Elder. During his childhood, his family lived at Germanicus' posting on the Rhine, where the general's troops gave the young boy the nickname "Caligula," meaning "little boot," in reference to the small uniform in which his parents dressed him.

Caligula was almost 25 years old when he became emperor in 37

C.E. Initially, he was well-liked in Rome. He had announced political reforms and had recalled all political exiles. But in October of 37 C.E., he suffered from a severe illness that totally affected and unhinged Caligula, leading him to spend the remaining four years of his reign exploring the worst attributes of his nature.

Caligula was especially harsh to the Senate, the nobility, and the equestrian order. According to historians at the time, these actions led to a series of failed conspiracies against the emperor. Eventually, officers within the Praetorian Guard, led by Cassius Chaerea, managed to assassinate Caligula. The plot was devised by three men but was known by many in the Senate, the army, and the equestrian order. The situation worsened in 40 C.E. when Caligula decided to leave Rome and move permanently to Alexandria, Egypt, where he hoped to be worshipped as a living god. Rome was aghast at the prospect of losing its emperor and political power. This was the final straw for many, and Chaerea convinced the other conspirators to move forward with their plans.

On this day, Chaerea and some other soldiers attacked Caligula during the latter's address to an acting troupe beneath the palace. It is recorded that Chaerea stabbed the emperor first, followed by some of the conspirators. One historian records that the scene resembled the assassination of Julius Caesar. It was recorded that Caligula was stabbed 30 times. By the time the emperor's loyal Germanic guard arrived, Caligula was already dead, but they managed to kill several of the conspirators, along with some innocent senators and bystanders. The assassins also sought out and killed Caligula's wife, Caesonia, and their daughter, Julia Drusilla, by smashing her head against a wall. They could not find the emperor's uncle, Claudius, who was hidden by several Praetorian Guards.

The Senate attempted to capitalize on Caligula's death and restore the Republic. Unfortunately for them, the military supported the idea of an imperial monarchy, and thus Caligula's uncle, Claudius, became the new emperor with the support of the Praetorian Guard. The Julio-Claudian dynasty would remain secure for another 17 years until Nero's suicide in 68 C.E.

JANUARY 25
1947

On this day in history, American gangster Al Capone died eight days after his 48th birthday. After suffering for years from paresis (a late stage of syphilis), which reduced him to the mental capacity of a 12-year-old, he finally died of an apoplectic stroke complicated by pneumonia and heart failure.

Alphonse Gabriel Capone was born in New York City in 1899 to Italian immigrant parents who came to America from Naples in 1893. Al was the fourth of nine children who grew up in Brooklyn, New York. He went to school until the sixth grade when he dropped out at age 14 for hitting a teacher. He would work at several menial jobs – as a candy store clerk, a bowling alley pin boy, a laborer in an ammunition plant, and a cutter in a book bindery – all while being a member of a couple of youth gangs named the South Brooklyn Rippers and the Forty Thieves Juniors. They were groups of delinquent children known for vandalism and petty crime that was rampant in New York at the time.

He joined the Five Points Gang as a teenager, and then he became a bartender and bouncer in organized crime establishments such as brothels and bars. In 1917, while working at both jobs at a Coney Island bar, Capone insulted the sister of a man who retaliated by cutting Al's face with a razor. As a result, he earned the name "Scarface," which he always detested, but a name that would last for his entire life.

In his early twenties, he went to Chicago, where he worked for Johnny Torrio, head of the Unione Siciliana, the predecessor to The Outfit. Not long after, Torrio retired after nearly being murdered in a gangland hit, and he gave the reins to Capone. Soon Al became the most formidable gangster in Chicago as he expanded his reach and influence in the criminal underworld.

It is estimated that "The Outfit" under Capone was bringing in over 100 million dollars annually. But Al always maintained he was providing a public service. He stated, "Ninety percent of the people drink and gamble, and my offense has been to furnish them with those amusements."

To ensure that he could continue doing his criminal business, Capone ordered hits on many of his enemies, and he never hesitated to get rid of those who threatened his enterprises. The most famous retaliation attributed to him was the St. Valentine's Day Massacre of 1929. Six members of rival gangland leader George "Bugs" Moran, in addition to a garage attendant, were lined up against a wall and summarily executed by men carrying shotguns and Tommy guns. Two of the gunmen were also dressed as police.

Leading citizens in Chicago and Government officials demanded something be done. Capone was given the moniker of "Public Enemy No. 1". Capone had been bribing city and state officials for years, so there seemed like little would be done. However, President Herbert Hoover was determined to make Capone pay for his crimes.

Unable to find any evidence against Capone for murder, racketeering, extortion, or other crimes, they noticed that Al had not been filing tax returns. Capone was therefore charged with tax evasion, and on October 17, 1931, Capone was found guilty on five of twenty-three charges against him. He was sentenced to eleven years in prison and a $50,000 fine (equal to $780,000 in 2020). At the time, it was the harshest penalty ever given for tax evasion.

In May 1932, a 33-year-old Capone began serving his sentence in an Atlanta prison. After two years and several bribe attempts made toward guards, Scarface was transferred to the maximum-security prison at Alcatraz in San Francisco Bay.

By 1939 the lingering effects of syphilis had ravaged Capone's body and mind, and he was released to seek medical treatment. After several weeks of inpatient and outpatient care at a Baltimore, Maryland hospital, Capone was released, and he went to live at his Florida mansion. In 1942, after mass production of penicillin began, Capone was among the first to receive a course of the drug. While it helped with the syphilis, it did nothing for the brain damage that he had suffered. He still had the mentality of a 12-year-old child.

On January 21, 1947, Capone suffered a stroke. He began to improve but contracted pneumonia. He suffered a heart attack on January 22, and on January 25, with his family at his side, Capone died of heart failure due to apoplexy. His body was taken to Chicago for burial the following week.

His obituary stated that "He was 48. Death had beckoned to him for years, as stridently as a Cicero whore calling to a cash customer. But Big Al had not been born to pass out on a sidewalk or a coroner's slab. He died like a rich Neapolitan, in bed in a quiet room with his family sobbing near him and a soft wind murmuring in the trees outside."

JANUARY 26
1863

On this day in history, Massachusetts Governor John Andrew received permission from United States Secretary of War Edwin M. Stanton to begin recruitment of an African American regiment to fight in the American Civil War. Such a move was authorized by the enactment of the Emancipation Proclamation on January 1, 1863. With Stanton's authorization, Governor Andrew created the 54th Massachusetts Infantry Regiment, the second all-African American unit after the 1st Kansas Colored Volunteer Infantry Regiment.

The unit began recruiting in February 1863 when Governor Andrew called for Black soldiers. Massachusetts did not have an overabundance of African American residents, but by the time the 54th Infantry Regiment headed off to training two weeks later, there were over 1,000 recruits. Many had come from other states like New York, Ohio, Indiana, and Pennsylvania; some even enlisted from Canada. One-quarter of the volunteers came from slave states and the Caribbean. Fathers and sons would enlist together, some as young as 16 years old. The most famous volunteers were Charles and Lewis Douglass, the two sons of abolitionist Frederick Douglass.

Governor Andrew also sought out white officers with similar antislavery views as his own to lead the 54th Regiment. Captain Robert

Gould Shaw of the 2nd Massachusetts Infantry Regiment was chosen to lead the 54th and was promoted to full Colonel. The son of very prominent anti-abolitionists, Shaw had seen combat and had been wounded at the Battle of Antietam. Shaw and the 28 other officers trained the men of the 54th Infantry Regiment from March until late May 1863. On May 28, 1863, the regiment received its colors, marching through Boston before a crowd of twenty thousand onlookers before loading onto the transport ship Demolay for their voyage south.

Initially, the 54th was intended to be used strictly for manual labor and raids. The regiment was forced to lead a very violent attack on the town of Darien, Georgia. Shaw protested this ill-use of his troops to his affluent father, the Governor of Massachusetts, and Union General George Strong. The result was a commitment that the 54th would see combat. In July 1863, they participated in the Battle of Grimball's Landing in James Island, South Carolina.

The next engagement the regiment would participate in was the attack on Battery Wagner. This would be a more challenging and more violent fight than their previous battle had been. Ultimately, they suffered 42% casualties in a horrific confrontation against a vigorously defended position. Of 600 men, over 280 men were killed, wounded, captured, and missing, and presumed dead. Union soldiers were briefly able to penetrate Wagner itself but could not exploit the 54th's breakthrough due to the dogged determination of the Confederate defenders. Finally, in the early hours of July 19, Union troops withdrew, and the battle ended, but not before the 54th's commander, Colonel Shaw, was struck down and killed during the fight.

As a result of the immense bravery shown in battle by the men of the 54th Regiment, the U.S. Army decided to increase the number of African American enlistments so that by 1865 nearly two hundred thousand Blacks had served at some point during the Civil War. This would roughly be ten percent of the total number of American soldiers fighting for the Union Army.

The men of the 54th also fought the American government for pay equity. When they signed up, they were promised the same pay and allowances as their Caucasian equivalent. This was supposed to amount to maintenance and $13 a month. Instead, when they arrived in South Carolina, they were informed that they would be paid $10 a month, with $3 of that held back for uniforms, while white soldiers did not pay for their uniforms.

Therefore, the men of the 54th refused their pay for over a year in protest until finally, on June 16, 1864, by a Congressional bill, equal pay was granted to all who had enlisted as freemen as of April 19, 1861. After swearing an oath that "you owed no man unrequited labor," the men were paid their 18 months of back wages.

The 54th would serve on the southeast coast for the balance of the war. Although most of their time was in Charleston, South Carolina, they did serve in Florida for a time. They also battled at Honey Hill and Boykin's Mill, South Carolina, in the final months of the war. On August 20, 1865, the 54th Regiment was finally mustered out of service in Mount Pleasant, South Carolina, and they returned to Boston in September.

The 54th Massachusetts Infantry Regiment was immortalized in the Hollywood film *Glory*, starring Matthew Broderick and Denzel Washington. The movie made popular the image of the combat role that African Americans played in the Civil War. The 54th, often represented in historical battle re-enactments, is now called the "Glory" regiment.

JANUARY 27
1945

On this day in history, Auschwitz concentration camp – a Nazi concentration camp and extermination camp in occupied Poland where 1.1 million people were murdered as part of the Nazi's "final solution to the Jewish question" – was liberated by the Soviet Red Army during the Vistula-Oder Offensive. Despite most of the camp's prisoners being forced onto a "death march" by the Nazis prior to the Soviet army's arrival, about 7,000 souls too sick to move were left behind. The Soviet soldiers who had liberated Auschwitz tried to help those left behind and were shocked at the scale of the Nazi depravity and cruelty. The date is recognized as the International Holocaust Remembrance Day.

Auschwitz was a group of camps designated I, II, and III. There were also about 40 smaller "satellite" camps. It was at Auschwitz II, called Birkenau, established in October 1941, that the SS created an intricate, grotesquely orchestrated killing ground: 300 prison barracks; four "bathhouses" in which the prisoners were gassed; corpse cellars; and cremating ovens. Thousands of unfortunate prisoners were also used for medical experimentation, overseen by the camp doctor, Josef Mengele, the "Angel of Death."

The Soviet Red Army had been moving through Poland since mid-

January. They had liberated Warsaw and Krakow and were on a path toward Auschwitz, although the latter was not a stated goal. The SS officers at Auschwitz, anticipating the Soviet arrival, went on a killing spree, shooting sick and infirmed prisoners and destroying the crematoria in a desperate bid to destroy the evidence of their many crimes.

The first soldier entered Auschwitz III from the 100th Infantry Division at 9 p.m. on Saturday, January 27, 1945. The 60th Army of the 1st Ukrainian Front (also a part of the Red Army) arrived at Auschwitz I and II around 3 p.m. In total, they found 7,000 prisoners alive in the three main camps, 500 in the other subcamps, and over 600 corpses. They also found 837,000 women's garments, 370,000 men's suits, 44,000 pairs of shoes, and 7,000 kilograms of human hair, estimated to have come from 140,000 people. Traces of hydrogen cyanide, the main ingredient of Zyklon B, the chemical used to gas the prisoners, were found in some of the hair left behind. The Forensic Science Institute had examined the hair in Krakow, Poland.

In later years, Georgii Elisavetskii, a Red Army soldier who had entered one of the barracks, stated that he could hear other soldiers telling the prisoners: "You are free, comrades!" But they did not believe them, so he tried in Russian, Polish, German, and Ukrainian. Then he spoke to them in Yiddish: "They think that I am provoking them. They begin to hide. And only when I said to them: 'Do not be afraid, I am a colonel of the Soviet Army and a Jew. We have come to liberate you'.... Finally, as if the barrier collapsed... they rushed toward us shouting, fell on their knees, kissed the flaps of our overcoats, and threw their arms around our legs."

The liberation of Auschwitz received very little press attention then, with the Red Army focusing its advance on Germany. Liberating the camp had not been one of its key objectives. The Soviet newspaper Pravda, reporting on the liberation of Auschwitz on February 2, 1945, did not mention the Jewish prisoners; inmates were described collectively as "victims of Fascism." It was only when the British and the Americans arrived in Buchenwald, Dachau, and Bergen-Belsen in April 1945 that the deliverance of the camps would receive extensive reporting.

JANUARY 28
1918

On this day in history, Canadian soldier, physician, and poet Lieutenant-Colonel John McCrae died of pneumonia and meningitis while serving during World War1 in Wimereux, France. He was 45 years of age. Best known for his 1915 poem "In Flanders Fields," quite possibly the best poem written during the war, McCrae was a talented doctor and soldier who was "ungirded by the highest standards of loyalty, service, and duty."

The grandson of Scottish pioneers on both sides of his family, he inherited his father's love of soldiering, his immense pride in the British Empire, his mother's intelligence, and their sense of duty to others. After successfully completing a BA in 1894 and an MD in 1898, he worked briefly as an intern at the Johns Hopkins Hospital in Baltimore, Md. Within a year, he was off to South Africa with the Royal Canadian Field Artillery and took part in battles, quickly rising the ranks from Captain to Major. In one incident during the war, McCrae nearly drowned while crossing a river on horseback. He returned to Canada in 1901 and gave a public lecture about the employment of artillery during the war.

Over the next 13 years, he worked as a pathologist and a doctor of infectious diseases as well as in his own private practice. With the onset of the First World War in 1914, McCrae used his connections from the South African war to be appointed a Major and brigade surgeon in the 1st Brigade, Canadian Field Artillery, in the Canadian Expeditionary Force. After attending the battle at Neuve Chapelle, France, his brigade was moved to the Ypres salient, where on April 22, 1915, the Germans used chlorine gas for the first time. Half of McCrae's brigade, including his friend Alexis Helmer, would be killed over a 17-day battle.

Lieutenant Alexis Helmer's burial inspired the poem "In Flanders Fields," which was written on May 3, 1915, the day after Helmer's funeral, which was presided over by McCrae. It was subsequently published in the London magazine *Punch* in December 1915, and very quickly, it became the most famous poem written during the war, used in countless fundraising campaigns, and frequently translated. Originally placed very poorly within the magazine and initially without McCrae's name, and when it was included, it was misspelled.

The poem made the poppy the most famous symbol of the war dead of the British empire. The Poem reads as follows:

In Flanders Fields
n Flanders Fields, the poppies blow
Between the crosses, row on row,
That mark our place; and in the sky
The larks, still bravely singing, fly
Scarce heard amid the guns below.

We are the dead, short days ago
We lived, felt dawn, saw sunset glow,
Loved and were loved, and now we lie
In Flanders Fields

Take up your quarrel with the foe:
To you from failing hands we throw
The torch; be yours to hold it high.
If ye break faith with us who die

*We shall not sleep, though poppies grow
In Flanders Fields.*

McCrae, now "a household name, albeit a frequently misspelled one," thought little of his newfound fame, instead wishing "they would get to printing 'In F.F.' correctly: it never is nowadays"; but (writes his biographer) "he was satisfied if the poem enabled men to see where their duty lay."

By January 1918, McCrae had spent three long years providing medical care near the front in France and Belgium. Finally noticed for his unwavering service and duty, on January 24, 1918, he was appointed the consultant physician to the First British Army – the first Canadian named to this post. McCrae, however, would not live long enough to take on his new duties. John McCrae died of pneumonia and meningitis four days later at the No. 14 British General Hospital in Wimereux, France. He was only 45 years old.

McCrae was buried the next day in the Commonwealth War Graves Commission section of Wimereux Cemetery, just two kilometers up the coast from Boulogne, with full military honors. His flag-draped coffin was placed upon a gun carriage, and the mourners included General Arthur Currie and many of McCrae's friends and colleagues. The procession was preceded by McCrae's charger, "Bonfire," with McCrae's boots reversed in the stirrups. Bonfire had been with McCrae from training camp in Valcartier, Quebec, until his death and was much loved. Nursing sisters found a few poppies to put on McCrae's grave on that very unseasonably warm and sunny winter's day.

JANUARY 29
1863

On this day in history, as many as 500 Northwestern Band of the Shoshone Nation lay dead after the worst massacre of Native Americans by the U.S. military in American history. Most people have never heard of the Bear River Massacre near Preston, Idaho. The Natives were killed after soldiers rode into a valley where they lived for the winter and attacked, leaving about 100 women and children among the dead. Even at the lower end of casualty estimates, the Bear River Massacre outnumbered the likes of the Sand Creek Massacre (230 Cheyenne dead in 1864), Marias Massacre (173-217 Blackfeet killed in 1870), and even the Wounded Knee Massacre (150-300 Sioux killed in 1890).

In one account of the death and destruction, Danish immigrant Hans Jasperson, in his 1911 autobiography, stated that he had walked amongst the bodies, counting 493 Shoshone Indians dead. Jasperson wrote that "I turned around and counted them back and counted just the same." It is recorded that only two dozen American soldiers were killed at Bear River.

Following a story that is all-to-familiar in the annal of America's West, relations between Natives and whites were friendly, if cautious at first. But when white settlers were lured by gold and cheap land, they began encroaching on the Shoshone during the 1840s and 1850s. It was then that the relationship became strained and then violent. During this era, the Mormons, led by Brigham Young, settled near the Shoshone, and claimed the land. Young told his followers that they should feed them rather than fight their Native brethren. But the large influx of settlers and the native Shoshone put a strain on the available food resources in the area.

Hunger crept into the equation and soon violence. In 1862 Shoshone Chief Bear Hunter decided it was time to hit back against the white people and began conducting raids on cattle herds and attacking bands of miners.

The locals soon asked for federal help with their Native problem. Colonel Patrick Connor was chosen to "make clean work of the savages." They began their trek north towards the Shoshone encampment. Even until the end, Chief Sagwitch was sure he could conclude the situation peacefully.

On the morning of January 29, 1863, Chief Sagwitch saw on the horizon a strange fog gathering on a bluff above the river in the sub-zero temperatures. The fog was moving too quickly for it to be anything but the breath of American soldiers and their horses. The chief shouted for his people to prepare themselves, but it was too late.

As 300 soldiers charged down the ravine, they fired at every living thing: men, women, and children were all killed without mercy. The Indians had "very few rifles." They fought with tomahawks, spears, bows, and arrows. Some Shoshone tried to flee by jumping into the frigid river, which was soon full of "dead bodies and blood-red ice," according to one village elder.

One Shoshone chief – Bear Hunter - faced extreme torture after being captured by American troops. Whipped and kicked, he said "not a word, nor did he cry out," according to one tribal elder. "To him, that would have been a sign of cowardice." Because he did not fear the pain, one soldier heated a rifle bayonet and "ran it through his head from ear to ear."

According to tribal historians, about 150 Shoshones survived the attack. According to Connor's final report that he sent to the U.S. War Department, they had destroyed 70 Indian lodges and captured 175 horses. He said he left "a small quantity of wheat for the sustenance of 160 captive squaws and children whom I left in the field."

Despite the number of Shoshone killed at the Bear River Massacre, it remains a relatively little-known event today. Historians surmise that is because it happened during the American Civil War: Americans were far more interested in the battles between the Union and the Confederate States than in what was happening in the West. It only received cursory coverage in papers in Utah and California.

The area was finally declared a National Historic Landmark in 1990. The land where the massacre took place has remained in private hands since 1863. In 2018 the Northwestern Band of the Shoshone Nation purchased about 550 acres of Bear River land. The tribe, with a current population of 560, plans to construct an interpretive center to honor the history and those lost at Bear River.

JANUARY 30
1945

On this date in history, 134 U.S. Army Rangers and Alamo Scouts, along with about 280 Filipino guerilla fighters, successfully raided a Japanese prisoner of war camp near Cabanatuan City, Philippines, extricating more than 500 Allied POWs. This World War II rescue mission became known as "The Great Raid."

Many prisoners at the Cabanatuan prisoner-of-war camp consisted of American and Filipino soldiers who had capitulated to the Japanese Army following the Battle of Bataan. Japanese forces had invaded the Philippines within hours of their attack on the American installation at Pearl Harbor, Hawaii, on December 7, 1941. The Battle of Bataan began a few weeks later, in January 1942. The Imperial Japanese Army eventually defeated the American and Filipino forces, and about 76,000 Allied soldiers surrendered to the Japanese. The result of the defeat was the "Bataan Death March," which was a 70-mile forced trek by the American and Filipino prisoners who were exposed to grotesque and unspeakable atrocities at the hands of the Japanese. It is estimated that up to 20,000 prisoners died on that march.

As the war progressed, the Americans began to regain control of the Philippines by the fall of 1944. By this time, the Japanese had transferred all fit and able prisoners to other prison camps in Japan to perform slave labor. This left about 500 weak and ill prisoners at the Cabanatuan camp. The Japanese High Command ordered all their forces to kill their prisoners so that they could not be liberated by the Americans. After the order was given, 139 American POWs were killed near the city of Puerta Princesa in what would become known as the Palawan Massacre. One hundred fifty prisoners were put in a trench, doused with gasoline, and set alight. If they tried to escape, they were machine-gunned. 11 prisoners managed to escape and warn the American military about what was happening.

Facing brutal conditions, including disease, torture, and starvation, the prisoners feared that the Japanese would execute them before General Douglas MacArthur and his American forces returned to Luzon. Plans were made to rescue the prisoners at Cabanatuan, but the earliest they could arrive was January 31 or February 1. As a result, Colonel Horton White assembled a special force to get to the POW camp by January 29, 1945.

Lt. Col. Henry Mucci, leader of the 6th Ranger Battalion, was tasked with leading the rescue mission. Capt. Robert Prince of the 6th Ranger Battalion led the main force into the camp. On January 28th, the main force of 121 Rangers, led by Prince, began the mission by driving 60 miles to Guimba. They would cross Japanese lines and travel 30 miles to the Cabanatuan prison camp. Filipino guerillas would serve as guides for the Americans, helping them find their way to the camp while avoiding the Japanese. Before their departure on the 29th, Mucci addressed the Rangers by stating: "Remember, these boys have been in that (expletive) hole beaten and starved for nearly three years. If they can't walk to the river, carry them. We don't leave one of them behind. Not a single one! We attack tomorrow night. I think the date of January 30, 1945, will long be remembered. Go with God – and bring our boy's home. They have not been forgotten."

Capt. Juan Pajota of the Luzon Guerilla Army Force (LGAF) noticed that the Japanese soldiers would become quite distracted whenever an American plane flew over. He suggested to his superiors that an aircraft flyover could distract the Japanese long enough for the force to crawl up to the camp perimeter without being detected. A plan was devised to have a P-61 Black Widow aircraft provide a flyover for the raid. The flyover took place on January 30, and the force crept up to the edge of the camp. The P-61 provided the distracting flyover for about 45 minutes before the final assault at 7:45 p.m.

At the appointed time, the Rangers attacked the facility, surprising the Japanese guards in and around the camp. The Americans were able to render the Japanese forces neutral and extricate the prisoners from the camp in 30 minutes. The prisoners were gathered up, and using 106 donkey carts, they got everyone back to American lines.

One deaf British prisoner had managed to sleep through the entire raid unaffected. When he woke up in the morning, he noticed the camp shattered and empty. Realizing what had occurred, he shaved and put on his best clothes, which he had been saving for such an occasion, and proceeded to sit and wait for help to arrive. Fortunately for him, he had been missed, and a request was radioed to Filipino guerillas to doublecheck the camp for stragglers. They found him sitting quietly in a chair and quickly shuffled him off to safety.

The final count revealed 522 prisoners evacuated from the camp. When the smoke cleared, it was determined that more than American soldiers were there. There were: 464 American soldiers, 22 British soldiers, 3 Dutch soldiers, 28 American civilians, and 2 Norwegian civilians, along with 1 British, 1 Canadian, and 1 Filipino civilian.

Between 500 and 1000 Japanese soldiers were killed in the raid. Casualties on the American side were very light: 2 American soldiers had been killed and four wounded, while 9 Filipino guerillas had also been wounded. Two of the prisoners, however, unfortunately, had died from exhaustion, illness, excitement, or a combination thereof.

Mucci was recommended for the Medal of Honor; however, he and Prince were awarded the Distinguished Service Crosses. Mucci was approved for promotion to colonel and was given control of the 1st Regiment of the 6th Infantry Division. All other American officers and some enlisted men received Silver Stars. The remaining American enlisted men and the Filipino guerillas were awarded Bronze Stars. The 13 Alamo Scouts received Presidential Unit Citations.

JANUARY 31
1874

On this day in history, Cole and John Younger, Frank and Jesse James, and Art McCoy pulled off the first peacetime train robbery in Missouri history at the whistle-stop town of Gads Hill. They would manage to steal $12,000.

Fresh from a stagecoach holdup committed January 15, 1874, near Hots Springs, Arkansas, the James-Younger Gang had crossed into Missouri planning to rob a train. Gads Hill was a small town comprising 15 people, three crude houses, a store/post office, and a little railroad platform. Passing trains only usually slowed down marginally to exchange mailbags, but this day would be different. On this cold Saturday afternoon, the southbound Little Rock Express was scheduled to stop and let off a passenger – State Rep. L.M. Farris of adjoining Reynolds County.

Five armed riders approached from the southeast as some children played by the road. With hats pulled low and faces covered, their first stop was the store, where they stole a rifle and $800 from the shopkeeper. The masked men moved all the town's citizens out of the buildings to the outside, where they had them build a large bonfire on the tracks. Then they pried the switches so the oncoming train would be forced on a sidetrack. After that, everyone waited. It was 4 p.m.

Finally, at 4:45 p.m., the four-car train with 25 passengers approached Gads Hill. The conductor noticed a masked man waving a red flag on the station platform, which immediately caused him some concern. The conductor jumped off the train and approached the podium. Just as he was almost there, four other masked men appeared and seized the conductor by the collar, saying, "Stand still, or I'll blow the top of your damned head off!"

As the train stopped, the engineer and fireman were forced off the locomotive. Several curious passengers stuck their heads out of the train to see what was going on and were told in no uncertain terms to get back on the train and do not interfere if they knew what was best. Three outlaws boarded the train and began to pillage the safe. They asked express agent Bill Watson for his receipt book and promptly wrote on a blank page, "Robbed at Gads Hill."

Then they proceeded to the passenger cars. At first, they announced they would only rob the "sons of bitches" who wore high silk hats (or "plug hats" as they called them), but then they added "Goddamned Yankees," regardless of their hat styles, to the list of people to be robbed. "Workingmen" and ladies were to be spared.

The masked men walked about joking with the passengers, patting children's heads, and bowing politely to ladies. One drunk Irishman even offered the robbers a drink, which was declined. But it was not all fun and games. The masked men thought a famous Chicago detective was aboard and repeatedly asked, "Where's Mr. Pinkerton?" For 2 ½ years, Allan Pinkerton and his Pinkerton National Detective Agency had been trying to apprehend the James-Younger Gang, and they were intent on doing him in. Several male passengers suspected of being the detective were threatened. One was even taken into a private compartment and strip-searched for a Pinkerton secret mark. Everybody proved their identities and lived to travel another day.

Just before leaving the train, one of the robbers asked a preacher aboard to pray for them, and then he quoted some lines from William Shakespeare. Although we do not know which lines were mentioned, they may have been from King Henry IV. In that play, the bard used Gad's Hill, England, after which the Missouri village (without the apostrophe) was named, as a setting for a highway robbery pulled off by Sir John Falstaff and friends. It has been suggested that perhaps Frank James' love for that play, or Shakespeare in general, was a determining factor in selecting Gads Hill, Missouri, as the robbery site.

When everything was almost done, one of the robbers took a piece of paper from one of the passengers. A detailed account of the train holdup was written on it, complete with a headline. The bandit stated that he wrote it for the newspapers to make sure the facts were reported correctly this time.

It read:

"THE MOST DARING ROBBERY ON RECORD

The southbound train on the Iron Mountain Railroad was boarded here this evening by five heavily armed men and robbed of _____ dollars. The robbers arrived at the station a few minutes before the train arrived, arrested the agent, put him under guard, and then threw the train on the switch.

The robbers were all large men, none of them under six feet tall. They were all masked and started in a southerly direction after they had robbed the Express. They were all mounted on fine-blooded horses. There's a hell of an excitement in this part of the country."

The passenger passed the paper over to the conductor, and the contents would appear in several newspapers as part of their coverage of the holdup. After finishing their business, the robbers shook hands with the engineer and thanked him for his hospitality, and they then proceeded to ride out of town.

By the following day, a posse of 25 men was formed to ride after the desperados, but they would have no luck. Pinkerton's Agency would send in detectives with little chance of tracking down the James-Younger Gang. The town of Gads Hill has changed its look many times over the years. Once a town of 600 people with three sawmills, a water-powered gristmill, a hotel, a blacksmith shop, and a railroad depot, it now consists of only one house, a bar and grill, and two "City Limits" signs. There is also a historical marker near the robbery site that reads: "Gads Hill Train Robbery. Jesse James and Four Members of His Band Carried Out the First Missouri Train Robbery Here, January 31, 1874."

FEBRUARY 1
1968

On this day in history, South Vietnamese General Nguyen Ngoc Loan, in charge of the national police, executes assumed Viet Cong officer Nguyen Van Lem on a Saigon street early in the Tet Offensive. Captured on NBC TV cameras and by Associated Press photographer Eddie Adams, the picture and film footage were sent worldwide, quickly symbolizing the Vietnam War's stark brutality.

However, what most people at the time, and even now, do not realize about the events leading up to the "Saigon Execution" photo illustrate a very different picture from what was shown to the public at first glance.

By 1968, America was up to its neck in Vietnam. What began as a limited advisory deployment soon became full-scale combat between U.S. forces and a mix of North Vietnamese regular forces and Viet Cong guerillas. The latter operated in the shadows all over South Vietnam, and the Americans could not stop them.

With the Tet Offensive in early 1968, 80,000 communist troops struck over 100 targets nationwide. Saigon was overrun, allowing the Viet Cong to eliminate its political adversaries and settle some old scores. General Loan, as chief of South Vietnam's National Police Force, was part of the effort to drive out the Viet Cong and re-capture the city.

On the morning that the "Saigon Execution" photo was taken, Loan led a police unit in Saigon looking for civilians and the Viet Cong, who might be a definite threat to them. Nguyen Van Lem was precisely the type of enemy fighter Loan was looking for. According to the soldier's who captured Lem, he was caught red-handed leading a Viet Cong hit team tasked with killing National Police members or, if they could not locate any, their families were used instead.

On the day of the "Saigon Execution" photo, Nguyen Van Lem's death squad had recently killed 34 people – seven police officers, two or three Americans, and several police officers' family members, all bound by the wrists and shot in the head over an open pit – and they may have been looking for Loan himself.

According to the Geneva Convention of 1949, Lem was fighting as a war criminal because he was not in uniform. Because of his actions that morning, he was subject to summary execution when or if South Vietnamese forces caught him. The Viet Cong were indiscriminately killing people. Summary execution of partisans was allowable under the Geneva Convention.

The "Saigon Execution" photo would become a symbol of the anti-war movement in America, and it was taken largely by accident. Photographer Eddie Adams was out looking for possible images to take, and he saw what he surmised was an ordinary Viet Cong soldier being brought out into the street. Adams decided to start taking pictures. He stated that he:

> "...followed the three of them as they walked toward us, making an occasional picture. When they were close – maybe five feet away – the soldiers stopped and backed away. I saw a man walk into my camera viewfinder from the left. He took a pistol out of his holster and raised it. I had no idea he would shoot. It was common to hold a gun to the head of prisoners during questioning. So, I prepared to make that picture – the threat, the interrogation. But it didn't happen. The man just pulled the pistol out of his holster, raised it to the VC's head, and shot him in the temple. I made a picture at the same time."

Interviewed in May 1968, Loan was asked about the execution. He stated that "He wasn't wearing a uniform and I can't respect a man who shoots without wearing a uniform. Because it's too easy: you kill, and you're not recognized. I respect a North Vietnamese because he's dressed as a soldier, like myself, and so he takes the same risks as I do, but a Viet Cong in civilian clothes – I was filled with rage."

Eddie Adams' "Saigon Execution" photo was a worldwide journalistic sensation. However, it was stripped of its context and presented as a war crime caught on film for the world to judge. The "world" did not know who the victim was or why he was shot, and the public was left to assume that he was just a random person being murdered by a bloodthirsty villain. Adams' photo won him the 1969 Pulitzer Prize for Spot News Photography. Adams later stated that he regretted that he was unable to get a picture "of that Viet Cong (Lem) blowing away the (Tuan) family."

A few months after the "Saigon Execution" photo, Loan was seriously wounded near Saigon by machine gun fire, and the result was the amputation of his leg. He spent time convalescing in Australia and the United States. He returned to South Vietnam, and in 1975, with Saigon's fall, he fled to the United States. He settled in Dale City, Virginia, and eventually opened a pizzeria in a suburb of Washington, D.C.

In 1978 Loan was almost deported from the U.S. for war crimes based on the "Saigon Execution" photo, but through the intervention of Eddie Adams and President Jimmy Carter, General Loan was able to stay in America. In 1991, he closed his restaurant and retired following increased notoriety about his past caused a decline in business and threats made upon him and his family. Adams remembered that on his last visit to the pizza parlor shortly before it closed, he had seen written on a toilet wall, "We know who you are, you f***er."

Nguyen Ngoc Loan died of cancer on July 14, 1998, aged 67, in Burke, Virginia.

Eddie Adams wrote a eulogy to Loan in *Time*:

"The general killed the Viet Cong; I killed the general with my camera. Still, photographers are the most powerful weapon in the world. People believe them, but photographs do lie, even without manipulation. They are only half-truths. What the photograph didn't say was, 'What would you do if you were the general at that time and place on that hot day, and you caught the so-called bad guy after he blew away one, two, or three American soldiers?'"

FEBRUARY 2
1945

On this day in history, 500 Soviet Army officers, who had revolted and escaped from the Mauthausen concentration camp, were hunted down, and murdered. Local citizens, local Nazi organizations, and Wehrmacht and SS soldiers hunted down the escapees for three weeks after the initial escape. Only eleven prisoners would remain free until the end of the war from the original 500 escapees.

Inside Mauthausen, there was a special block, designated as "K" or Block No. 20, intended for Soviet officers. The letter "K" in the designation meant that all prisoners were subject to immediate liquidation. Block No. 20 was built in 1944 according to an order via Field Marshal Wilhelm Keitel which stated that 5700 Soviet officers were to be sent to the Mauthausen concentration camp and shot. Some were shot immediately, and the rest were in Block No.20.

Prisoners in this block only received one-quarter the amount of food that other prisoners were given. One witness stated that "They had no spoons or plates. From the cauldrons, the Germans threw out the spoiled food to the prisoners directly on the snow and waited for it to freeze. After that, the Russians were ordered to rush for food…." In addition, the block was sectioned off from the rest of the camp with a

2.5-meter wall, on top of which was electrified barbed wire going around it. The prisoners were given no ventilation in the summer and no heat in the winter. They had to sleep on the floor piled up to four people high, as no bunks were provided. The detainees acted as living mannequins during the training of SS officers and soldiers. They practiced various kinds of interrogation and torture techniques. Roughly ten people a day died from the "training." During the winter, the SS hosed the floor with water and forced the prisoners to lie down so the SS soldiers could walk on them so they would not get their boots dirty. The men imprisoned in this block were forced to "exercise" non-stop all day by running or crawling around the compound. The prisoners referred to it as the "death barracks."

On the night of February 2, 1945, the remaining 500 prisoners in the camp from Block No. 20 attempted to escape after learning that the Germans planned to exterminate the remainder of the prisoners. Using fire extinguishers from the barracks, blankets, and boards as projectiles, one section attacked and successfully occupied a watch tower. In contrast, a second group used wet blankets and bits of clothing to cause a short circuit in the electrified fence. The prisoners then climbed over the wall.

Of the remaining 500 prisoners, 419 managed to escape the block, but many of the prisoners, already in a pre-existing weakened state, collapsed in the snow outside the camp, where they were subsequently shot by SS guards that very night. Those who did not make it to the woods, along with the 75 prisoners who were too weak to attempt the escape and still in the barracks, were all executed that night. Over 300 prisoners reached the woods that first night.

The SS camp commandant immediately called out the SA detachments, the Gendarmerie, the Wehrmacht, the Volkssturm, and the Hitler Youth to hunt down the escapees. The local citizenry was encouraged to help, which they willingly did. The SS camp Commandant ordered everyone "not to bring anyone back alive."

Most of the fugitives were captured, and most were shot or beaten to death on the spot. Members of the Volkssturm who brought escapees back to Mauthausen were chastised for not having beaten them to death instead. Only 11 Soviet officers are known to have survived the manhunt until the end of World War II. Despite the very high risk, a few farm families and civilian forced laborers hid escapees or brought food to those hiding in the woods. After three months, the war ended, and the fugitives were safe.

FEBRUARY 3
1882

On this date in history, Phineas T. Barnum of the Barnum & Bailey Circus purchased the world-famous elephant "Jumbo" from the London Zoo for $10,000 U.S. The decision to sell resulted from Jumbo's growing aggression and the possibility of a public disaster. The sale of Jumbo, however, caused a great uproar in London as they viewed it as a significant loss for the British Empire. Over 100,00 schoolchildren wrote to Queen Victoria begging for her intervention in the matter. A court case was launched to prevent the sale of the elephant, alleging the sale was in contravention of multiple zoo bylaws, and even the zoo tried to renege on the deal, but the court eventually upheld the sale.

Jumbo, the African elephant, was born on the Ethiopia – Sudan border in late 1860. Captured as an infant after hunters killed his mother, Jumbo was apprehended by Sudanese elephant hunter Taher Sheriff and German big-game hunter Johann Schmidt. Then he and other animals were sold to the Paris Zoo Jardin des Plantes. In 1865 he was then re-sold to the London Zoo and arrived there on June 26. Jumbo would quickly become a crowd favorite due to his immense popularity.

Jumbo's trainer and keeper was Matthew Scott, who created an incredible bond with the animal, which would pay dividends in the years ahead. Jumbo spent much of his time taking small children for rides, including a young Winston Churchill, Theodore Roosevelt, and some of Queen Victoria's children. In his early 30s, when he first took charge of Jumbo, Scott would regularly sleep in the elephant's stall at night, and they grew to share an extraordinary bond, based not the least on their mutual love of alcohol. Jumbo was said to enjoy a keg of beer each day, and Scott liked to share a bottle of Scotch with him at night.

By 1881 Jumbo was beginning to exhibit signs of distress. Whether it was a tooth problem due to his soft diet. Elephants grew up to six sets of molars over their lifetime, and their diet in the African bush helped to grind down their current set of teeth, thus allowing the new set of teeth to grow up. The soft diet he was given in captivity did not allow his teeth to grind down, thus blocking the new set of teeth from coming in and bending out of shape, causing tremendous pain for the elephant. Another possible problem was that Jumbo had reached elephant adolescence and experienced his first annual outbreak of "musth," the tsunami of testosterone which impels bull elephants to mate.

Scott and the zoo's superintendent, Abraham Bartlett, feared that Jumbo might harm the keeper or, worse, a visitor. That is when the decision to sell Jumbo occurred. After the transaction was finished, Jumbo was prepared for transport across the Atlantic Ocean. Once in New York, Jumbo was immediately taken to Madison Square Gardens and exhibited, earning more than enough in three weeks from the enormous crowds to recover the money he spent to buy the elephant. On May 17, 1884, Jumbo was one of Barnum & Bailey's 21 elephants that crossed the Brooklyn Bridge to demonstrate that it was safe after 12 people were killed during a stampede caused by mass hysteria over collapse fears a year earlier.

Jumbo died at a railway yard in St. Thomas, Ontario, Canada, on September 15, 1885. At that time, the circus traveled North America using the train. Jumbo and the other animals had finished their nightly performance and were returned to their boxcar accommodations for the night. Jumbo was bringing up the rear and as he was crossing the railway tracks when an unscheduled freight train came roaring by and struck Jumbo, and he was mortally wounded, dying within minutes.

Barnum, never one to pass up the opportunity to make a dollar, had pieces of his star attraction separated to have multiple sites attracting curious spectators. Jumbo's skeleton toured with Barnum & Bailey's circus, and when that was done, it was donated to the American Museum of Natural History in New York City, where it remains to this day. Jumbo's heart was sold to Cornell University. The elephant's hide was stuffed by William J. Critchley and Carl Akeley, both of Ward's Natural Science, who made Jumbo bigger by stretching the coat during the mounting process. The stuffed and mounted version of Jumbo toured with Barnum & Bailey's circus for two years.

The stuffed and mounted Jumbo was eventually donated to Tufts University by P.T. Barnum, where it was displayed for many years. It was destroyed by fire in 1975. They collected the ashes from the stuffed Jumbo, which is stored in a 14-ounce Peter Pan Crunchy Peanut Butter jar in the Tuft's athletic director's office. Jumbo's taxidermied tail, previously removed during earlier renovations, is stored in the holdings of Tufts Digital Collections and Archives. Jumbo is also the Tufts University mascot.

FEBRUARY 4
1880

On this date in history, five members of the Donnelly family from Biddulph Township, Ontario, Canada, were murdered by six members of the local Vigilance Committee. Those killed that unfortunate evening were farmer James Donnelly, his wife Johannah, his sons Thomas and John, and his niece Bridget Donnelly. Two eyewitnesses, eleven-year-old Johnny O'Connor and James Donnelly's eldest son, William, claimed to have identified six of the murderers, who were subsequently brought to trial in London, Ontario, later in the year.

Even for the rough and tumble times in which they lived, the Donnellys were a violent bunch. Living on what was locally known as the "Roman Line," called such because of the large number of Catholics residing there, most of the conflict was with other Catholics, and not Protestants, as one might otherwise surmise.

Donnelly and his seven sons and one daughter were linked to many robberies, arsons, assaults, and even mutilation of horses, not to mention attempted murders, murders, trespassing, theft, and assaulting a police officer. They constantly engaged in fisticuffs, causing trouble with local girls, and intimidating their adversaries. In 1879 Michael Donnelly was the first in the family to face justice. He was killed in a bar fight. As of February 3, 1880, Thomas was on trial for robbery, and John was awaiting trial for perjury. The Donnelly parents were to have gone on trial on an arson charge the very next day.

By this time, the locals had just about had enough of the Donnelly family. It was decided by the local Vigilance Committee, an offshoot of the Biddulph Peace Society, led by James Carroll and included at least two justices of the peace and the parish priest. Six men gathered at the Cedar Swamp Schoolhouse late on the night of February 3 before proceeding to the Donnelly homestead. The final straw was the allegation against the Donnellys of the destruction of Patrick Ryder's barn. Since they had an airtight alibi, the group planned their revenge. After drinking a lot of liquid courage in the form of liquor, the group proceeded to the Donnellys, where they planned to hang them from a tree until they confessed their crimes against the community.

Things never go according to plan. The Vigilance Committee did a bit of surveillance on the Donnelly's home. On the night of the attack, things immediately went awry. James Donnelly, 63, wife Johannah, 56, son Thomas, 25, and niece Bridget, 21, were home, as was an 11-year-old hired boy named Johnny O'Connor. As soon as they opened the door and handcuffed Thomas, the killing began. It became a bloodbath, with only young Johnny O'Connor managing to hide and avoid being murdered.

After dispatching four members of the Donnelly family, they went on to kill William at his home, five kilometers away. They knocked at the door, and instead of William answering, his brother John did and was immediately shot and killed. The six assailants thought they had killed William and promptly left feeling their work was done.

The first trial began on Monday, October 4, 1880, in London, Ontario, Canada, with James Carroll being accused of the murder of Johannah Donnelly. Despite the eyewitness testimony of Johnny O'Connor and William Donnelly, the jury decided after deliberating for four and a half hours that they could not reach a verdict. They felt they could not convict Carroll based on Johnny O'Connor's words alone. One juror stated that he would not have found him guilty even if he had seen him kill Johannah Donnelly himself.

The second trial occurred on February 2, 1881, with the same witnesses taking the stand. This time the jury deliberated for three hours, and Carroll was found not guilty. There were such negative feelings towards the Donnellys in the county that it was virtually impossible to get a guilty verdict.

Today the Donnelly's are well known in Canadian history, and the story of their murder is widely known throughout Canadian and American farming communities. However, despite this popularity, the residents of Lucan and Biddulph Township have tried to keep hidden the story altogether. Until today, even among those born in that local area, many had never even heard of the Donnelly murders until adulthood. The accounts of that day were purposely suppressed because of the number of local residents who had ancestors who were intimately involved with the massacre.

History was not kind to the Donnelly family in the years afterward. The victors wrote the story, and the family, blamed for all the violence, became known as the "Black Donnellys."

Today, the Black Donnellys is a mix of history and legend. Their exploits and gruesome deaths are the sort of stories that mothers use to scare their children. Their story has immersed itself into the fabric of Lucan and the neighboring counties.

FEBRUARY 5
1983

On this day in history, Klaus Barbie, the former Nazi Gestapo chief of German-occupied Lyon, France, better known as the "Butcher of Lyon," was extradited from Bolivia to stand trial in France for crimes against humanity. As chief of Nazi Germany's secret police in Lyon, Barbie sent 7,500 French Jews and French Resistance partisans to their deaths in concentration camps while executing some 4,000 others. Barbie individually tortured and executed many of his prisoners.

Barbie joined the *Sicherheitsdienst* (SD), the SS security service, which acted as the intelligence-gathering arm of the Nazi Party in 1935. After the German occupation of the Netherlands at the beginning of World War II, Barbie was posted in Amsterdam. In late 1942 he was assigned to Lyon, France, as the head of the local Gestapo. His headquarters was located at the Hotel Terminus in Lyon, where he would personally torture adult and child prisoners. He soon became known as the "Butcher of Lyon."

In 1943, Barbie captured the head of the French Resistance, Jean Moulin, and subsequently had him beaten to death. In 1944, he caught 44 young Jewish children and their seven teachers at an orphanage in Izieu. And then he had them sent to Auschwitz concentration camp.

Only one survived out of the 51 sent to the extermination camp. As the Germans prepared to retreat from Lyons in August 1944, Barbie arranged one last deportation train that ferried hundreds of Jews and partisans to the death camps.

At the war's end, Barbie returned to Germany, where he decided to burn off his SS identification tattoo and assume a new identity since he was a wanted man in France. In conjunction with fellow former SS officers, they took part in anti-communist activity. In June 1947, Barbie was recruited by the U.S. Counter-Intelligence Corps (CIC) to provide intelligence services against the communists in exchange for money and protection from prosecution. By 1949 things were heating up for Barbie, and the French were getting close, so the Americans facilitated Barbie and his family's removal via the "Rat Line" to South America.

Barbie finally settled in Bolivia and continued to work for the U.S. CIC using the alias, Klaus Altmann. He went into business and advised the military regime in Bolivia. By 1971 Barbie was helping the Bolivian government to set up internment camps for its many political prisoners. During his thirty-plus years in Bolivia, Barbie also worked as an officer in the Bolivian Secret Police, took part in the drug cartel business, and founded a rightist death squad. He regularly traveled to Europe and France using a diplomatic passport with impunity. The French government, meanwhile, tried and convicted Barbie in absentia and sentenced him to death for his war crimes.

In 1972 Barbie was located in Bolivia by Nazi hunters, but the rightist Bolivian government refused to extradite him to France. In the early 1980s, a change in government in Bolivia saw a leftist government willing to extradite Barbie in exchange for French aid. On January 19, 1983, Barbie was arrested, and on February 5, he was deported to France to be put on trial. Later that year, the American government apologized to the French for its part in allowing Barbie to remain free for nearly 40 years.

After a series of legal delays, Barbie finally went on trial for 41 different counts of crimes against humanity based on the statements of 730 Jews and French Resistance survivors who described how he tortured and murdered various prisoners. The trial began on May 11,

1987, just over four years since his arrest in Bolivia. Swiss pro-Nazi financier Francois Genoud funded his defense. Remarkably, Barbie was represented by three minority lawyers – an Asian, an African, and an Arab – who amazingly made the case that the French and the Jews were just as guilty of crimes against humanity as Barbie or any other Nazi was. During his trial, Barbie declared, "When I stand before the throne of God, I shall be judged innocent."

In France, though, Barbie's lawyers' arguments were rejected. On July 4, 1987, he was convicted and condemned to life in prison. He died in jail in Lyon four years later, in 1991, of leukemia and spine and prostate cancer at the age of 77.

(Photo: SS-Obersturmführer Klaus Barbie during his military service. Wikimedia Commons)

FEBRUARY 6
1928

On this day in history, a lady named Anastasia Tschaikovsky, declaring herself to be the youngest child of the slain Russian Czar Nicholas II, arrives in New York City. This woman held a press conference aboard the liner Berengaria, explaining that she was there to have her damaged jaw reset. She claimed that a Bolshevik soldier broke the jaw during her harrowing escape during the execution of her whole family – the Romanovs – at Ekaterinburg, Russia, in July 1918. Tschaikovsky was greeted in New York by Gleb Botkin, who was the son of the Romanov family doctor who was killed along with his patients in 1918. Botkin called her "Your Highness" and stated that, without a doubt, she was the Grand Duchess Anastasia with whom he played as a child.

Between 1918 and 1928, several women came forward, claiming to be the lost Romanov daughter. So many had come forward that people were naturally suspicious of Tschaikovsky's assertions. Despite this, she was treated as a celebrity during her stay in New York, and she was often invited to society parties and fashionable hotels worthy of a Romanov heir. While registering at one hotel, she used the name Anna Anderson, which later became her permanent alias.

After the Romanovs were executed, the Bolsheviks' stated that Nicholas II had been killed and that Alexandra and their five children were taken to a safe location. Later it was revealed that the whole family had perished, but a persistent rumor spread throughout Europe that Anastasia, the youngest child, had survived. Several pretenders came forward trying to cash in the Romanov fortune tucked away in European banks, but they were very quickly exposed as the frauds that they were. But then there was Anna Anderson.

On February 17, 1920, it began. A young lady attempted suicide by jumping off a bridge in Berlin, Germany. She was rescued from the Landwehr Canal by police and taken to a medical clinic for treatment. She refused to tell anyone her identity and was committed to the Dalldorf Asylum, where she lived anonymously until 1922. Then she announced that she was Anastasia, to the surprise of many.

In Europe at the time, there were a great many Russian exiles who had fled Russia when the revolution occurred. Several of them rallied around the young Anna Anderson, who, at first glance, very well could have been the lost Anastasia. She had stated that a Bolshevik soldier, noticing that she was still alive after the execution of her family, helped her to reach Europe. A few months after claiming to be Anastasia, she was released from the asylum and moved in with the first of a long line of supporters.

During the following years, her entourage of Russian emigres grew exponentially. Also, during this time, several Romanov relatives and acquaintances interviewed Anna, and many were impressed by both her resemblance to Anastasia and her knowledge of many of the small details of the Romanov family life. Others, however, had serious reservations about her when she continuously failed to remember important events regarding young Anastasia's life. Anna's skills in speaking English, French, and Russian were severely lacking, while the young Anastasia was fluent in all those languages. However, many blamed this deficiency on the fact that she had spent several stays in an asylum.

At the same time, her supporters were waging a campaign to have her legally declared the true Anastasia. This recognition would give her access to whatever wealth the Romanovs had outside of Russia and make her a strong political pawn of czarist exiles who still hoped to overthrow the communist regime in Russia.

The Grand Duke of Hesse, Alexandra's brother, and Anastasia's uncle were huge skeptics of this campaign. The Grand Duke hired a private investigator to learn the true history of Anastasia Tschaikovsky's life. The investigator found out that she was, in fact, Franziska Schanzkowska, a Polish-German factory worker from Pomerania who had disappeared in 1920. Schanzkowska had a long history of mental instability and was injured in an ammunition factory explosion in World War 1, which accounted for the multiple scars on her body.

Over the following years, until she died in 1984, she lost every lawsuit she brought to prove she was Anastasia. Anna Anderson would spend her final years in the United States married to an eccentric history professor named J.E. Manahan.

In 1991 Russian investigators found what they thought were the remains of the Romanov family. With the help of British DNA experts, they could prove that the remains were, in fact, the Romanovs using blood from Prince Philip, the consort of Queen Elizabeth II, who was the grand nephew of Alexandra. To prove that it was Nicholas II, he exhumed his brother's body, Grand Duke George, and extracted a DNA sample which proved that it was the czar.

Everyone was accounted for except for one of the Romanov daughters. Was it possible that Anastasia had escaped and resurfaced as Anna Anderson? In 1994 British and American scientists obtained a tissue sample of Anderson's from a Virginia hospital and compared it to the DNA of the Romanov females and sons. As well, American scientists tested a strand of Anna Anderson's hair. The British and the American scientific teams came to the same conclusion: Anna Anderson was not a Romanov.

After that, the scientists compared Anna Anderson's DNA with that of Karl Maucher, the grand nephew of Franziska Schanzkowska, and it was a match, which proved the theory put forth by the German investigator in the 1920s. One of the significant mysteries of the 20th century was partially solved.

FEBRUARY 7
1964

On this day in history, the British singing group, the Beatles, departed from London's Heathrow Airport with 4,000 jubilant fans waving and screaming as the aircraft took off. Upon landing at New York's John F. Kennedy Airport, a boisterous crowd of 3,000, primarily teenage girls, nearly started a riot when the band disembarked the plane and walked onto American soil. This was the Beatle's first visit to the United States, and the British rock-and-roll quartet, dressed in mod suits and sporting their trademark mop-top haircuts, had just had its first No. 1 U.S. hit six days prior with "I Want to Hold Your Hand."

In two days, John Lennon, age 23, Paul McCartney, 21, George Harrison, 21, and Ringo Starr, 25, would make their first of three appearances on the *Ed Sullivan Show*, a wildly popular television variety show. Even though the band was difficult to hear over teenage girls screaming in the studio audience, an estimated 73 million people in America, or roughly 40 percent of the American population, viewed the Beatles on the program. The group made its first public concert appearance in America on February 11 at the Coliseum in Washington, D.C., and 20,000 people attended. The next day the Beatles gave two performances at New York's Carnegie Hall, and police were forced to close off all the streets around the illustrious music hall because of fan frenzy. On February 22, the Beatles returned to Great Britain.

The Beatles' first American tour significantly impacted the nation's cultural mosaic. Beatlemania had arrived. American youth were ready to break away from the rigid norms of 1950s society. The Beatles, with their upbeat music and good-natured rebellion, were the perfect mechanism to create that shift. Their singles and albums sold in the millions, and at one time in April 1964, all five best-selling U.S. singles were Beatles songs. In August 1964, when the Beatles' first feature film, A Hard Day's Night, was released, Beatlemania became a global phenomenon. Later that same month, the Beatles returned to America for their second tour, playing at sold-out venues across the country.

In 1966 the Beatles gave up touring and devoted themselves to an increasingly experimental approach to their recording. One rock and roll historian, when speaking about the Beatles' 1967 album *Sgt Pepper's Lonely Hearts Club Band*, stated that

"The overwhelming consensus is that the Beatles had created a famous masterpiece: a rich, sustained, and overflowing work of collaborative genius whose bold ambition and startling originality dramatically enlarged the possibilities and raised the expectations of what the experience of listening to popular music on record could be. Based on this perception, *Sgt. Pepper* became the catalyst for an explosion of mass enthusiasm for album-formatted rock that would revolutionize both the aesthetics and the economics of the record business in ways that far outstripped the earlier pop explosions triggered by the Elvis phenomenon of 1956 and the Beatlemania phenomenon of 1964."

The Beatles' music remained very relevant to youth throughout the massive cultural upheaval of the 1960s, and the songwriting team of Lennon-McCartney was seen as the best in the music industry. In 1970 the Beatles broke up, leaving a heritage of 18 albums and 30 Top 10 U.S. singles. After the group's break-up, the former members of the group enjoyed success as solo artists and some partial reunions occurred.

The Beatles are by far the best-selling music act of all time, with an estimated sales of 600 million units worldwide. They have received much praise over the years, including seven Grammy Awards, four

Brit Awards, an Academy Award (for Best Original Song Score for the 1970 documentary film *Let it Be*), and fifteen Ivor Novello Awards. In 1988, the band was initiated into the Rock and Roll Hall of Fame, and each band member was individually inducted between 1994 and 2015. In 2004 and 2011, the Beatles were at the top of *Rolling Stone's* lists of the greatest artists in history. *Time* magazine included them among the 20th century's 100 most influential people.

FEBRUARY 8
1587

On this date in history, Mary, Queen of Scots, after being held prisoner for 19 years, is beheaded at Fotheringhay Castle in England after being found guilty of plotting to kill Elizabeth I in 1586.

Central to the story is the fact that Mary, a Roman Catholic, was regarded by Roman Catholics as the legitimate heir to the English throne. Mary was made Queen of Scotland when she was just six days old after her father's death, King James V. She was sent to be raised in the French Court, and in 1558 she married the French dauphin, who became King Francis II of France in 1559. Francis would widow Mary, the Queen's consort, the following year when he died from an ear infection. Mary then returned to Scotland to take on the role of Queen of that country.

In 1565 Mary married her English cousin Lord Darnley, who was also related to Queen Elizabeth, to bolster her claim of succession to the English throne after Elizabeth's death. Two years later, Darnley died in an explosion at his home, and Mary's lover, the Earl of Bothwell, was considered the prime suspect. Bothwell was absolved of complicity in the matter due to a lack of evidence. He would wed Mary that same year which enraged the country's nobility. Mary raised an army against the nobles and was soundly defeated and imprisoned at Lochleven, Scotland. She was then forced to abdicate her throne for the son she had with Darnley, James.

In 1568 Mary escaped her captors and raised another army which was handily defeated and forced her to flee to England and request Elizabeth's help. Initially, Queen Elizabeth welcomed Mary, but it soon became evident that Mary, along with English Catholics and amid Spanish plots, was hoping to overthrow her.

In August 1586, Mary was arrested and taken to Staffordshire after being incriminated in the Babington Plot. In a successful attempt to entrap her, Elizabeth's principal secretary, Sir Francis Walsingham, had intentionally arranged for Mary's letters to be carried out of Chartley. Mary was made to believe that they were secure, while in fact, they had been deciphered and read by Walsingham. From these letters, it became clear that Mary had sanctioned the attempted assassination of Elizabeth.

In October 1586, Mary was sent to be tried for treason at Fotheringhay Castle by 46 English lords, bishops, and earls. She was not given legal counsel, nor was she permitted to review the evidence against her, nor to call witnesses. Portions of the translated letters were read at the trial. Mary was convicted of treason against England. One English Lord voted not guilty. Elizabeth signed her cousin's death warrant, and the date of her execution was set for February 8, 1587.

On the appointed day and time, before 300 witnesses, Mary was brought out to the scaffold, where the executioner awaited her. Her servants prepared her, and then her head was positioned on the block with her arm stretched outwards. Her final words were, *In manus tuas, Domine, commendo spiritum meum* ("Into thy hands, O Lord, I commend my spirit.")

Mary was not beheaded with one swing of the axe. The first blow hit the back of her head, missing her neck. The second strike severed the neck, except for a tiny bit of sinew, which the executioner cut through using the axe. He held her head up and declared, "God save the Queen." At that moment, the auburn hair in his hand turned out to be a wig, and Mary's head fell to the ground, showing all her short, grey hair. One observer noted that after Mary's death, "Her lips stirred up and down a quarter of an hour after her head was cut off."

Mary requested that she be buried in France. Elizabeth denied this request. She was embalmed and placed in a secure lead coffin until she was buried in a Protestant service at Peterborough Cathedral in July 1587. Her body was disentombed in 1612 when her son, King James VI, and I decided she should be reinterred at Westminster Abbey in a chapel across from Elizabeth's tomb. In 1867, her tomb was opened to find the final resting place of her son, James I of England. He was eventually found with the remains of Henry VII. Several of her other descendants were interred in her vault, namely Prince Rupert of the Rhine, Elizabeth of Bohemia, and the children of Anne, Queen of Great Britain.

FEBRUARY 9
1971

On this day in history, pitcher Leroy "Satchel" Paige became the first Negro League player to be recommended for the Baseball Hall of Fame in Cooperstown, New York. In August of that same year, Paige, a pitching legend known for his incredible fastball, dramatic presence, and the longevity of his playing career, which lasted more than five decades, was inducted into the Baseball Hall of Fame. New York Yankees' outfielder Joe DiMaggio once described Paige as the "best and fastest" pitcher he had ever played against.

A native of Mobile, Alabama, Leroy Robert Page was born in 1906 and grew up with 11 siblings. He was given the nickname "Satchel" for a contraption he made for carrying passengers' bags at the local train station. The family added the "I" to the spelling of their last name when he was young.

Satchel Paige was taught to pitch by Reverend Moss David while at reform school. When he was released from there when he was 18 years old, he went to play semi-pro baseball for the Mobile Tigers. In one of baseball's most famous incidents, in the ninth inning of a game where Paige had a 1-0 lead with two outs, his teammates made three consecutive errors, loading the bases. Paige then called his outfielders in and told them to sit down in the infield. He struck the final batter out to win the game. Paige was subsequently signed by the Chattanooga White Sox of the Negro Southern League, a Negro League farm club. His contract was quickly purchased by the Birmingham Black Barons of the Negro National League. Paige was an outstanding pitcher, drawing large crowds to the games he pitched in. He changed teams a lot over the next few years. He played for one year in Cuba and then returned to the U.S., where he would play for appearance money. Paige would mix playing for different leagues, barnstorming tours, and prominent Negro league teams.

In 1948, at 42, Satchel Paige was signed by Bill Veeck of the Cleveland Indians, who were in a tight pennant race and who needed pitching. He became the first black pitcher in the American League. The games in which he pitched were always sell-outs, often breaking attendance records. He became the first Negro League player to pitch in the World Series that very same year. He would later play for the St. Louis Browns and the Kansas City A's before retiring in 1953. In 1965, at the age of 59, he returned to the majors to pitch three innings, making him the oldest person ever to play in the Major Leagues. He did not allow a run. In 1968, the Atlanta Braves added the then 62-year-old Paige to their roster. The color line had caused Paige to start his Major League career late, and he was about five months short of qualifying for a pension. The Braves added him to their roster as a tribute for all he had done for the game. The rule was soon changed, and Paige was eligible for his MLB pension.

Paige was married three times. He and his third wife, LaHoma Jean Brown, had seven children. Leroy "Satchel" Paige died in Kansas City, Missouri, on June 8, 1982.

Willie Mays, one of baseball's all-time greatest players and Alabama native, described when, as a 17-year-old, he faced Satchel Paige for the first time: "It was 1948. Satchel had a very, very good fastball. But he threw me a little breaking ball just to see what I could do, and I hit it off the top of the fence. And I got a double. When I got to second, Satchel told the third baseman, 'Let me know when that little boy comes back up.' "Three innings later, I go to kneel in the on-deck circle, and I hear the third baseman say, 'There he is.' Satch looked at the third baseman, and then he looked at me."

Willie Mays continued: "I walk halfway to home plate, and he says, 'Little boy.' I said, 'Yes, sir?' because Satch was much older than I am, so I was trying to show respect. He walked halfway to home plate and said, 'Little boy, I'm not going to trick you. I'm going to throw you three fastballs, and you're going to go sit down.' And I'm saying in my mind, 'I don't think so.' If he threw me three of the same pitch, I'm going to hit it somewhere."

"He threw me two fastballs, and I just swung… I swung right through it. And the third ball he threw, and I tell people this all the time, he threw the ball, and then he started walking. And he says, 'Go sit down.' This is while the ball was in the air.

"He was just a magnificent pitcher."

Photo: Leroy "Satchel" Paige. Wikimedia Commons)

FEBRUARY 10
1946

On this date in history, American Mafia leader Charles "Lucky" Luciano agrees to be deported from the United States for Italy after a plea bargain with New York Governor Thomas E. Dewey for services rendered by the mob on the docks of New York during World War II. Luciano, the Italian-born American mobster best known for creating the structure of modern organized crime in the United States, would never touch the ground again in America during his lifetime.

Luciano was born Salvatore Luciana in 1897 in the Sicilian town of Lercara Friddi. In 1906, at the age of 8, he and his family immigrated to the United States and settled in New York's Lower East Side, where a large contingent of Italian immigrants lived. Unable to speak English, the young Luciano learned how to survive on the streets, and by the age of 14, he had garnered a lengthy list of arrests.

By 1916 he was a top member of the Five Points Gangs and a friend of rising Jewish mobster Meyer Lansky. Along with gangster Benjamin "Bugsy" Siegel, Luciano ran bootlegging rackets and other criminal ventures. By 1927 he had been chosen as the top lieutenant of Giuseppe "Joe the Boss" Masseria, the head of New York's most prominent crime family. But Luciano did not care for Masseria's traditional business ways, and he was a man who would let grudges get in the way of profits.

During the 1920s, with prohibition in place, Luciano became one of the "Big Six" of bootlegging along with childhood friends Lansky, Siegal, Louis "Lepke" Buchalter, Jacob "Gurrah" Shapiro, and Abner "Longy" Zwillman. These men dominated the illegal liquor trade on the East Coast.

In 1929, Luciano lived up to his nickname "Lucky" by surviving a vicious attack by a group of men who beat and stabbed him. It was unclear who ordered the attack, and Luciano never said, but it was thought to be either the police or Masseria. Masseria was in a turf war with rival boss Salvatore Maranzano. Luciano had switched allegiances and now supported Maranzano. In 1931 he arranged for Masseria to meet his maker in a not-so-friendly way.

Luciano was made Maranzano's top lieutenant, but it was not long before the latter put a hit out on Luciano. When Luciano learned of the assassination plot, he sent some men to kill Maranzano. Luciano now became the top boss in the New York Mafia. He tried to achieve an equitable distribution of power between the five newly formed crime families, all led by veterans of the Castellammarese War. The families took names from the men in charge: Vito Genovese, Joe Profaci, Joe Bonanno, Carlo Gambino, and Luciano.

Luciano now focused on improving how criminal gangs did business. He created a national organized crime network to prevent conflicts, manage disputes and establish guidelines between the different organizations. In addition to the heads of the five families, Luciano brought in crime figures from around the country, like Al Capone from Chicago. This new entity, sometimes called the Commission, took organized crime to a new level.

By 1935 Luciano was living the good life. He lived at New York's luxurious Waldorf-Astoria under the name of Charles Ross. Overflowing with cash, wearing custom-made suits, and being driven around by a chauffeur, Luciano played the part of a wealthy businessman to the hilt. But that would soon end, as Thomas E. Dewey was appointed a special prosecutor to investigate organized crime.

In May 1936, he and eight members of his crime family were

brought to trial on charges of extortion and prostitution. Found guilty in June, Luciano was sentenced to 30 to 50 years in prison.

During World War II, the American government entered a confidential deal with the incarcerated gangster. In 1942 the Office of Naval Intelligence was worried that German and Italian agents would enter the U.S. through the New York waterfront. Sabotage was also another concern at the waterfront facilities. Knowing that the Mafi controlled the waterfront, the U.S. Navy contacted Luciano about a deal. He was moved to a facility closer to New York City to facilitate the deal.

The deal they struck was that Luciano would be a commutation of his sentence in exchange for the complete assistance of his criminal organization in providing intelligence to the Navy. They promised that there would be no dockworker strike for the duration of the war. In planning for the 1943 allied invasion of Sicily, Luciano allegedly provided the U.S. military with Sicilian Mafia contacts. This cooperation between the Navy and the Mafia became known as Operation Underworld.

On January 3, 1946, as a reward for his wartime cooperation, now Governor Dewey reluctantly commuted Luciano's pandering conviction on the condition that he agree to be deported to Italy. Luciano accepted the deal but still maintained that he could not legally be deported as an American citizen. On February 10, Luciano's ship sailed from New York Harbor for Italy. After a 17-day voyage, his ship arrived in Naples.

After being deported to Italy, Luciano hopped on a plane and headed for Cuba in October 1946. He wanted to get in on the blossoming Havana hotel and casino industry. He also wanted to talk to other mob bosses about the heroin trade and what to do about Siegel and his floundering Flamingo Hotel project in Las Vegas. The Conference lasted more than a week at the Hotel Nacional de Cuba.

However, it would be less than a year before the former American Mafia boss would suffer the same scrutiny from Cuban authorities as in the U.S. On the afternoon of February 23, 1947, Luciano was arrested at a restaurant in Havana. The head of Cuba's secret police revealed Luciano was detained because he might cause a public disorder.

Less than a month later, Luciano was deported back to Italy from

Cuba. He would spend the rest of his days in Italy. In January 1962, while meeting a film and television producer at the Naples Airport about his life story, Luciano suffered a heart attack and died.

After 300 people attended Luciano's funeral in Naples, his family was permitted by the U.S. government to bury his body in New York City. He was buried in St. John's Cemetery in Middle Village, Queens. More than 2,000 mourners attended his funeral. He was buried beside his parents under his birth name, Salvatore Lucania.

FEBRUARY 11
1990

On this day in history, Nelson Mandela, the leader of the campaign to end South African apartheid, is released from prison by South African President F.W. De Klerk after 27 years behind bars. His very dramatic walk from the gates of the Victor Verster Prison in Cape Town, hand in hand with his wife Winnie, captured the world's imagination.

Nelson Mandela was born in 1918 in the town of Mvezo, Union of South Africa. He studied law at the University of Witwatersrand and the University of Fort Hare. He then worked as a lawyer in Johannesburg. There, he became entangled in anti-colonial and African nationalist politics while joining the African National Congress (ANC) in 1943. He co-founded the ANC's Youth League in 1944.

After South Africa's National Party's white-only government created apartheid, a system of racial segregation that rich whites, Mandela and the ANC committed themselves to its destruction. He was named president of the ANC's Transvaal chapter, gaining fame for his work with the 1952 Defiance Campaign and the 1955 Congress of the People. It was during this time that Mandela was repeatedly arrested for "seditious activity" and was found not guilty during the 1956 Treason Trial. As a pro-Marxist, he joined the banned South African Communist Party (SACP). Initially, he was committed to non-violence; in league with SACP, he co-founded the militant uMkhonto we Sizwe in 1961 and then led a sabotage campaign against the government. Mandela was detained in 1962 and convicted in 1964 of conspiring to overthrow the state. For more than 18 of those years, Mandela endured the very harsh conditions of Robben Island. By the late 1970s, the almost invisible prisoner had become a symbol of South African oppression. During the 1980s, "Free Nelson Mandela" became a worldwide campaign.

The first 18 of his 27 years in prison were spent at the terrible Robben Island Prison. He was restricted to a small cell without a bed or plumbing, and he was forced to do hard labor in a stone quarry. He was allowed to write and receive one letter every six months, and once a year, he could have a 30-minute visit with one guest. However, Mandela could not be broken, and while being the symbolic leader of the anti-apartheid movement, he led a campaign of civil disobedience at Robben Island Prison that helped convince South African officials to change conditions at the prison radically. He was later moved to another facility and lived under house arrest.

In 1989, F.W. de Klerk became South African president and began the process of tearing apartheid apart. De Klerk lifted the prohibition on the ANC, suspended executions, and in February 1990, ordered Nelson Mandela's release from prison.

Mandela then led the ANC in its negotiations with the minority government to set about dismantling apartheid and for the creation of a multiracial government. Mandela and De Klerk were jointly awarded the Nobel Peace Prize in 1993. In 1994 the ANC won an electoral majority in the country's first democratically held elections. Mandela was elected as South Africa's president.

Mandela would only serve one presidential term, retiring from politics in 1999. Globally he was seen as an icon and a global advocate of democracy and social justice. He received more than 250 honors in his lifetime and is often referred to as the "Father of the Nation."

Nelson Mandela passed away on December 5, 2013. He was 95.

FEBRUARY 12
1912

On this day in history, Hsian-T'ung, the six-year-old last emperor of China, is forced to abdicate following the Xinhai Revolution. A provisional government was created in his place, ending 267 years of the Qing Dynasty and over 2100 years of imperial rule in China. The former emperor was allowed to keep his residence and servants in Beijing's Forbidden City until 1924, when he was forced into exile and took the name of Aisin-Gioro Puyi.

Puyi became emperor in November 1908 after the demise of his half-uncle, the Guangxu Emperor. Aged two years and ten months, Puyi was forcibly taken from his family and moved to the Forbidden City in Beijing by a procession of officials and eunuchs. Only his wet nurse was permitted to travel with him the entire journey. After his abdication, his life centered around the Forbidden City.

Very briefly, in July 1917, Puyi was restored to the throne as Qing emperor by the loyalist General Zhang Xun. After twelve days, republican troops overthrew the royalist forces. In 1922 it was decided that Puyi should be married. He was given a selection of photographs of potential brides, and after much deliberation, he chose Gobulo Wanrong, the teenage daughter of one of Manchuria's wealthiest aristocrats. The pair were engaged in March 1922, and they married that autumn. The very first time the teenagers met was at their wedding.

In 1924, a coup d'état saw Beijing seized and Puyi's imperial titles abolished, reducing him to a mere private citizen. After falling in with those from the Japanese Legation (essentially the Japanese embassy in China), who were sympathetic to his cause, and he moved from Beijing to neighboring Tianjin. He was courted by Chinese warlord General Zhang Zongchang and Russian and Japanese powers, all of whom flattered him and promised him the restoration of the Qing dynasty.

Imprudently manipulated by the Japanese, Puyi ventured to Manchuria in 1931, expecting to be installed as head of state by Imperial Japan. In 1932 he was made a puppet ruler, called "Chief Executive' rather than the imperial throne that was promised him when the Japanese invaded Manchuria. He was given the era name of "Datong" (Ta-tung). He had little understanding of the complicated political situation in the region at the time or realized that the state was just a colonial tool of Japan.

From 1934 until the end of World War II, Puyi was given the title of Emperor of Manchukuo, with the era name "Kangde" (Kang-te). When the Red Army arrived in Manchuria at the end of WWII, Puyi abdicated his throne and declared Manchukuo part of China again. He tried to escape but was captured by the Soviets, who refused repeated requests from the Chinese to have him returned home. This refusal most likely saved Puyi's life, as the Chinese were keen to execute members of the Qing dynasty.

He subsequently testified at the Tokyo War Trials in a vain attempt to justify his actions. Those present stated he was "prepared to go to any lengths to save his skin." Eventually, he was repatriated to China in 1949 and spent the next ten years imprisoned and re-educated as a war criminal. He was released from prison and lived simply as a street sweeper in Beijing. He supported the Communist regime in China and did all he could to forward their agenda.

Regretful for the pain and suffering he had inflicted; his newfound kindness and humility were legend. He repeatedly told people that "yesterday's Puyi is the enemy of today's Puyi." In his autobiography, written with the permission of the Chinese Communist Party, he declared that he regretted the testimony he had given at the Tokyo War Trials because he had covered up many facts to protect himself from justice.

Puyi died on October 17, 1967, from a combination of kidney cancer and heart disease. He was 61 years old.

FEBRUARY 13
1945

On this day in history, over 800 Royal Air Force Lancaster's descended on Dresden, Germany, "the Florence of the Elbe," and with its lethal cargo, turned the city into a raging inferno killing approximately 25,000 innocent people and completely flattening eight square miles that was once the city center. The city's air defenses were so ineffectual that only six British Lancaster's were shot down that horrible night.

One school of thought maintains that as a major center for Nazi Germany's rail and road network, Dresden's destruction was intended to overwhelm Nazi authorities and services and clog all transportation routes with a mass of refugees. The Allied assault on Dresden happened less than a month after over 19,000 Allied troops were killed in Germany's last-ditch offensive at the Battle of the Bulge and three weeks after the terrible discovery of the atrocities committed by German forces at Auschwitz.

Some saw the bombing of Dresden as an attempt to force a surrender; it was intended to terrorize the civilian population locally and, indeed, nationwide. While Dresden was known for culture and art, it was also the home to over 100 factories that produced everything from poison gas to munitions to aid the war effort. Furthermore, it was the last city in the country to be bombed. According to an internal RAF memo, this made it a valuable target.

Just after 6 p.m. on February 13, 1945, the 800 RAF planes took off from England and headed for Dresden. At 10 p.m., the city's air raid sirens began to wail. Within minutes, thousands of tons of bombs began to fall on the city, starting many small fires which would soon combine into a firestorm that decimated the city center. It is estimated that the temperature reached 1800 degrees Fahrenheit. This would not be the last attack. Within hours at least 500 U.S. Army Air Force planes headed for Dresden to rain down further carnage.

One Dresden bombing survivor, Lothar Metzger, who was ten years old at the time, recalled the events of that day this way:

"We saw terrible things: cremated adults shrunk to the size of small children, pieces of arms and legs, dead people, whole families burnt to death, burning people ran to and fro, burnt coaches filled with civilian refugees, dead rescuers, and soldiers, many were calling and looking for their children and families, and fire everywhere, everywhere fire, and all the time the hot wind of the firestorm threw people back into the burning houses they were trying to escape from. I cannot forget these terrible details. I can never forget them."

By the time the Dresden bombing ended on February 15, 1945, the Allies had deposited nearly 4,000 tons of bombs, and over 90 percent of the city center was destroyed. According to the city of Dresden's report of 2010, 25,000 people had been killed, though they did note that there were many unaccounted refugees in the city, and because so many victims had been vaporized, the true count could be as high as 35,000 dead. American author Kurt Vonnegut, who was present as a prisoner of war in Dresden during the Allied bombing of the city and wrote about the contentious event in his book Slaughterhouse-Five, observed of postwar Dresden, "It looked a lot like Dayton, Ohio, more open spaces than Dayton has. There must be tons of human bone meal in the ground."

Some call the bombing of Dresden a war crime – that no valuable military target existed to warrant such a harsh bombing of a relatively defenseless city. As previously noted, others believed it was a city producing weapons of war and a transportation hub that needed to be dealt with.

Many historians feel that one purpose for the devastating attack on Dresden was to show Russia the strength, willingness, and power of the British and American forces and to act as a warning to Stalin not to renege on any agreements made at Yalta or elsewhere. One memo summed it up: "The intention of the attack is to hit the enemy where he will feel it the most, behind an already partially collapsed front, to prevent the use of the city in the way of further advance – and incidentally to show the Russians when they arrive what Bomber Command can do."

FEBRUARY 14
1929

On this day in history, a black Cadillac drove up to the SMC Cartage Company garage at 2122 North Clark Street in Chicago at around 10:30 a.m., and four or five men, two wearing police uniforms, got out of the vehicle. Once inside, they ordered the seven men there to line up facing the north wall. At that point, the intruders opened fire with two Thompson submachine guns and a shotgun, hitting the seven men with over seventy bullets. Moments later, the unknown assailants walked out with their hands up, prodded by the alleged cops, and drove away. Nobody was ever tried in the case, leaving the St. Valentine's Day Massacre the most sensational unsolved crime in gangland history.

It was immediately assumed that Al "Scarface" Capone was responsible for the slayings of his rival gangster, George "Bugs" Moran, and seven associates. Gang wars ruled the streets of Chicago during the late 1920s as the top gangster, Al Capone, sought to consolidate control by getting rid of his rivals in the illegal trades of bootlegging, gambling, and prostitution. Throughout this decade, both Capone and Moran survived multiple attempted murders. On one notorious occasion, Moran and some of his associates drove six cars past a hotel in

Cicero, Illinois, where Capone and his associates were having lunch. They showered the building with more than 1,000 bullets. A $50,000 bounty on Capone's head was the final straw for the Chicago gangster. He ordered that Moran's gang be destroyed.

On February 14, the seven victims – mob accountant Adam Heyer, second-in-command Albert Kachellek; nightclub owner Albert Weinshank, enforcers Peter and Frank Gusenberg, mechanic John May and Reinhardt Schwimmer, an optometrist who liked to hang out with them — were waiting for a delivery of bootleg liquor that was expected at Moran's North Clark Street garage. But Moran was running late, and the hitmen's spotter mistook one of the seven men for Moran and gave the signal to proceed with the massacre. As Moran arrived, he noticed the police officers going into the garage. He went to a local coffee shop and waited for the situation to clear, as he thought his men were being arrested in a raid. However, little did he know that the disguised assassins were killing his associates inside.

If they were there to receive and unload bootleg liquor, they certainly were not dressed for the occasion. Most were dressed in expensive suits, the kind you would wear to a business meeting. If Moran's men were frightened by the new arrivals, they did not show it. Most of Moran's associates were armed. But not one reached for his weapon in time to do anything with it. Maybe they had been expecting the company. Perhaps they knew their guests. Or seeing men in police uniforms, they decided to play it cool. If it was money the officers wanted, Moran's men had plenty of it. But it was not about money. They were lined up against the wall, and in a brief moment, it was over.

After hearing popping noises and seeing the faux police leave with apparent prisoners, some neighbors entered the garage. They were faced with six dead men mutilated on the floor. Only Frank Gusenberg remained alive. Sergeant Thomas J. Loftus, a veteran of the 36th District station, was first on the scene. After moving the neighbors out of the way of the bodies, he spied Frank Gusenberg, who was shot 14 times, but still hanging on to life. "Do you know me, Frank?" the sergeant asked.

"Yes, you're Tom Loftus," the gangster stated between gulps of air. Then Gusenberg added: "I won't talk," as if he knew the sergeant's next question.

Yet after sucking in more air, Gusenberg (according to some newspaper accounts) did talk briefly. "Cops did it," he said.

Loftus pressed for more details but had yet to get any.

"For God's sake, get me to a hospital!" said Gusenberg.

He got to the hospital and died three hours later without saying another word.

Capone had an airtight alibi at the time of the murder. He was in a Dade County courthouse that morning being questioned by prosecutors about a New York murder. Of course, with his history of animosity with Moran, Capone could have easily ordered the hit from Florida.

In subsequent years, many theories were put forth about who committed the St. Valentine's Day Massacre. Some involve Capone, some the police for revenge for killing a sergeant's son, and some even include Moran himself doing some housecleaning of some unruly associates. What the Valentine's Day Massacre did do was set off a public outcry over mob violence which posed a problem for all mob bosses. February 14, 1929, was the last confrontation between Capone and Moran. Capone was imprisoned in 1931, and Moran lost so many influential men that he could no longer control his territory and ceased to be a force in the criminal world.

The simple fact remains that no one was ever brought to trial for the murders. It remains one of the most significant unsolved crimes in history.

(Photo: Bodies from the St. Valentine's Day Massacre in Chicago on February 14, 1929. Wikimedia Commons)

FEBRUARY 15
1564

On this day in history, Italian astronomer, physicist, mathematician, natural philosopher, and observational astronomer Galileo Galilei was born in Pisa, Duchy of Florence, Italy. He was a leading force in the Scientific Revolution, and he would go on to improve the telescope and make many significant discoveries in astronomy. Galileo's findings would result in his championing the Copernican heliocentrism (Earth rotating daily and revolving around the sun), which was met with significant opposition from the Catholic Church and some astronomers. The Church investigated the matter in 1615, ultimately concluding that heliocentrism was foolish, absurd, and heretical since it contradicted Holy Scripture. He would later defend his views again on the same topic in 1633 after he wrote *Dialogue Concerning the Two Chief World Systems* (1632). This time though, he would be found guilty of heresy and would spend the rest of his life under house arrest.

Galileo was born the son of Vincenzo Galilei, a musician, composer, and scholar, and Giulia Ammannati, who married in 1562. In 1581 he began studies at the University of Pisa at age 16 to study medicine but soon found mathematics more to his liking, much to his father's chagrin. From 1589 to 1610, Galileo taught mathematics at the universities of Pisa and then Padua. He was able to pursue his interests in astronomy and mechanics.

During this time, Galileo made important discoveries about gravity, inertia and developed the thermometer. He also created the pendulum clock and worked on the science of gnomonics (telling time by shadows) and the laws of motion.

Galileo would make his most significant impact on astronomy. His support for heliocentrism would garner the ire of the Catholic Church. He came to the same conclusion as Copernicus – that the sun was the center of the universe and not the Earth.

When he invented the world's first powerful telescope, Galileo was able to make many ground-breaking discoveries. His telescopes increased magnification from around 2x to around 30x magnification. By using his new telescope, he found that Saturn had a colorful ring of clouds around it, that the moon was not flat but had mountains and craters on the surface; he discovered that Jupiter had four moons that revolved around the planet and not the sun. To support the theory of heliocentrism, Galileo not only used the mathematical proofs of Copernicus but also had new proofs from the science of astronomy. Yet, Galileo knew that he was taking a risk with the Catholic Church by publishing his findings. He did not seem to mind risking the church's displeasure. In the *Letter to the Grand Duchess Christina*, Galileo wrote, "I do not feel obliged to believe that the same God who has endowed us with sense, reason, and intellect has intended for us to forgo their use."

Galileo was a devout Catholic. He had even considered becoming a priest as a young man. Yet, he believed the church was wrong to use the Bible as a literal source for all scientific studies. Galileo stated, "The Bible shows the way to go to heaven, not the way the heavens go." The church opposed heliocentrism based on Bible passages like "the world, if firmly established, it cannot be moved." 1 Chronicles 16:30. He believed this was a mistaken view of faith and the bible.

After the publication of *Dialogue Concerning the Two Chief World Systems* in 1632, the Vatican had Galileo arrested and imprisoned for several months. He was convicted of heresy and forced to recant his beliefs. One fanciful story relates how Galileo, after rejecting his scientific ideas, muttered under his breath – the rebellious phrase: "And yet it moves." He would spend the remaining years of his life under house arrest at Arcetri.

Galileo had three children with Maria Gamba, whom he never married: Two daughters, Virginia (Later "Sister Maria Celeste") and Livia Galilei ("Sister Arcangela"), and a son Vincenzo Gamba. Despite his later troubles with the Catholic Church, both of Galileo's daughters became nuns and were embraced by the convent of San Matteo in Arcetri.

Despite the censure at the hands of the Catholic Church, and even though he was 70 years of age, Galileo continued to make discoveries. He was able to write, while under house arrest, *Two New Sciences*; this summarised his earlier work on the new science of kinematics and the strength of materials. One significant contribution he made to the Scientific Revolution was to depict the laws of nature in mathematical terms and effectively use experiments and observation to develop theories.

His law, "A body moving on a level surface will continue in the same direction at constant speed unless disturbed," was incorporated into Sir Isaac Newton's laws of motion. His influential work led many to call him the father of "Modern Physics."

Galileo was blind when he died on January 8, 1642, in Arcetri, near Florence, Italy, at 77, after being troubled with heart palpitations and fever.

FEBRUARY 16
1942

On this day in history, 22 Australian Army nurses and 60 Australian and British soldiers, and crew members who managed to survive the sinking of the freighter *Vyner Brooke* were machine-gunned by soldiers of the Imperial Japanese Army. Australian nurse Sister Lt. Vivian Bullwinkel, American Private Eric Kingsley, and Stoker Ernest Lloyd RN were the only survivors of the carnage. A fact not reported at the Tokyo War Crimes Tribunal in 1947 nor included in subsequent re-telling of events was the rape of the 22 nurses before they were killed in the massacre, which was discovered by research in 2019.

On the afternoon of February 14, 1942, the British ship *SS Vyner Brooke* left Singapore before its fall to the Imperial Japanese Army. The ship carried many injured soldiers, the 65 nurses of the Australian Army Nursing Service taken from the 2/13th Australian General Hospital, and the remaining civilian men, women, and children. In total, there were 300 people on that ship. As the ship sailed through the difficult and treacherous strait between Bangka Island and Sumatra, she was attacked and sunk within 15 minutes by Japanese bombers.

In the mad scramble to save the wounded and to protect all the passengers, Sister Lt. Bullwinkel managed to jump ship and find a partially submerged lifeboat to hold on to along with some fellow nurses and two civilian women and one civilian man and a ship's officer managed to cling to the same life raft until it made it to shore over eight hours later. As three various groups of survivors converged at the same place on the beach, they were joined by 20 British soldiers who had swum ashore from their sunk vessel. By now, there were about 100 survivors on the beach.

By the morning of Monday, February 16, an officer from the *Vyner Brooke* suggested that as they had no food, no help for the injured, and no chance of escape, they should give themselves up to the Japanese Army. He said he would walk to Muntok, a town on the northwest of the island, and contact the Japanese. While he was gone, it was suggested by the most senior Australian nurse, Matron Irene Drummond, that all women and children should walk to Muntok. That same morning the ship's officer returned with about 20 Japanese soldiers who proceeded to separate the men from the women. They then took about 60 men down the beach and behind a headland. The nurses heard a quick succession of gunshots before the Japanese soldiers returned, sat down in front of them, and cleaned their bayonets and rifles.

One Japanese officer instructed the 22 Australian nurses and one civilian woman to walk down the beach and into the sea until they were waist-deep in the water. No one complained as the women walked into the waves, leaving ten or twelve stretcher cases on the beach and fully aware of their coming fate. All put on a brave face. Their matron, Irene Drummond, called out: "Chin up girls. I'm proud of you, and I love you all." At this point, the Japanese had begun firing the machine gun they had set up on the beach. Vivian Bullwinkel later described what happened next: "(They) started firing up and down the line with a machine gun.... They just swept up and down the line, and the girls fell one after the other. I was towards the end of the line, and a bullet got me in the left loin and went straight through and came out towards the front. The force of it knocked me over into the water, and there I lay. I did not lose consciousness.... The waves brought me back onto the edge of the water. I lay there for 10 minutes, and everything seemed quiet. I sat up and looked around, and there was no sign of anybody. Then I got up and went in the jungle and lay down and either slept or was unconscious for a couple of days."

By Wednesday, while she was examining her wounds and searching for food and water, she came across another survivor, Private Kingsley. He was one of the stretcher cases on the beach suffering from mortar wounds to the chest. After the nurses were machine-gunned, the Japanese proceeded to bayonet all those on stretchers on the beach. Kingsley was lucky as they did not hit any vital organs when they bayonetted him, and he crawled into the jungle. Realizing their prospects were grim, the two decided to turn themselves over to the Japanese while vowing never to mention what they had seen on the beach on February 16.

Bullwinkel was taken initially to Muntok, where she saw the initial group of women and children safe in Japanese hands. She also met 31 other Australian nurses who had landed at different points on Bangka Island. Of the 65 nurses on the *Vyner Brooke*, twelve were presumed drowned, 21 had been shot, and 32 had been taken to prison in Muntok before being shipped to Palembang in southern Sumatra. Over 80 people had been killed on the beach: a quarter of them women.

Bullwinkel and the others who survived spent over three years in a prisoner-of-war camp. They managed to keep the secret of what happened on Bangka Island. She kept the secrets of the rapes as the Australian government had demanded much to her everlasting pain and sorrow. Vivien Bullwinkel returned to Bangka Island in 1993 to attend an unveiling of a memorial to the nurses who died, and she donated her diaries to the Australian War Memorial; the uniform she wore when she was shot, complete with bullet holes, is also part of the Australian War Memorial's permanent collection. She died on July 3, 2000, at the age of 84.

FEBRUARY 17
1909

On this day in history, Geronimo, Chiricahua Apache leader and medicine man, died of pneumonia; while riding home on his horse, he was thrown off. He survived the night out in the cold, but Geronimo's health was deteriorating rapidly when a friend found him the next day. He passed away six days later, with his nephew at his side.

"I should never have surrendered," Geronimo, still a prisoner of war, said on his deathbed. "I should have fought until I was the last man alive."

Geronimo was born in 1829 to the Bedonkohe band of the Apache near Turkey Creek, in the modern-day state of New Mexico, then part of Mexico. However, the Apache did dispute Mexico's claim to the territory. His given name was Goyaale, meaning "the one who yawns." How he came to be called Geronimo is a historical mystery with several far-flung explanations floating around out there. His grandfather, Mahko, had been chief of the Bedonkohe Apache.

As a boy, the story goes, Geronimo swallowed the heart of his first kill to ensure a lifetime of success on the chase. Belonging to the smallest band within the Chiricahua tribe, the Bedonkohe (numbering only 8,000 people), they were surrounded by enemies – not just Mexicans but also other tribes, including the Navajo and Comanches. Raiding their neighbors was part of Apache life. As a result, the Mexicans placed a bounty on Apache scalps, but this did little to deter the frequency and viciousness of the raiding. By 17, Geronimo had already led four successful raiding operations.

On March 5, 1851, a group of 400 Mexican soldiers from Sonora under the command of Colonel Jose Maria Carrasco attacked Geronimo's camp outside Janos, Chihuahua, while the men were in town trading. According to Carrasco, this was in response to a raid that Geronimo and his men conducted at Sonora. Among those killed in Carrasco's attack at Janos were Geronimo's wife, three children, and aged mother. The loss of his whole family devastated Geronimo and led him to hate all Mexicans for the rest of his life, even more than Americans. As a show of grief, he set fire to his family's belongings and then headed into the wilderness to grieve his loss. There, it is said, alone and crying, a voice came to Geronimo that promised him: "No gun will ever kill you. I will take the bullets from the guns of the Mexicans… and I will guide your arrows."

Feeling invigorated by this newfound power, Geronimo gathered a force of 200 men and stalked the Mexican soldiers who killed his family. This continued for the next ten years as Geronimo exacted his revenge against the Mexican government.

By the 1850s, the face of the enemy had changed. With the end of the Mexican American War in 1848, the United States took over large amounts of land from Mexico, including areas belonging to the Apache. The discovery of gold in the Southwest spurred many settlers and miners to move into the territory, thus causing friction with the Apache and other Native Americans. Geronimo kept up his raiding ways, and by 1877 Geronimo was caught by the American Army and banished to the San Carlos Apache reservation. He struggled with reservation life for four years until 1881, when he finally escaped.

Over the next five years, Geronimo and his small band of Chiricahua eluded American soldiers. Perceptions of Geronimo were nearly as complicated as the man himself. His followers saw him as the last great defender of the Native American way of life. Yet others, including several fellow Apaches, viewed him as a stubborn holdout, violently driven by revenge and foolishly putting the lives of people in constant danger. At one point, nearly one-quarter of the American Army and 3,000 Mexican soldiers were engaged in the effort to hunt him down.

By September 1886, after having grown tired of the chase, Geronimo finally surrendered, this time for good. The rest of the Chiricahua Apache had been captured and sent to Florida, including some of his wives and children (Geronimo would marry nine times over his lifetime). General Nelson Miles pledged to Geronimo that he would be reunited with his family in Florida, but this would not occur for two more years.

Geronimo would spend the remaining 27 years of his life as a prisoner of war with the American government. He would never be free again. Later, he became a celebrity, with people paying for the privilege of seeing him. He would sell them photos of himself and hats that he had worn. He would even allow his picture to be taken with tourists for a fee. They would even pay 25 cents for a button off his coat.

In 1905 Geronimo rode horseback down Pennsylvania Avenue in President Theodore Roosevelt's Inaugural Parade. He rode with five other chiefs and wore a headdress and painted faces. Later in the week, Geronimo met with President Roosevelt and asked him for permission to be relieved of their status as prisoners of war and return to their homeland in Arizona. President Roosevelt refused, speaking about the continued animosity that the people of Arizona had against Geronimo and the Apache who took part in the Apache Wars. Through an interpreter, Roosevelt told Geronimo that the Apache had a "bad heart. "You killed many of my people; you burned villages...and were not good Indians." Roosevelt then told him he would "see how you and your people act" on the reservation.

He died on a reservation at Fort Sill, Oklahoma, on February 17, 1909, at age 79.

A legend is spoken of until this day that Geronimo may have managed one final escape. When an army reporter visited the monument to Geronimo at Fort Sill in 1943, he spoke to an elderly Apache man who claimed that not long after Geronimo died, some Chiricahua compatriots removed his body from Fort Sill and took it back to the Apache homeland in the rugged desert of the Southwest. Even in death, Geronimo had eluded his captors.

(Photo: Geronimo (Goyaalé), a Bedonkohe Apache, kneeling with rifle, 1887. Wikimedia Commons)

FEBRUARY 18
1943

On this day in history, Hans Scholl, his sister Sophie, and Christoph Probst, the German youth group Weisse Rose (White Rose) leaders at the University of Munich, are arrested by the Gestapo for opposing the Nazi regime. They distributed leaflets and used graffiti to denounce Nazi crimes and the political system while calling for opposition to the Nazi state and the war. On February 22, 1943, the three agitators were beheaded after a sham trial for treason.

The White Rose was comprised mainly of university medical students who spoke out against Adolf Hitler and his political and military apparatus. The founder of the movement, Hans Scholl, was a one-time member of the Hitler Youth who grew disenchanted with Nazi ideology once its true aims became apparent. As a student at the University of Munich in 1940-1941, he met two Roman Catholic professors who helped to redirect and focus his life. Leaving his medical studies for religion, philosophy, and the arts, Hans Scholl began to associate with like-minded friends who also disliked and despised the Nazi regime, and thus the White Rose was born.

The group's first leaflet was the text of a sermon by Bishop August von Galen, which Hans Scholl had read in 1941. The bishop wrote a withering treatise on the Nazis, especially their practices regarding mercy killing for the sake of eugenics and the belief that they were improving and strengthening the German race. White Rose published their first pamphlet in 1942. Over the next year, they published four more leaflets denouncing the Nazi and SS atrocities, including the extermination of Jews and Polish nobility. They called for outright resistance to the regime. These leaflets mainly targeted the educated elite in Germany. They would leave them in public phone booths, mail them to academic colleagues and send them to other universities across the country.

The risks involved in this type of endeavor were humungous. The lives of average Germans were closely watched for any deviation from absolute loyalty to the state. Even an off-hand remark critical of Hitler or the regime could result in arrest by the Gestapo, the Nazi's secret police. Yet the students of the White Rose, despite their idealism and high moral and ethical principles, risked everything, especially for their Jewish friends and neighbors. Despite the significant risks, Hans Scholl's sister Sophie, who was 21 years old, and a biology major at the University of Munich, begged her brother to allow her to participate in the group's covert endeavors.

In January 1943, White Rose printed between 6,000 and 9,000 copies of their fifth leaflet. On February 18 of that year, Hans and Sophie placed stacks of this literature around their university campus just before classes ended. They realized they had some leaflets left over, so Sophie pushed a stack off a top banister into the open Atrium below. As she did this, she was spotted by the building janitor, who was a rabid Nazi supporter. Sophie and Hans were reported to and arrested by the Gestapo and taken in for interrogation. A quick investigation into items on their person and in their home led to the arrests of most other White Rose members.

The Scholls and Christoph Probst were ordered to stand trial before the Volksgerichtshof – the Nazi's "People's Court" infamous for its unfair political practices, which more times than not ended with a death sentence – on February 22, 1943. The head of the People's Court, Roland Friesler, asked Sophie a final question whether she hadn't "indeed come to the conclusion that (her) conduct and the actions along with (her) brother and other persons in the present phase of the war should be seen as a crime against the community?" Sophie replied: "I am, now as before, of the opinion that I did the best that I could do for my nation. I, therefore, do not regret my conduct and will bear the consequences that result from my conduct." They were found guilty of treason and sentenced to death. The trio were executed the same day by guillotine at Stadelheim Prison. Sophie went under the guillotine first, followed by Hans and then Christoph. While Sophie and Christoph were silent as they died, Hans yelled, "Es lebe die Freiheit!" (Long live freedom) as the blade fell.

Sophie Scholl's last recorded words are: "How can we expect righteousness to prevail when there is hardly anyone willing to give himself up individually to a righteous cause? Such a fine, sunny day, and I have to go, but what does my death matter if, through us, thousands of people are awakened and stirred to action?"

Two more trials of White Rose members in April 1943 would result in the death sentence for many and long prison terms for others. The White Rose's sixth leaflet had been circulating, and one copy made it to London, where the Allies retitled it "The Manifesto of the Students of Munich." It printed millions of copies and dropped them from planes over Germany. Thus, the activities of the White Rose became well known in wartime Germany but, like other attempts at resistance, failed in causing widespread opposition against the Nazi regime. Yet, it continued to be an important inspiration for acts of individual resistance throughout the remaining war years.

(Photo: Sophie Scholl. Wikimedia Commons)

FEBRUARY 19
1847

On this day in history, the first rescuers reached the surviving members of the Donner Party, a group of American Midwest pioneers who were California-bound and trapped by snow in the Sierra Nevada Mountains. Detained by several unfortunate circumstances, they resorted to cannibalism to survive the long winter, eating the bodies of those who perished to starvation, sickness, and extreme cold.

In May 1846, the Donner and Reed families set out from Springfield, Illinois, amid a trend encompassing the United States to head west to California. Eighty-nine souls – including thirty-one members of the Donner and Reed families – set out by wagon train on what should have been a four-to-six-month journey. After arriving at Fort Bridger, Wyoming, the travelers were persuaded to avoid the usual route to California and decided to take a new trail recently blazed by California author and promoter Lansford Hastings, the so-called "Hastings Cut-off."

The bypass was anything but a shortcut: it was meant to shorten the journey by 350 miles but, in actuality, lengthened it by twenty-five miles. It set the Donner Party back nearly a month and cost them much-needed supplies. After suffering great deprivations in the Wasatch Mountains, the Great Salt Lake Desert, and through the

Humboldt River, the group finally reached the Sierra Nevada Mountains in early October.

Despite the lateness of the season, the Donner Party was still able to reach the slopes of the Sierra Nevada Mountains by early November 1846. They only had a mere one hundred miles remaining on their journey, but before the pioneers could drive their wagons through the mountains, an early blizzard covered the Sierras in several feet of snow. Mountain passes that were traversable twenty-four hours earlier soon transformed into icy roadblocks, forcing the Donner Party to retreat to nearby Truckee Lake and wait out the winter in dilapidated tents and cabins. Most of the group's supplies and animals had already been lost on the trail, and it was not long before the first settlers began to perish due to starvation.

On December 16, 1846, after a month of being snowbound, fifteen of the strongest members of the settlers put on makeshift snowshoes and tried to walk out of the mountains and find help for the others. After walking for several days, they were starving and on the verge of collapse. The group decided that cannibalism was their only option and decided to draw lots for a human sacrifice or even have two men square off in a duel. A few of the settlers died naturally, though, thus saving them from making a choice, so the survivors cooked and consumed their corpses. The meat, however displeasing the thought of it may have been, sustained them. After thirty-three days of walking, seven of the original fifteen made it to a Native American encampment. From a neighboring town, they could coordinate help for the others. Historians have called this trek "The Forlorn Hope."

As their food stockpile diminished, the group stranded at Truckee Lake increasingly resorted to eating bizarre meals. They killed and ate their livestock, cooked their dogs, gnawed on leftover bones, and even boiled the animal hide roofs of their cabins into a foul paste to eat. Several people died of malnutrition, but the rest managed to exist on morsels of boiled leather and tree bark until rescuers arrived in February and March 1847. Not all the settlers were robust enough to endure such measures, however, and those left at the rear were forced to cannibalize the frozen corpses of their friends while awaiting help.

In total, roughly half of the Donner Party's survivors eventually resorted to eating human flesh.

News of the stranded Donner Party made it to California quickly, and a rescue party set out at the end of January 1847. Arriving at Truckee Lake twenty days later, they found the camp completely snowbound and the surviving settlers happy with relief at their being saved. The rescuers fed the group, and then they started to evacuate them. Three more rescue parties would arrive to help with the withdrawal of settlers. Still, the return to California proved equally difficult, and the last survivors did not reach security till late April.

Of the eighty-nine original members of the Donner Party, only forty-five would reach California.

Virginia Reed, one of the settlers in the group, wrote a letter to her cousin in Illinois about "our troubles getting to California" shortly after the journey. She wrote:

> "I have not wrote to you half the trouble we have had, but I have wrote enough to let you know that you don't know what trouble is. But that God we have all got through and the only family that did not eat human flesh. We have left everything, but I don't care for that. We have got through with our lives but don't let this letter dishearten anybody. Never take no cutoffs, and hurry along as fast as you can."

> — Virginia Reed to Cousin Mary Keyes, May 16, 1847

FEBRUARY 20
1939

On this day in history, 22,000 people attended a pro-Nazi demonstration at Madison Square Garden in New York City. Organized by the German American Bund (Federation), a Nazi organization established in 1936 as a vehicle to allow American citizens of German descent a way to promote a favorable view of Nazi Germany in America. The Bund promoted the event, which incidentally took place two days before George Washington's birthday, as a "pro-Americanism" rally; the stage at the event featured a 30-foot high portrait of Washington with swastikas on both sides.

The Gardens were filled with banners that called out "Stop Jewish Domination of Christian Americans," as well as "Wake Up America. Smash Jewish Communism," were draped from the ceiling. That night, it was a full house for German American Bund leader Fritz Kuhn, who had become a household name as the "American Hitler."

Aside from its admiration for Adolf Hitler and the achievements of Nazi Germany, the German American Bund program included antisemitism, strong anti-Communist sentiments, and the demand that America remain neutral in any impending war. The group combined Nazi imagery with American patriotic imagery.

The pro-Nazi organizations in the United States were vigilantly countered by anti-Nazi organizations led by American Jews and pro-Communist groups who opposed Hitlerism and supported a boycott of German goods and services. The Joint Boycott Committee held a rally at Madison Square Garden in 1937.

There were dozens of the German American Bund's drum and bugle corps marching down the center aisle of the Gardens that night in February 1939, which featured the aforementioned 30-foot-tall portraits of George Washington surrounded by American and Bund flags. There were color guards bearing more Nazi flags following behind the drum corps.

In addition, there were 3,000 Ordnungsdienst (OD), the Bund's equivalent of Hitler's SS protection squadron troops. They were marching in SS-like uniforms of black pants, black shoes, gray shirts, Sam Browne military cross straps, and swastika insignia.

"Sieg Heil!" the OD and the crowd shouted in unison, with arms outstretched in a sea of Nazi salutes.

New York City May LaGuardia readily understood the dangers posed by a rally of this nature. Therefore, he dispatched the largest number of police to a single event in the city's history. One thousand seven hundred uniformed police officers patrolled outside the Gardens, 600 undercover detectives and non-uniformed officers were scattered throughout the hall, and even 35 firefighters, armed with a heavy-duty fire hose in preparation for a riot. Bomb squads also roamed the venue as a threat was received a week earlier, boasting of a series of time-activated devices to explode during the event. LaGuardia felt sure that New York was ready for the influx of Nazi rally attendees and was prepared to protect their guaranteed rights at all costs.

About 100,000 anti-Nazi protesters gathered outside the Gardens in protest of the Bund, carrying signs stating, "Smash Anti-Semitism," "Drive the Nazis out of New York," and "Give me a gas mask, I can't stand the smell of Nazis." Three times the protesters attempted to break the arm-linking lines of the police; the first of these, some First World War veterans wrapped in the Stars and Stripes, were held back by police on mounted horseback. Next, there was a "burly man carrying an American flag," and finally, a Trotskyist group known as the Socialists Workers Party, who, like those before them, were pushed back by police.

The rally occurred just as the Bund's popularity waned; Kuhn hoped a high-octane event would turn the group's fortunes around. The pro-Nazi Bund was highly unpopular in New York, and some called for the event to be banned. Mayor La Guardia allowed the event to go forward, correctly predicting that the Bund's high-profile spectacle would discredit them in the eyes of the public.

The rally began at 8 p.m. with a rousing rendition of "The Star-Spangled Banner." The first speaker stated that "if George Washington were alive today, he would be friends with Adolf Hitler." Speaker after speaker came to the podium spewing their anti-government and anti-Semitic diatribe to the delight of the pro-Nazi crowd. West Coast Bund leader, for instance, chose to denounce the Jewish control of Hollywood and news industries: "Everything inimical to those Nations which have freed themselves of alien domination is "News" to be played up and twisted to fan the flames of hate in the hearts of Americans, whereas the Menace of Anti-National, God-Hating Jewish Bolshevism, is deliberately minimized."

The last to speak was the Bundesfuhrer himself, Fritz Kuhn. He immediately continued the antisemitic theme of the evening, going so far as to call President Roosevelt "Rosenfeld" and the man to whom he promised to make no antisemitic remarks, Fiorello "Jew Lumpen" LaGuardia himself. Everything came to a sudden halt in the middle of Kuhn's speech when a man broke through the lines of the OD men, ran onto the stage, and charged toward Kuhn. He was quickly swarmed by the Ordnungsdienst; he was subdued amid a rollicking cascade of kicking and punching, exemplifying an "uncanny replication of Nazi thuggery as a pack of uniformed men blasted away with fists and boots on a lone Jewish victim." He was later identified as 26-year-old plumbing assistant Isadore Greenbaum, the lone victim was pulled away by a team of police and arrested. He was given ten days in jail or a $25 fine.

Kuhn finished his speech by advocating for an America ruled by White Gentiles, free from a Jewish Hollywood and news. "The Bund is open to you, provided you are sincere, of good character, of White Gentile Stock, and an American Citizen imbued with patriotic zeal. Therefore: Join!" As Kuhn left the stage, 22,000 Bund members yelled, "Free America! Free America! Free America!" in the biggest Nazi rally in American history.

FEBRUARY 21
1965

On this day in history, civil rights leader Malcolm X was assassinated after taking the stage at the Audubon Ballroom in New York City to address his Organization of Afro-American Unity. In the front row of the venue was his wife, Betty Shabazz, who was pregnant with twins, and their four daughters, who took cover as three men gunned the African American nationalist and religious leader to death shortly after 3 p.m. He was 39 years old.

Malcolm X was born Malcolm Little, on May 19, 1925, in Omaha, Nebraska, and was the civil rights era's most prominent voice for Black nationalism. He rose through the ranks of the Nation of Islam, leaving the group in 1964, following a deep rift with leader Elijah Muhammad over political ideology (Malcolm believed that the Nation of Islam should join in civil rights protests), as well as morals (he also disliked the fact that Muhammad had fathered several children by multiple women). When Malcolm called the assassination of John F. Kennedy "chickens coming home to roost," Muhammad disliked that Malcolm had disobeyed a direct order not to comment on the President's death. Muhammad silenced Malcolm for 90 days, after which a considerable rift opened between the two men.

After this incident, Malcolm broke away from the Nation of Islam.

During a trip to Mecca in 1964, Malcolm converted to Sunni Islam, taking the name el-Hajj Malik el-Shabazz. He then formed the secular Organization of African American Unity, which blamed racism and not the white race for injustices. The group also adopted a more moderate stance on civil rights.

Malcolm's leaving the Nation of Islam and the starting of his own organization prompted death threats to be made against him. On February 14, 1965, Molotov cocktails were thrown through the windows of his home in Queens while he and his family slept. They all manage to get out safely. Malcolm felt that the incident was done "upon the orders of Elijah Muhammad." Malcolm told reporters, "I live like a man who is dead already."

Preceding his talk at the Audubon Ballroom on February 21, 1965, Malcolm X had instructed his security detail not to perform security checks at the entrance. These searches of all attendees were a long-standing practice enacted by the Nation of Islam at their rallies. One that Malcolm had, in the beginning, continued after he left the organization. By January 1965, however, he had decided to stop them, even though he retained a personal security detail.

There were roughly 400 people in the audience that day for Malcolm's speech, but there was no visible law enforcement presence in the Audubon Ballroom. This was very unusual since police were usually highly visible at his rallies.

When Malcolm was about to start his speech, an altercation took place in the crowd that drew his security team away from him to calm the dispute. Just then, a lone man with a sawed-off shotgun jumped onto the stage and shot Malcolm. Two other men quickly followed with semi-automatic pistols and began shooting at Malcolm. He was shot a total of 21 times. Mujahid Abdul Halim (aka Thomas Hagan) was shot in the leg by a security guard, held and beaten by the crowd, and was subsequently arrested at the scene. While the two other gunmen escaped, they were captured five days later. Muhammad A. Aziz (aka Norman 3x Butler) and Khalil Islam (aka Thomas 15x Johnson) were arrested. All three men were members of the Nation of Islam and were charged with first-degree murder.

During their 1966 trial, Halim confessed to the crime but swore that

Islam and Aziz were innocent. Witness accounts were contradictory. The New *Times* reported that there was no physical evidence tying Islam and Aziz to the crime. Both men gave plausible alibis for their whereabouts. Halim told the jury that "I just want to testify that Butler (Aziz) and Johnson (Islam) had nothing to do with it.... I was there, I know what happened, and I know the people who were there."

Despite the lack of evidence and Halim's testimony, the three men were found guilty on March 11, 1966, and sentenced to 20 years to life in prison.

Aziz and Islam continued to maintain their innocence throughout their whole incarceration. Aziz was released from prison in 1985, at age 46, after serving 20 years. Islam, released in 1987, died in 2009. Halim was released in 2010.

Others have maintained and championed Aziz and Islam's innocence for decades. Once again, Halim asserted their innocence in a pair of affidavits filed in 1977 and 1978 and offered a partial list of his accomplices, but the judge denied the motion for a new trial. Calls from experts and authors went unheeded until February 2020 when Manhattan district attorney Cyrus R. Vance Jr. began a review of the case based on the Netflix documentary "Who Killed Malcolm X?" which supported the innocence of Aziz and Islam.

On November 18, 2021, Aziz and Islam were absolved after an investigation discovered important FBI documents held back from the defense and prosecution during the trial. Aziz was 83 years old when he was pardoned.

FEBRUARY 22
1898

On this day in history, U.S. Postmaster Frazier B. Baker and his two-year-old daughter Julia Baker were lynched and died at their home in Lake City, South Carolina, after a white mob attack on their home. The mob set fire to the Baker home in an effort to drive them out. Baker's wife and two of his other children were hit by gunfire and were wounded but managed to escape the burning house.

When the attack started at 1:00 AM on February 21, 1898, the fire had consumed the rear wall of the Baker home, which also contained the local post office. Frazier Baker knew precisely what the fire had meant. Born in nearby Effingham, he had assumed the postmastership of Lake City as a patronage appointment brought about by the state Republican Party establishment several months before. Local whites, angry by the elevation of a black man – and an "outsider" to boot – to a position of authority, had burned down the first post office building Baker maintained, had shot his black assistant, and had made repeated threats on his life. After the 1896 Presidential election, William McKinley's Republican administration appointed hundreds of blacks to postmasterships across the American South. These appointments were opposed by local whites, who disliked any black Republican officeholders. They felt that the increased political power of black postmasters would encourage them to proposition white women. The people of Lake City, South Carolina, had had enough, and they were doing something about this affront to civilized society, or so they thought.

As the smoke thickened that night, Baker's eldest son Lincoln opened the front door to cry out for help, only to retreat when several gunshots rang out. They could not douse the fire with what little water they had on hand. Baker told his wife, Lavinia, "We might as well die running as...standing still." He attempted to take his family safely out of the inferno, but backlit by the flames, he was an easy target for the well-armed whites congregated around the front of the house who opened fire. Frazier Baker, postmaster, collapsed, fatally wounded in the deluge of bullets. Whites continued to fire, inflicting severe gunshot injuries on the children Rosa, Cora, and Lincoln before they could run from their home into the sheltering darkness. (Two other children, Sarah, and Willie, were miraculously unharmed.) Lavinia tried to follow, holding their infant daughter Julia, but a bullet passed through her hand, killing the baby, and forcing her to drop the child from her arms. Struck in the leg by a second bullet, Lavinia Baker collapsed outside the building as the flames consumed the house and the bodies of her husband, Frazier, and daughter Julia. As the white mob left, local African Americans drawn by the gunfire offered refuge in their homes to the new widow and her five surviving children.

The lynching was rebuked by many in the country, including across the South. Those in the South, though, agreed with South Carolina Senator Benjamin Tillman, who stated that the "proud people" of Lake City refused to receive "their mail from a n****r." Journalist Ida B. Wells-Barnett condemned the murders and said the mob had not even pretended Baker had committed a crime. She organized mass protests in Chicago and even met with President McKinley, telling him that Baker's murder "was a federal matter, pure and simple. He died at his post of duty in defense of his country's honor, as truly as did ever a soldier on the field of battle."

The lynching of the Bakers had to compete for newspaper coverage with the sinking of the *USS Maine*, which had occurred a few days before. White newspapers in South Carolina called the murders "dastardly" and "revolting," while the *Williamsburg County Record* characterized the matter as "the darkest blot upon South Carolina's history." It also stated that the McKinley administration was also guilty of "thrusting venal negro henchmen into Southern offices of trust."

A grand jury was assembled in Williamsburg County, but no indictments were returned. The McKinley administration conducted a vigorous investigation into the murders, even offering $1500 ($48,858 today) for information leading to the arrest and conviction of any members of the white mob. Even though witnesses refused to testify, prosecutors indicted seven men for killing Frazier Baker and his daughter, Julia. Eventually, thirteen men were indicted on charges of murder, conspiracy to commit murder, assault, and the destruction of mail on April 7, 1899, after two men turned state's evidence in exchange for immunity.

The trial occurred in federal court from April 10-22, 1899. There was an all-white jury presiding over the trial. Witnesses told how events transpired that evening, and despite testifying against their neighbors, they showed no remorse for the events of that evening. Henderson Williams, an African American witness, testified that he had seen a group of white men at the post office on the night of the lynching. Williams was threatened and fled Lake City after a local businessman threatened to "do (him) like they did Baker."

The jury deliberated for about 24 hours before declaring a mistrial; the jury was hopelessly deadlocked in reaching a verdict of five to five. The case would never be retried.

Following the mistrial, Lake City whites petitioned for the post office to be reopened and mail service restored. Local African Americans ridiculed this request as hypocritical.

Lavinia Baker and her five remaining children were assisted by Charleston doctor Alonzo C. McClennan, who chaired a committee in charge of the Baker's welfare. Eventually, the Baker family moved to Boston, where a house was purchased for them. In Boston, they remained out of the public eye. The surviving Baker children would fall victim to a tuberculosis epidemic, with four children, William,

Sarah, Lincoln, and Cora, dying from the disease between 1908 and 1920. Rosa Baker, the last surviving child, would die in 1942. After her last child died, Lavinia moved back to South Carolina, where she lived until she died in 1947.

FEBRUARY 23
1836

On this day in history, a Mexican force of 6000 soldiers led by General Antonio Lopez de Santa Anna began a blockade of the fort at the Alamo. Although the Texan force of 200 was grossly outnumbered, the Alamo's defenders – commanded by James Bowie and William Travis, as well as the presence of celebrated frontiersman and Tennessee senator Davy Crockett – held out for thirteen days before the Mexican army finally overpowered them. For Texans, the Battle of the Alamo became a long-lasting representation of their fight against tyranny and their struggle for independence, which they would attain later that same year. The "Remember the Alamo" battle cry became popular ten years later during the Mexican-American War of 1846-1848.

For several months before the Mexican arrival at the Alamo, Texians had forced all Mexican troops out of Mexican Texas. At the time, there were about 100 Texians encamped at the Alamo. The Texian force grew marginally when reinforcements showed up with Bowie and Travis; for the next ten days after the Mexican force showed up at the Alamo, the two armies engaged in many skirmishes with minimal casualties. Travis knew his small force could not withstand such a significant Mexican attack, so he wrote several letters begging for more men and supplies from Texas and the United States. The head of the

Texian forces in Texas, Sam Houston, could not afford to spare any of the few men he had. As a matter of fact, Houston had initially ordered Bowie and Travis to leave the Alamo and destroy the facility on their way out of town. They had refused, feeling that the fort was defensible. Ultimately, the Texians at the Alamo were only reinforced with 100 men because the United States also had a treaty with Mexico that prevented them from supplying men and arms, which would be considered an act of war.

Early on the morning of March 6, the Mexican Army launched their final attack against the Alamo. Playing the El Deguello bugle call and flying a red flag, Santa Anna signaled that no quarter would be given to the defenders. He sent 1400-1600 men forward in four columns which overwhelmed the Alamo's tiny garrison. One column, led by General Cos, broke through the fort's north wall, and poured into the Alamo. Historians believe that Travis died while resisting this breach. During brutal hand-to-hand fighting, Mexican forces entered the Alamo until nearly the entire Texian force had been wiped out. Any Texians trying to escape were promptly cut down by Mexican cavalry as they attempted to flee. All 200 defenders were killed, while an estimated 600 soldiers from the Mexican Army were killed. Records indicate that seven men may have survived the fighting, but Santa Anna promptly executed them.

Mexican soldiers were interred in the local cemetery, Campo Santo. The Texian bodies were stacked and burned, with the ashes left where they fell until February 1837, when Juan Seguin returned to Bexar to examine the remains. He filled a simple coffin with the ashes from the funeral pyres and inscribed it with the names Travis, Crockett, and Bowie. According to an article in the Telegraph and Texas, dated March 28, 1837, Seguin buried the coffin under a peach tree grove. The spot was never marked and cannot now be found. Seguin later claimed that he had placed the coffin before the altar at the San Fernando Cathedral. In July 1936, a coffin was found at that location, but according to historian Wallace Chariton, it was unlikely to comprise the remains of the Alamo defenders. Snippets of uniforms were found in the coffin, and it is known that the Texian soldiers from the Alamo did not wear uniforms.

Several non-combatants were sent to the town of Gonzales, where Sam Houston was to spread the word of the Texian defeat. The news of the Texian loss had the exact opposite effect that Santa Anna hoped for. Recruitment to the cause went wild; many men signed up to avenge the deaths of their compatriots at the Alamo. Conversely, when news of the defeat hit Gonzales, panic ensued, which became known as "The Runaway Scrape," where the Texian army, the settlers, and the government of the new, self-declared but officially unrecognized Republic of Texas fled toward the United States ahead of the advancing Mexican Army.

Despite their losses at the Alamo, the Mexican Army in Texas still outnumbered the Texian forces by six to one. Santa Anna thought that this fact and what had happened to the Texian men at the Alamo would curtail the fighting spirit of the Texians. On April 21, 1836, the Texian Army assaulted Santa Anna's Camp near Lynchburg Ferry. The Mexican Army was caught off-guard, and the Battle of San Jacinto was basically over in 18 minutes. During the fighting, the Texian Army could be heard yelling, "Remember the Alamo!" as they slaughtered fleeing Mexican troops. As a bonus, Santa Anna was captured the next day and apparently told Houston: "That man may consider himself born to no common destiny who has conquered the Napoleon of the West. And now it remains for him to be generous to the vanquished." Houston replied, "You should have remembered that at the Alamo." Santa Anna received a reprieve, and he was forced to order his army out of Texas, thus ending Mexican control of the territory and giving some legitimacy to the new republic.

FEBRUARY 24
1841

On this day in history, former U.S. President John Quincy Adams rose in the Supreme Court to argue the Amistad case. Adams was the son of America's second president, founding father, and declared abolitionist John Adams. At age 73, John Quincy Adams was still a practicing lawyer and a member of the U.S. House of Representatives. Although he downplayed his abolitionist leanings, he believed the practice was irreconcilable to the nation's core principles of freedom and equality. Adams served one term as president between 1825 and 1829 and was then elected to the House of Representatives, where he served until he died in 1848. During his time in the House, he repealed a rule preventing any debate about slavery on the House floor.

In August 1839, the revenue cutter *Washington*, a U.S. ship, seized the schooner *Amistad* off Montauk Point in Long Island, New York. Aboard the Spanish ship was a group of Africans seized and sold illegally as enslaved people in Cuba. The enslaved Africans rebelled against their captors at sea, killing the ship's captain and cook (who promised to kill the Africans, cook them, and serve them as a meal) and taking control of the *Amistad*. American authorities seized the ship and imprisoned the Africans, beginning a legal and diplomatic fight that would rock the foundations of the nation's government and bring the hot issue of slavery to the forefront of American politics.

Joseph Cinque and the other Africans were charged in Connecticut court with murder and piracy and jailed in New Haven. These charges were quickly dropped, but the detainees were kept in jail. At the same time, the courts determined their legal status, as well as the grappling property claims of the *Washington*, the plantation owners who had allegedly purchased the Africans, Pedro Montes and Jose Ruiz, and the Spanish government.

While U.S. President Martin Van Buren tried to deport the Africans to Cuba to appease Spain, a faction of abolitionists in the North, led by Lewis Tappan, Rev. Joshua Levitt, and Rev. Simeon Jocelyn, began raising money to mount a legal defense for the Africans, arguing that they had been illegally kidnapped and exported as enslaved people from West Africa.

In January 1840, a judge in the U.S. District Court in Hartford, Connecticut, ruled that the Africans were not enslaved Spanish people but had been illegally captured and should be returned to West Africa. The decision was appealed to the Circuit Court, which upheld the lower court's decision, and then the U.S. attorney was instructed by Van Buren to appeal the verdict to the United States Supreme Court, which heard the case in early 1841.

In an eight-hour argument lasting two days, John Quincy Adams assailed Van Buren's blatant abuse of executive power. He tore apart the U.S. attorney's position that the 1795 anti-piracy treaty with Spain should override American principles of individual rights. In appeasing a foreign country, Adams argued that Van Buren committed the "utter injustice (of interfering) in a suit between parties for their individual rights." In a very dramatic moment, Adams faced the justices, pointed to a copy of the Declaration of Independence hanging on the courtroom wall, and stated: "(I know) no law, statute or constitution, no code, no treaty, except that law…which (is) forever before the eyes of your Honors." He stated, "The moment you come to the Declaration of Independence, that every man has a right to life and liberty, an inalienable right, this case is decided. I ask nothing more on behalf of these unfortunate men than this Declaration."

On March 9, 1841, the United States Supreme Court ruled 7-1 to preserve the lower court's verdicts in favor of the Africans of the *Amistad*, based on Adam's skillful arguments. Justice Joseph Story delivered the majority opinion, stating that the Africans had been unlawfully transported and held as slaves, and had rebelled in self-defence. He went on to state that "There does not seem to us to be any ground for doubt, that these negroes ought to be deemed free."

But the one thing that the court did not do was to require the government to make provisions for the Africans to get back to Sierra Leone. Salvage rights for the ship were, however, given to the U.S. Navy officers who arrested the men and their ship. After Van Buren's successor, John Tyler refused to pay for the Africans' repatriation, abolitionists again raised funds, as they had for their defense. In November 1841, Joseph Cinque and the other 34 surviving Africans of the *Amistad* (the others perished at sea or in prison awaiting trial) left New York aboard the ship *Gentleman*, escorted by several Christian missionaries, to return to their homeland.

FEBRUARY 25
1855

On this day in history, Bowery Boys gang leader William "Bill the Butcher" Poole was shot in the chest by a gang from arch-rival John Morrissey's Irish American-led political group Tammany Hall. Poole, the local leader of the Know Nothing political movement in mid-19th-century New York City, would die 11 days later. "Bill the Butcher" is mainly remembered today by the villainous performance of Daniel Day-Lewis in the movie Gangs of New York. Lewis's character, Bill "The Butcher" Cutting, was inspired by the real William Poole.

William Poole was born in New Jersey on July 24, 1821, the son of a butcher. At age 10, his family relocated to New York City, where Poole followed in his father's footsteps and ultimately took over the family shop in Lower Manhattan. By the 1850s, he was married and had a son. Considered a big man for the times, Poole was over six feet in height and weighed more than 200 pounds.

He was considered violent and totally uncontrolled emotionally. According to the *New York Times*, Poole frequently argued, was considered a demanding customer, and loved to fight. The *Times* wrote, "He was a fighter, ready for action on all occasions when he fancied, he had been insulted. And while his manners, when he was not aroused, were generally marked with much politeness, his spirit was haughty and overbearing.... He could not brook an insolent remark from one who thought himself as strong as he."

Poole's fighting style made him remarkably and generally admired as one of the best "rough and tumble" fighters in the country. He particularly enjoyed gouging out an opponent's eyes and was very proficient with using knives due to his line of work. Poole was also known as a heavy drinker and gambler. He closed his family's butchery business in the 1850s and opened a drinking saloon called the "Bank Exchange."

William Poole became the leader of the Bowery Boys, a nativist, anti-Catholic, anti-Irish gang in antebellum Manhattan. The street gang was associated with the xenophobic, pro-Protestant Know Nothing political movement, which thrived in New York in the 1840s and 1850s. They felt that the thousands of Irish immigrants pouring into the United States would wreak havoc on America's democratic and Protestant values.

For his part, Poole became a lead "shoulder hitter" who would enforce the nativists' rule at the ballot box. He and other Bowery Boys would constantly be street-fighting with their Irish rivals, then known as the "Dead Rabbits." Poole's main rival was John "Old Smoke" Morrissey, an Irish-born American and bare-knuckle boxer who had won the heavyweight title in 1853. Morrissey was ten years younger than Poole and was a "shoulder-hitter" for the Tammany Hall political movement that ran the Democratic Party in New York City. Tammany Hall was pro-immigrant; by the mid-19th century, most of its leaders were Irish American.

Poole and Morrissey were arrogant, vicious, and explosive, but they occupied different sides of the political spectrum. Partisan differences and bigotry aside, deadly fighting between them was almost certain because of their egos.

Poole and Morrissey locked horns in July 1854 at the Amos Street docks. After a spirited and dirty eye-gouging affair, Poole came out on top after Morrissey gave up after being battered mercilessly by Poole.

According to newspaper accounts, John Morrissey met William Poole again on February 25, 1855, at Stanwix Hall. When Poole entered the establishment, Morrissey immediately confronted Poole and yelled obscenities at him. Morrissey then drew a gun, pointed it at Poole's head, and pulled the trigger three times, each time failing to discharge. The police were called, and both men were taken to different police stations, but neither were charged, and they were released.

By 1 a.m. Poole was back at the Stanwix. It is unclear where Morrissey was at this time. Shortly after that, six of Morrissey's associates came into the saloon – including Lewis Baker, James Turner, and Patrick "Paudeen" McLaughlin. Each of these men had had previous contact with Poole, pleasant or otherwise. According to witnesses, Paudeen tried to goade Poole into a fight but refused because he was outnumbered, even though Paudeen had spit in Poole's face three times and called him a "black-muzzled bastard."

At that point, Turner pulled out his Colt revolver and pointed it at Poole. Turner was pushed just as he squeezed the trigger. The shot accidentally went through his left arm, shattering the bone. Turner then fell to the floor and then fired again. This time he hit Poole in the right leg above the kneecap, and then he hit him in the shoulder with another bullet.

William Poole began to move for the door but was intercepted by Lewis Baker, who said, "I guess I will take you anyhow." He then shot Poole in the chest. It took Bill the Butcher 11 days to die. The bullet did not enter his heart but lodged into its protective sac. On March 8, 1855, William Poole finally fell victim to his wounds. His purported last words were, "Goodbye, boys, I die a true American." He was buried with thousands of spectators in Brooklyn's Green-Wood Cemetery on March 11, 1855.

Lewis Baker was indicted along with John Morrissey, James Turner, Cornelius Linn, Charles Van Pelt, John Huyler, James Irving, and Patrick "Paudeen" McLaughlin for feloniously killing William Poole with a loaded pistol. The trial lasted fifteen days; the jury deliberated for just over a day but could not reach a verdict. It was reported that nine jurors voted for conviction and three for acquittal. The three for acquittal were of foreign birth.

Baker was tried twice more, but each time resulted in a hung jury.

He was eventually released. Morrissey went on to open several Irish pubs and stockpile a fortune of $1.5 million. He would serve two terms as a New York state senator and two more terms in the U.S. House of Representatives. Morrissey died in 1878 and was buried in a Roman Catholic cemetery in his boyhood hometown of Troy, New York.

FEBRUARY 26
1846

On this day in history, William Frederick Cody, better known as "Buffalo Bill," was born in Le Claire, Iowa Territory (now the U.S. state of Iowa). He was an American soldier, a recipient of the Medal of Honor, a performer, a bison hunter, a pony express rider, and a U.S. Army scout. He eventually became a Knight Templar and had a 32nd degree in the Scottish Rite branch.

He was one of the most famous and well-known personages of the American Old West. Buffalo Bill's legend began to grow when he was a mere 23 years old. Soon afterward, he started to perform in shows that displayed cowboy themes and events from the frontier and Indian Wars. He founded *Buffalo Bill's Wild West* in 1883, taking his huge company on tours of the United States and, beginning in 1887, to England and Europe.

In 1847, when William was one year old, his parents, Isaac, and Mary Cody, moved the family back to Isaac's birthplace in what is now Mississauga, Ontario, Canada. After several years there, the family moved back to Iowa to sell their land, and then in 1853, they all moved to Fort Leavenworth, Kansas Territory. While the territory dealt with the slavery issue, Isaac gave an anti-slavery speech in a trading post, a known den for pro-slavery advocates. Warned to stop his speech, Isaac was stabbed twice when he refused. But now he was a marked man, having survived the stabbing. Continuously on the run from his attackers, Isaac finally succumbed to a respiratory infection compounded by the nagging effects of his stabbing and complications from kidney disease, which led to his death in April 1857. William was 11 years old and now the man of the family. It was time to find a job.

By the age of 19, William had already worked as an army scout, cattle driver, teamster, fur trapper, prospector, and Indian fighter. After he joined the Russell, Majors, and Waddell firm as a teamster and a cattle driver, Cody became a Plainsman and frequently accompanied military supply trains bound for the West.

In 1864, Cody enlisted in the Seventh Kansas Volunteer Cavalry. After one and a half years as a private, he met Louisa Frederici in St. Louis, and after a brief courtship, the two were married in 1866. The couple would stay together for over fifty years despite some definite rough patches, especially when Cody tried to sue for divorce but was unsuccessful. They would have four children, but two would die when they were young.

In 1866 Cody would reunite with his old friend "Wild Bill" Hickok in Kansas, and they both became army scouts. Making $75 monthly, Cody guided troops, carried messages, and hunted game. For the next ten years, he remained a proficient and reliable scout for the United States Army. After he became Chief of Scouts for the Fifth Cavalry, he took part in several conflicts with the Plains Indians.

His involvement in the 1869 Battle at Summit Springs saw him kill Chief Tall Bull, the notorious leader of the Cheyenne Dog Soldiers. Three years later, the United States Congress awarded Cody the Medal of Honor for his total contributions as a civilian scout.

During this time, figures like "Wild Bill" Hickok and William "Buffalo Bill" Cody created the beginnings of American celebrity. Cody began cultivating his Wild West persona on the back of Hickok's, growing his hair, and wearing similar buckskin outfits. Cody's nickname grew out of an 18-month stint buffalo hunting in Kansas. He claimed to have killed 4,282 buffalo.

In the early 1870s, Cody was noticed by an author who wrote a fictionalized account of his life in a newspaper serial. Under the nom de plume Ned Buntline, the author's *Buffalo Bill, King of the Border Men* overstated Cody's character and was regularly published in New York Weekly. These tales of Buffalo Bill would be compressed into dime novels that sold well. Over the next four decades, Cody would create and craft a prolific career as a caricature of himself.

In 1872 Buntline invited Cody to play himself in the western Scouts of the Prairie melodrama on stage in Chicago. It was a rousing success at the box office. Because of the success, Cody decided to create his own troupe called The Buffalo Bill Combination, and it toured around the country with alternating casts for ten years. The dramatizations were usually centered around triumphant gunplay between Native Americans and a mythical version of Buffalo Bill. Touring was seasonal, so he spent time with his family in his downtime. After the death of Custer at Little Big Horn, Cody returned to his scouting duties with the Fifth Cavalry.

In 1883 Cody founded *Buffalo Bill's Wild West*, a circus-like attraction that toured annually throughout the United States and continental Europe. In 1893, Cody changed the title of his show to Buffalo Bill's Wild West and Congress of Rough Riders of the World. This show began with a parade on horseback, with people from horse-culture groups that included the U.S. and another military, cowboys, American Indians, and performers from all over the world in their best dress. Turks, Georgians, gauchos, Arabs, and Mongols displayed their distinctive horses and colorful costumes. Visitors would see main events, feats of skill, staged races, and sideshows. Many historical Western figures took part in the show. One example is Sitting Bull, performed with a band of 20 braves.

Cody performed for Queen Victoria, Kaiser Wilhelm II of Germany, Pope Leo XIII, The Prince of Wales, later King Edward VII, and the future King George V. His show played before millions of people on both sides of the Atlantic and made Cody a wealthy man for a while. A series of bad investments would drive his net worth to a mere $100,000 by the time he died.

Cody passed away on January 10, 1917. He was christened in the Catholic Church the day before his death. He received a full Masonic funeral. On June 3, 1917, Cody was buried on Lookout Mountain in

Golden, Colorado. In 1948 the Cody Chapter of the American Legion offered a $10,000 reward to anyone who would steal Cody's body and take it to Cody, Wyoming. In reaction, the Denver chapter of the American Legion placed a guard over the grave. Rumors persist that Buffalo Bill is buried at Cedar Mountain in Cody, Wyoming.

FEBRUARY 27
1854

On this date in history, German composer Robert Schumann is saved during a suicide attempt on the Rhine River in Dusseldorf, Germany. Schumann suffered from a mental disorder that began in 1833 as a serious, melancholic depressive episode. It recurred many times, staggering between phases of "exaltation" and increasingly also paranoid ideas of being poisoned or terrorized with metallic items. It is now thought that he suffered from bipolar disorder and perhaps mercury poisoning from a possible case of syphilis, which led to "manic" and "depressive" periods in Schumann's compositional productivity.

In addition to being a composer, Robert Schumann was a pianist and prominent music critic with his own publication (Neue Zeitschrift fur Musik (New Journal for Music)). He is widely viewed as one of the greatest composers of the Romantic era. For a time, Schumann studied law, but he soon grew tired of those studies thrust upon him by his family. His heart truly lay with pursuing a career as a virtuoso pianist. His teacher, Friedrich Wieck, a German pianist, had assured him that he could, with hard work, become the greatest pianist in Europe, but an injury to his right hand derailed his dream permanently. Schumann then decided to focus his musical energies on composing.

Until 1840, Schumann wrote expressly for the piano. Later, he composed piano and orchestral works and many Lieder (songs for voice and piano). He composed four symphonies, one opera, and other orchestral, choral, and chamber works. His best-known works include *Carnaval, Symphonic Studies, Kinderszenen, Kreisleriana,* and the *Fantasie in C.* Schumann became well-known for infusing his music with characters through motifs and references to works of literature. These characters worked their way into his editorial writing in the (Neue Zeitschrift fur Musik (New Journal for Music), a Leipzig-based publication he co-founded.

Schumann's nervous constitution had never been strong. He had considered suicide at least three times during the 1830s, and from the mid-1840s on, he suffered from periodic attacks of severe depression and nervous exhaustion. His musical capabilities had declined by the late 1840s, though some of his work still displayed flashes of his former genius. By 1852 a general decline of his nervous system was becoming evident. On February 10, 1854, Schumann complained of a "very strong and painful" attack of the ear malady that had troubled him before; aural hallucinations followed this. On February 26, he asked to be taken to a lunatic asylum.

Around noon on February 27, 1854, Robert Schumann left his study and exited his family's first-floor apartment on Bilker Strasse in Dusseldorf without explanation. He was still wearing his floral-patterned dressing gown and slippers and was hatless in the frigid February weather. He walked to a wooden pontoon bridge on the Rhine River for about ten minutes through pouring rain. It was carnival time in the city, so his bizarre clothing would have easily blended in with the crowds than maybe it might have otherwise done.

Schumann arrived at the bridge without money to pay the toll collector. In lieu of the toll, he offered the collector his silk handkerchief and was allowed to continue. The specific details of what happened next are not clear. At some point on his way across the bridge, Schumann halted, stepped over the wooden railing, and jumped into the Rhine, possibly via one of the pontoon boats below.

The sudden impact with the ice-cold river would have been immediate, and Schumann would undoubtedly have drowned or died of hypothermia had help not been close at hand. It came from Joseph Jungermann, a local river worker who reacted swiftly by pulling the composer from the fast-flowing current into his vessel. According to witnesses, Schumann resisted Jungermann's efforts to save him but was eventually brought ashore and taken home in a cart.

While the news of Schumann's apparent suicide attempt was shocking to both his friends and his family. His wife, Clara Schumann, stated that "What I felt is indescribable, it was as if my heart had stopped beating." But his attempt to end his life certainly was not surprising. For years he had suffered from mental instability, which had grown alarmingly worse in the weeks immediately preceding the Rhine incident.

Schumann had reported suffering from "very strong and painful auditory disturbances" and began hearing music "more wonderful than one ever hears on earth." He claimed one theme was dictated to him by Schubert – dead for a quarter of a century – and he began writing variations on it. But demon voices also assailed Schumann, accusing him of sinfulness and causing him to scream out fearfully— more than once, he worried that he might harm his beloved Clara.

External factors may have played a part in his mental collapse as well. A few months before this, Schumann had been forced to step down as municipal music director in Dusseldorf, where his tenure had not inspired much confidence. The humiliation was huge and had financial ramifications, especially as Clara was pregnant with the couple's seventh child. Any or all these circumstances may have triggered Robert's final collapse. The truth is we will never know precisely why Schumann acted as he did on that fateful February morning in 1854.

Five days later, he was admitted into a mental asylum nearly 40 miles away in Endenich, near Bonn, a move Schumann himself had suggested to his doctors. There he spent the remaining 28 months of his life, occasionally lucid but more often delusional and sometimes straitjacketed.

Clara, strongly advised by doctors to stay away from Endenich, visited her husband just once on July 27, 1856. "He smiled at me," she wrote, "and wrapped his arm around me – never will I forget that." Two days later, Robert died, aged 46. Despite living for another 40 years, Clara never remarried.

FEBRUARY 28
1906

On this date in history, American gangster Benjamin "Bugsy" Siegal was born. He began his life of crime on the streets of New York City. He created the Bugs-Meyer gang with his friend Meyer Lansky as a teenager; then, he rose to prominence within Mafia kingpin Charles "Lucky" Luciano's national syndicate. Siegal relocated his gambling rackets and bootlegging to the West Coast after numerous death threats were made against him. While there, he maintained a lavish lifestyle as in New York. In 1945 he moved his operations to Las Vegas to supervise the syndicate-funded construction of the Flamingo Hotel and Casino. With mob bosses on the East Coast very unhappy with his management of the construction of the Flamingo, Siegal was shot to death in his girlfriend's Beverly Hills home.

He was the second of five children of Jennie and Max Siegal, a poor Jewish family that emigrated from the Galicia region of the then-Austro-Hungarian Empire. With the creation of the Bugs-Meyer Gang, the two small-time gangsters became involved in gambling, car theft, and bootlegging. Siegal hired himself out to other gangs as a hitman almost a decade before Murder Inc. was created. He first smoked opium during his youth and became involved in the drug trade. By age 21, he made a lot of money and was not shy about bragging about it. He purchased an apartment at the Waldorf Astoria Hotel and a Tudor-style Scarsdale, New York home. He wore flashy clothes and jewelry and participated in New York City nightlife.

On January 28, 1929, Siegal married Esta Krakower, his childhood sweetheart. They had two daughters, Millicent, and Barbara. He had a well-deserved reputation as a womanizer, and the marriage ended in 1946. His wife moved with their daughters from California to New York.

By the late 1920s, Lansky and Siegal had ties to Luciano and Frank Costello, the future bosses of the Genovese crime family. Siegal was part of a crew that killed New York mob boss Joe Masseria on Luciano's orders on April 15, 1931, ending the Castellammarese War. On September 10 of that same year, Luciano hired a crew of four from the Bugs-Meyer mob to murder mobster Salvatore Maranzano, thus creating Luciano's rise to the top of the Mafia and signifying the beginning of the era of modern American organized crime.

After Maranzano's death, Luciano and Lansky formed the National Crime Syndicate, an organization of crime families that brought power to the underworld. The Commission was established to divide Mafia territories and prevent future gang wars. With his associates, Siegal created Murder, Inc. This was the enforcement arm of the National Crime Syndicate and, between 1929 and 1941, committed between 400 and 1,000 murders, often within organized crime.

By the late 1930s, Siegal's enemies were closing in on him. The East Coast mob decided that Siegal should go to California and head up their West Coast operations. Upon arriving, he soon took over Los Angeles's numbers racket. He used money from the syndicate to help establish the drug trade route from Mexico and organized circuits with the Chicago Outfit's wire services. By 1942 $500,000 US per day was coming in via the syndicate's bookmaking wire operations.

Siegal was welcomed into the highest circles in Hollywood and befriended movie stars. He associated with George Raft, Clark Gable, Gary Cooper, Cary Grant, and studio executives Louis B. Mayer and Jack L. Warner. Actress Jean Harlow was a friend of Siegal's and a godmother to his daughter Millicent. Siegal also threw lavish parties at his Hollywood Hills home. He gained the admiration of young celebrities, including Tony Curtis, Phil Silvers, and Frank Sinatra.

In Hollywood, Siegal devised a plan to extort the movie studios; he would take control of the local trade unions (such as the Screen Extras Guild and the Los Angeles Teamsters) and stage strikes to force studios to pay him off so that unions would return to work. Siegel would also borrow money from celebrities, knowing they would never ask for repayment. During his first year in Hollywood, he received more than $400,000 U.S. in loans from movie stars.

In 1939, Siegal attempted to sell Atomite, a new type of explosive substance that detonated without sound or flash, to Benito Mussolini and the Axis powers. Mussolini advanced $40,000 to Siegel to have the atomite scaled up, but during a demonstration for Mussolini, Joseph Goebbels, and Hermann Goring, the atomite failed to detonate. Mussolini demanded the return of his $40,000.

In 1946, Siegel found a way to reinvent his image after the Harry Greenberg assassination debacle of 1939. Siegel had been charged with murder after a crewmember ratted on him. He lived like a king in jail, and two witnesses ended up dead, but in the end, he was found not guilty due to a lack of evidence. Siegel's idea was to diversify into a legitimate business with William R. Wilkerson's Flamingo Hotel. He had big plans for the Flamingo Hotel, and they did not include Wilkerson, who was coerced into selling his stake in the Hotel under the threat of death. Wilkerson went into hiding in Paris for a time. From this point on, the Flamingo became syndicate-run.

The Flamingo needed an investment of 1.2 million dollars to finish. The East Coast mob agreed to pay; however, by the time Siegel was done, it cost 6 million dollars. The Flamingo finally opened on December 26, 1946, during a massive wind and rainstorm. Few people showed up, and not the Hollywood stars that were expected to show up. The Casino was shut down after losing $275,000 at the gaming tables during the first two weeks of operation. On March 1, 1947, the operation reopened and was immediately profitable; however, the mob bosses had had enough of Siegel.

On the evening of June 20, 1947, as Siegel sat with his friend Allen Smiley in his girlfriend Virginia Hill's Beverly Hills home reading the

Los Angeles Times, an unknown gunman shot him through the window, striking him many times, including twice in the head. No one has ever been charged with Siegel's death, and the crime remains unsolved.

The prominent theory is that Siegal's death resulted from his massive cost overruns and possible theft of mob funds during the Flamingo Hotel construction. In 1946, a conference was convened with the "board of directors" of the crime syndicate in Havana, Cuba, so Luciano, exiled in Sicily, could attend, and participate. A contract on Siegel's life was the conclusion. It is said that Lansky reluctantly agreed with the decision. Another theory is that Siegel was shot to death pre-emptively by Mathew "Moose" Pandza, the lover of mobster Moe Sedway's wife Bee, who went to Pandza after learning that Siegel would kill her husband. Siegel had grown tired of Sedway's influence over his finances and thus planned to get rid of him.

The day after Siegel's murder, David Berman and his Las Vegas mob associates, Sedway and Gus Greenbaum, walked into the Flamingo and took over the operation of the Hotel and casino.

FEBRUARY 29
1940

On this day in history, Hattie McDaniel became the first African American actor to win an Oscar for Best Supporting Actress for her role as Mammy in *Gone With The Wind*, which went on to win 8 Oscars that night. This was an impressive feat considering the racist overtones of the book of the same name by Margaret Mitchell and the movie and Hollywood's attitude toward African American actors in the film industry. In 1940, years before the civil rights movement altered the nation's perceptions of African Americans, McDaniel's win was groundbreaking in white Hollywood. Yet, it would not be enough to shatter the prevalent racial stereotypes.

McDaniel's career would produce two stars on the Hollywood Walk of Fame (one for radio and one for film), and in 1975 she was included in the Black Filmmakers Hall of Fame, and she was the first Black Oscar recipient honored with a U.S. postage stamp in 2006. McDaniel also recorded 16 blues records from 1926 to 1929 and was a radio performer and a television personality; she was the first Black woman to sing on radio in America. Even though she appeared in more than 300 movies, she only received on-screen credits for 83. In addition to *Gone With The Wind*, her other significant films are *Alice Adams*, *In This Our Life*, and *Since You Went Away*.

Hattie McDaniel was born to formerly enslaved people on June 10, 1895, in Wichita, Kansas. Her father, Henry McDaniel, fought with the 122nd United States Colored Troops during the Civil War, while her mother, Susan Holbert, was a singer. In 1900 the family moved to Denver, Colorado. It was here that Hattie learned that she desired to be an actress.

At 15, she quit high school to pursue her acting career, but she was not the only one in the family interested in acting. McDaniel went on the road with her brother, Otis, when he joined up with a touring carnival.

In 1914, Hattie created a women-only minstrel show with her sister Etta Goff titled the McDaniel Sisters Company. McDaniel took on extra work as a maid and laundress to make ends meet. Then, in 1929, Hattie was hired as lead singer in George Morrison's Melody Hounds, a traveling jazz orchestra based in Denver. Their tours took her to Hollywood, where she landed her first uncredited role in *The Impatient Maiden* in 1932. Two years later, her name was in the movie credits for the first time in Judge Priest, but it was misspelled as "McDaniels."

Hattie McDaniel continued to grab minor roles throughout the 1930s. But like most African Americans at the time in the lily-white film industry, McDaniel was primarily typecast as the help. She would portray a maid 74 times throughout her career.

Finally, she scored her biggest gig in playing "Mammy" in 1939's *Gone With The Wind*. Upon hearing about the planned production of this movie, the NAACP fought hard for the film's producer and director to delete racial epithets from the film (in particular, the offensive n-word) and to change scenes that might be incendiary and that were historically inaccurate. The Ku Klux Klan is portrayed as a savior in one scene with Scarlett O'Hara. The settings were altered, and some of the language was deleted ("darkie" was still used despite the protestations of the NAACP), yet the film's message about slavery stayed much the same.

The premiere of *Gone With The Wind* was held at Loew's Grand Theater on Peachtree Street in Atlanta, Georgia, on Friday, December 15, 1939. Studio head David O. Selznick requested that McDaniel be permitted to attend, but MGM told him no because of Georgia's segregation laws. Clark Gable promised to boycott the Atlanta premiere unless McDaniel was allowed to participate, but McDaniel convinced Gable to attend anyway. While Jim Crow laws kept McDaniel from the Atlanta premiere, she participated in the movie's Hollywood opening on December 28, 1939. Selznick insisted that her picture feature prominently in the program.

For her performance as the house servant in which she won the 1939 Academy Award for Best Supporting Actress, she was the first Black American actor to be nominated and to win an Oscar. When speaking about the part, McDaniel stated, "I loved Mammy.... I think I understood her because my own grandmother worked on a plantation not unlike Tara." Her performance upset some Southern whites, who felt she had become too "familiar" with her white owners. But that was essentially the character that Margaret Mitchell created in her novel.

When McDaniel attempted to take her "Mammy" character on a road show, Black audiences were not open-minded. While many Blacks were happy about McDaniel's personal victory, they also viewed it as bittersweet, feeling that the movie praised the slave system and disliked the forces that demolished it. For them, the award McDaniel had won suggested that only those who did not fight Hollywood's systemic use of racial generalizations could find work and success there.

The Twelfth Academy Awards occurred at the Ambassador Hotel's Coconut Grove Restaurant in Los Angeles. When she turned up at the hotel, McDaniel was taken to "a small table set against a far wall," where she spent the remainder of the night with her black companion, F.P. Yober, and her white agent, William Meiklejohn. She was not permitted to sit with her fellow cast members, who were all white.

Hattie McDaniel accepted her Oscar, dressed in a beautiful turquoise gown embellished with rhinestones and white gardenias in her hair. To thunderous applause, she appeared on stage to receive her honor. At the podium, she stated:

"Academy of Motion Picture Arts and Sciences, fellow members of the motion picture industry and honored guests: This is one of the happiest moments of my life, and I want to thank each one of you who had a part in selecting me for one of their awards, for your kindness. It has made me feel very, very humble; and I shall always hold it as a beacon for anything that I may be able to do in the future. I sincerely hope I shall always be a credit to my race and to the motion picture industry. My heart is too full to tell you just how I feel, and may I say thank you and God bless you."

She made her final movie appearances in *Mickey* (1948) and *Family Honeymoon* (1949). She stayed active on radio and television in her later years, becoming the first Black American to feature in her own radio show with the comedy series "Beulah." That show was very controversial: Critics stated that it perpetuated negative stereotypes of black men as lazy and shiftless. She repeatedly asked her disparagers, "Why should I complain about making $700 a week playing a maid? If I didn't, I'd be making $7 a week being one."

McDaniel died of breast cancer at age 59 on October 26, 1952, at the hospital on the premises of the Motion Picture House in Woodland Hills, California. It was her wish to be buried at Hollywood Cemetery, on Santa Monica Boulevard in Hollywood, but the owner at the time, Jules Roth, forbade it as it was a "Whites Only" cemetery. Alternately, she was buried at Rosedale Cemetery (now known as Angelus-Rosedale Cemetery), where she lies today.

In 1999, Tyler Cassity, the new owner of the Hollywood Cemetery (now known as the Hollywood Forever Cemetery), offered to have McDaniel re-interred there. Her family refused to disturb her remains and declined the offer. Instead, Hollywood Forever Cemetery built a large cenotaph on the lawn overlooking its lake. It is one of Hollywood's most popular tourist attractions.

MARCH 1
1912

On this day in history, New York City police department "police matron" Isabella Goodwin was appointed the NYPD's first female detective and ranked 1st-grade lieutenant. As a matron, she was previously responsible for caring for the station house and the women and children held there. Goodwin got her big break in 1912 when the so-called "taxi bandit" managed to pull off a bank heist and get away with $25,000 ($600,000 U.S. in today's funds). Goodwin would go undercover and secure the needed evidence to put the heist's mastermind behind bars, thus securing her detective's shield.

Goodwin was born Isabella Loghry in Manhattan on February 20, 1865, to Anna Monteith and James Harvey Loghry, who operated a restaurant and hotel on Canal Street. When she was young, Isabella hoped to be an opera singer. When she was 19, she married John W. Goodwin, an NYPD patrolman. But unfortunately, he died in 1896, leaving a 30-year-old widow with four children to support on her own.

Shortly after the death of her husband, Goodwin decided she, too, would work for the NYPD. It was common for police departments to hire widows of fallen officers; Goodwin was not just handed the job. She studied for and passed the required civil service exam and, in May of 1896, was assigned as a police matron.

Even as a matron, Isabella Goodwin was recognized for her sleuthing skills. One contemporary newspaper account described Goodwin as possessing "a kind, motherly face. Her dark hair is not yet streaked with gray. And her gray eyes are full of expression and sympathy. A broad forehead denotes intelligence, and her manner would lead one to take her for a married woman of the well-to-do class."

In 1910 Goodwin was transferred to the detective bureau to help with investigations, all for less than half of a detective's pay. Standing just 5'1", Goodwin put her kindly, sympathetic appearance and demeanor to good use in her new job. She was given special investigations to work at, posing as a naïve society matron to uncover fortune tellers, quack healers, astrologers, Hindu magicians, and surgeons. She even went undercover as a degenerate gambler to help raid a women's-only betting parlor. She gained evidence against over 500 swindlers while working as a police matron.

One morning in February of 1912, a bank robbery took place in broad daylight on a busy street in the heart of Manhattan's Financial District would change the trajectory of Isabella Goodwin's life and police career.

A gangster named Eddie "the Boob" Kinsman and some accomplices managed to hijack a taxi, robbing the driver and his guard while beating them up, before speeding away in a waiting getaway car. (The NYPD had no vehicles in their department, so they could not give chase.) The East River National Bank robbery netted Kinsman a cool $25,000, the equivalent of about $600,000 U.S. today.

The robbery stunned Manhattan and made national news when the fugitives managed to elude police not long before the press started railing against the NYPD and its being "seemingly helpless" in its ability to crack the case.

Before long, the NYPD got a tip that Kinsman was hanging around the rooming house where "Swede Annie" Hull and her companion Myrtle Hoyt were hanging out. This was when they called in Isabella Goodwin. She was tasked with going undercover to find Kinsman's girlfriend, Swede Annie, by hiring on as a maid in the rooming house where she lived. Her job there was scrubbing floors, cleaning rooms, collecting rent, emptying the garbage, running errands for the lodgers, and cooking meals for $6 per week. In return, she would stay rent-free in a dark, miserable little hole in the wall.

The New York Times interviewed Goodwin, who stated how she looked the part "with slatternly clothing and frowsy hair." She wore an old kimono from her house as she worked, and she watched the boarders all day and roamed the halls by night, standing outside doorways, listening at keyholes, and clandestinely leaving in the early hours to report back to the NYPD. In one of her evening forays in the hallways of the boarding house, she heard Swede Annie regale to her roommate, "Well, Eddie the Boob turned the trick all right."

Goodwin knew from her many years as a matron that down-on-their-luck women often confided in the hired help. So, when she saw Myrtle Hoyt in a funk in her room, she knew this was the opening she was looking for. "What's wrong?" Isabella asked Myrtle. By the time Hoyt stopped speaking, Goodwin had learned that Eddie Kinsman and Swede Annie had embarked on an upstate shopping spree. When Swede Annie returned in fancy new clothes and flashing a wad of cash, she told Hoyt she was leaving and that she and Kinsman were living in a downtown hotel before heading West.

Because of Isabella Goodwin, four NYPD detectives were at Grand Central Station ready to arrest Eddie "the Boob" Kinsman as he was about to buy two tickets to California. He was arrested for highway robbery and assault with an attempt to kill and was eventually sentenced to three to six years in prison.

Goodwin was summoned to the commissioner's office the morning after the arrest and given a promotion; she was now a detective lieutenant with a hefty pay raise of $2,250 yearly (a male detective made $3,300 annually). She was not only New York's first female detective, but as *The Brooklyn Daily Eagle* proclaimed, she was "the best-known woman sleuth in the United States."

In 1921 Goodwin was picked to lead the new Women's Bureau, a department of 26 female officers overseeing cases involving prostitutes, runaways, truants, and victims of domestic violence. In 1924, she investigated fraudulent medical practices to help clinch several high-profile arrests before retiring after 30 years with the NYPD.

Goodwin died of colon cancer on October 26, 1943. She was 78. She was buried in Green Wood Cemetery in Brooklyn as Isabella Seaholm. (Her gravestone lists her birth year as 1871, but census and other records support the 1865 date.)

Goodwin once said that women made strong detectives because of their ability to "sense things for which at first you have no actual proof.... I think that the reason why a woman sometimes succeeds where a man fails is because she is more strongly endowed with this intuition." She added that she was proud to "show just what a woman can do when the chance comes her way."

MARCH 2
1882

On this day in history, a Scotsman named Roderick Maclean attempted to assassinate Queen Victoria by gunshot while sitting in her carriage at Windsor railway station after she arrived by train from London. Over Victoria's 63-year reign, there were no less than eight assassination attempts on her life, all unsuccessful. The worst she received was a black eye and a bump on the head from the cane of Robert Pate during his attempt in June 1850. Maclean's motive, in 1882, allegedly was a curt reply from the Queen to some poetry that he had mailed her.

Maclean came from a respectable family, spoke French and German, and was 28 years old when the attempt on Victoria's life occurred. His conduct had always been "irregular and eccentric, according to friends and relatives." his family got so tired of him that they had long ago "turned him off, allowing him a very small weekly pittance." After that, he led a sedentary life roaming around aimlessly from town to town. He had been committed to an asylum a couple of times, once at Somersetshire about six months before the attack on the Queen and once in Dublin. He was even known to beg for money despite the allowance given to him by his family.

When Maclean was arrested, a letter was found on him dated March 2, 1882. He addressed it to no one, and he wrote:

"I should not have done this crime had you, as you should have done, allowed the 10s. per week instead of offering the insultingly small sum of 6s per week, and expected me to live on it. So, you perceive the great good a little money might have done had you not treated me as a fool and set me more than ever against those bloated aristocrats ruled by the old lady, Mrs. Vic, who is a licensed robber in all senses."

He asserted that he never intended to harm the Queen. Instead, he only wanted to "alarm the public." He also maintained that he attempted the assassination because his grievances were not respected, "such as the pecuniary straits in which I have been situated."

Victoria remained in her carriage at the train station for a few minutes after arrival. Then she walked across the platform through the waiting room to the royal carriage in the station yard. The carriage, drawn by a couple of grey ponies, was closed. The weather was very cold. Her Majesty and Princess Beatrice took their seats, and the carriage proceeded. While the bystanders were raising cheers, a man standing at the gateway of the yard raised a pistol and fired at Victoria's carriage, which was fifteen yards away.

The shot missed its mark, and the carriage driver took off all the quicker for Windsor Castle. In the meantime, the shooter, Roderick Maclean, was arrested by Superintendent Hayes, chief of the Windsor police. Eyewitnesses at the scene claim that a photographer named James Burnside took the pistol away from Maclean. Also, two Eton students were standing behind Maclean, and they "flew at him with great fury, and one beat him fiercely over the head with an umbrella." A locomotive foreman, John Frost, also helped secure the would-be assassin, who, when seized, cried out, "Don't hurt me."

At the police station, Maclean was searched by detectives. On him were found fourteen ball cartridges inside a piece of paper, and several other documents and valueless articles were also discovered. In addition, the seized weapon was described as a medium-sized, six-chambered revolver of German origins. Two of the chambers held ball cartridges, and two others were empty. He was presumed to have acted alone.

The Queen sent a reassuring telegram to her eldest son that read:

"From the Queen, Windsor Castle, to the Prince of Wales, Marlborough House. In case the exaggerated report should reach you, I telegraph to say that as I drove from the station here a man shot at the carriage, but fortunately hit no one. He was instantly arrested. I am not the worse."

Soon after his arrest, on April 20, 1882, the trial of Robert Maclean took place. It generated great interest amongst the public, and large crowds gathered to watch the judges and officials enter the courthouse.

At trial, Robert Maclean was described as medium height, dark-complected, with short hair and a mustache. He was charged with high treason for having made an attempt on the Queen's life. Moreover, according to the Glasgow Evening Citizen:

"The charge against the prison was of the most aggravated kind, he is having directly attempted to compass the life of Her Majesty. Detailing the facts of the case, the prisoner appeared to have taken advantage of seeing Her Majesty sitting inside the open window of the carriage and firing the pistol directly towards the carriage in which the Queen was sitting, and the bullet was found in a direct line with carriage. Apparently, the crime had been one of premeditation, prisoner having purchased days before the pistol and ammunition to commit the crime, and a document in his possession showed his intention to commit the deed."

When Maclean was brought into the courtroom, he immediately pleaded "not guilty." His solicitor, Montagu Williams, stated that his client was insane and then supported this declaration by calling several witnesses who had examined Maclean. Several doctors were called who had examined Maclean over the years, and all found him insane. They even mentioned that he had been restrained at the Bath and Summerside Asylum for a time.

After the witnesses testified about his insanity, the prosecution practically confirmed that their assessments were accurate and that Maclean was insane. Thus, the jury was out for five minutes before delivering their verdict. It was probably no surprise when they found Roderick Maclean "not guilty on the grounds of insanity."

After Maclean was declared insane, he lived out the rest of his life at the Broadmoor Asylum, a psychiatric hospital in Crowthorne, Berkshire. However, the verdict did not sit well with the Queen. She was often the target of attacks by mentally ill individuals. She wanted a change made to English law so that offenders charged in similar cases, who were found to be "guilty, but insane" would be kept in custody as "criminal lunatics." She hoped such sentences would serve as a deterrent. Her request for a new law resulted in the *Trial of the Lunatics Act 1883*.

MARCH 3
1887

On this day in history, Anne Sullivan began teaching six-year-old Helen Keller, who lost her hearing and sight after a dreadful illness at the age of 19 months. Under Sullivan's guidance, which included her revolutionary "touch teaching" techniques, Keller prospered, eventually graduating from college, and becoming an international writer, lecturer, and activist. Sullivan, often called "the miracle worker," remained Keller's interpreter and constant companion until the older woman died in 1936.

Sullivan, born in Massachusetts in 1866, also knew what it meant to be handicapped. When she was five years old, Sullivan developed the bacterial eye disease trachoma, which caused severe infections and, over time, made her nearly blind. After her mother's death when she was eight and her father abandoned her and her two siblings, her and her brother were placed in an almshouse in Tewksbury, Massachusetts. After some unsuccessful operations meant to correct her sight and her brother's death, Sullivan endured years of terrible care. By 1880 she managed to get placed in the Perkins School for the Blind, where she flourished. There, Anne Sullivan learned the manual alphabet to converse with a classmate who was deaf and blind. Eventually, she had several operations that improved her diminished eyesight.

Helen Keller was born on June 27, 1880, in Tuscumbia, Alabama, to Arthur Keller, a newspaper publisher, and a one-time Confederate army officer, and his wife Kate, whose father was Charles W. Adams, a Confederate general. The Keller family was part of the slaveholding elite before the war but lost their status after the conflict. As a child, Helen had an illness described by doctors then as "an acute congestion of the stomach and the brain," now categorized as either scarlet fever or a type of bacterial meningitis, left the 19-month-old Helen unable to see, hear, or speak. She was considered a bright but strong-willed and spoiled child. At that time, Keller could communicate a little with the daughter of the family cook, who was two years older, and she understood the girl's signs. By the time Helen was seven, she had more than 60 home signs to communicate with her family and could differentiate between people by the vibrations of their footsteps.

It was during this time that Keller became difficult to handle. She would kick and scream when upset and laugh uncontrollably when elated. She tormented her friend and inflicted raging tantrums on her parents. Many family members and relatives felt that she should be institutionalized.

Looking for answers and help with Helen, Keller's mother sent Helen and her father to see Dr. J. Julian Chisholm in Baltimore, Maryland. After a complete examination, he suggested that they visit Alexander Graham Bell, the inventor of the telephone, who worked with deaf children at the time. Bell met with the Keller's, and he suggested that they meet with officials at the Perkins Institute for the Blind in Boston, Massachusetts. There, the family met with the school's director, and he felt that Helen would benefit from working with one of the institute's most recent graduates, Anne Sullivan.

On March 3, 1887, Sullivan went to Keller's home in Alabama and immediately started work. She began by teaching the six-year-old finger spelling. After much trial, this was ultimately unsuccessful. Helen grew frustrated, and the tantrums increased. After isolating her and Helen from the rest of the family in a cottage on the plantation,

Sullivan began to make inroads with her student. She taught Helen the word "water" by running water over the child's hand and spelling the word on her hand. It was the breakthrough they needed. By nightfall, Helen had learned thirty words.

In 1890, Keller began taking speech classes in Boston, Massachusetts. Helen worked hard for over twenty-five years to learn to speak so that people could understand her. From 1894 to 1896, Keller was enrolled at the Wright-Humason School for the Deaf in New York City. There, she improved her communication skills and studied regular academic subjects. It was at this time that Helen became resolved to go to college. In 1896, she went to Cambridge School for Young Ladies, a preparatory school for women.

As Keller's story became more widely known, she began to meet famous and influential people. She met the writer Mark Twain, who was very impressed with her, and they became friends. Twain introduced her to Henry H. Rogers, a Standard Oil executive. Rogers was so impressed with Helen's talent, drive, and determination that he and his wife agreed to pay for her to attend Radcliffe College at Harvard University. There, she was joined by Sullivan, who sat with her to interpret lectures and textbooks. By this time, Keller had mastered numerous methods of communication, and speech, including touch-lip reading, Braille, typing, and fingerspelling.

Keller graduated cum laude from Radcliffe College in 1904 at 24 years of age.

With the help of Sullivan and her future husband, John Macy, Keller penned her first book, The *Story of My Life*. It was published in 1905 and covered Keller's life until the age of 21 when she was a student.

In the first half of the 20th century, Keller attacked social and political issues, including women's suffrage, pacifism, birth control, and socialism. She became a well-known celebrity and lecturer who shared her experiences with audiences and helped to advocate for those with disabilities. In 1920, Helen co-founded the American Civil Liberties Union. In 1924 she joined the American Federation for the Blind and helped raise awareness and funds for the organization. In 1946, she was assigned to be a counselor of international relations for the American Foundation of Overseas Blind. Between 1946 and 1957, she visited thirty-five countries on five continents.

During her lifetime, she was given many honors for her achievements, the least of which was the Presidential Medal of Freedom in 1964. She received honorary doctoral degrees from universities worldwide, including Temple University and Harvard University.

Helen Keller died peacefully in her sleep on June 1, 1968, just weeks prior to her 88th birthday. She had suffered several strokes in 1961 and spent the remainder of her life at her home in Connecticut.

(Photo: Keller (left) with Anne Sullivan vacationing on Cape Cod in July 1888. Wikimedia Commons)

MARCH 4
1870

On this day in history, Irish Protestant and member of the anti-Catholic Canadian Party, Thomas Scott, age 28, is executed by order of the President of the Provisional Government of Assiniboia (then on the cusp of being the Canadian province of Manitoba) and Metis leader Louis Riel for insubordination. His execution led to the Red River Expedition; a 1200-strong military force sent to Manitoba by Canadian Prime Minister Sir John A. Macdonald to confront the Metis at Red River. From that point on, Protestant Ontarians, especially members of the influential Orange Order, wanted retribution from Riel for Scott's death. Scott's execution led to Riel's exile and ultimately to Riel's execution for treason in 1885.

Thomas Scott was born in Clandeboye, near Belfast, Ireland 1842. In 1863, at age 21, he arrived in Canada West, now Ontario, and settled near Belleville. He became a member of the powerful, anti-Catholic Orange Order. Scott eventually traveled west, and in the spring of 1869, he landed at the Red River Colony near the Assiniboine and Red Rivers. It was home to 5,000 relatives of French explorers and fur traders who had wedded Indigenous women. Most Metis were Catholic and French speaking, but a large minority were English-speaking Protestants.

The Red River was part of a vast region called Rupert's Land, owned by the Hudson Bay Company. In March 1869, just prior to Scott's arrival, it had been sold to the British government, who, in turn, sold it to the Dominion of Canada. The Canadian purchase would be official on December 1.

Between March and December 1869, people were perplexed about who owned the land. The Canadian government sent a survey crew to the area, which upset the Metis people greatly. This added to the resentment among the populace at Red River, who had never been consulted about the sale. Racial, religious, and ethnic tensions were worsened by the belief that the deal would bring even more Protestant migrants from Ontario. Some people in the area wished to join Canada, others lobbied for the colony to be independent, while others wanted to join the United States.

Scott had found work as a laborer and a bartender. According to some, he was already becoming known in the area for his fighting, drinking, and spewing of anti-Catholic and anti-Metis hate.

Meanwhile, Scott met doctor and entrepreneur John Schultz. Schultz led the Canadian Party, a small group of English Protestants who wanted Red River to join Canada and be led by English Protestants. In early December 1869, sixty-seven Canadian Party followers gathered at Schultz's warehouse in Lower Fort Garry to plan an attack on the Metis government.

The Metis founded the Provisional Government of the Metis Nation with Riel as president. On December 7, Riel had Schultz and his followers arrested and detained. Scott had not been there at the time of their arrest, but when he learned, he demanded their release. When Riel refused, Scott began yelling racist insults, and he, too, was subsequently arrested. After being detained, he continued with the insults and tirades, even threatening to shoot Riel at one point.

On January 9, 1870, Scott and 12 others managed to escape. He eventually joined up with Canadian Major Charles Boulton and 60 others who were determined to free Schultz and the others from Upper Fort Garry. Along the way, they were joined by another 100-armed men whose collective goal was to overthrow Riel and his government in addition to freeing the captives.

Upon arrival, they learned that Riel had already released his prisoners. That caused many men to go home, but Scott, Boulton, and the remaining 45 men demanded that Riel step down. Riel had them arrested instead.

Riel and the other leaders decided that Boulton was guilty of treason and sentenced to death. After pleas for mercy from the Canadian government, Riel chose to commute the sentence. The incident, and Riel's compassion, helped to improve support for the provisional government in Red River.

Meanwhile, Thomas Scott languished in jail, where he constantly shouted racist insults and violent threats at his jailers. He even assaulted one of the guards, which drew a beating that Riel had to stop. On March 3, Scott was charged with insubordination and treason by a six-man council. He was not given a lawyer, and the proceedings were in French. Witnesses were not cross-examined, and at the end of the trial, Riel summarized proceedings for Scott in English. One council member voted for acquittal, another for banishment, and the remaining four found him guilty. They stated that he would be executed by firing squad.

Many pleas were made for mercy, but all went ignored by Riel. He told the Canadian government official, Donald Smith, that Scott's execution would demonstrate the power of Riel's government to the people of the Red River and, as he said to Smith, "We must make Canada respect us."

At 1 p.m. on March 4, 1870, Thomas Scott's hands were tied behind his back, and he was led from his cell and taken to the courtyard outside. With Riel watching, Scott knelt in the snow, and a white cloth was tied around his eyes. Scott yelled out, "This is horrible. This is cold-blooded murder." Six Metis raised their guns, but only a few shots rang out when the order to fire came. Scott was hit twice – once in the shoulder and once in the chest – and he crumpled to the ground but was still alive. Francois Guillemette, a firing squad member, stepped forward, withdrew his revolver, and ended Scott's life.

The uproar caused by Scott's execution did not change Prime Minister Macdonald's mind about allowing Manitoba into Confederation. He met with a delegation from Red River and agreed to Riel's conditions, including the formation of the province of Manitoba; promised protection for Metis land, the Catholic religion, and the French language; and treaties with Indigenous nations be negotiated. Manitoba entered Confederation in July 1870.

The execution of Thomas Scott caused a division to occur in Canada along linguistic lines. Quebec supported the French-speaking Riel while the pro-Protestant, anti-Catholic Orange Order whipped up anti-French sentiment in Ontario.

Riel's part in Scott's death destroyed his capacity to participate in Canadian politics. Riel was elected three times between 1873 and 1874 as the Member of Parliament for Provencher. However, because of a $5,000 bounty on his head, placed there by Ontario's Orangemen, Riel feared arrest or assassination, so he never took his seat in the Canadian House of Commons.

Riel returned to Canada from exile in the United States, and in 1885 he led Saskatchewan's Metis in the North-West Rebellion. This caused Ontario's Protestants to demand Riel's arrest again. Riel was seized and charged with high treason when the rebellion was stopped. Scott's execution significantly affected Riel's trial and death sentence. It was also part of why Prime Minister Macdonald allowed Riel's death sentence to be carried out.

(Photo: The execution of Thomas Scott at Fort Garry, March 4, 1870. Wikimedia Commons.)

MARCH 5
1770

On this day in history, a confrontation between nine British soldiers and a crowd of three to four hundred Bostonians led to five people from the crowd being shot and killed, with six injured. The mob verbally abused the soldiers and threw various projectiles at them. The event was quickly labeled the Boston Massacre by leading Patriots like Paul Revere and Samuel Adams. It would be a turning point in relations between American colonists and British authorities. The incident provided one of the sparks that would ignite the American Revolution.

Two regiments of British troops had been garrisoned in the city of Boston, in the Province of Massachusetts Bay, since September 1768, after residents had resisted taxes levied by the British Parliament on staples like tea and paper to pay for the expensive French and Indian War (1754-1763). Sent to enforce these taxes and keep the peace, Bostonians hated the over one thousand British soldiers who were seen as an affront to their local autonomy.

From the start of the occupation, conflicts intermittently flared up between soldiers and townspeople, and by early 1770, fights had become commonplace. The death of an 11-year-old boy, Christopher Seider, during one such skirmish the previous month only worsened tensions and put most of the town on edge.

On the cold, snowy evening of March 5, 1770, Private Hugh White was the lone soldier protecting the King's money stored inside the Custom House on King Street in downtown Boston. Before long, 50-60 locals surrounded him and began insulting and threatening him violently. At one point, White fought back and hit one of the colonists with the butt of his rifle. The locals pummelled him with snowballs, ice, and stones in retaliation. Bells from the cathedral began ringing throughout the town – usually a warning of fire – drawing a multitude of male colonists into the streets. As the attack on White continued, he eventually fell and called for reinforcements.

In response to White's plea for assistance and fearing large riots and the loss of the King's money, Captain Thomas Preston arrived at the Custom House with several soldiers, and they promptly took up position on the front steps. Worried that bloodshed was unavoidable, some colonists pleaded with the soldiers to hold their fire while others urged them to fire. Preston later stated that a colonist told him the agitators planned to "carry off (White) from his post and probably murder him."

The violence escalated, and the colonists started striking the soldiers with clubs and sticks. Reports on what happened next tend to differ, but after someone reportedly exclaimed the word "fire," a soldier fired his gun, although it is unclear if the shot was on purpose.

When the first shot rang out, other soldiers opened fire, killing five colonists – including Crispus Attucks, a local sailor and dockworker of mixed racial heritage – and the wounding of six. Among the other victims of the Boston Massacre was Samuel Gray, a rope maker with a hole in his head the size of a fist. Sailor James Caldwell, Samuel Maverick, and Patrick Carr were mortally wounded.

Within hours, Captain Preston and his soldiers were seized and jailed, and the propaganda machine began churning in full force on both sides of the conflict. Preston wrote his version of the events in his jail cell for publication. At the same time, Sons of Liberty leaders such as John Hancock and Samuel Adams whipped up colonists' sentiments to keep agitating against the British. As tensions rose, British troops were ordered from Boston and sent to Fort William. Paul Revere inspired anti-British attitudes by etching the famous engraving depicting British soldiers murdering American colonists. It showed the British as the instigators even though the colonists had started the melee. The engraving also portrayed the soldiers as vicious men and the colonists as gentlemen. It was later discovered that Revere had plagiarized his engraving from one drawn by Boston artist Henry Pelham.

Captain Preston and his soldiers finally came to trial seven months later for their part in the Boston Massacre. To give the appearance of a fair trial, American colonist, lawyer, patriot, and future President of the United States, John Adams, agreed to defend the British soldiers. Adams did not care for the British, but he did want Preston and the other British soldiers to have a fair and equitable trial. In this case, the death penalty was at stake, and the colonists did not want the British to have a reason to even the score. Convinced that impartial jurors did not exist in Boston, Adams convinced the judge to use a jury of non-Bostonians.

During Captain Preston's trial, Adams argued that confusion that night reigned supreme. Eyewitnesses presented conflicting evidence on whether Preston had ordered his soldiers to fire on the colonists. Witness Richard Palmes asserted..."After the Gun went off, I heard the word "fire!" The Captain and I stood in front about halfway between the breech and muzzle of the Guns. I don't know who gave the word to fire," Adams maintained that reasonable doubt existed; Preston was ultimately found not guilty.

The remaining soldiers asserted self-defence and were all found not guilty of murder. Hugh Montgomery and Mathew Kilroy were found guilty of manslaughter and branded on the thumbs as first offenders per English law. To Adams and the jury's praise, the British soldiers received a fair trial despite the hatred directed towards them and their country.

The Boston Massacre profoundly affected relations between Britain and the American colonies. It further incensed colonists already tired of British rule and unfair taxation, encouraging them to fight for independence.

Over the next five years, the colonists continued their rebellion.

They held the Boston Tea Party, created the First Continental Congress, and safeguarded their militia arsenal at Concord against the British, effectively starting the American Revolution. Today, Boston has a Boston Massacre site marker at Congress Street and State Street intersection, a few yards from where the first shots were fired.

MARCH 6
1951

On this day in history, the trial of alleged Soviet spies Julius and Ethel Rosenberg begins in the U.S. District Court for the Southern District of New York. Charged with conspiracy to commit wartime espionage, the Rosenbergs were ultimately convicted of giving top-secret information to the Soviet Union about radar, sonar, jet propulsion engines, and valuable nuclear weapon designs. Convicted in 1951the couple would ultimately be executed by the U.S. government at Sing Sing prison in New York state. They became the first American citizens to be executed for espionage during peacetime.

Julius Rosenberg was born in New York City on May 12, 1918, to Jewish immigrants from Russia. While living in the Lower East Side of New York, Julius attended Seward Park High School. He became a leader in the Young Communist League USA while attending City College of New York during the 1930s. In 1939, he graduated from CCNY with a degree in electrical engineering.

Ethel Greenglass was born in Manhattan, New York, on September 28, 1915. She had a brother, David Greenglass. She aspired to become an actress and a singer but eventually settled into a secretarial position at a shipping company. She joined the Young Communist League USA and met Julius in 1936. They married in 1939.

Julius signed up for the Army Signal Corps Engineering Laboratories at Fort Monmouth, New Jersey, in 1940, where he labored as an engineer-inspector until 1945. He was discharged from the army when they found out about his earlier membership in the Communist Party. Significant research occurred at Fort Monmouth during World War 2 regarding electronics, communications, radar, and guided missile controls.

Rosenberg was recruited to spy for the Soviet Union by spymaster Semyon Semyonov on Labor Day, 1942. Julius also recruited several sympathetic individuals with access to pertinent classified information like documents from Emerson Radio, the National Advisory Committee for Aeronautics, and a complete set of design and production drawings for Lockheed's P-80 Shooting Star, America's first operational jet fighter. His handler also learned that Ethel's brother, David Greenglass, had been working at the Los Alamos National Laboratory on the top-secret Manhattan Project; he ordered Julius to recruit Greenglass. The U.S. and the USSR were allies during World War 2, but the Americans did not share any information with, or seek assistance from, the Soviet Union regarding the Manhattan Project. The U.S. was shocked by the speed with which the USSR could hold their first nuclear test, "Joe 1", on August 29, 1949.

The first bit of unraveling of the Rosenberg spy ring was the arrest of Klaus Fuchs, the German-born British physicist, on February 2, 1950. Fuchs had also been employed at Los Alamos and had passed information to the Soviets independently of the Rosenbergs, though they shared a critical connection with their courier, Harry Gold.

In May 1950, the FBI arrested Gold, who incriminated David Greenglass, who was arrested on June 15 and charged with espionage. He very quickly confessed to passing information on to the USSR through Gold. The dominoes continued to fall with Julius' arrest in July and Ethel's seizure in August. Julius' friend and co-conspirator, Morton Sobel, was discovered to be hiding in Mexico at the time, and he was turned over to the FBI by Mexican authorities.

After Greenglass pleaded guilty, the legal proceedings for the Rosenbergs and Sobell started on March 6, 1951, in New York. Showing no impartiality, Judge Irving R. Kaufman opened the proceedings by stating: "The evidence will show that the loyalty and alliance of the Rosenbergs and Sobell were not to our country, but that it was to Communism."

The case against the Rosenbergs heavily relied upon the testimonies of Gold and Greenglass. Gold stated that he met Greenglass in Albuquerque, New Mexico, in June 1945, with the password "I come from Julius." After each confirmed to the other their shared allegiance by producing a piece of a cut-off Jell-O box top, Gold paid $500 for details on the atomic device.

Greenglass testified that the Rosenbergs began asking his wife, Ruth, to get her husband involved in the spy ring by November 1944. In January 1945, he showed Julius his notes and a sketch of a high-explosive lens. Even more damning was that Greenglass related meeting the Rosenbergs in September 1945, during which time Ethel supposedly typed up his shoddy, hastily scribbled notes.

Until now, the government had no case against Ethel; now, her brother had shown her to be a willing participant. Chief prosecutor Irving Saypol leaped over these details, dramatically thrilling the jury how Ethel "sat at that typewriter and struck the keys, blow by blow, against her country in the interests of the Soviets."

The Rosenbergs took the stand in their defense, but other than denying the charges, they essentially invoked the Fifth Amendment, their silence only amplifying the testimony against them.

On March 29, 1951, the jury found the three conspirators guilty. Judge Kaufman imposed the death penalty against Julius and Ethel, stating to them, "I consider your crimes worse than murder." He spared Sobell's life, who was not directly involved in the movement of atomic secrets and sentenced him to 30 years in prison.

A considerable outcry erupted for leniency worldwide towards the Rosenbergs. Despite the pleas from people like Albert Einstein and Pope Pius XII, President Truman, then President Eisenhower was not swayed. After a last-minute attempt at a stay of execution was denied, on June 19, 1953, Julius and Ethel Rosenberg were electrocuted in Ossining, New York, at Sing Sing Prison, making them the first U.S. civilians to be executed for espionage during peacetime.

In 1995 the NSA released an assortment of decrypted Soviet

communications from the Venona Project, which established Julius' espionage. In 2001 David Greenglass admitted that he lied about his sister's role in the affair. It had been his wife, Ruth, who had typed up the notes in question. He stated that the prosecutor had persuaded him to change his initial testimony and blame everything on the Rosenbergs. In 2008 Sobell confirmed that Ethel was only guilty of "being Julius' wife."

These new disclosures have given Michael and Robert Meeropol, the Rosenbergs' surviving sons, to fully re-double their efforts to exonerate their mother. They could not convince President Obama, but there may be hope for the future.

MARCH 7
1876

On this day in history, Alexander Graham Bell received a patent for his invention of the telephone. Born from his work on the harmonic telegraph – a device that allowed multiple messages to be sent over a wire at the same time (1871) – the invention of the telephone would revolutionize society like no other invention before it. Bell, as his father, grandfather, and brother before him, had all been associated with work on elocution and speech, and his mother and wife were both deaf, profoundly influencing Bell's life work. His research on hearing and speech would lead him to experiment with hearing devices, ultimately helping him to invent the telephone in 1876. Bell regarded the telephone as such an encroachment on his real work as a scientist that he refused to have one placed in his workshop.

Alexander Graham Bell was born on March 3, 1847, in Edinburgh, Scotland. His father was a professor of speech elocution at the University of Edinburgh, and his mother, despite her deafness, was an accomplished pianist. Alexander was a curious child who studied piano and began inventing things early on. Both of his brothers died from tuberculosis when Bell was in his twenties. In his early years, he was homeschooled. Alexander did not thrive academically, yet he was an astute problem solver from an early age.

At 12, Alexander invented a device with rotating paddles and nail brushes to remove husks from wheat grain. It was used in a friend's family's flour mill. His friend's father gave the boys space to work on their inventing in exchange for the husking device.

At 16, Bell began studying the mechanics of speech. He attended Royal High School and the University of Edinburgh. In 1870 Bell, along with his family, moved to Canada. The next year he moved to the Boston, Massachusetts area. While in the United States, Alexander implemented a system that his father created to teach deaf children called "visible speech" – a set of symbols that represented speech sounds.

In 1872, Bell started the School of Vocal Physiology and Mechanics of Speech in Boston, where he taught deaf people to speak. At age 26, the budding inventor became a Professor of Vocal Physiology and Elocution at the Boston University School of Oratory, despite having no university credentials. During his teaching, Bell met Mabel Hubbard, a deaf student. The couple would marry on July 11, 1877. They would go on to have four children.

At the time, Western Union began working with inventors Elisha Gray and Thomas Edison to find a method to transmit multiple telegraphs on each telegraph line to avoid the horrendous cost of building new lines. When Bell divulged to Gardiner Hubbard and Thomas Sanders that he was working on sending multiple voices on a telegraph wire using a multi-reed device, the two wealthy patrons began to support Bell's work financially.

Bell and Pollok visited scientist Joseph Henry in March 1875 at the Smithsonian Institution, and they asked his advice on the electrical multi-reed apparatus that Bell hoped would convey the human voice by telegraph. Henry told Bell he had "the germ of a great invention." When Bell told Henry he did not have the necessary knowledge, Henry replied, "Get it!" However, a meeting in 1874 between Bell and Thomas Watson, an experienced electrical designer and mechanic, changed everything.

With funding from Hubbard and Sanders, Bell hired Thomas Watson as his assistant, and both worked on acoustic telegraphy. In 1875 Bell created an acoustic telegraph and filed a patent application for it. He first applied for a patent in Britain because Britain would only issue patents for discoveries not previously patented elsewhere. Meanwhile, Elisha Gray also experimented with acoustic telegraphy and found a way to transmit speech using water. On February 14, 1876, Gray filed a warning with the United States Patent Office for a telephone device that used a water transmitter. Bell had submitted his patent request a few hours before Gray, thus beating out Gray.

Bell's patent, 174,465, was issued to him on March 7, 1876, by the U.S. Patent Office. Bell's patent covered "the method of, and apparatus for, transmitting vocal or other sounds telegraphically...by causing electrical undulations, similar in form to the vibrations of the air accompanying the said vocal or other sounds."

On March 10, three days after his patent was given to him, Bell succeeded in getting his telephone to work. Bell spoke the sentence "Mr. Watson – Come here – I want to see you" into the transmitter; Watson, listening on the receiving end in an adjoining room, heard the words clearly.

By 1877, the Bell Telephone Company, today known as AT&T, was created. In 1915 Bell executed the first transcontinental telephone call to Watson from New York City to San Francisco.

The inventor faced a 20-year legal battle with other scientists, including Elisha Gray and Antonio Meucci, who claimed they created telephone prototypes before Bell's patent. In 1887, the U.S. government tried to remove the patent issued to Bell, but after a series of legal rulings, the Bell company won a Supreme Court decision. While the Bell Company faced over 600 court clashes, in the end, none were successful.

Alexander Graham Bell died on August 2, 1922, at 75, in Nova Scotia, Canada. The cause of his death was problems with diabetes. His wife and two daughters survived him.

MARCH 8
1951

On this day in history, Raymond Fernandez, and Martha Beck, better known as "The Lonely Hearts Killers," were executed by electric chair at Sing Sing Prison in Ossining, New York, for the murder of Janet Fay, 66, of Long Island, New York. The couple had conspired to seduce, rob, and kill women who placed personal ads in newspapers and magazines. Fernandez and Beck boasted of killing as many as twenty women in this manner during a spree between 1947 and 1949. Several television shows and films are based on this case.

Raymond Martinez Fernandez was born in Hawaii on December 17, 1914, to Spanish parents. His family moved around the United States several times, and eventually, Fernandez moved to Spain to work on his uncle's farm. While there, he married and started a family, all by the age of 20.

Fernandez served in World War II before deciding to return to the U.S., abandoning his wife and four children. On the ship to America, he suffered a head injury when a steel hatch fell on him, smashing his skull and injuring his frontal lobe. This damage may well have affected his social and sexual behavior. Because of his accident, he spent three months in hospital recuperating from his injuries. He then fell into a life of crime and was sent to prison for theft. While there, his Haitian cellmate reportedly taught him voodoo and black magic, which be believed gave him irresistible power and charm over women.

Martha Jule Beck was born in Milton, Florida, on May 6, 1920. A glandular condition caused her to be overweight and to undergo puberty prematurely. Beck later claimed during her trial that her brother had sexually assaulted her at a young age and that her mother abused her.

Beck completed studies for her nursing degree, but she struggled to secure a job because of her weight, so she bounced around the country for a time. She eventually returned to Florida while pregnant with her first child. Shortly after, she became pregnant with her second child. Beck married the second baby's father, but the marriage only lasted a few months. In 1946, as a single mother of two, Martha Beck landed a job at the Pensacola Hospital for Children. A year later, she placed a lonely-hearts ad in a magazine and soon received a reply from Raymond Fernandez.

Fernandez came to Florida from New York City and stayed with Beck briefly but returned to the city shortly after that. Beck was then unexpectedly fired from her position at the Children's Hospital, so she impulsively packed up her belongings and moved in with Fernandez. She doted on him, and he subsequently confessed his life of crime to her. Influenced by her new love for Fernandez, Beck gave up her children to the Salvation Army and committed everything she had to him. Beck was devoted to Fernandez until the end.

Fernandez continued to answer lonely hearts ads, and Beck often posed as his sister, claiming that he was just a guest, and the home was hers. The lie enabled him to maintain an air of respectability, making his victims more comfortable having someone else in the house with them.

Beck's love for Fernandez made her intensely jealous, and if he ever slept with a mark, Beck would fly into a rage. In 1949, Fernandez got engaged to Janet Fay, and she moved into his apartment in Long Island. When Beck discovered them in bed together, she attacked Fay by striking her on the head with a hammer, after which Fernandez finished the job by strangling her. They buried her in the basement of his apartment building. The pair were forced to flee to Michigan after

Fay's family grew suspicious when she went missing. The couple ended up locating in Wyoming Township, just outside Grand Rapids.

In February 1949, Fernandez and Beck met a widow, 28-year-old Delphine Downing. Things initially went well. Downing soon invited the pair to move in with her. She then took them to Nebraska to meet her mother and planned to sell her home in Michigan, so the threesome could all move to California.

The turning point came when Downing entered her bathroom on Saturday, February 26, 1949, and discovered that Fernandez had been keeping a secret from her. Because of his head injury years earlier, the swindler had worn a toupee to keep his damaged pate a secret. As Downing beheld his bald, scarred head under the bathroom light, she became distressed and accused "Charles" and his sister of deceiving her.

Fearing that Downing would contact the police and end their charade, Beck and Fernandez decided murder was their only way out. To quiet the agitated woman, Beck urged Downing to take sleeping pills. Downing did so. After falling asleep, Fernandez grabbed a blanket, wrapped it around Downing's dead husband's pistol, put it to her head, and fired, all while Downing's 2-year-old daughter watched. Fernandez and Beck buried Downing in the basement and encased the grave in cement.

With Downing gone, the two fraudsters had free reign of the house. The dead woman's daughter was crying for her mother incessantly, so Fernandez told Beck to kill her, which she did by drowning in a basin two days later. The young girl was buried in the basement beside her mother.

Raymond Fernandez and Marta Beck were arrested by Wyoming Township police soon after at the home after neighbors reported the young mother missing.

During the interrogation, Fernandez confessed to multiple murders across the country but later retracted his confession. He told police he was trying to protect Beck but knew that Michigan did not have the death penalty and used the confession to stay there. However, the pair were extradited to New York for the murder of Janet Fay, a state with the death penalty. They were tried and convicted of murder and sentenced to the electric chair. Soon after, they were remanded to Sing Sing Prison.

Fernandez and Beck were executed on March 8, 1951, at Sing Sing Prison for the murder of Janet Fay. Though police had Fernandez's confession to the deaths of multiple women, there is no way to know the exact number of victims.

MARCH 9
1862

On this day in history, the Battle of Hampton Roads occurred between the U.S.S. *Monitor* and the C.S.S. *Virginia* during the American Civil War and was history's first naval battle between ironclad warships. It was an effort by the Confederate States to smash the Union blockade of Southern ports, including Richmond and Norfolk, Virginia that had been inflicted upon them at the beginning of the war. Even though the results of the battle were inconclusive, it had begun a whole new era in naval warfare.

The C.S.S. *Virginia*, originally the U.S. Navy ship the U.S.S. *Merrimack*, was a 40-gun frigate launched in 1855. The *Merrimack* initially worked in the Caribbean and had been the flagship of the Pacific fleet in the 1850s. In early 1860, the vessel was decommissioned for repairs in Norfolk, Virginia. The ship was still in the naval yard when the Civil War started in April 1861, and Union sailors scuttled the vessel as the facility was vacated. The boat was raised six weeks later, and the Confederates reconstructed it.

The Confederates enveloped the vessel in heavy armor plating above the waterline and equipped it with various high-powered guns. Renamed *Virginia* upon its launch in February 1862, it was an intimidating ship. The ship's commander, Franklin Buchanan, was the only admiral in the Confederate Navy during the American Civil War.

The battle began when the large and cumbersome C.S.S. *Virginia* headed into Hampton Roads on the morning of March 8, 1862. C.S.S. *Virginia* was joined by the *Raleigh* and *Beaufort* at Hampton Roads by the James River Squadron, *Teaser, Patrick Henry,* and *Jamestown*. At this time, the Union Navy had five warships in the area. The sloop-of-war *Cumberland* and frigate *Congress* were berthed near Newport News. The sail frigate *Lawrence* and the steam frigates *Minnesota* and *Roanoke* were near Fort Monroe, along with the storeship *Brandywine*.

The *Virginia* headed directly for the Union squadron. There was some skirmishing between the Union tug *Zouave* and the *Beaufort*. The *Virginia* did not fire until she was in range of the *Cumberland*. Return fire from the *Cumberland* and *Congress* simply bounced off the iron plates of the *Virginia* without piercing, although later, some of *Cumberland's* gunfire managed to damage *Virginia* lightly.

Virginia slammed *Cumberland* below the waterline, and she sank quickly, "gallantly fighting her guns as long as they were above water," according to Buchanan. *Cumberland* went down with 121 seamen on board; those wounded increased the casualty total to nearly 150. Ramming *Cumberland* almost ended with the scuttling of *Virginia* as well. *Virginia's* bow ram got caught in the enemy vessel's hull, and as *Cumberland* listed and began to sink, she almost pulled *Virginia* down with her. *Virginia* broke free; however, her ram broke off as she backed away.

Buchanan then turned his attention to *Congress*. Joined by the James River Squadron, they and the *Virginia* took only an hour before *Congress* surrendered. While the *Congress* removed their surviving crew members, a Union battery on shore opened fire on the *Virginia*. In retaliation, Buchanan ordered *Congress* to fire upon, with hot shots, cannonballs heated red-hot. *Congress* caught fire and was aflame the rest of the day. Near midnight she exploded and sank, stern first. One hundred-ten crew members were killed or went missing and were presumed drowned. Another 26 were injured, ten of whom died within a few days.

C.S.S. *Virginia* was not completely undamaged. Fire from *Cumber-*

land, Congress, and Union troops ashore had pierced her smokestack, reducing her to an even slower speed. Two of her guns were incapacitated, and several armor plates had been loosened. Two of her crew had been killed, and more were wounded. One of the injured was Admiral Buchanan, whose left leg was pierced by a rifle shot.

The tide was now falling, and the darkness was setting in, so the Confederate ships sailed for friendly waters off Sewell's Point for the night. The Union Navy had lost 250 men and two vessels, while the Confederates only lost two men. The United States Navy's most significant defeat (up until World War II) had caused great panic in Washington. Secretary of War Edwin Stanton even feared that C.S.S. *Virginia* might attack east coast cities, sail up the Potomac, and shell the White House. He was assured that the *Virginia* could not make it close to the White House and that the Union had an ironclad and was on its way to meet *Virginia*.

The next day, March 9, the *Monitor* steamed into Chesapeake Bay to protect the remainder of the Union Navy's wooden fleet, including the *Minnesota*, which had run aground and was a sitting duck. The *Monitor* had left Brooklyn three days earlier under the command of Lieutenant John L. Worden. Swedish engineer John Ericsson designed the ship with a uniquely low profile, only rising from the water 18 inches. The flat iron deck had a 20-foot round turret in the middle of the vessel, sheltering two 11-inch Dahlgren guns. The *Monitor* had a draft of fewer than 11 feet to operate efficiently in the shallow harbors and rivers of the South. It began its career on February 25, 1862, and arrived in Chesapeake Bay just in time to fight the *Virginia*. On March 9, Worden exclaimed to the *Minnesota's* captain, "I will stand by you to the last if I can help you."

The fight between the *Monitor* and the *Virginia* began on the morning of March 9 and lasted four hours. The ships encircled one another, jockeying for position as they fired their guns. However, the cannon balls merely deflected off the ironclads. In the early afternoon, the *Virginia* pulled back into Norfolk. Neither ship was severely damaged, but the *Monitor* ended the short period of alarm that the Confederate ironclad had brought to the Union fleet.

Both ships met undignified ends. The withdrawing Confederates sank the Virginia when the Union conquered the James Peninsula after the Battle of Hampton Roads. The Monitor went down in a terrible storm off Cape Hatteras, North Carolina, at the end of the year. Though they existed for relatively short periods, the naval battle between the Ironclads brought in a new period of naval warfare. By the end of the Civil War, the Confederacy and the Union launched over 70 ironclads, signaling the end of wooden warships.

MARCH 10
1913

On this date in history, American abolitionist, social activist, and underground railroad conductor Harriet Tubman died of pneumonia in Auburn, New York. Born into slavery, Tubman escaped bondage and helped upwards of 70 people escape captivity, including friends and family, using the network of antislavery advocates and safe houses indicated as the Underground Railroad. She was also a nurse, an armed scout, a Union spy during the American Civil War, and a women's suffrage supporter. Tubman remains one of the most recognized figures in 19th-century America, and her legacy continues to inspire to this day.

Born Araminta Ross about 1820 in Dorchester County, Maryland, Tubman was one of nine children of slave parents, Harriet ("Rit") Green and Benjamin Ross. Rit labored as a cook in the plantation's "big house," and Benjamin travailed as a timber worker. Nicknamed "Minty" as a child, she changed her first name to Harriet in honor of her mother. Rit tried to keep her nine children together, but the nature of slavery and its mercantile ways made it difficult for Rit to keep the family together.

When Harriet was merely five years old, she was hired out as a nursemaid, where she was beaten when the baby cried, leaving her with permanent emotional and physical scars. At seven, Harriet was leased out to a planter to set muskrat traps and was later used as a field hand. She later stated that she preferred physical plantation work to indoor domestic chores. When she was twelve, an overseer threw a large metal weight at another enslaved person. It missed and struck Harriet in the head. She later stated that "the weight broke my skull.... They carried me to the house, all bleeding and fainting. I had no bed, no place to lie down on at all, and they laid me on the seat of the loom, and I stayed there all day and the next."

As a result of this incident, Harriet was left with constant headaches, seizures, and narcolepsy for the rest of her life, causing her to fall asleep at a moment's notice. She also started having realistic dreams and hallucinations, which she often asserted were religious visions (she was a staunch Christian). Her infirmity caused her to be less attractive to potential slave buyers and renters.

In 1844, Harriet wedded John Tubman, a free black man, so she changed her last name from Ross to Tubman. The marriage was not a good one. Two of her brothers – Ben and Henry – were about to be sold, inspiring Harriet to plan an escape. On September 17, 1849, Harriet and her two brothers left their Maryland plantation. After two weeks, the brothers changed their minds, and Harriet returned them to their home. Harriet kept to the original script and escaped using the Underground Railroad and traveled 90 miles north to Pennsylvania and freedom.

Tubman found life as a housekeeper in Philadelphia unfulfilling – she also wanted her friends and family to know freedom. She soon returned south to lead her niece and children to Philadelphia via the Underground Railroad. At one point, she tried to escort her husband John north, but he had already remarried and was unwilling to leave Maryland with his new wife.

The 1859 Fugitive Slave Act permitted fugitive and freed workers in the North to be caught and re-enslaved. This made Harriet's position as an Underground Railroad conductor even more challenging and required her to take enslaved people farther north to Canada, moving at night, usually in the spring or fall, when the days were shorter. She began and ended her rescues in St. Catharines, Ontario, Canada, where she started living in 1851. "I wouldn't trust Uncle Sam with my people no longer, but I brought 'em clear off to Canada," she said.

St. Catharines was one of the Canadian end points of the Underground Railroad. When Tubman arrived in December 1851, she found a job and rented a house on North Street. At the time, there was already a small Black community in the town, multiplying due to freedom-seekers arrival.

In 1858, in Ontario, she met John Brown, the leader of the attack on Harper's Ferry, West Virginia. Tubman endorsed the plan to begin an insurgency against enslavement in the American South. She hosted a meeting at her home to find Brown recruits and share information that would be helpful to his rebellion. Brown wanted "General Tubman" to go with him in the uprising, but her health prevented her from participating.

Tubman lived in St. Catharines between 1851 and 1861 for varying periods while she continued her rescue missions in Maryland.

Tubman found more ways to fight enslavement after the American Civil War broke out in 1861. She was enlisted to assist fugitive enslaved people at Fort Monroe and labored as a nurse, scout, and laundress. Harriet used her skill and expertise with herbal medicines to help treat ill soldiers and enslaved people.

In 1863, Harriet oversaw an espionage network for the Union Army. She gave critical intelligence to Union commanders about Confederate Army supply routes and troops and even helped liberate 700 enslaved people during the Combahee Ferry Raid in South Carolina. Some of those formerly enslaved people joined black battalions to fight the Confederates.

For almost three decades, Tubman would not be recognized for her gallant military efforts in the Civil War.

After the Civil War, Harriet lived with her family and friends in Auburn, New York. She married a former enslaved man and Civil War veteran Nelson Davis (who was twenty years her junior) in 1869, and they adopted a young girl named Gertie a few years later.

Harriet helped anyone in need, even though she lived near poverty most of her life. In 1896, Tubman purchased an adjacent lot to her home and opened the Harriet Tubman Home for the Aged and Indigent Colored People with funds raised by friends and the public. Her head injury as a youth continued to plague her, and she underwent brain surgery in Boston, which helped relieve some of the symptoms. Yet, her health continued to decline, and eventually, she was admitted into the home that bore her name in 1911.

On March 10, 1913, Harriet Tubman succumbed to pneumonia in Auburn, New York.

(Photo: Carte-de-visite showing a considerably younger Harriet than normally seen in the known images of her, just coming off her work during the Civil War, 1868. Wikimedia Commons)

MARCH 11
1971

On this day in history, Doors frontman Jim Morrison leaves the U.S. for Paris, France. The controversial singer abandons America immediately after recording all the vocals for the group's sixth studio album, "L.A. Woman," and with the mindset of giving up his music career to become a writer. However, his "escape" from the United States also has to do with the court case that he was just sentenced to six months in jail for indecent exposure and profanity before a six-person jury after a sixteen-day trial. The sentence resulted from his actions during his 1969 performance at a Doors concert in Miami.

Morrison checked into the Hotel George V with his girlfriend, Pamela Courson, who had been preparing things for his arrival in Paris. Shortly after, they moved into their rented apartment at 17-19 Rue Beautreillis in Le Marais, 4th arrondissement. In messages to friends, he described long walks through the city alone, even though he is often recognized as The Doors singer. He had hoped to leave all the trappings of celebrity behind in the United States, but it was not to be. During this time, he shaved off his beard and shed some of the weight he had gained in the previous months. To his friends, he seemed to find peace. He wrote every day. During this time, he also tries to get sober and get his life back on track.

Morrison spent his last months traveling across Europe and Northern Africa (where he lost his passport and documents). He gathers a small circle of friends around him, including the Belgian film director Agnes Varda and a couple of French music journalists. Despite his efforts to clean himself up from his drug and alcohol habit, he discovers a different drug scene in Europe, eventually leading to his demise.

Morrison spends much time in Paris alone, something he is not accustomed to. His open relationship with Pamela allows her to often spend weekends with lovers or with her European gay friends, leaving Morrison alone in their apartment most of the time. Courson's growing heroin habit begins to influence Morrison. Bloated from years of alcohol abuse, Morrison, who had never indulged in heroin, reportedly started using it in Paris when the drug became trendy in Europe.

During his last days, in the summer of 1971, his health began to fade quickly. Although the album "L.A. Woman" was praised by critics and fans alike, he had not yearned to return to the United States, despite his loneliness in Paris.

The events of Morrison's last hours on July 3, 1971, remain a blur and are wrapped in mystery. What is certain is that Jim Morrison died at 27 and that paramedics were called into his apartment, where he was found in the bathtub. The official cause of death was listed as cardiac arrest, but no autopsy was ever performed. Few could view the body that left the apartment in a sealed coffin. The official story, as told by Pamela, was that they had a quiet evening after going out to dinner at a Chinese restaurant and to the movies. She said they relaxed, watched their home movies, and listened to music at home. Still, during the early hours of July 3, Morrison felt ill and went to take a bath, where he vomited blood with his supper and remained in the bathtub while Pamela went to sleep, possibly passed out from heroin. She woke up at 5 a.m., found him in the same position in the bathtub, and noticed that he was deceased.

Courson then called her local friends in Paris, including long-time Morrison friends Alain Ronay and Agnes Varda. Ronay went to the apartment, and only then was an ambulance called. Within days Morrison was placed in a sealed coffin and discretely buried at Pere

Lachaise cemetery in Paris with a small group of eight people in attendance. The Doors manager Bill Siddons was asked by Door's member Ray Manzarek to go to Paris and confirm if Morrison was indeed dead. He never saw the body. His death only became public one week later.

Those events have led to several theories about his death. One is that several persons claimed that in the hours before his death, Jim Morrison was alone at the Paris club Rock n'Roll Circus, a trendy nightclub frequented by rock stars like Mick Jagger, and also a place where heroin use was rampant. Pamela had spent the night with one of her lovers, possibly Jean de Breiteuil, a count who was also a drug supplier to rock stars. Reportedly, some witnesses state that Morrison went to take heroin that night in the club's toilets and overdosed as he was not used to the drug (a potent variant named China White). Two drug dealers tried to revive him but were unable to. They then carried him through the club and back to his apartment, where they put him in a bathtub full of ice (something that is used to reanimate drug overdose victims). No ambulance was called, and Morrison's body was left there alone.

When Pamela returned home, she found him and began making her phone calls. More recently, Mick Jagger's 1960s girlfriend and singer-actress, Marianne Faithful, says she knows who killed Morrison: her then-boyfriend, Pamela's lover, and drug supplier Jean de Breiteuil inadvertently sent the singer on a final ride. Faithful said that when de Breitreuil went to visit Morrison for the last time, she skipped the trip. She was woken up in the early hours of July 3 by a phone call from Pamela asking Jean to help her. He went to the apartment and found Morrison dead, and when he returned to his place, he told Faithful that they had to flee the country, and he never told her why or the details of what happened to Morrison.

Jim Morrison became one of Rock's most mythological figures and remains to this day an absolute icon and influential singer and artist. His gravesite at the Pere Lachaise is one of Paris' most visited sites, with daily pilgrimages of fans worldwide. Morrison's death happened two years to the day after the demise of Rolling Stones guitarist Brian Jones and roughly nine months after the deaths of Jimi Hendrix and

Janis Joplin. All these famous musicians died at the age of 27, leading to the debut of the 27 Club.

MARCH 12
1945

On this day in history, the Commander in Chief of the Replacement Army (German Home Army), General Friedrich Fromm, is executed by firing squad for his role in the July plot to assassinate Adolph Hitler in 1944. The fact that Fromm's participation in the conspiracy was lukewarm at best did not save him from the firing line.

By 1944, many high-ranking German army officers and government officials had decided that Hitler had to be removed from power. He was steering Germany towards destruction with his two-front war, and they firmly believed that assassinating the Fuhrer was the only way to stop him and save Germany. According to their plan, a coup d'état would follow the assassination, and a new government would be put in place in Berlin, saving Germany from destruction at the hands of the Allies. Everything would not go as planned, however. Colonel Claus von Stauffenberg was the coordinator of the plot by this time, and it was his job to plant a bomb during a meeting that was being held at Hitler's holiday retreat, Berchtesgaden (but was later moved to the Fuhrer's headquarters at Rastenburg). Stauffenberg was assigned chief of staff to General Friedrich Fromm at the Home Army headquarters in central Berlin. This position allowed Stauffenberg to attend Hitler's military meetings, either at the Wolfsschanze in East Prussia or at Berchtesgaden, thus allowing him, perhaps the last that would present itself, to kill Hitler with an explosive or a pistol.

As Commander in Chief of the Home Army (composed of reservists who remained behind the front lines to help preserve order in Germany), Fromm was predisposed to the conspirators' plot but agreed to cooperate actively in the coup once Hitler was dead. He did not have any direct involvement in the conspiracy.

On July 15, Stauffenberg again flew to Wolfsschanze. The plan was for Stauffenberg to hide the briefcase with the bomb in Hitler's meeting room with a timer engaged, excuse himself from the meeting, wait for the explosion, then travel back to Berlin and join the other conspirators at the Benderblock. Operation Valkyrie would be mobilized, the Home Army would take the reigns in Germany, and the other Nazi leaders would be arrested. The conspirators would appoint an interim head of state, chancellor, and armed forces commander-in-chief. Yet again, on July 15, the attempt was called off at the last moment. Himmler and Goring were present, but at the last minute, Hitler was called out of the room. Stauffenberg was able to block the placement of the bomb and prevent its discovery. When the attempt to proceed with the mutiny on July 15, 1944, failed, Fromm refused to have any further part in the plot.

On July 20, Stauffenberg placed an explosive-filled briefcase under a table in the conference room at Rastenburg. Hitler was looking over a map of the Eastern Front as Colonel Heinz Brandt, attempting to get a better look at the map, moved the briefcase out of place, further away from where Hitler was positioned. At 12:42 p.m., the bomb exploded. A stenographer was killed immediately. More than 20 people in the room were injured, with three officers later dying. As did everyone else shielded by the conference table leg from the explosion, Hitler survived. His trousers were burnt and torn, and he experienced a perforated eardrum, as did most of the other 24 people in the room.

Meanwhile, Stauffenberg flew to Berlin to meet with his co-conspirators to carry out Operation Valkyrie, overthrowing the central government. At 4:00 p.m., Fromm learned from Field Marshal Wilhelm Keitel that Hitler was still alive. Keitel wanted to know Stauffenberg's location, which indicated to Fromm that they had traced the plot to his headquarters and that he was in grave danger. Fromm stated that he thought Stauffenberg was with Hitler. To protect himself, Fromm changed sides and ordered the arrest of Stauffenberg and his men, but Fromm was located and locked in an office by Nazi police.

Fromm was freed from this room, and fighting broke out in the headquarters of the Home Army between officers supporting and opposing the coup; Stauffenberg was wounded in the shootout. As the fighting was ongoing, Fromm's forces received reinforcements, and the conspirators were overwhelmed and arrested; by 11 p.m., Fromm had regained control of the building.

Perhaps hoping that a brave show of loyalty would save him, Fromm convened an impromptu court-martial consisting of himself, and he sentenced four conspirators, including Stauffenberg and two of his aides, to death for high treason while arresting General Beck. Beck realized the situation was hopeless and asked for a pistol and shot himself – the first of many attempted suicides in the coming days. At first, Beck only wounded himself, and then some soldiers shot and killed him. Despite protests from other officers, who had been ordered by Hitler to only arrest the conspirators, at 00:10 on July 21, the four officers were executed outside the building, possibly to prevent them from revealing Fromm's involvement in the plot. Others would have also been executed, but at 00:30, Waffen-SS personnel led by Obersturmbannfuhrer Otto Skorzeny arrived, and further executions were forbidden.

After the execution of Stauffenberg and the others, Fromm went to Goebbels to take credit for stopping the coup, to which Goebbels glibly replied, "You have been in a damn hurry to get your witnesses below ground." On the morning of July 22, 1944, Fromm and other conspiracy members were arrested. Because the court failed to prove a direct association with the July 20 plotters, he was instead charged and convicted of cowardice before the enemy. However, because he had executed the conspirators, he was not tortured and executed by hanging with a thin rope and sentenced to military execution.

On March 12, 1945, Fromm was executed at the Brandenburg-Gorden Prison by firing squad as part of the post-insurgency purge. His final words before the firing squad were reported, "I die because it was ordered. I had always wanted only the best for Germany."

MARCH 13
1881

On this day in history, Czar Alexander II, the Emperor of Russia since 1855, was assassinated in Saint Petersburg, Russia, while going home to the Winter Palace from Mikhailovsky Manege in a closed carriage. The deed was done by bombs thrown by members of the revolutionary "People's Will" group. The People's Will, formed in 1879, used terrorism and assassination to attempt to continually overthrow Russia's czarist autocracy. They murdered government officials and tried several times to end the Czar's life before finally assassinating him on March 13, 1881.

As Czar, Alexander achieved much to modernize and liberalize Russia, including abolishing serfdom, for which he became known as Alexander the Liberator. He was also responsible for other reforms, including reorganizing the judicial system, promoting local self-government through the Zemstvo system, setting up elected local judges, abolishing corporal punishment, promoting university education, imposing universal military service, and ending some privileges of the nobility. After an attempt on his life in 1866, Alexander adopted a somewhat more reactionary stance until his death. When his authority was challenged, he turned repressive and vehemently opposed calls for political reform. Ironically, on the day he was assassinated, he signed a proclamation – the so-called Loris-Melikov constitution – that would have given rise to two legislative commissions made up of indirectly elected representatives. Upon taking the throne after his dead father, Alexander III would repeal the Loris-Melikov constitution, stating it was too progressive.

On August 25-26, 1879, on the anniversary of his accession to the throne, the 22-member Executive Committee of Narodnaya Volya (People's Will) assassinated Alexander II, hoping it would cause a revolution amongst the masses. Over the next year and a half, the various attempts on Alexander's life failed. The Committee then decided that they would assassinate him. At the same time, he was on his way back to the Winter's Palace following his regular Sunday visit to the Mikhailovsky Manege. Andrei Zhelyabov was the main organizer of the plot. They observed his movements for a couple of months and deduced two possible routes the party would take. The group planned for all possible contingencies to achieve their goal of assassinating Alexander II.

In one scenario, the group would plant a large stash of bombs under the street on one route, and as the procession passed, they would detonate the explosives. To further ensure the plot's success, four bomb throwers were to loiter at the corners of the street; after the explosion, they were to close in on the Czar and use their bombs if necessary. If, on the other hand, the Czar passed the canal, the bomb throwers alone were to be relied upon. Ingnacy Hryniewiecki, Nikolai Rysakov, Timofey Mikailov, and Ivan Yemelyanov volunteered as bomb throwers.

The Czar traveled to and from the *Manege* in a closed two-seater carriage drawn by two horses. He was attended by five mounted Cossacks and Franciszek Jackowski, a Polish noble, with a sixth Cossack sitting on the coachman's left. The Czar's carriage was followed by three sleighs carrying the chief of police Colonel Dvorzhitzky and two officers of the Gendarmerie.

On the afternoon of March 13, after having watched the maneuvers of two Guard battalions at the *Manege*, the Czar's carriage turned into

Bolshaya Italyanskaya Street, thus avoiding the cache of bombs under the street in Malaya Sadovaya. On his way back, the Czar visited his cousin, the Grand Duchess Catherine. This allowed the conspirators enough time to get set up at their alternate place of attack.

At 2:15 p.m., one of the bomb-thrower hurled a bomb under the carriage carrying the Czar, killing one Cossack, and injuring a 14-year-old boy who was a bystander. This bomb only damaged the carriage. After the explosion, Alexander exited the carriage shaken but unharmed. The bomb thrower was captured immediately. The perpetrator yelled out to one of his accomplices in the gathering crowd. The coachman implored the Czar not to get out of the carriage, but he was adamant that he view the perpetrator and the damage to the carriage. He expressed concern for the victims of the bombing. To the anxious inquiries of his entourage, Alexander replied, "Thank God, I'm untouched."

The Czar was preparing to depart when a second bomber rushed forward and threw a bomb at the emperor's feet. The Czar and his assassin fell to the ground, mortally wounded. Because people had crowded close after the first explosion, there were many more injuries with the second bomb. According to one observer, there were about 20 people injured by the blast. Alexander was leaning on his right arm. His legs were shattered below his knees, from which he was bleeding abundantly. His abdomen was torn open, and his face was mutilated. The bomber, also gravely wounded from the blast, lay next to the Czar, as was a 14-year-old boy.

Bystanders rushed to hear the Czar's barely audible cries for help; he could scarcely whisper: "Take me to the Palace...there...I will die." Alexander was taken by sleigh to his study in the Winter Palace, where twenty years earlier, he had proclaimed the Emancipation Edict freeing the serfs. Other members of the Romanov family rushed to the Palace. The dying Czar was given Communion and Last Rites. When the physician, Sergey Botkin, was asked how long before he would die, he replied, "Up to fifteen minutes." At 3:30 p.m. that day, the personal flag of Alexander II was taken down for the final time.

His 36-year-old son, Alexander III, succeeded him. Alexander II's assassins were arrested and hanged immediately, and the People's Will was thoroughly destroyed. Vladimir Lenin's Bolshevik revolutionaries finally achieved the peasant revolution advocated by the People's Will in 1917.

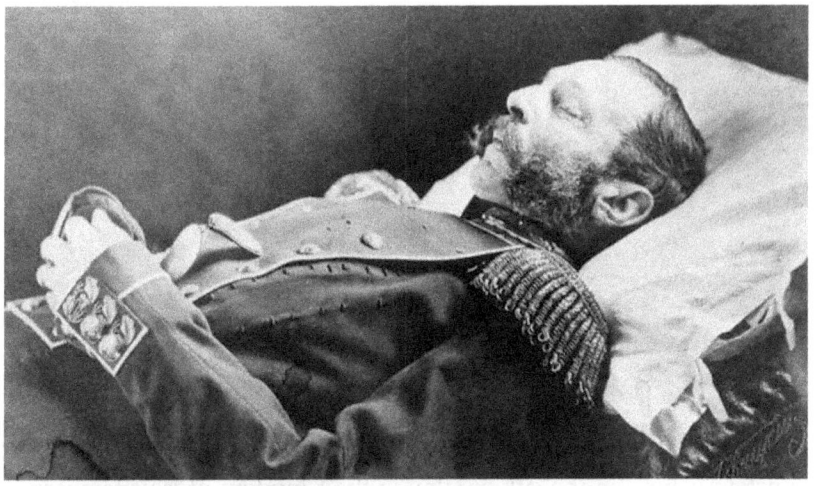

(Photo: Czar Alexander II laying in state. Wikimedia Commons)

MARCH 14
1879

On this day in history, German-born theoretical physicist Albert Einstein is born in the city of Ulm, in the Kingdom of Wurttemberg in the German Empire. The son of a Jewish electrical engineer, Einstein's theories of special and general relativity immensely changed human comprehension of the universe, and his work in particle and energy theory helped to make attainable quantum mechanics and, ultimately, the atomic bomb. Relativity and quantum mechanics together are the two pillars of modern physics. His mass-energy equivalence formula $E=mc2$, which arises from relativity theory, has been dubbed "the world's most famous equation." His body of work is also known for its immense impact on the philosophy of science. In 1921 he won the Nobel Prize in Physics "for his services to theoretical physics, and especially for the discovery of the law of the photoelectric effect," a significant step forward in developing quantum theory. His intellectual achievements and originality made " Einstein " interchangeable with "genius."

Albert Einstein was raised in a middle-class Jewish family in Munich. When he was young, music captivated him, especially playing the violin, mathematics, and science. He was a poor student, and subsequently, in 1894, he dropped out of school and moved to

Switzerland, where he resumed his schooling, and he later gained admission to the Swiss Federal Polytechnic Institute in Zurich. In 1896, he relinquished his German citizenship and effectively remained stateless until 1901, when he became a Swiss citizen.

While at the Polytechnic Institute in Zurich, Einstein fell in love with a student named Mileva Maric. His parents opposed this union, and Einstein had insufficient funds to get married. The couple gave birth to an illegitimate daughter, Lieserl, born in 1902, of whom little is known. He secured employment as a clerk at the Swiss patent office in Bern, which allowed him and Maric to get married in 1903. They would subsequently have two more children, Hans Albert (born 1904) and Eduard (born 1910).

While employed at the patent office, Einstein did some of the most brilliant work of his life. In 1905, a year sometimes referred to as his *annus mirabilis* ("miracle year"), Einstein published four groundbreaking papers. In his first article, he applied the quantum theory (developed initially by German physicist Max Planck) to light to describe the occurrence known as the photoelectric effect, by which a material will discharge electrically charged particles when struck by light. The second paper contained Einstein's hypothetical proof that atoms exist, which he got by examining the Brownian motion phenomenon, in which tiny particles were suspended in water.

In the third and arguably most famous paper, titled "On the Electrodynamics of Moving Bodies," Einstein argued that the apparent contradiction between two main theories of physics: Isaac Newton's concepts of absolute time and space and James Clerk Maxwell's idea that the speed of light was continuous. To do this, Einstein introduced his theory of relativity, which held that the laws of physics are the same even for objects moving in different inertial frames (i.e., at constant speeds relative to each other) and that the speed of light is a constant in all inertial frames. The fourth paper discussed the fundamental association between mass and energy, previously considered unconnected concepts. Einstein's well-known equation $E=mc^2$ (where "c" was the constant speed of light) related to this relationship.

Einstein worked at the patent office until 1909, when he found a full-time academic post at the University of Zurich. In 1913, he landed at the University of Berlin and was made director of the Kaiser Wilhelm Institute for Physics. This move corresponded to the beginning of his romantic relationship with his cousin, Elsa Lowenthal, whom he would marry after divorcing Mileva. In 1915, Einstein published his theory of relativity, which he considered his masterpiece. This theory states that gravity, as well as motion, can affect time and space. According to his equivalence principle – which held that gravity's pull in one direction is equal to an acceleration of speed in the opposite direction – if light is bent by acceleration, it must also be bent by gravity. In 1919, two expeditions sent to perform experiments during a solar eclipse found that light rays from distant stars were deflected or bent by the sun's gravity, just as Einstein had foretold.

The general theory of relativity was the first significant theory of gravity since Newton's, more than 250 years before, and the result had a resounding effect worldwide. He began touring the world, speaking before thousands of people. Einstein was awarded the Nobel Prize in 1921 for his work on the photoelectric effect, as his work on relativity remained highly controversial.

A long-time pacifist and a Jew, Einstein became the target of hostility from those inside Germany suffering from the after-effects of defeat during World War I. In 1933, Adolf Hitler assumed power in Germany while Einstein was visiting the United States. Einstein, as Jewish, objected to the policies of the newly elected Nazi regime, so he decided to emigrate. He ultimately accepted a job at the Institute for Advanced Study in Princeton, New Jersey. He would not return to Germany again in his lifetime.

Einstein's wife, Elsa, died in 1936. After a decade of concentrated work on trying to find a unified field theory, which would consolidate all the laws of the universe and those of physics into a single framework, Einstein had become isolated from many of his colleagues, who were focused on quantum theory and its implications, rather than relativity.

By the late 1930s, Einstein's theories, including his equation $E=mc2$, helped form the origin of the development of the atomic bomb. In 1939, Einstein endorsed a letter to U.S. President Franklin D. Roosevelt alerting him to the potential German nuclear weapons program and recommending that the U.S. begin similar research. Einstein became an American citizen in 1940 while retaining his Swiss citizenship. He was not asked to participate in the Manhattan Project, as the U.S. government opposed his socialist and pacifist views. In 1952, Einstein refused an offer by David Ben-Gurion, Israel's premier, to assume the presidency of Israel.

Albert Einstein died of an aortic aneurysm on April 18, 1955, at 76. Since his death, Einstein's reputation, and stature in the world of physics have only grown as physicists continue to unravel the mystery of the so-called "strong force" (the missing piece of his unified field theory), and space satellites further verify the principles of his cosmology.

MARCH 15
1493

On this day in history, explorer, and navigator Christopher Columbus returns to Spain after his first voyage to the New World. He would ultimately make four trips across the Atlantic Ocean from Spain: 1492, 1493, 1498, and 1502. He was resolute in finding an uninterrupted water route west from Europe to Asia, but he never did. Instead, he faltered upon the Americas. Though he did not "discover" the so-called New World – millions of people already lived there – his voyages marked the beginning of centuries of exploration and colonization of North and South America.

Columbus was born in Genoa in 1451. Little is recognized of his early life, but he worked as a seaman and then as a maritime businessman. He became fixated on the possibility of discovering a western sea route to India, Cathay (China), and Asia's gold and spice islands. At this time, Europeans knew of no direct sea route to southern Asia, and the thoroughfare via Egypt and the Red Sea was not available to Europeans by the Ottoman Empire, as were many land routes.

Columbus remained at sea until 1476, when pirates attacked his ship as it sailed along the Portuguese coast. The boat sank, but Columbus floated ashore by holding on to an errant piece of wood from his vessel. Eventually, he made his way to Lisbon (he based himself there from 1477 to 1485), where he studied mathematics, astronomy, cartography, and navigation. He also began to devise a plan that would change the world forever.

In 1478 he married Felipa Perestrello e Moniz, daughter of Bartolomeu Perestrello, a Portuguese nobleman of Lombard origin who had been the donatary captain of Porto Santo. In 1480, Columbus's son Diego was born. He continued to work for the Centurione family. He traded along the coasts of West Africa, reaching the Portuguese trading post of Elmina on the Guinea coast (in present-day Ghana). By 1484 he returned to Porto Santo to find that his wife had died. He went back to Portugal to settle her estate and collect his son. He left Portugal for Castile in 1485, where he found a mistress in 1487, a 20-year-old orphan named Beatriz Enriquez de Arana.

Being ambitious, Columbus eventually learned to speak Portuguese, Latin, and Castilian. He read widely about history, astronomy, and geography, including the works of Claudius Ptolemy, the travels of Marco Polo and Sir John Mandeville, Pierre Cardinal d'Ailly's Imago Mundi, Pliny's *Natural History*, and Pope Pius II's *Historia Rerum Ubique Gestaram*. According to historian Edmund Morgan,

"Columbus was not a scholarly man. Yet he studied these books, made hundreds of marginal notations, and came out with ideas about the world that were characteristically simple, strong, and sometimes wrong."

Like most others, Columbus underestimated the world's size, calculating that East Asia must lie where North America sits on the globe (he was unaware that the Pacific Ocean existed). With only the Atlantic Ocean lying between Europe and the riches of the East Indies, as was his thinking, Columbus tried to convince King John II of Portugal to fund his "Enterprise of the Indies," as he called his plan. He was turned down as the Spanish King and Queen, Ferdinand, and Isabella twice turned him down as well. However, after the Spanish victory over the Kingdom of Granada in January 1492, the Spanish King and Queen agreed to support his mission to the East Indies.

On August 3, 1492, Columbus left Spain with three small ships, the *Nina*, the *Pinta*, and the *Santa Maria*. On October 12, the expedition reached land, most likely in the Bahamas. Later that month, Columbus viewed Cuba, which he thought was China, and in December, the three ships landed on Hispaniola, which Columbus thought might be Japan. He founded a small colony called La Navidad in present-day Haiti with 39 of his crew. The explorer returned to Spain with spices, gold, and "Indian" captives in March 1493 and received the highest honors from the Spanish monarchs. He was the first European to have explored the Americas since the Vikings set up colonies in Newfoundland and Greenland in the 10th century.

When Columbus arrived back in Spain on March 15, 1493, he promptly announced his discoveries to King Ferdinand and Queen Isabella in a letter. He noted that "I discovered many islands inhabited by numerous people. I took possession of all of them for our most fortunate King by making public proclamation and unfurling his standard, no one making any resistance." In his letter, he also spoke of the native culture and lack of weapons, noting that "they are destitute of arms, which are entirely unknown to them, and for which they are not adapted; not on account of any bodily deformity, for they are well made, but because they are timid and full of terror." Columbus wrote that because the native people are "fearful and timid... guileless and honest," the land could easily be conquered by Spain. The natives "might become Christians and inclined to love our King and Queen and Princes and all the people of Spain."

Columbus led four expeditions to the "New World" during his lifetime but never accomplished his original goal – a western ocean route to Asia. Columbus died in Spain in 1506 without understanding the scope of his achievements: He had discovered the New World, whose wealth over the next century would help make Spain the richest and most powerful nation on the planet. He also released centuries of vicious colonization, the transatlantic slave trade, and the demise of millions of Native Americans from disease and murder.

MARCH 16
1881

On this day in history, Francisco "Chico" Forster is shot to death on a downtown Los Angeles Street by his former lover, eighteen-year-old Lastenia Abarta. The forty-year-old Forster was the son of a wealthy Los Angeles landowner with a considerable reputation for womanizing, who had falsely promised Lastenia marriage only to be deceived and blackmailed to obtain her sexual favors.

Lastenia Abarta was born in 1863 in Los Angeles, the daughter of Pedro Abarta, born Pierre Abartachipy in Ustaritz, France, and Maria Ysabel Rada, born in Hermosillo, Sonora, Mexico. Pedro Abarta, who was considered one of the original settlers of Los Angeles, died at age 56 of heart disease on January 3, 1877.

Lastenia worked in her parents' pool hall, singing, and playing guitar. She would meet a frequent customer of the business, Francisco Pio "Chico" Forster, 40, one of Southern California's wealthiest landowners at that time, and son of a prominent rancher and land developer John Juan Forster and Ysidora Pico, who was a member of California's prominent Pico family and sister of Pio Pico, California's last Mexican governor.

It was at the pool hall that Lastenia caught Chico's eye. Chico was a lady's man in the Los Angeles area of the 1870s and 1880s. Chico was known to be a womanizer who had already fathered two children out of wedlock. He would begin courting Lastenia, but due to the moral and religious standards of the time, she would not agree to sexual relations with Chico unless he promised to marry her. Forster agreed and promised to marry her as requested. But Lastenia's widowed mother, Ysabel, disapproved of the relationship because she wanted her to marry lawyer (and former newspaper editor) Francisco P. Ramirez.

On March 15, 1881, Lastenia sang at a party given by Pio Pico, California's last Mexican governor. Pico had just lost his Rancho Santa Margarita (now Camp Pendleton) to Chico Forster's father in a famous lawsuit; he had lost the governorship decades before. Being in love with the son of the man to whom he had lost that land, Lastenia insulted him further. She changed one line in the lyrics of the last song she sang that night – changed the words so that it took a sizable dig at the party's host. She sang, "I salute your loving lips," knowing how sensitive he was about his prominent mouth. No sooner had she sung the changed lyric than she ended the song and rushed off the stage and straight into the arms of Chico. The crowd never had time to react before she was gone.

Lastenia and Chico ran to the Moiso Mansion Hotel, where Chico had reserved a room. There, he made love to Lastenia, taking her virginity but promising to marry her. By the following morning, Lastenia was grieved by her choice to give herself to this man before they had wed, so Chico pledged to leave immediately to find a priest and rectify the situation. Ashamed, Lastenia hid away in the hotel while she waited. But too much time had passed, and Chico never returned by late afternoon. Lastenia went home and told her the story. Her mother was angry and told her, "If you are not married today, I don't want to see you anymore." Depressed, Lastenia went to John Leiver's gun shop to buy a gun so she could commit suicide. She purchased a Smith and Wesson .38 caliber revolver and, knowing that she did not know how to use it asked the gun shop owner how to use the gun. She went home intending to commit suicide and was interrupted by her sister, Hortensia, who saw her sister with the gun and inquired as to the problem. Lastenia told her the story, and her sister promised to help her.

On March 16, 1881, the Abarta sisters searched the city and found the man who had deceived and abandoned her, gambling his money away at the horse tracks and gambling on racehorses. Angry, the sisters forcibly put Chico into their carriage and tried to head to the Plaza Church to be married. Only Chico did not want to go, so he jumped out of the conveyance partway to their destination. Both young women followed, yelling at him. When he finally stopped and turned to face them, Lastania drew her pistol from her skirt pocket and shot Chico in the right eye, killing him instantly. There were several witnesses to the crime, and she was arrested and put on trial.

Chico's father, intent on getting justice for his son, hired a special prosecutor, the soon-to-be U.S. Senator Stephen M. White, for $500. Defending Lastenia were two of the city's most prominent criminal defense attorneys, G. Wiley Wells, a former consul in Shanghai, and John F. Godfrey, former city attorney. Together they saw a way to win this case that others thought a sure loser. Prosecutors said the murder was premeditated, and the motive was revenge. The defense argued that Abarta had been driven mad -not by disgrace but by biology.

Nineteenth-century American medicine – monopolized by males – was obsessed with what it viewed as female "hysteria," which medical journals of the time linked to sexual deprivation and the evil influences of an oversexed uterus. Some popular medical theories even held that the mental strain of higher education would have dire effects on the natural development of women's reproductive organs. By the 1880s, American physicians believed that female hysteria was an epidemic in the land.

Abarta's lawyers sought to build their defense in that climate of misguided medical opinion. First, they provided the blood-soaked sheets from the hotel that proved that Lastenia was "an innocent young woman." One after another, seven medical experts took the stand, most agreeing that hysteria was a uterine disorder brought about by irregular menstrual periods that "tended to disease the mind." Some experts went further, testifying that Abarta's behavior was a classic display of "hysterical symptoms" – fury, combativeness, and paranoia.

One physician testified that Lastenia's condition was "unavoidable because her brain was undoubtedly congested with blood.... Disappointment is the great incentive to hysteria; disappointment in love is the great cause of insanity."

But the testimony of Dr. Joseph Kurtz, a local physician of formidable reputation, cemented the jurors' decision. "Any virtuous woman when deprived of her virtue would go mad, undoubtedly," he said.

The spectators in the court applauded.

After a three-week trial, the all-male jury, swayed by Kurtz's forthright testimony, took 20 minutes to find Abarta had been insane at the time of the shooting.

A dispirited John Forster died less than a year after his son's death.

After the trial, Lastenia and Hortensia left Los Angeles for good, moving to El Paso, Texas. There, on January 20, 1883, she married the Frenchman Auguste Cazaux, with whom she would have four children. For diplomatic reasons, in 1889, they moved to Mexico City, where they fit perfectly into the Porfiriato aristocracy. Lastenia would die on January 30, 1947, at 84. She is buried in the French Pantheon of Piety in Mexico City in a tomb where the remains of her husband Auguste, who died in 1918, and her son Augustin Cazaux Abarta, who died in 1935, now rest.

MARCH 17
1955

On this day in history, the Richard Riot (named after Montreal Canadian hockey star Maurice Richard) occurred in Montreal, Quebec, Canada. After a brutal confrontation on March 13 in which Richard hit a referee, NHL president Clarence Campbell suspended him for the balance of the 1954-1955 NHL season, including the playoffs. Montreal fans felt that the suspension was too harsh. After the next Montreal home game on March 17, 1955, a large crowd of Montreal supporters decided to riot outside the team's arena, causing significant damage and injuries. Hostilities finally lessened after Richard made a personal and public appeal accepting his punishment and promising to return the following year to help his team win the Stanley Cup. The incident cost Richard that year's league scoring title, and the circumstances surrounding the riot contributed to the leaving of long-time Canadian head coach Dick Irvin and was a forerunner to Quebec's Quiet Revolution.

On March 13, 1955, during a game in Boston, Richard fought with Hal Laycoe after he was high-sticked in the head. Richard needed five stitches to close the wound to his forehead. When the play ended, Richard skated over to Laycoe and struck him in the face with his stick. A linesman tried to restrain Richard, who repeatedly tried to attack

Laycoe. Richard eventually broke his hockey stick over the body of Laycoe. Linesman Cliff Thompson tried to contain the Canadian player, and Richard hit him twice in the face, knocking him out. The referee gave Richard a match penalty and an automatic $100 fine.

In the dressing room after the game was over, Boston police tried to arrest Richard but were stopped from accessing the dressing room by Canadiens players. Eventually, the Boston team convinced the police officers to let the Canadiens leave, providing the NHL would take care of the issue. Richard was never arrested for the incident. Richard was instead sent to the hospital by team doctors after Richard complained of headaches and stomach pains.

The Laycoe incident was Richard's second confrontation with an official that season. The previous December, in a game in Toronto, Richard slapped a linesman across the face, which resulted in a $250 fine. Upon hearing the referee's report in the Laycoe incident, league president, Clarence Campbell, ordered all individuals involved to appear at a March 16 hearing at league headquarters in Montreal.

After the hearing, Campbell issued a statement to the press. In it, he stated that

"Whether this type of conduct is the product of temperamental instability or wilful defiance of the authority in the games does not matter. It is a type of conduct that cannot be tolerated by any player – star or otherwise. Richard will be suspended from all games, both league, and playoff, for the balance of the current season."

Within minutes of the judgment, the NHL head office was deluged with hundreds of telephone calls from angry fans, many of whom made death threats against Campbell. While many in Montreal felt that the suspension was too harsh and unduly severe, the general feeling around the league was that the punishment was insufficient. Some even thought that he should have been suspended for life.

Public outrage continued to boil over in Montreal over the extreme suspension. Many Quebecois felt that the punishment was the English majority's attempt to suppress the French minority while attempting to demean French Canadians by "excessively punishing their favorite player." Despite the death threats, Campbell was adamant that he would attend the Canadiens next home game versus the Detroit Red Wings on March 17, despite strong advice that he should not. Hundreds of demonstrators had gathered in front of the Montreal Forum two hours before game time. They tried to crash the gate but were repulsed by the police. They then gathered at Cabot Square across the street from the Forum; before long, there were 6,000 protestors.

Campbell arrived at the game at the halfway mark of the first period. The packed house of 15,000 immediately began booing, and those nearby started throwing eggs, vegetables, shoes, and debris at Campbell and his party for close to 10 minutes. At one point, a fan got by Campbell's security and walked up to him with his hand extended as if he wanted to shake his hand. At the last moment, the fan withdrew his hand and slapped Campbell across the face, then punched him in the head. The police immediately arrested the man and removed him from the Forum. Shortly after that incident, a tear gas bomb was set off inside the Forum, close to Campbell's seat. The Montreal Fire Department ordered the game to be stopped, and the building emptied for everyone's safety. Campbell forfeited the game in Detroit's favor.

The departing crowd joined the protestors outside, and a riot resulted outside the Forum. Windows were smashed, bystanders were attacked, newsstands were set on fire, and cars were overturned. Over fifty stores within a fifteen-block radius of the Forum were looted and vandalized. Twelve police officers and twenty-five civilians were wounded. The riot finally ended at 3 a.m. Between 41 and 100 individuals were arrested, and $100,000 in damage was done ($1,000,000 in today's dollars).

Richard gave the following statement to reporters on March 18 in the hopes that any further rioting would cease:

"Because I always try so hard to win and had my troubles in Boston, I was suspended. At playoff time, it hurts not to be in the game with the boys. However, I want to do what is good for the people of Montreal and the team. So that no further harm will be done, I would like to ask everyone to get behind the team and to help the boys win from the New York Rangers and Detroit. I will take my punishment and come back next year to help the club and the younger players to win the Cup."

The suspension came when Richard led the NHL scoring title, and the Canadians were battling Detroit for first place. Richard lost the scoring title of 1954-55 to teammate Bernie Geoffrion by one point, who scored the winning point in the season's final game. The Canadiens fans booed him when he scored despite being a teammate.

The points from the forfeiture allowed Detroit to win first place overall in the league, and they were guaranteed home-ice advantage throughout the Stanley Cup Playoffs. That season, Detroit defeated the Canadiens in seven games to win the 1955 Stanley Cup Finals. Montreal would win the next five Stanley Cups, a record that still stands today. Richard retired from playing in 1960 after the Canadiens' fifth straight Stanley Cup.

MARCH 18
1837

On this day in history, Grover Cleveland, the 22nd and 24th president of the United States, was born. He was an American lawyer and political reformer who served as president from 1885 to 1889 and 1893 to 1897. He was the only president to date to serve two non-consecutive terms and the only Democratic president to win an election during a time of Republican control of the White House that stretched from Abraham Lincoln's (1809-1865) election in 1860 to the end of William Howard Taft's (1857-1930) term in 1913.

Cleveland worked as an attorney and then served as mayor of Buffalo, New York, then governor of the state of New York before becoming the president of the United States in 1885. His record in the White House was mixed at best. His battle for political reform and fiscal conservatism made him popular with American conservatives at the time. Cleveland was admired for his honesty, integrity, self-reliance, and dedication to the principles of classical liberalism. He fought against political corruption, patronage, and bossism. He considered himself a watchdog over Congress rather than an initiator. During his second term, he angered many of his earliest supporters and seemed overcome by the Panic of 1893 and the depression that followed. He declined the invitation to run for a third term.

Stephen Grover Cleveland was born in Caldwell, New Jersey on March 18, 1837. He was the fifth of nine children of Richard Falley Cleveland (1804-1853), a Presbyterian minister, and Anne Neal Cleveland (1806-1882). The family moved to upstate New York in 1841, where Cleveland's father served several congregations before his untimely death in 1853. He became known as Grover in his adult life.

After his father died, Cleveland left school to help support his family. He was employed as an assistant teacher at the New York Institute for the Blind with the help of his brother, who had already worked there. In 1855 he moved to Buffalo, New York, and took a job as a clerk in the law firm of Rogers, Bowen, and Rogers, read law with them, and was admitted to the New York Bar in 1859. In 1862, he started his own law firm. Cleveland did not fight in the American Civil War (1861-1865); when the Conscription Act was passed in 1863, he could hire a substitute to fight for him in the war. Cleveland paid $150 (equivalent to $3301 in 2021) to George Benninsky, a thirty-two-year-old Polish immigrant, to serve in his place. Benninsky survived the war.

Cleveland's first taste of political life came in 1871 when he was elected sheriff of Erie Count, New York. He carried out the death sentence during his two-year term by hanging three convicted murderers. In 1873 he returned to his law practice. Then he was elected mayor of Buffalo and subsequently governor of New York from 1882 to 1884 when he became known as "Uncle Jumbo." Cleveland was soon regarded as presidential material.

During his first term as president, 1885-1889, Cleveland continued the policy of his predecessor, Chester Arthur, in basing political appointments on merit rather than party connections. He tried to decrease government spending, using the veto more often than any other president up to that point. Cleveland was a noninterventionist in foreign policy and fought to have protective tariffs lowered.

In 1886, he married Frances Folsom (1864-1947), a student at Wells College in New York who was 27 years younger than he was. Although Cleveland was not the first president to marry while in office, he was the only president to get married in the White House. At age 21, Frances became the youngest first lady in U.S. history. The Clevelands would go on to have five children.

In the election of 1888, former U.S. Senator Benjamin Harrison (1833-1901) of Indiana won, primarily due to heavy turnout by voters in the industrial states of the Northeast who saw their jobs threatened by lower tariffs. Cleveland even lost his home state of New York in that election. He returned to New York City and took a position in a law firm for the next four years.

Cleveland's second term opened during the worst financial crisis in the country's history. The Panic of 1893 started with a railroad bankruptcy in February 1893, followed rapidly by bank failures, a nationwide credit crisis, a stock market crash, and the failures of three more railroads. Unemployment soared to 19 percent, and strikes crippled the coal and transportation industries in 1894. He became unpopular with organized labor when he employed federal troops to crush the Pullman railroad strike in 1894. The American economy recovered in 1896-1897 when the Klondike gold rush in the Yukon began a decade of rapid expansion.

Cleveland was an honest and hard-working president, but he is criticized for being unimaginative and having no overarching vision for American society. Against using legislation to bring about social change, he is best known for strengthening the federal government's executive branch in relation to Congress.

By the fall of 1896, Cleveland had become unpopular with some factions in his party. Other Democrats wanted him to run for a third term, as there were no term limits for presidents at that time. Cleveland declined, and former U.S. Representative William Jennings Bryan of Nebraska won the nomination. He ended up losing the 1896 election to Governor William McKinley of Ohio.

After vacating the White House in 1897, Cleveland retired to his home in Princeton, New Jersey, and served as a trustee of Princeton University from 1901 until his death. He refused overtures from his party to run again for the presidency in 1904. His health began to fail rapidly at the end of 1907, and he died of a heart attack at 71 on June 24, 1908. His last words were recorded as being: "I have tried so hard to do right."

MARCH 19
1945

On this day in history, USS *Franklin* (CV-13), an *Essex*-class aircraft carrier, was severely damaged by a Japanese air attack at 7:05 a.m. on March 19, 1945, with a loss of over 800 crewmembers and over 400 wounded. Named after Founding Father Benjamin Franklin and nicknamed "Big Ben," the *Franklin* was the most heavily damaged United States aircraft carrier to survive World War II. After the attack, she was returned to the New York Navy yards for repairs, missing the rest of the war. She was decommissioned in 1947, was never modernized and overhauled, and never again saw active service. *Franklin* and *Bunker Hill* (impaired by two kamikazes) were the only two of twenty-four *Essex*-class aircraft carriers not to see active service in the post-war era.

At 7:05 a.m. on the morning of March 19, 1945, the aircraft carrier USS Hancock transmitted a sighting of an unknown twin-engine aircraft to the ships of Task Force 58, positioned for attack 50 miles southwest of the Japanese coast. The *Franklin* crew had been brought to battle stations twelve times within six hours that night, and Captain Gehres downgraded the alert status to Condition III, allowing his men to eat or sleep. However, gunnery crews remained at their stations. The Japanese dive-bomber broke from the clouds at 2,000 feet, about 1,000 yards off *Franklin's* bow. The ship's 5-inch antiaircraft guns started firing, and two bombs hurtled toward the ship from the dive-bomber.

One of the two 550-pound semi-armor-piercing bombs struck the deck in the center, penetrating the hangar deck, causing much destruction, igniting voracious fires throughout the second and third decks. The second bomb hit aft, tearing through two decks. When she was struck, the *Franklin* had 31 armed and fuelled aircraft warming up on her flight deck, and the planes caught fire almost immediately. The hangar deck contained planes, 16 were fuelled, and five were armed. The hangar deck exploded and set fire to the aircraft's fuel tanks, and a gasoline vapor explosion occurred and devastated the deck. Only two crewmen survived the fire.

Franklin was soon dead in the water, without radio communications, broiling in the heat from the surrounding fires. Captain Gehres ordered *Franklin's* magazines to be flooded, but this could not be executed because the ship's water mains had already been destroyed by fire or explosions. Cruisers USS Santa Fe and USS Pittsburgh, with destroyers USS *Marshall*, USS *Miller*, USS *Hickox*, and USS *Hunt*, left the task group formation to assist *Franklin*. Rear Admiral Davison transferred his flag from the *Franklin* to the USS *Miller* by breeches buoy and suggested abandoning the ship. However, Gehres refused to scuttle the *Franklin* as many men were still alive below deck.

Many of the other ships stayed astern of the carrier to rescue the members of the crew of the Franklin who had been thrown overboard or jumped off to avoid the fire. Many crew members were killed or wounded, but hundreds of officers and enlisted men stayed aboard and saved the ship. Recent scholarship tallies the number of dead in this incident on the Franklin as being 807 and more than 487 wounded. Casualty figures would have been much higher had it not been for the efforts of some brave individuals. One of these was the Medal of Honor recipients Lieutenant Commander Joseph O'Callahan, the ship's Catholic Chaplin, who gave last rites, organized, and directed firefighting and rescue parties, and took men below to water down magazines that threatened to explode. There was also Lieutenant Junior Grade Donald Gary, who discovered 300 men trapped in a destroyed mess compartment and, finding an exit, repeatedly returned to lead groups of sailors to safety. Gary later organized and led firefighting details to fight fires on the hangar deck. Fifty-nine planes were destroyed on the *Franklin* that day in the conflagration. The crew received two Medal of Honors, 19 Navy Crosses, 22 Silver Stars, 116 Bronze Stars, 235 Letters of Commendation, 347 Purple Hearts, and 808 Posthumous Purple Hearts.

Still under tow on the morning of March 20, 1945, *Franklin* regained steering control in her pilothouse at 9:30 a.m., and then at 12:33 p.m., she cast off her towline as she could now make "15 knots under her own power," a true testament to the will and strength of her remaining crew. Entering Ulithi Lagoon in a column on March 24, *Franklin's* crew stood "in straight ranks, chins up and heedless of the drizzling rain..." living proof of their captain's words that "A ship that will not be sunk, cannot be sunk." The following day, standing amid the charred wreckage of the carrier's hangar deck, Chaplain O'Callahan led a memorial service for the dead.

On March 27, 1945, *Franklin*, able to proceed under her own power, began her voyage back to the United States. The aircraft carrier steamed from Ulithi to Pearl Harbor (27 March-3 April), Pearl Harbor to Colon, Panama (9-17 April), and then from Colon to New York City (19-28 April).

Upon *Franklin's* arrival in New York, a long-brewing dispute over the ship's crew conduct during her efforts finally came to a head. Captain Gehres had held culpable many of those who had left the ship on March 19, 1945, of desertion, even though those who had leaped into the ocean to escape a sure death by fire or had been believed that "abandon ship" had been ordered. While sailing from Ulithi Atoll to Hawaii, Gehres had pronounced that 704 crew members were part of the "Big Ben 704 Club" for staying with the severely damaged warship. Still, investigators in New York later discovered that only about 400 were onboard *Franklin* continuously. The others had been brought back aboard either before or during the stop at Ulithi. All the charges against the crew members were silently dropped. Captain Gehres retired with the rank of rear admiral. He would never receive the command of another Navy ship again.

MARCH 20
1852

On this day in history, Harriet Beecher Stowe's anti-slavery novel, *Uncle Tom's Cabin*, is published. The novel sold nearly 300,000 copies in its first three months in America alone and was so popular that when President Abraham Lincoln met Stowe at the White House in 1862, he purportedly stated, "So this is the little lady who made this big war." It was the first American novel to be translated into Chinese.

Harriet Beecher was born in Litchfield, Connecticut, on June 14, 1811. Her father was the Calvinist preacher Lyman Beecher. Her mother was his first wife, Roxanna Foote Beecher, a deeply religious woman who died when Harriet was five. Writing came naturally to Harriet, as it did to her father and many siblings. Yet it was not until the family moved to Cincinnati, Ohio, that she found her authentic writing voice. In her new city, Harriet taught at the Western Female Institute, a school established by Catharine. There Harriet wrote many short stories and articles and co-authored a textbook.

Ohio was located just across the river from Kentucky, a slaveholding state. Harriet often encountered runaway enslaved people in Ohio and heard their heartbreaking and depressing stories. It was this and a visit to a Kentucky plantation that fueled her abolitionist zeal and laid the first seeds for her anti-slavery book, *Uncle Tom's Cabin*.

Harriet and Calvin were married on January 6, 1836. She met Calvin at the Semi-Colon Club, a co-ed literary group of leading writers. He encouraged her to write, and she continued producing short stories and sketches. The Stowes would have seven children together, including twin daughters.

In 1850, Calvin accepted a teaching job at Bowdoin College in Brunswick, Maine, and the family moved east. Also, that year, Congress passed the Fugitive Slave Act, which permitted runaway enslaved persons to be hunted, caught, and taken back to their owners, even in states where slavery was prohibited. In 1851, Stowe's 18-month-old son, Samuel Charles Stowe, died. This tragedy cemented in her mind the heartbreak enslaved mothers must experience when their children are taken from them and sold. The Fugitive Slave Law and her significant loss led Stowe to write about the dilemma of enslaved people. Stowe claimed to have envisioned a dying enslaved person during a communion service at her church, which inspired her to write his story.

The Stowes were passionate critics of slavery and endorsed the Underground Railroad, temporarily housing several fugitive slaves in their homes. One enslaved fugitive, John Andrew Jackson, wrote of hiding with Stowe in her home in Brunswick, Maine, as he attempted to escape to Canada in his narrative titled *The Experience of a Slave in South Carolina*.

On March 9, 1850, Stowe wrote to the editor of the weekly antislavery magazine *The National Era*, that she intended to write a story about the issue of slavery: "I feel now that the time is come when even a woman or a child who can speak a word for freedom and humanity is bound to speak.... I hope every woman who can write will not be silent."

Uncle Tom's Cabin tells the tale of Tom, an honorable, unselfish middle-aged enslaved person who's removed from his wife and children to be sold at auction. On a ship, he saves Eva's life, a white girl from a wealthy family. Eva's father buys Tom, and Tom and Eva become excellent friends. In the meantime, Eliza_ another slave worker from the same plantation as Tom – learns of plans to sell her son Harry. Eliza escapes with her son, but they are eventually hunted down by a slave catcher whose views on slavery are ultimately changed by Quakers who nurse him back to health after a severe injury.

Eva became ill, and on her deathbed, she asked her father to free all his enslaved workers. He agrees but dies before he can accomplish this, and Tom is sold to a ruthless new owner who uses violence and coercion to keep his slaves in line. After helping two other enslaved people escape, Tom is beaten to death for not revealing where the escaped enslaved people are. Tom clings to his steadfast Christian faith throughout his life, even as he lay dying. *Uncle Tom's Cabin's* strong Christian approach reflected Stowe's belief that slavery and the Christian faith were at odds; in her mind, slavery was clearly a sin.

The book appeared in serial form in 1851-1852 in *The National Era* and then was published as a two-volume novel. The book sold 10,000 copies in the first week. And over the next three months sold over 300,000 copies in America while selling over 1 million copies in Britain (for which she did not receive a dime due to a lack of an international copyright agreement).

Stowe became successful immediately and soon toured the United States and Britain, promoting the book and her abolitionist standpoint. The book brought slavery into the limelight like never before, especially in the northern states. The book shone a light on enslaved person's lives. It made people uncomfortable as they realized enslaved people had families, hopes, and dreams like white people, yet were considered chattel and exposed to terrible living conditions and violence. Uncle Tom's Cabin made slavery intimate and relatable instead of just some strange institution in the South.

The book sparked outrage and anti-slavery views in the North. Abolitionists grew from a small group to a large and potent political force. In the South, *Uncle Tom's Cabin* infuriated enslavers who preferred to keep the darker side of slavery to themselves. They stubbornly held tight to the thought that slavery was economically crucial to the South and that enslaved people were somehow inferior people incapable of taking care of themselves. In large parts of the South, the book was deemed illegal. By the mid-1850s, the Republican Party was created to help prevent slavery from spreading.

It is speculated that abolitionist sentiment fuelled by the release of

Uncle Tom's Cabin helped put Abraham Lincoln into the presidency after the election of 1860 and played a role in igniting the Civil War.

In 1853, Stowe published two more books about slavery: *A Key to Uncle Tom's Cabin*, which put forward documents and personal testimonies to verify the book's accuracy, and *Dred: A Tale of the Great Dismal Swamp*, which spoke about her belief that slavery demeaned society.

In 1864, Calvin retired and moved the family to Hartford, Connecticut – their neighbor was Mark Twain. Still, the Stowes spent their winters in Mandarin, Florida, where Stowe and her son Frederick established a plantation and hired ex-slaves to work it.

In 1871, Stowe's lost her son Frederick who drowned at sea, and in 1872, Stowe's brother Henry, who was a preacher, was accused of adultery with one of his parishioners. But no impropriety ever diminished the considerable impact her writing had on slavery and the literary world.

Harriet Beecher Stowe died on July 2, 1896, at her home in Connecticut from complications from Alzheimer's Disease. She was 85 years old.

MARCH 21
1945

On this day in history, Dutch resistance fighter Hannie Schaft is arrested by Nazi Police at a military checkpoint in Haarlem, Netherlands. Early in the war, Schaft became an active member of a Communist resistance cell, hiding and assisting Jews who were being rounded up for "resettlement" to the death camps of the East (1941); with Freddie and Truus Oversteegen, carried out assassinations and became known to the German forces as the "red-haired girl" (1942-1943), and encouraged student solidarity that led to the closing of Dutch universities in 1943. She was so deadly and destructive that Adolf Hitler ordered her capture and elimination.

Hannie Schaft was born on September 16, 1920, in Haarlem, Netherlands.

Due to her parents' socialist leanings Hannie, from a very early point, developed a very keen hatred of fascism. Schaft would often discuss politics and social justice with her parents, thus encouraging her to pursue a law degree and to become a human rights lawyer working for the League of Nations (forerunner to the United Nations). When the Nazis overtook the Netherlands in 1940, Schaft studied law at the University of Amsterdam. There she became friends with Jewish students Sonja Frenk and Philine Polak, which made her feel strongly about actions against Jews. By 1941, the mistreatment of Jews by the Nazis convinced Schaft to join the small, Communist-leaning Raad van Verzet (Council of Resistance) cell in Haarlem, one of the many illegal groups organized to resist the Nazi occupation forces and their Dutch collaborators. It was also the most militant. Although not officially a Communist organization, the group was allied with the Communist resistance movement, and its members were sympathetic to the political Left.

In 1943, university students were required by the Nazis to sign a declaration of allegiance to their overlords. When Schaft refused to sign the petition supporting the occupation forces, like 80% of the other students, she had to stop her studies. In the summer of 1943, she moved in with her parents again, bringing Frenk and Polak, who went into hiding.

Schaft's work at first involved assisting Jews who were trying to escape the tightening dragnet as the Germans gathered them up to be sent to concentration camps and eventually to extermination facilities farther to the East. Sometimes, like with her university friends, she would hide Jews in her parents' home, where they were given food, encouragement, and false documents. She also collected funds from sympathetic individuals in Haarlem to support these activities. She learned to speak German and became involved with German soldiers.

Over time, Hannie, Truus, and Freddie began more radical resistance, specializing in assassinating German Nazi officers and Dutch traitors. The Germans began taking and shooting many Dutch hostages in retaliation. There were even objections within the resistance movement, and some members felt women should not be assassins. Schaft and the Oversteegens' strongly disagreed with this viewpoint, and in time the trio became notorious in German and Dutch Nazi circles for their bold effectiveness. They were branded as dangerous terrorists, and Hannie in particular – the "red-haired girl" – was singled out as a special target, and many resources were committed to her capture.

Schaft did not, however, accept every assignment. When she was asked to kidnap the children of a Nazi official, she steadfastly refused. If the plan failed, then the children would have to be killed, and Schaft felt that that was too close to the Nazis' brand of horror.

On June 21, 1944, Schaft and Jan Bonekamp, a co-resistance fighter, were assassinated in Zaandam by a Dutch police officer and collaborator, Willem Ragut. Schaft hit Ragut with a shot to the back, but it failed to kill him. Bonekamp was hit by a bullet in the stomach by Ragut before finally killing him. Mortally wounded, Bonekamp left the scene but was captured shortly afterward and taken to hospital. There he was drugged into giving a Dutch Nazi nurse faking to be a resistance member the home address of Hannie Schaft. To force a confession from Schaft, German authorities arrested her parents and assigned them to the Vught concentration camp near Den Bosch. The anguish of this situation and her grief over Bonekamp's death (with whom she had feelings for) caused Schaft to stop resistance work for a brief while. Her parents were released after two months.

After recovery, Schaft dyed her hair black and began to wear glasses to hide her appearance, and she then returned to resistance work. She once again started committing assassinations and sabotage, courier work, the transportation of illegal weapons, and disseminating illicit newspapers. On March 1, 1945, NSB police officer Willem Zirkzee was murdered by Hannie Schaft and Truus Oversteegen near the Krelagehuis in Haarlem. On March 15, they wounded Ko Langendijk, a hairdresser from Ijmuiden who provided information for the Sicherheitsdienst (SD), a Nazi intelligence agency. He survived that attack, and in 1949 he was sentenced to life in prison.

On March 21, 1945, Schaft was bicycling to Ijmuiden when she was stopped at a German military checkpoint and could not get rid of her handbag, which contained copies of the underground Communist paper De Waarheid. Worse, she was also discovered to be carrying a pistol. Taken to a prison cell, she maintained her composure through relentless interrogation but was then sent to Amsterdam and interrogated by Emil Ruhl. Recognized as the "red-haired girl," she was warned that five Dutch girls would be executed without a complete confession, and Hannie broke down and confessed. After the war, Ruhl noted that despite the harsh treatment, the longtime resistance fighter behaved with dignity throughout her ordeal.

On April 17, 1945, Hannie Schaft was executed by Dutch Nazi officials. Even though there was an agreement between the occupier and the Dutch resistance to stop any further executions, she was shot dead three weeks before the cessation of the war in the dunes of Overveen, near Bloemendaal. Mattheus Schmitz and Maarten Kuiper escorted her to the execution site to be killed. Schmitz fired the fatal bullet into her head at close range. However, the bullet ended up only grazing Schaft. She is said to have allegedly told her executioners: "Idiots! I shoot better," after which Kuiper delivered the final shot to the head. Schaft's murder was directly ordered by Willy Lages, who would end up being freed from prison in 1966 for health reasons, and he would spend the rest of his life in Germany.

On November 27, 1945, Hannie Schaft was reburied at a state funeral at the Dutch Honorary Cemetery Bloemendaal. The Dutch government and royal family members attended, including Queen Wilhelmina, who referred to Schaft as "the symbol of resistance."

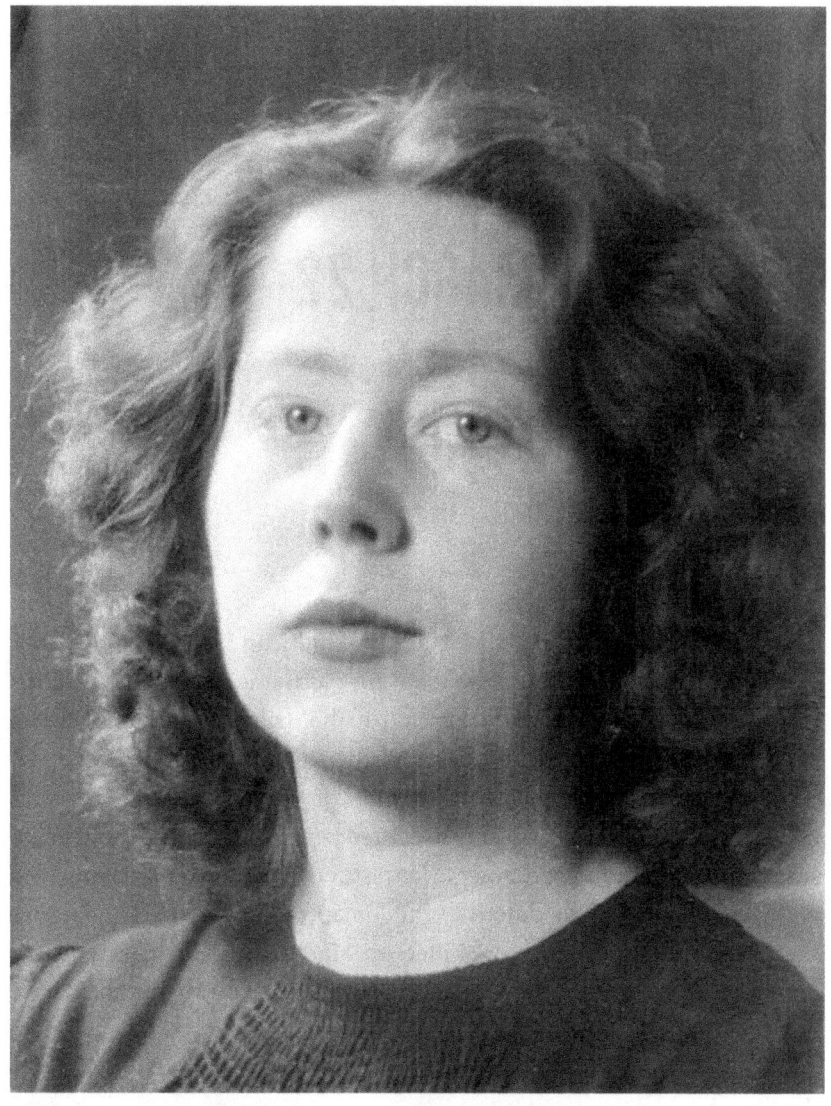
(Photo: Hannie Schaft, Dutch communist and resistance fighter. 1940s. Wikimedia Commons.)

MARCH 22
1622

On this day in history, the Native American Massacre of 1622 occurred, which was an attack on the settlements of the Virginia Company in Jamestown, Virginia, by the tribes of the Powhatan Confederacy under their leader Opechancanough (pronounced: O-pee-can-can-no) resulting in the deaths of 347 colonists. The attack was meticulously planned and executed with great speed and precision so that only one settlement, Jamestown, received a warning and was able to prepare a defense. Out of approximately 1,250 English colonists in the area, 347 were killed on March 22, 1622, mainly before noon, and hundreds more would perish in the next few months due to malnutrition, starvation, and disease because of the destruction of their crops as well as further military engagements with the Powhatan.

The attack was an utter and complete surprise and a total victory for the Powhatan Confederacy. Peace existed between the colonists and the natives since the end of the First Powhatan War in 1614. Natives and colonists partnered in trade and visited each others' settlements, and natives were often guests in colonists' homes. Since 1610, the colonists had begun moving out of their original settlement at Jamestown, extracting more and more lands from the Powhatan

Confederacy, mistreating the people, stealing food, and letting livestock ruin crops and desecrating sites sacred to native rituals.

Early on the morning of March 22, 1622, groups of Powhatans gathered near English settlements and waited patiently for a signal. When it finally came, they began walking towards the colonists' houses, apparently in no hurry. Since many of them had been trading with the English for years, dropping by when they had something to trade, share or borrow, nothing seemed abnormal. Once inside the settlements, at about 8 a.m., Opechancanough's warriors began attacking the colonists with whatever weapon was available in their homes. After the initial attacks, fifty to a few hundred warriors joined the fighting to kill the remainder of the survivors, burn settlements, and slaughter livestock.

Opechancanough never expected that one day's attack, even such a well-executed one, would succeed in removing the English from his lands immediately and permanently. Warriors continued to raid and ransack settlements over the next few months while the English wobbled from the disaster.

Colonists left their homes and sought refuge at better-protected plantations nearby, following Governor Sir Francis Wyatt's general order of late April to clear out all outlying settlements and move to eight strongly fortified locations along the James River. Local leaders even felt that moving their populations to the Eastern Shore may be a good idea, where Indians were still friendly with the colonists, to reduce further harm.

Meanwhile, Opechancanough continued to plan. In the summer of 1622, he sent gifts to the chief of the Patawomecks, a strong tribe living on the Potomac River, urging him to join his war against the English, bragging that "before the end of two Moons there should not be an Englishman in all their Countries." By demolishing plantations and industrial sites and cutting off food supplies, he felt they could weaken and demoralize the English so they would either become victims of his warriors or be forced to leave the colony.

The colonists began to regroup and rebuild and traded again with the tribes that had attacked and decimated them. However, they had little choice as their crops had been burned. The massacre's aftermath had claimed as many as seven hundred more lives. Because the attack had disrupted spring planting, the colonists grew even less maize than usual. Meanwhile, the Virginia Company tried to rebuild Jamestown by sending over a thousand new settlers. Incredibly, they came to Virginia with no food supplies.

Reinforcements could not help against the guerilla tactics of the natives in the Second Powhatan War, however, so the colonists resorted to trickery. In May 1623, a proposal was made with Opechancanough to negotiate peace and attain the release of the 20 missing women who were taken from the settlement of Martin's Hundred on March 22, 1622. He released Mistress Boyse as a good-faith gesture, with the implied message that he would mediate for the release of the remaining women. Captain Tucker and a group of musketeers arranged a meeting with Opechancanough and members of a Powhatan tribe along the Potomac River on May 22. Dr. John Potts prepared a batch of poisoned wine to prepare for the occurrence. Captain Tucker and English officers offered ceremonial toasts, and 200 Powhatans were killed after consuming the wine. Another 50 natives were shot and killed. Opechancanough escaped, but numerous tribal leaders were murdered. The English retaliated by attacking and burning down several Powhatan villages. Tribal members and the captive women escaped the English attacks.

The colonists, in revenge for the massacre, continued to attack the Powhatan through "the use of force, surprise attacks, famine resulting from the burning of their corn, destroying their boats, canoes, and houses, breaking their fishing weirs and assaulting them in their hunting expedition, pursuing them with horses and using bloodhounds to find them and mastiffs to seize them, driving them to flee within reach of their enemies among other tribes, and assimilating and abetting their enemies against them."

In 1624, because of the massacre, Virginia was declared to be an English royal colony by King James I. This meant that the Crown took direct control rather than allowing guidance from the Virginia Company. The Crown could exercise its philanthropy for royal favorites. Settlers continued encroaching on the land of the Powhatan tribes, and the colonial government habitually changed or ignored agreements with the natives when they were no longer in the colony's interest. The tribes were increasingly frustrated with the colonists.

The next major confrontation with the Powhatans was the Third Powhatan War, occurring in 1644, resulting in the death of 500 colonists. While similar to the death toll of 1622, the loss twenty-two years later represented less than ten percent of the total population and had far less impact on the colony. This time, the elderly Opechancanough, who was almost 100 years old and being moved about by litter, was captured by the colonists. Imprisoned at Jamestown, he was shot in the back and killed by one of his English guards.

His demise marked the beginning of the fast decline of the once-strong Powhatan. Its member tribes eventually left the area altogether, gradually living amongst the colonists or living on one of the few reservations in Virginia. Most of these were also subject to attack and land seizure by the ever-growing European population.

MARCH 23
1944

On this day in history, the day which marked the 25th anniversary of the founding of Mussolini's Fascist movement, 17 members of an Italian partisan cell, the Patriotic Action Group (Gruppi d'Azione Patriotica, or GAP), a Communist-dominated group led by Rosario Bentivegna, detonated 40 pounds of TNT near a column of 150 SS Police Regiment Bozen marching down the Via Rasella in German-occupied Rome, killing 33 soldiers. The next day, the Germans gathered up 335 Italian civilians and transported them to the Adeatine caves. They were subsequently shot dead as revenge for the death of the 33 soldiers. Of the civilian victims, 253 were Catholic, 70 were Jewish, and 12 were unidentified. They ranged in age from 15 to 70 years old.

Although reported as being thrown from a building, the bomb had been concealed in a rubbish cart, put into position by a Partisan dressed as a street cleaner while others functioned as lookouts. The fuse was lit when the police, marching towards them, were forty seconds away from the bomb. The Partisans, who had ties to Italy's underground communist movement, dispersed into the crowd of bystanders when the bomb exploded and evaded capture. The explosion caused the immediate deaths of 28 German SS policemen (more would subsequently die) and wounded 100 more. The bombing quite possibly killed two civilian onlookers, one of whom, Piero Zuccheretti, was an eleven-year-old boy, although stray German police bullets may have killed him during the melee; it is unknown.

On the evening of March 23, the Commander of the Security Police and Security Service (Sicherheitsdienst – SD) in Rome, SS Lieutenant Colonel Herbert Kappler, and Lieutenant General Kurt Malzer, the Wehrmacht commandant in Rome, recommended a retaliation action in which ten Italian civilians would be shot for each policeman killed in the Partisan act. They suggested that the potential victims be chosen from people already condemned to death and awaiting execution in the prisons of the Security Police and SD. Colonel General Eberhard von Mackensen, the Commander of the Fourteenth Army, whose jurisdiction included Rome, approved the proposal.

When he became aware of the incident that evening, Adolf Hitler suggested the destruction of Rome. Defendants accused of perpetrating the massacre claimed after the war that Hitler ultimately endorsed Kappler and Malzer's retribution plan but that it must be completed within 24 hours. Evidence suggests that Hitler quickly forgot about the matter and left the final decision to Colonel General Alfred Jodl, Chief of the Operations Staff of the Armed Forces High Command (Oberkommando der Wehrmacht, or OKW).

Whatever Hitler's level of involvement, Field Marshal Albert Kesselring, Commander-in-Chief South, presumably interpreted Hitler's initial reaction as a guideline and authorized the retribution plan as initially conceived. Kappler assured him that sufficient prisoners were available.

By noon on March 24, Kappler only had created a list of 271 victims, each with his crime and name listed, except for the Jews, who were simply listed as "Jew." By now, the death toll from the Via Rasella bombing had risen to 32. (One more would die during the reprisal period.) To even up the numbers, *Questore* Pietro Caruso, head of the Fascist police in Rome, offered some Italian prisoners from his Regina Coeli prison, among them Maurizio Giglio, who had once been one of his lieutenants, before being detected as a double agent operating for the American OSS in charge of radio communications for the Fifth Army. To reach the required quota, they rounded up civilians found on the streets of Rome. The oldest of the condemned was in his seventies; the youngest was fifteen. Because of the time limit that Hitler had imposed, Malzer and Kappler agreed that the victims would need to be shot in the back of the head at close range rather than the conventional firing squad. The men of the Bozen regiment, the unit hit in the attack, were offered the chance to avenge their comrades, but they refused to do it that way.

On the afternoon of March 24, 1944, personnel from the headquarters of the Security Police and SD in Rome, led by SS Captain Erich Priebke and SS Captain Karl Hass, assembled 335 Italian male civilians near a series of man-made caves on the outskirts of Rome on the Via Ardeatina. The *Fosse* Ardeatine, or Ardeatine Caves, were the remnants of ancient Christian catacombs and served as a convenient venue to carry out the retribution killings in secrecy and conceal the victims' bodies.

As the group assembled at the cave, Priebke and Hass discovered that they had inadvertently gathered 335 prisoners instead that the 330 prescribed in the order. The SS men decided that releasing the five hostages might compromise the secrecy of the action and therefore included the five among their victims.

Those condemned to die showed up at the caves with their hands tied behind their backs. Before reaching the site, Priebke and Hass had decided against using a firing squad because it would take too much ammunition. Instead, they instructed the shooters to pick a victim and shoot him at close range, saving time and ammunition. The German police officials brought the victims into the cave and forced them to kneel in rows of five. The shooters then killed each one with a shot at close range to the base of the skull. As the killing proceeded, the German police officials forced the hostages to kneel on top of the bodies of those previously shot to conserve space.

Following the shootings, Priebke and Hass ordered engineers to seal the mouth of the cave through the detonation of explosives, killing any victims who had managed to survive and interring the dead.

The Ardeatine Caves Massacre, as it became known, remained hidden until after the United States Fifth Army liberated Rome on June 4, 1944. Then the atrocity came to light. Attilio Ascarelli, an expert in forensic medicine, led the effort to exhume and identify the dead. On July 26, 1944, they set to work. Remarkably, Ascarelli's team determined the identity of 326 of the 335 victims.

MARCH 24
1874

On this day in history, escape artist, magic man, and stunt performer Erik Weisz, better known as Harry Houdini, was born in Budapest, Hungary. He remains, to this day, one of the most famous magicians in history. Although he could perform card tricks and traditional magic acts, he was widely known for escaping from what seemed like anything and everything, including ropes, jail cells, water-filled milk cans, handcuffs, straitjackets, and even nailed-shut boxes that had been thrown into a river. After World War I, Houdini turned his knowledge about deception against Spiritualists who claimed to be able to contact the dead. Then, at age 52, Houdini died mysteriously after being struck hard in the abdomen by a college student in Montreal, Quebec.

Houdini was one of seven children of Rabbi Mayer Samuel Weisz and Cecilia Steiner, who arrived in the United States from Hungary on July 3, 1878. The family altered their name to the German spelling Weiss, and Erik became Ehrich. The family moved to Appleton, Wisconsin, where his father was the Zion Reform Jewish Congregation rabbi. Young Houdini would later claim that he was born in Appleton. At 13, he and his father moved to New York City after his father lost his position as rabbi. They performed odd jobs and resided in a boarding house before the rest of the family could join them in New York.

In 1894 he began his career as a professional magician, and this was when he first started using the name "Harry Houdini." He chose that name because Harry was a derivative of his first name, "Ehrie," and the last name was an homage to the great French magician Jean Eugene Robert-Houdin. (He would later write a book, *The Unmasking of Robert-Houdin*, debunking the magician's skill and talent.) Though Houdini's magic achieved little in the way of success, he soon drew attention to his skills as an escape artist with handcuffs. He married fellow performer Wilhelmina Beatrice Rahner in 1893, who would serve as Houdini's lifelong stage assistant under Beatrice "Bess" Houdini.

Houdini's breakthrough was in 1899 when vaudeville impresario Martin Beck hired him to perform on a tour of the United States and Europe. On Beck's advice, escaping constraints was the central theme of his act. He began asking audiences to bind him up or secure him in handcuffs, and he promoted his shows by performing escapes from local jails, usually after a strip search and being put in shackles by police. The act was a resounding success, and he became the highest-paid performer in American vaudeville.

The newly dubbed "King of Handcuffs" played to sold-out audiences across Europe. He later bolstered his fame by staging several high-profile escapes in the U.S. One stunt saw him jump into a Rochester, N.Y. river with his hands restrained behind his back; in another, he broke out of a jail cell that had once imprisoned Charles Guiteau, the man who murdered President James A. Garfield.

Houdini continued his act in the United States in the early 1900s, constantly raising the stakes from handcuffs and straitjackets to locked, water-filled tanks and nailed packing crates. He was able to escape because of his unique strength and his unique ability to pick locks. In 1912, his act reached its zenith, the Chinese Water Torture Cell, which would be the highlight of his career. In it, Houdini was hung by his feet and put upside-down in a locked glass cabinet full of water, requiring him to hold his breath for more than three minutes to escape. The performance was so daring and crowd-pleaser that it remained in his act until he died in 1926.

By the late 1900s, Houdini had become a rich man. This wealth allowed him to pursue other desires, such as aviation and film. He bought a plane in 1909 and decided to become the first person to fly an aircraft in Australia. In 1910 he achieved his goal, but it was later found that Captain Colin Defries had made a short flight in December 1909.

Houdini also began a movie career, releasing his first movie in 1901, *Merveilleux Exploits du Celebre Houdini Paris*, which documented his escapes. He starred in several other films, such as *Terror Island, The Master Mystery, and The Grim Game*. He started his own production company, the Houdini Picture Corporation, and a film lab called The Film Development Corporation, but both were unsuccessful. In 1923, Houdini started and became president of Martinka & Co., America's oldest magic company.

Houdini's writing career did not end with his critique of Jean Eugene Robert-Houdin, as he later penned *Miracle Mongers and Their Methods* (1920) and *A Magician Among the Spirits* (1924).

Houdini was the president of the Society of American Magicians and an ardent crusader against fraudulent psychic mediums. He debunked renowned medium Mina Crandon, better known as Margery. This act turned him against former friend Sir Arthur Conan Doyle, an ardent believer in spiritualism. Despite his activism against spiritual charlatanism, Houdini and his wife did, in fact, experimented with otherworldly spiritualism when they decided that when the first of them died, they would try to communicate from beyond the grave with the survivor. Before her 1943 death, Bess Houdini declared the experiment a failure.

There are different theories about what caused Harry Houdini's death, but one is that he suffered from acute appendicitis. Whether his death can be attributed to the McGill University student testing Houdini's stomach muscles by punching him repeatedly (with permission) or by poison from a group of angry Spiritualists is unknown. What is known is that Houdini succumbed from peritonitis because of a ruptured appendix on October 31, 1926, at 52, in Detroit, Michigan.

Bess Houdini would spend years trying to contact her dead husband before finally giving up, purportedly stating, "Ten years is long enough to wait for any man." Many others have continued the search, however, and since the 1930s, fans have held Houdini seances on Halloween to communicate with the magician. There is also an "Official Houdini Séance" that occurs in a different city each year.

(Photo: Harry Houdini and his wife Bess, 1922. Wikimedia Commons.)

MARCH 25
1931

On this day in history, nine young black men were taken off the Southern Railway line in Paint Rock, Alabama, and arrested for throwing a group of white teens off the train further up the line. Two white women aboard the train, Victoria Price, and Ruby Bates, told the police posse assembled at the Paint Rock station that a group of black teenagers had raped them. The posse brought the women to the jail where the teenagers were held and positively identified them as their attackers. A doctor was called to examine the women for signs of rape, but none was found.

The nine teens – Charlie Weems, Ozie Powell, Clarence Norris, brothers Andrew and Leroy Wright, Olen Montgomery, Willie Roberson, Haywood Patterson, and Eugene Williams - were moved to a jail in Scottsboro, Alabama, to await trial.

The trials and repeated retrials that the "Scottsboro Boys," as they became known as, were subjected to sparked international turmoil. They produced two landmark United States Supreme Court verdicts, even as the defendants were obliged to endure years of battling the courts and suffering through the harsh conditions of the Alabama prison system.

There was absolutely no evidence (beyond the women's testimony) pointing to the guilt of the teens, yet that did not matter because of the prevalent racism in the South at the time, according to which white men were constantly policing black men for any signs of sexual interest in white women, which could easily be punishable by lynching. The two women may have told the police they were raped to escape police attention. They were both suspected of being prostitutes and risked being arrested for it. Still, they could also have been charged for breaking the Mann Act by crossing a state line "for immoral purposes."

In the first set of trials in April 1931, an all-white, all-male jury quickly convicted the Scottsboro Boys and sentenced eight of them to death. The trial of the youngest, 13-year-old Leroy Wright, ended with a hung jury when one juror favored life imprisonment over death. A mistrial was declared, and Leroy Wright would remain in prison until 1937, awaiting the final verdict on his co-defendants.

At this point, the International Labor Defense (ILD), the legal wing of the American Communist Party, took on the boy's case, hoping to stimulate public opinion against racism. That June, the court gave the teens a stay of execution, awaiting an appeal to the Alabama Supreme Court. In March 1932, the Alabama Supreme Court confirmed the convictions of seven of the accused; it granted Williams a new trial, as he was a minor at the time of his judgment.

In November 1932, the U.S. Supreme Court ruled in *Powell v. Alabama* that the Scottsboro defendants had been denied the right to counsel, which violated their right to due process as per the 14th Amendment. The Supreme Court overturned the Alabama verdicts and remanded the cases to the lower courts.

The second round of trials began in Decatur, Alabama, 50 miles west of Scottsboro, under Judge James Horton. One of the boys' accusers, Ruby Bates, disavowed her original testimony and agreed to testify for the defense. But even with the changed testimony and confirmation from the initial medical examination of the women that disproved the rape charge, another all-white jury convicted the first defendant, Patterson, and recommended the death penalty.

After reviewing the evidence, Judge Horton suspended the death sentence and awarded Patterson a new trial. (The judge would be rewarded for this brave act by losing his re-election bid the following year.)

Again, Patterson and Norris were retried, and once again, they were found guilty and sentenced to death in late 1933. With prominent defense attorney Samuel Leibowitz arguing the case for the ILD, the Alabama Supreme Court unanimously refused the defense's motion for new trials, and the case went for a second hearing at the U.S. Supreme Court.

In January 1935, the Supreme Court again overturned the guilty verdicts, ruling in Norris v. Alabama that the systematic exclusion of blacks on Jackson County jury rolls denied a fair trial to the defendants and suggesting that the lower courts review Patterson's case. This second landmark decision in the Scottsboro Boys case would help integrate future juries across the nation.

The National Association for the Advancement of Colored People (NAACP) and other civil rights groups joined the ILD that year to form the Scottsboro Defense Committee, which reorganized the defense effort for the next set of trials.

In 1936, Patterson was convicted for a fourth time but sentenced to 75 years. The day after the guilty verdict, Ozie Powell was shot in the head after he attacked a deputy sheriff with a knife: both men lived.

After the Alabama Supreme Court confirmed Patterson's conviction in June, and Norris's third trial ended with another death sentence, Weems and Andy Wright were found guilty of rape and sentenced to lengthy prison terms. Prosecutors dropped the rape charges against Powell, but he was convicted of attacking the deputy sheriff and sentenced to 20 years.

Rape charges were also dropped against Montgomery, Roberson, Williams, and Leroy Wright, and all four were released. Alabama Governor Bibb Graves commuted Norris' sentence to life imprisonment in 1938 and denied pardon applications by all five convicted defendants that same year.

Alabama officials eventually agreed to let four convicted Scottsboro Boys – Weems, Andy Wright, Norris, and Powell – out on parole. After escaping from prison in 1948, the FBI arrested Patterson in Detroit, but the Michigan governor refused Alabama's request to extradite him.

Convicted of manslaughter after a barroom brawl in 1951, Patterson died of cancer in 1952.

The trials of the Scottsboro Boys, the two Supreme Court verdicts they produced, and the international uproar over their treatment helped fuel the fuse of the civil rights movement later in the 20th century. They left a lasting imprint on the nation's legal and cultural landscape.

Clarence Norris, who received a pardon from Governor George Wallace of Alabama in 1976, would outlive all the other Scottsboro Boys, dying in 1989 at 76.

In 2013, the Alabama Board of Pardons and Paroles voted unanimously to issue posthumous pardons to Weems, Patterson, and Andy Wright, ending one of the most heinous cases of racial injustice in American history.

(Photo: The Scottsboro boys, 1931. Wikimedia Commons.)

MARCH 26
1827

On this day in history, German pianist and composer Ludwig van Beethoven dies in Vienna at 56. He is widely deemed one of the greatest musical geniuses of all time. His groundbreaking compositions blended vocals and instruments, expanding the sonata, symphonies, concertos, and quartets range. His works are amongst the most played in the classical music collection and span the transition between the Classical and Romantic periods in classical music. A battle against deafness marred Beethoven's personal life, and some of his most important works were composed during the last ten years of his life when he was deaf.

Beethoven was born in Bonn, archbishopric of Cologne (Germany), on or about December 16, 1770. Although his date of birth is unknown, Beethoven was baptized on December 17, 1770. Baptizing babies within 24 hours of birth was customary, so December 16 is his most probable birthdate. Of Johann and Maria Magdalena von Beethoven's seven children, only Ludwig, the second-born, and two younger brothers survived into adulthood: Kaspar, born in 1774, and Johann, born in 1776.

Ludwig's father, Johann van Beethoven, was an unexceptional court singer known more for his alcoholism than his musical ability.

His mother, Maria Magdalena Beethoven, was a slender, sophisticated and profoundly moralistic woman.

Beethoven's father began teaching him music with astonishing vigor and ruthlessness that affected him for the rest of his life. Neighbors stated that they often observed the young boy crying while playing the clavier, standing atop a footstool to reach the keys, and his father thrashing him for each hesitation or error. Almost daily, Beethoven was flogged, locked in a cellar, and deprived of sleep for several hours of practice. His father taught him the violin and clavier, and he took additional lessons from organists around town. Despite, or because of his father's oppressive methods, Beethoven was an immensely talented musician from his earliest days.

Beethoven's father hoped the young Ludwig would be compared to the musical prodigy Wolfgang Mozart. He arranged his first public recital for March 26, 1778, and he billed it as "a little son of 6 years," even though he was in years 7-years-old. Beethoven played well, but his recital received no press whatsoever.

At school, Beethoven was an average student. Some biographers have stated that he was mildly dyslexic. He said, "Music comes to me more readily than words." In 1781, at age 10, Beethoven withdrew from school to study music full-time with Christian Gottlob Neefe, the newly appointed Court Organist. At 12, Beethoven published his first composition, a set of piano variations built on a theme by an obscure classical composer named Dressler.

There is no conclusive evidence to prove that Beethoven ever met Mozart. In 1787, the court dispatched Beethoven to Vienna to facilitate his musical development, where he had hoped to study with Mozart. After hearing Beethoven, Mozart said, "Keep your eyes on him; someday, he will give the world something to talk about." After a little while in Vienna, Beethoven's mother died, and he returned home to Bonn. Remaining there, Beethoven continued to build his reputation as the city's most promising young musician.

In 1792, Beethoven returned to Vienna, and he began to study piano with Haydn, vocal composition with Antonio Salieri, and counterpoint with Johann Albrechtsberger. Not yet recognized as a composer,

Beethoven rapidly created a reputation as a virtuoso pianist who was remarkably gifted at improvisation.

He made his long-awaited public debut in Vienna on March 29, 1795. He is believed to have played his "first" piano concerto in C Major. Then he published three piano trios and named it his Opus 1, an enormous critical and financial success. Beethoven composed many pieces that marked him as a great composer. It was also around 1801 that Beethoven discovered he was losing his hearing.

Beethoven never married or had children. He was, however, madly in love with a married woman named Antonie Brentano. Over two days in July 1812, Beethoven wrote her a long, beautiful love letter he had never sent. Addressed "to you, my immortal Beloved," the letter stated in part, "My heart is full of so many things to say to you – ah – there are moments when I feel that speech amounts to nothing at all – Cheer up – remain my true, my only love, my all as I am yours."

The demise of Beethoven's brother Kaspar in 1815 created one of the great trials of his life, a prolonged legal battle with his sister-in-law, Johanna, over the custody of Karl von Beethoven, his nephew, and her son. The struggle stretched for seven years, during which both sides spewed hateful speech at each other. Ultimately, Beethoven won the boy's custody, though not his affection.

Despite his extraordinary output of magnificent music, Beethoven was lonely and miserable throughout most of his adult life. Beethoven quarreled with his brothers, publishers, housekeepers, pupils, and patrons; he was absent-minded, short-tempered, greedy, and suspicious to the point of paranoia.

By the turn of the 19th century, Beethoven was trying to come to terms with and hide the fact that he was going deaf. In a letter to his friend Franz Wegeler in 1801, he showed, "I must confess that I lead a miserable life. For almost two years, I have ceased to attend any social functions just because I find it impossible to say to people: I am deaf. If I had any other profession, I might be able to cope with my infirmity; but in my profession, it is a terrible handicap."

Almost astoundingly, despite his rapidly growing deafness, Beethoven continued to compose at a furious rate despite frequent and prolonged bouts of illness during the last part of his life.

Beethoven's death occurred on March 26, 1827, at 56, of post-hepatitic cirrhosis of the liver. An autopsy revealed Beethoven had major liver damage, most likely because of his heavy drinking and substantial dilation of the auditory and other related nerves.

Summing up his life and impending death during his last days, Beethoven, who was never as eloquent with words as music, borrowed a tagline that concluded many Latin plays at the time. *Plaudite, amici, comoedia, finita est*, he said. "Applaud friends, the comedy is over."

MARCH 27
1829

On this day in history, the seventh president of the United States, Andrew Jackson, defied Washington society leaders and chose scandal-plagued John Eaton as his secretary of war.

Earlier that same year, Eaton had married a former tavern worker with a supposedly colorful past. Margaret "Peggy" Eaton had been raised in a boarding house patronized by Washington politicians and became an intelligent observer of politics and a gifted musician and dancer. She enthralled many of the boarding house's tenants, including then-Senator Andrew Jackson and his friend John Eaton. She was believed to have had many forbidden affairs before her first marriage. She was 23 and the wife of a Navy sailor when she first met Jackson and Eaton. Eaton enjoyed Margaret's intelligence and wit and accompanied her to social gatherings while her husband was at sea.

When Margaret's first husband died of pneumonia without warning, rumors ran rampant that he had committed suicide over his wife's supposed affair with Eaton. Both Eaton and Margaret denied the relationship, arguing that they were nothing more than friends. In addition to Margaret's tarnished character, her passionate disposition and seductive and forthrightness irked Washington's society ladies at a time when those qualities were considered inappropriate in women.

When Eaton and Margaret married just nine months after the death of her husband, the women of Washington society shunned the new couple.

The couple's marriage on January 1, 1829, provoked new condemnation of the couple. Louis McLane, a prominent Maryland politician (who would hold the positions of secretary of the treasury and secretary of state in Jackson's second Cabinet), was critical that the 39-year-old Eaton had "just married his mistress- and the mistress of 11 dozen others!" Margaret Bayard Smith, a Washington society maven whose husband was president of the local branch of the Bank of the United States, pronounced Eaton's reputation "totally destroyed" by this marriage with a woman who did not even wait a considerate amount of time before walking down the aisle again.

Jackson commiserated with and backed his friend Eaton. Jackson's late wife Rachel – whom he had unknowingly married before her divorce from her first husband was legal – had also been the victim of society gossip when she first came to Washington. When someone advised Jackson against making Eaton his secretary of war because of Margaret's character, Jackson firmly stated, "Do you suppose that I have been sent here by the people to consult the ladies of Washington as to the proper persons to compose my cabinet?!" Secretary of State Martin Van Buren also sided with Eaton. Vice President John Calhoun's wife led Washington's elite in rebuffing the Eatons at social gatherings. For the rest of Jackson's first term, his adversaries used the Eaton Affair or Petticoat Affair, as it was known, to attack the president's ethical judgment and, by extension, his administration's programs, and political candidates.

At a grand ball on inauguration night, "the other ladies in the official family tried not to notice as Peggy Eaton swept into the room and startled everyone with her presence and beauty." Even Emily Donelson, Jackson's beloved niece and his choice as the new mistress of the White House, turned a chilly shoulder to Margaret. She claimed that Eaton's elevation to the cabinet had given his wife airs, making her "society too disagreeable to be endured."

During his early months in office, Jackson intended to replace corrupt bureaucrats. Instead, he was tormented by what Secretary of

State Martin Van Buren called "Eaton Malaria." Jackson decided to delay his formal post-inaugural cabinet dinner, fearing tensions between Mrs. Eaton and the other political wives. Jackson was constantly distracted from the nation's business by having to defend Margaret – despite her declarations that she did "not want endorsements (of virtue) any more than any other lady in the land."

President Jackson was very annoyed after Vice President John Calhoun's wife, Floride, refused to reciprocate Margaret Eaton's social call. Most of the cabinet that opposed the Eatons was aligned with Calhoun, a man Jackson was beginning to distrust. Indeed, when combined with policy differences between her husband and Jackson, Floride Calhoun's obstinacy–especially on whether states should be allowed to nullify federal laws – drove a deep wedge between the nation's two highest-ranking officials. At the same time, Calhoun was falling from grace with the president, and Secretary of State Martin Van Buren's fortunes were rising. The former governor of New York, charming in person and a skilled behind-the-scenes strategist Van Buren had won the president's regard by respecting John and Margaret Eaton. He became Jackson's "dear friend," someone the president felt was "well qualified" to one day fill his shoes.

For two years, the press and pundits savaged the administration over Jackson's support for the Eatons. If the president got rid of the anti-Eaton minority from his cabinet, he risked alienating Calhoun's contingent of the party. If he dumped his secretary of war after all this time, he would have caved into his critics. The dispute was finally resolved in April 1831 when Van Buren offered to resign along with Eaton. The president asked the remainder of his Cabinet to resign to allow for a reorganization. Though a few members resisted, later protesting their departures in print, they all gave up their positions. Eaton was eventually appointed governor of Florida Territory and then as minister to Spain.

Van Buren would resurface in 1832 as Jackson's Vice President when the latter won a second term as president. Calhoun resigned as Vice President in 1832 and returned to South Carolina, where he was quickly voted into the U.S. Senate and became a regional leader who lobbied in favor of states' rights and the expansion of slavery.

Regarding the Petticoat affair, Jackson later stated, "I (would) rather have live vermin on my back than the tongue of one of these Washington women on my reputation." To Jackson, Margaret Eaton was just another of many wronged women he had known and defended over his lifetime. He believed every woman he had supported, including her, had been the victim of motives tied to his political enemies who were content to bring him down.

MARCH 28
1939

On this day in history, the three-year-old Spanish Civil War ended when the Republican defenders of Madrid surrendered after a hard-fought battle.

The Spanish Civil War was fought in Spain from 1936 to 1939 between the Republicans and the Nationalists factions. The Republicans were staunch supporters of the left-leaning Popular Front government of the Second Spanish Republic. They comprised various communist, socialist, republican parties, separatists, and anarchists, some of whom had opposed the government in the pre-war era. The opposing Nationalists were a coalition of conservatives, Falangists, monarchists, and traditionalists led by a military junta, among whom General Francisco Franco swiftly attained a more significant role. Due to the worldwide political climate at the time, the war had many aspects. It was viewed as a struggle between dictatorship and republican democracy, class and religious struggle, revolution, counterrevolution, fascism, and communism. Even then, it was seen as a "dress rehearsal" for World War II.

In 1931, Spanish King Alfonso XIII approved elections to determine the government of Spain, and voters compellingly chose to terminate the monarchy for a liberal republic. Alfonso slipped into exile, and the

Second Republic, initially controlled by middle-class liberals and moderate socialists, was declared. During the first two years of the Republic, leftist militants and organized labor imposed pervasive liberal reforms, and the independence-leaning region of Catalonia and the Basque provinces realized virtual autonomy.

The landed aristocracy, the church, and a sizeable military faction opposed the Republic, and in November 1933, conservative forces recovered control of the government in elections. In response, socialists began a revolution in Asturias, and Catalan nationalists revolted in Barcelona. General Franco crushed the October Revolution in the name of the conservative government, and in 1935 he was assigned army chief of staff. In February 1936, new elections brought the leftist coalition, the Popular Front, to power, and Franco, a staunch monarchist, was sent to an obscure command in the Canary Islands off Africa.

Afraid the liberal government would give way to the Marxist revolution, army officers conspired to seize power. After a period of uncertainty, Franco joined the military plot to overthrow the government, which was supposed to begin in Morocco at 5 a.m. on July 18 and in Spain 24 hours later. The discrepancy in time was to permit the Army of Africa time to seize Morocco before being shipped to Spain's Andalusian coast by the navy.

Though a critical backer of the coup, Franco did not originate the plot and was never expected to lead the country. However, the rebels' intended first choice for head of state, General Jose Sanjurjo, died in a plane crash just days after the rebellion began while returning from exile in Portugal. At about the same time, Republican forces took out several of Franco's other possible rivals, including monarchist politician Jose Calvo Sotelo, fascist politician Jose Antonio Primo de Rivera, and generals Joaquin Fanjul and Manuel Goded. By October 1936, Franco had been named commander in chief of the armed forces and head of the rebel Nationalist government. His final near-equal, General Emilio Mola, the practical architect of the coup plot, died in a June 1937 plane crash, leaving Franco firmly and exclusively in charge.

On July 18, Spanish garrisons rose in revolt across Spain. Workers and peasants battled the uprising, but in many cities, the Republican government denied their weapons, and the Nationalists soon achieved command. In conservative regions of Old Castile and Navarre, the Nationalists took control with little bloodshed. Still, in other regions, such as the intensely autonomous city of Bilbao, they were afraid to leave their garrisons. The Nationalist revolt in the Spanish navy was unsuccessful, and warships run by committees of sailors were able to secure several coastal cities for the Republic.

Nevertheless, Franco managed to transport his Army of Africa from Morocco to Spain. During the next few months, Nationalist forces quickly overran many Republican-controlled areas in central and northern Spain. Madrid was put under siege in November.

In 1937, Franco integrated the Nationalist forces under the governance of the *Falange*, Spain's fascist party, while the Republicans were under the control of the communists. Germany and Italy aided Franco with many military supplies, while the Soviet Union aided the Republican side. Thousands of communists and other leftists from France, the USSR, America, Canada, and elsewhere formed the International Brigades, to the tune of 40,000 men, to aid the Republican cause. The most significant input into the Civil War of these foreign units was their successful defense of Madrid until the war's end.

The Nationalists progressed from their strongholds in the south and west, taking most of Spain's northern coastline in 1937. They also laid siege to Madrid and the area to the south and west for much of the war. After much of Catalonia was seized in 1938 and 1939, and Madrid was isolated from Barcelona, the Republican military position became doomed. Following the fall, without fighting Barcelona in January 1939, the Francoist regime was acknowledged by France and the United Kingdom in February 1939. On March 5, 1939, in response to an alleged increasing communist supremacy of the republican government and the worsening military situation, Colonel Segismundo Casado conducted a military coup against the republican government with the aim of seeking peace with the Nationalists. These peace advances, however, were rejected by Franco. Following an internal conflict between Republican factions in Madrid in the same month, the Republicans surrendered Madrid on March 28, 1939. Hundreds of thousands of Spaniards sought refuge in southern France. The victorious Nationalists victimized those associated with the losing Republicans who stayed in Spain. Franco created a dictatorship where all right-wing parties were amalgamated into the structure of the Franco regime. Over a million lives were lost in the conflict, the most destructive in Spanish history. Franco then served as dictator of Spain until he died in 1975.

MARCH 29
1971

On this day in history, Lieutenant William L. Calley is found guilty after a six-officer jury (five of whom served in Vietnam) deliberated for 79 hours and found him guilty of premeditated murder at My Lai, South Vietnam, by a U.S. court-martial at Fort Benning, Georgia. Calley, a platoon leader, had led his men in slaughtering Vietnamese civilians, including women and children, at My Lai, a cluster of hamlets in Quang Ngai Province, on March 16, 1968.

Calley was indicted with six specifications of premeditated murder. During the trial, Chief Army prosecutor Captain Aubrey Daniel alleged that Calley ordered Sergeant Daniel Mitchell to "finish off the rest" of the villagers. The prosecution contended that all the killings were perpetrated even though Calley's platoon had met no opposition and that he and his men had not been fired upon.

Calley was found guilty of personally massacring 22 civilians and condemned to life imprisonment. Still, his prison term was reduced to 20 years by the Court of Military Appeals and lowered later to 10 years by the Secretary of the Army. Declared by much of the public as a "scapegoat," Calley was paroled in 1974 after serving about a third of his 10-year sentence in house arrest.

The My Lai massacre was one of the most horrendous instances of brutality perpetrated during the Vietnam War. A company of American soldiers viciously slaughtered most of the people – women, children, and older men – in the village of My Lai on March 16, 1968. Over 500 people were butchered during the incident, including young girls and women who were raped and dismembered before being slain. U.S. Army officers buried knowledge of the bloodbath for over a year before it was recounted in the American press, igniting a firestorm of international indignation. The viciousness of the My Lai massacre and the official cover-up energized anti-war sentiment and further split the nation over the Vietnam War.

Because the Quang Ngai province was believed to be a Viet Cong (VC) stronghold during the war, it was subjected to repeated bombing attacks and heavily strafed with Agent Orange. In March 1968, Charlie Company – part of the American Division's 11th Infantry Brigade – received notification that VC guerrillas had entered the area. Charlie Company was sent in on March 16 to conduct a search-and-destroy mission. At that time, morale among American soldiers was falling fast, especially in the wake of the VC-led Tet Offensive, launched in January 1968. Charlie Company had lost 28 soldiers to death or injuries and was down to just over 100 men.

Army commanders told Charlie Company that any people found in the My Lai area were to be considered VC or VC sympathizers and ordered them to destroy the village. When they arrived shortly after dawn, the soldiers, led by Lieutenant Calley, found no VC. Instead, they found a docile village filled with women, children, and older men preparing to eat breakfast. The residents were gathered up into groups as the soldiers examined their huts. Even though they only found a few guns, Calley ordered his men to shoot the village's inhabitants.

Despite some soldiers hesitating at the orders, a massacre had commenced within a few seconds, with Calley killing many men, women, and children. "I saw them shoot an M79 (grenade launcher) into a group of still-alive people. But it was mostly done with a machine gun. They were shooting women and children just like anybody else." Sergeant Michael Bernhardt, a soldier at the scene, later told a reporter. As well as killing unarmed men, women, and children, the soldiers butchered numerous livestock, raped an unknown number of women, and incinerated the village. Calley was said to have herded dozens of people, including young children, into a ditch before killing them. Not a single shot was fired against the men of Charlie Company at My Lai.

The My Lai massacre allegedly ended after Warrant Officer Hugh Thompson, an Army helicopter pilot on a reconnaissance mission, landed his aircraft between the soldiers and the fleeing villagers and threatened to open fire if they continued their attacks. Thompson and his crew flew dozens of survivors to receive medical care. In 1998 Thompson and his two crewmembers were given the Soldiers Medal for their efforts on that day.

By the time the My Lai massacre was over, 504 people had died. Among the victims were 182 women – 17 pregnant – and 173 children, including 56 infants.

Aware that the news of the massacre would cause a scandal, officers higher up in Charlie Company and the 11th Brigade immediately tried to downplay the bloodshed. Nonetheless, the U.S. Army began an internal investigation into the matter.

The cover-up of the My Lai massacre continued until Ron Ridenhour, a soldier in the 11th Brigade, investigated and broke the story to investigative journalist Seymour Hersh who published the report in several newspapers in November 1969.

Because of the international outcry, the Army was forced to investigate the My Lai massacre. In March of 1970, they recommended that 28 officers be charged for covering up the incident. The trial began on November 17, 1970. The Army would later only charge 14 men, including Calley, with crimes related to events at My Lai. All were acquitted except for Calley, despite his contention that he was only following the orders of his commanding officer, Captain Medina.

Later investigations have revealed that the massacre at My Lai was not an isolated incident. Other atrocities, such as a similar slaughter of villagers at My Khe, are less well known. A notorious military operation called Speedy Express killed thousands of Vietnamese civilians in the Mekong Delta, earning the commander of the operation, Major General Julian Ewell, the nickname "the Butcher of the Delta."

MARCH 30
1867

On this day in history, American Secretary of State William H. Seward signed a treaty with Russia facilitating the acquisition of Alaska for $7.2 million in gold. In modern terms, the cost was the equivalent of $140 million in 2021 dollars or $0.39 per acre. Notwithstanding the bargain price of roughly two cents an acre, the Alaskan purchase was derided in Congress and the press as "Seward's Folly," Seward's Icebox," and President Andrew Johnson's "polar bear garden." However, the reaction to the sale overall was generally positive, as many believed possession of Alaska would serve as a base to develop American trade in Asia. Russia also saw an opportunity to weaken arch-rival Great Britain's influence by causing British Columbia, including the Royal Navy base at Esquimalt, to become surrounded or annexed by American territory.

Alaska has been inhabited longer than any other location in North America, with the first people crossing over from Asia no later than 15,000 years ago. Nevertheless, it remained foreign to a good portion of the globe until 1741, when explorer Vitus Bering arrived as the leader of a rag-tag scurvy-induced expedition to Russia and claimed the land for Russia.

Russian fur traders began doing business there, but few stayed very long. No permanent colonial settlement would be created until 1784, and there were never more than a few hundred Russians living in Alaska at any time. Never self-sufficient, the colony depended on the British, native tribes, and the Americans for supplies.

Russian officials began to worry that American settlers would someday invade Alaska, much like they had in Texas. They also feared that Great Britain might take over the nearly defenseless colony. Since their defeat to the British in the Crimean War (1853-1856), Russia had been left devastated by debt. Then, the fur trade declined; even the czar's brother referred to Alaska as a luxury Russia could not afford. By the late 1850s, Russia had made an overture to the Buchanan administration about the sale of Alaska. Still, the timing could not have been worse with the pending American Civil War. Yet Senator William H. Seward, an ardent expansionist who would serve in the Lincoln and Johnson administrations, declared that Alaska would yet become American.

After the Civil War's end, Seward raised the matter of Alaska with Edouard de Stoeckl, the Russian minister to the United States, who then received permission from the czar to sell it. Secret discussions between Seward and Stoeckl began on March 11, 1867. After working through the night, the pair approved a treaty on March 30 stating that America would buy Alaska for $7.2 million in gold. (As was customary for the time, Alaska's vast Indigenous population was never consulted.) Seward hoped the Senate would endorse the treaty the same day. But the matter remained pending for a week and a half, during which Seward hosted opulent dinner parties to sway the senators attending.

The press, in the meantime, was having a field day. Most newspapers endorsed the deal. But a vocal minority, mainly related to the Radical Republican offshoot of the Republican Party, severely criticized it, referring to Alaska by names such as "Walrussia," "Johnson's Polar Bear Garden," and "Russian Fairy Land." (The term "Seward's Folly" was not used until many years after.)

Horace Greeley, the editor of the New York Tribune, was most vocal in his opposition, wrote that Alaska was a "burden... not worth taking as a gift." One senator joked that he would support the purchase only if Seward could "be compelled to live there." Yet that same senator failed to delay the purchase, and the Senate approved the treaty on April 9 by a 37-2 vote.

President Johnson selected General Lovell Rousseau to enable the handover of power in Alaska. Rousseau sailed via Panama to San Francisco and then to Sitka, Alaska, arriving on October 18. Later that day, the Russian flag was removed, and the American flag was raised in a ceremony attended by troops of both nations and a few Indigenous leaders. All interactions between the Russians and the Americans "were of the friendliest character," Rousseau reported, who went on to describe the people ("quiet, orderly and law-abiding"), the climate ("rains a great deal"), the potatoes ("small...but of the finest flavor"), the fisheries ("very fine"). The Russians left, and all Russian civilians remaining were allowed to become American citizens.

The story, however, did not end there. Focused on humiliating President Johnson, who was impeached in February 1868 (but survived removal from office by one vote), House Republicans declined to appropriate any cash for the acquisition of Alaska. Furthermore, a leading Massachusetts family asserted it should be given some of the $7.2 million as compensation for arms it purportedly sold to Russia during the Crimean War.

In July 1868, the House of Representatives voted 113-43 to pay Russia the sum owed. A congressional investigation later found that Stoeckl, the Russian minister to the U.S., bribed lobbyists, and journalists during this period. Private notes written by Johnson and another American official suggest that Stoeckl – with Seward's knowledge – likewise made thousands of dollars in illegal payments to members of Congress.

Alaska remained sparsely populated until the Klondike Gold Rush began in 1896. Organized initially as the Department of Alaska, the area was renamed the District of Alaska in 1884 and the Alaska Territory in 1912 before becoming the State of Alaska in 1959.

MARCH 31
1776

On this day in history, Abigail Adams wrote to her husband, John Adams, advising him and the other representatives of the Continental Congress not to forget about the nation's women when struggling for America's Independence from Great Britain.

Abigail herself enthusiastically supported independence and memorably argued that it should be applied to women and men. During the Second Continental Congress, when John Adams and his fellow members discussed declaring independence from Great Britain, Abigail sent a letter to her husband from their residence in Braintree, Massachusetts, on March 31, 1776. The future First Lady wrote, "I long to hear that you have declared an independency. And, by the way, in the new code of laws, which I suppose it will be necessary for you to make, I desire you would remember the ladies and be more generous and favorable to them than your ancestors. Do not put such unlimited power into the hands of the husbands. Remember, all men would be tyrants if they could. If particular care and attention is not paid to the ladies, we are determined to foment a rebellion and will not hold ourselves bound by any laws in which we have no voice or representation."

On the surface, John responded to Abigail's "remember the ladies" with playful banter. "As to your extraordinary code of laws, I cannot but laugh. We have been told that our struggle has loosened the bands of government everywhere," he wrote to her on April 14, 1776. "But your letter was the first intimation that another tribe more numerous and powerful than all the rest were grown discontented. – This is rather too coarse a compliment, but you are so saucy, I won't blot it out." He tried to soften the blow. "Depend upon it, we know better than to repeal our masculine systems. Although they are in full force, you know they are little more than theory."

Though her husband replied somewhat playfully to her appeal – expressing dread of the "Despotism of the Petticoat" – Abigail later made it clear that she was serious about what would happen to the status of women in a future independent republic.

She vociferously argued for women's education, writing to John in 1778 that "you need not be told how much female education is neglected, nor how fashionable it has been to ridicule female learning."

Abigail often expressed her thoughts on political affairs with her husband. Throughout her husband's career, Abigail served as his unofficial adviser. Their letters show that he sought her counsel on many issues, including his presidential aspirations.

One hundred fifty years before the 19th Amendment gave women the right to vote, Abigail Adam's letter was a private first step in the fight for women's rights. Recognized and admired as a formidable woman in her own right, the marriage between John and Abigail Adams lives on as a model of mutual respect and admiration; since that time, they have been called "America's first power couple." Their correspondence of over 1,200 letters written between 1762 and 1801 gives historians an essential perspective on domestic and political life during the Revolutionary period.

Abigail Smith was born on November 11, 1744, in Weymouth, Massachusetts, about 12 miles from Boston. Her father was William Smith, a minister with the First Congregational Church there, and he also made a living as a farmer. He and his wife, Elizabeth Quincy Smith, belonged to distinguished New England families. Elizabeth's father, John Quincy, was a titan in the colonial government and was Speaker of the Massachusetts Assembly for 40 years, and his public service career greatly influenced his granddaughter. Abigail was educated at home and read widely from the family library.

When Abigail was 19, she married a young lawyer, John Adams, who was 28. Nine months after they got married, Abigail gave birth to their first child, Abigail (called Nabby). She would have six children in total: four lived to adulthood, including Nabby Adams, John Quincy Adams (born 1767), Charles Adams (born 1770), and Thomas Adams (born 1772).

After the revolution, Abigail joined her husband in France and later in England, where he served as America's first minister to the Court of St. James from 1785 to 1788. When her husband became vice president the following year, Abigail stayed with him in the capital only part of the time, often returning to Massachusetts to take care of the farm and other business matters.

Abigail remained a supportive spouse and confidante after her husband became president in 1797. Some critics objected to Abigail's influence over her husband, calling her "Mrs. President." The nation's second first lady kept a busy schedule when she was in Philadelphia, the country's capital at that time. She still spent much time back in Massachusetts due to her health.

As far as matters of state, the couple did not always agree. They differed over the X, Y, Z Affair, where Abigail felt it right for America to go to war over bribery attempts by French officials. At the same time, John preferred a more diplomatic and less costly solution. However, they agreed on the Alien and Sedition Act of 1798. The three alien acts were aimed at immigrants increasing the waiting period for naturalization, allowing the government to detain foreign subjects, and permitting the deportation of any alien deemed dangerous. The Sedition Act federalized the ban against malicious anti-government writings inciting opposition to Congress or the president. Under the act, penalties included fines and jail time. Abigail, an ardent champion of her husband, thought those who published lies about John should be punished. President Adams signed these acts into law and has since been rebuked by historians for this anti-immigrant, anti-free speech legislation.

Around the time her husband was defeated in the 1801 presidential election by Thomas Jefferson, the family discovered that their second son Charles died due to his alcoholism. With great sadness, the family moved back to their family farm in Massachusetts.

With John now retired, the couple could now spend more time together. Abigail continued to run the farm and to care for family members, including their eldest child, Nabby, who eventually died of cancer at their home in 1814. Struggling with her health for decades, Abigail had a stroke in October 1818 and died at home with her family on October 28, 1818.

APRIL 1
1984

On this day in history, Marvin Gaye, an American musician who achieved worldwide stardom in the music industry, was shot and killed by his father, Marvin Gay Sr., the day before his 45th birthday at their home in Los Angeles, California. Gaye was shot twice after a confrontation with his father after he interceded in a disagreement between his parents. He was proclaimed dead on arrival at the California Hospital Medical Center. Gaye's father pleaded no contest to a charge of voluntary manslaughter.

Marvin Gaye had a terrible relationship with his father, Marvin Gay Sr., since early childhood. Marvin Sr. was a Christian minister who was a harsh disciplinarian and often physically abused his children. He was also a crossdresser, widely known in their Washington, D.C. neighborhood, making Marvin Jr. a target for bullying. It was because of this, and Gaye's own suspected homosexuality, that he added an "e" to his last name when he became famous. Gaye's father never approved of his career choice, and he certainly did not like that Marvin Jr. was close to his mother and had become the primary breadwinner for the family. Despite brief periods of calm, the two men would never find lasting peace.

By 1983 Gaye's career was on the upswing again with the release of his album *Midnight Love*, featuring the hit single "Sexual Healing." Never keen to hit the road, Gaye headed out in April of that year to tour supporting the album. He often wore a bulletproof vest until he was on stage because of an alleged attempt on his life. When the tour ended in August 1983, Gaye moved into the family home to help nurse his ailing mother. At that time, his father had been absent, returning from a business trip in October. The men tried to avoid each other and were successful for six months, but finally, an incident occurred where Marvin Sr. called the police to have Marvin Jr. removed from the house (a house he incidentally bought for his parents in 1973). Gaye eventually returned to the home determined to make peace with his father.

On Christmas Day, 1983, Gaye gifted his father a Smith & Wesson .38 Special pistol for protection against intruders. Friends and family contended that Marvin Jr. was often suicidal and suffered from paranoia and, by this point, was afraid of leaving his room and spoke of little except suicide and death. According to his sister Jeanne, Gaye tried to kill himself four days before his murder by jumping out of a speeding car, suffering only minor bruises. Jeanne stated that "there was no doubt Marvin wanted to die" and that he "couldn't take anymore."

In the days before his death, the tensions in the house had ratcheted up. Marvin Sr. and his wife were arguing over a missing insurance paper. Marvin Sr. was relentless in his badgering of his wife. Marvin Jr. finally had had enough, and after shouting and more words being stated between the two men Marvin Jr finally pushed Marvin Sr. out of his room and began to punch and kick him. Gay Sr. had stated publicly on more than one occasion that if anybody ever struck him, he would kill them. Eventually, Alberta, Gaye's mother, separated the men and got Marvin Jr. to return to his room.

Minutes later, at 12:38 pm, Marvin Sr. entered his bedroom, returning with the gun his son had previously purchased for him, pointed it at Gaye, and shot him right in the heart, as Alberta later explained to the police:

"I was standing about eight feet away from Marvin when my husband came to the door of the bedroom with his pistol. My husband didn't say anything, he just pointed the gun at Marvin. I screamed, but it was very quick. He, my husband, shot – and Marvin screamed. I tried to run. Marvin slid down to the floor after the first shot."

The first shot, which proved fatal, entered the right side of Gaye's chest, puncturing his right lung, heart, diaphragm, liver, stomach, and kidney before coming to rest against his left flank. Gaye's father moved nearer after first shooting him and then shot him a second time at point-blank range.

Running in fear of being the next person shot, Alberta exited the room, pleading with Marvin Sr. not to shoot her. Gay hid the pistol under his pillow in his room. Meanwhile, Gaye's brother, who lived in the guest house on the property, heard the gunshots and came into the place where he met a hysterical Alberta, who told him that his father had shot his brother. Frankie entered the house and went upstairs, finding the mortally wounded Marvin Jr. lying on the floor. He proceeded to hold him, and at that time, in barely a whisper, his brother told him, "I got what I wanted… I couldn't do it myself, so I had him do it… it's good, I ran my race, there's no more left in me." After police arrived, Marvin Jr.'s sister entered her father's bedroom and found the gun. The two went outside, where Irene threw the gun on the grass, and Marvin Sr. sat on the porch where he was arrested.

During his police interview, Gay told them that he feared for his life and that he was afraid of his son. He stated that he did not know the gun had any bullets. When asked if he loved his son, he stated, "Let's say I didn't dislike him." Marvin Sr. broke down and cried when told that his son was dead. Marvin Jr.'s sister stated that Gaye had forced his father's hand in the murder and that he had "accomplished three things. He put himself out of his misery. He brought relief to Mother by finally getting her husband out of her life. And he punished Father by making certain that the rest of his life would be miserable… my brother knew just what he was doing."

Marvin Sr. pleaded no contest to a charge of voluntary manslaughter on September 20, 1984. On November 2, 1984, the judge sentenced Gay to a six-year suspended sentence and five years of probation.

APRIL 2
1931

On this day in history, 17-year-old Jackie Mitchell was among the first female pitchers in professional baseball history. She pitched for the Chattanooga Lookouts Class AA, a minor league baseball team, in an exhibition game versus the New York Yankees and struck out Babe Ruth and Lou Gehrig one after the other during the match.

Jackie Mitchell was born August 29, 1913, in Chattanooga, Tennessee, to Virne Wall Mitchell and Dr. Joseph Mitchell. Her father escorted her to the baseball diamond and taught her how to play the game. Her next-door neighbor, Dazzy Vance, taught her how to pitch and instructed her to throw his "drop ball," a type of breaking ball. Vance was a major league pitcher and would ultimately be placed into the Baseball Hall of Fame.

At 17, Mitchell started playing for the Engelettes, a women's team based in Chattanooga, and went to a baseball training camp in Atlanta, Georgia. By doing so, she garnered the attention of team owner Joe Engel of the Chattanooga Lookouts, who was known for his publicity stunts used to draw crowds during the Great Depression. He saw Mitchell draw attention to the Lookouts, and keen on pumping up attendance at Engel Stadium, Engel signed her to the team on March 25, 1931. The nation's newspapers ate up the news – a photograph of

Mitchell signing the contract, with her optometrist father standing nearby, even appeared on the front page of the *New York Daily News*. She played in her first professional game on April 2, becoming the second woman to play organized baseball. She was behind Lizzie Arlington, who pitched for the Reading Coal Heavers versus the Allentown Peanuts in a minor league game in 1898.

Meanwhile, the *Chattanooga Daily Times* sports section pitched stereotypes of the era: "When not in uniform, Jackie dons an apron and joins in with the household chores," read a story below images of Jackie at home. "…Jackie can take that southpaw flipper and mix a mean batter or swing a wicked broom. Maybe that's where she got so much power in her flinging arm."

In early April 1931, while en route back to New York from spring training in Florida, the Yankees stopped in Chattanooga for exhibitions against the Lookouts. Engel announced he would pitch his newly signed lefthander against them. The consummate promoter eagerly stoked the fire for the story. "I think Jackie Mitchell will fool Babe Ruth as he is easily fooled, especially by a girl," he said, adding, "I don't think (our outfielders) will have anything to do."

Mitchell believed the Yankees showdown would put her biggest dreams within reach. She wanted to buy a roadster. She wanted money for college. She wanted to pitch in the World Series. It was a historic opportunity – infused with potential humiliation.

"There is no use to get nervous over a ballgame when I have been playing nearly all my life," Mitchell told the United Press. "I will just go out there and do my best and I believe I can fool the Babe."

Ruth was not concerned. He was just embarrassed for baseball. "Well, I don't know what things are coming to," Ruth said before the encounter. "I don't know what's going to happen if they begin to let women in baseball. Of course, they will never make good. Why? Because they are too delicate. It would kill them to play ball every day."

The ingrained misogyny of the era – only ten years had passed since the Nineteenth Amendment was adopted, granting women the right to vote – was captured throughout the male-dominated media.

"The Yankees will meet a club here that has a girl pitcher named

Jackie Mitchell, who has a swell change of pace and swings a mean lipstick," the *Daily News* wrote before the April 2 game. "I suppose that in the next town the Yankees enter, they will find a squad that has a female impersonator in left field, a sword swallower at short, and a trained seal behind the plate."

On April 2, 1931, 4,000 fans gathered at Engel Stadium to watch the exhibition game. A Universal film crew was there to document the event for showing in theaters. Fans did not have to wait long for Mitchell to face Ruth. To the crowd's roar, she took the mound as a reliever in the first inning. Ruth tipped his cap to Mitchell, who was composed despite the hoopla. Her first pitch was a ball inside.

Then Ruth swung, missed at two more pitches, and took a called third strike. Disgusted, he threw down his bat and stalked to the dugout. "Merely acting," the *Chattanooga News* described Ruth's "fit."

"The Babe performed his role very ably," reported the *New York Times*. "He swung hard at two pitches then demanded that Umpire Owens inspect the ball, just as batters do when utterly baffled by a pitcher's delivery." The next batter, Gehrig, went down swinging on three pitches. Mitchell's girlfriends at the game celebrated. After walking Tony Lazzeri, the Lookouts manager pulled Mitchell from the game. The Lookouts lost the game 14-4, but Chattanooga fans did not care. Their "feminine flinger" was the big story.

The debate has raged in the intervening years about whether Ruth and Gehrig flubbed their at-bats in favor of a "good show." Or was Mitchell the real deal? Shortly before she died in 1987, Jackie Mitchell insisted that her strikeout feat was legit. "Why, hell, they were trying – damn right," she said. "Hell, better hitters than them couldn't hit me. Why would they have been any different?"

Mitchell continued to play professionally; she barnstormed with the House of David, a men's team known for their very long hair and long beards. Mitchell retired in 1937 at 23 after becoming angry that her story about playing baseball was used as a sideshow. After baseball, she went to work in her father's optometry office.

APRIL 3
1882

On this day in history, Jesse James, one of America's most infamous felons, is shot dead by fellow gang member Bob Ford, who double-crossed James for the reward money. For a decade and a half, Jesse and his brother, Frank, perpetrated robberies, and murders all over the Midwest. Detective magazines and pulp novels painted a romanticized picture of the James gang, turning them into mythical Robin Hood-like figures driven to crime by unethical landowners and bankers. Jesse James was a cold-blooded killer who stole only for the benefit of himself and his gang.

The young James brothers joined southern guerrilla leaders when the Civil War began. Both took part in massacres of civilians and soldiers associated with the North. After the war, the quiet farming life of the James brothers' youth no longer seemed alluring, so the two brothers turned to crime. Jesse's first bank robbery happened on February 13, 1866, in Liberty, Missouri.

Over the next two years, the James brothers were accused of several bank robberies throughout western Missouri. However, locals, sympathetic to the plight of the ex-southern guerilla, corroborated the brother's alibi. All through the late 1860s and early 1870s, the James gang only robbed, on average, a couple of banks a year, the rest of the time maintaining a low profile.

In 1873, the James gang began robbing trains. During one robbery, the crew decided not to steal from any Southerners on the train. These, and subsequent train robberies, caught the attention of Pinkerton's Detective Agency, who was hired to capture the James gang. However, the Pinkerton detectives bungled the attempt to kill Jesse and only managed to injure an innocent woman and her child. This affair only created more public sympathy and support for the James brothers.

The James gang suffered misfortune in 1876 when they attempted to rob the bank in Northfield, Minnesota. The Younger brothers, the James brother's cousins, were shot and injured during the brash noontime robbery. After attempting to escape by running off in a different direction than the James brothers, the Younger brothers were arrested and sentenced to life in prison. The James brothers were the only two members of the gang who were not killed or captured during the robbery. After they got away, they headed for Tennessee to lay low for a while.

After farming for a few years, Jesse organized a new gang in 1881. Frank had decided to retire and move to West Virginia to live a calm life. By the spring of 1882, with his new gang diminished by arrests, deaths, and defections, James thought he could only trust the Ford brothers. Charles had been on raids with James before, but Bob was an eager recruit. The Fords resided with the James family in St. Joseph, Missouri, where Jesse went by the alias Thomas Howard.

James was planning another heist – the Platte City, Missouri bank – and had asked the Ford brothers to participate. Charles and Bob had decided to collect the $10,000 bounty on Jesse's head placed there by Missouri Governor Thomas Crittenden. In January 1882, Bob Ford and gang member Dick Liddil surrendered to the local sheriff. They were brought into a meeting with the Governor, as they had been around James's cousin Wood Hite the day Hite was murdered. Crittenden guaranteed Ford a full pardon if he would kill James, who was at that time the most wanted criminal in America. Crittenden had made capturing James's brothers his top priority. Barred by law from offering a large reward, he turned to the railroads to put up the $10,000 reward.

After eating breakfast on April 3, 1882, the Fords and James entered the living room before venturing onto Platte City. By reading the local newspaper, James had become informed of gang member Liddil's confession for participating in Hite's murder, and he grew increasingly suspicious of the Fords for not telling him of this development. According to Robert Ford, it became clear that James had discovered they were there to betray him. However, instead of criticizing the Fords, James walked across the living room to place his revolvers on the sofa. He turned around, noticed a dusty picture above the mantel, and stood on a chair to clean it. Bob Ford drew his weapon and shot James in the back of the head.

The Fords did not attempt to hide their role. Bob Ford wired the governor to claim his reward. Throngs of people crowded into the little house in St. Joseph to see the dead outlaw. The Ford brothers gave themselves up to the authorities and were upset to be charged with first-degree murder. All in one day, the Ford brothers were indicted, pleaded guilty, were condemned to death by hanging, and were given a full pardon by the Governor. None of this sat well with the public.

The Fords received a small amount of the reward and promptly left Missouri. Sheriff James Timberlake and Marshal Henry Craig, law officials in on the plan, were awarded most of the reward. Later, the Ford brothers had their touring stage show where they re-enacted the shooting. Suffering from tuberculosis (then untreatable) and morphine dependence, Charley Ford killed himself on May 6, 1884, in Richmond, Missouri. Bob Ford ran a tent saloon in Creede, Colorado. On June 8, 1892, Edward O'Kelley traveled to Creede, loaded a double-barrel shotgun, entered Ford's bar, and said "Hello, Bob" before shooting Bob in the throat, killing him immediately. O'Kelley was sentenced to life in prison but was subsequently released because of a 7,000-signature petition in his favor. The Governor of Colorado exonerated him on October 3, 1902.

James' original grave was on his family property but was moved to Kearney. James's mother, Zerelda Samuel, wrote the following inscription for his tombstone: "In Loving Memory of my Beloved Son, Murdered by a Traitor and Coward Whose Name is Not Worthy to

Appear Here." James's widow Zerelda Mimms James died lonely and in poverty.

APRIL 4
1841

On this day in history, William Henry Harrison, the ninth president of the United States, died just 31 days after his inauguration in 1841 and had the shortest presidency in American history. He was the first president to die in office, and a brief constitutional crisis erupted as presidential succession was not fully outlined in the American Constitution. Harrison was the last president to be born a British subject in the Thirteen Colonies and was the grandfather of Benjamin Harrison, the 23rd president of the United States.

Oddly, the man with the shortest presidency presented the lengthiest inaugural address in the nation's history, which may have been his downfall. The first presidential speech, given on an intensely cold March morning, lasted one hour and 45 minutes. Harrison was sent to bed at the end of inauguration day with a terrible cold that soon morphed into a fatal case of pneumonia. Some historians have maintained that a case of hepatitis or enteric fever may have also caused his death.

Harrison was born on February 9, 1773, at Berkeley, his family's plantation near Richmond, Virginia. His father, Benjamin Harrison (1726-1791), signed the Declaration of Independence and was governor of Virginia. William Harrison went to college intending to study medicine but decided to join the army before completing his degree. President John Adams took notice of Harrison's commendable service in the Indian Wars of the Northwest Territories and, in 1801, made him governor of the Northwest Territories (now Indiana and Illinois). Harrison later took up arms in the War of 1812 at the Battle of the Thames River. He became a congressman and then an ambassador to Colombia before running in the presidential election of 1840 with John Tyler on the Whig Party ticket.

Much to the chagrin of the political establishment, Harrison and Tyler campaigned in an aggressive style not usual for the period. They used Harrison's nickname, "Tippecanoe," which he earned during a brutal Indian War battle at Tippecanoe Creek, and they came up with the campaign slogan "Tippecanoe and Tyler, too." Harrison and Tyler held loud and energetic rallies, giving out free bottles of hard cider contained in little log cabin-shaped bottles. Their methods, however provocative, were effective, and on March 4, 1841, Harrison was confirmed as the ninth American president.

After three weeks in office, Harrison had become worn down by the many persistent office seekers and a brutal social schedule. Still, he had somewhat recovered from his inauguration-day cold. On Wednesday, March 24, 1841, Harrison went on his usual morning walk to the local markets without a coat or hat. Having been caught in a rainstorm, he did not change his wet clothes when he returned to the White House. On Friday, March 26, Harrison became sick with cold-like symptoms and was sent to his doctor. After taking medication for "fatigue and mental anxiety," Harrison felt better. The next day, the doctor was called again and found Harrison in bed with a "severe chill" after taking another early morning walk. The doctor applied a mustard plaster to his stomach and administered a mild laxative, and he felt better by the afternoon. By Sunday, Harrison continued to go downhill, so the doctor-initiated bloodletting until there was a drop in his pulse rate. The doctor then applied heated cups to the president's skin to enhance blood flow. He was then given castor oil and medicines to induce vomiting, and he diagnosed Harrison with pneumonia in the right lung. Several doctors were summoned on Monday, March 29, and they confirmed the diagnosis of pneumonia. The president was then given laudanum, opium, camphor, wine, and brandy.

On the evening of Saturday, April 3, Harrison developed severe diarrhea. He became delirious, and at 8:30 p.m., he spoke his last words to his doctor, assumed to be intended for Vice President John Tyler: "Sir, I wish you to understand the true principles of the government. I wish them carried out. I ask nothing more." Harrison died at 12:30 a.m. on April 4, 1841, nine days after becoming ill and precisely one month after taking the oath of office; he was the first president to die in office. His wife was still in Ohio packing for the journey to Washington when she was told of his death.

A 30-day period of mourning followed the death of the president. The White House held various public ceremonies modeled after European royal funeral practices. An invitation-only funeral service took place on April 7 in the East Room of the White House. Harrison's coffin was brought to the Congressional Cemetery in Washington, D.C., where it was put in the Public Vault. That June, Harrison's remains were moved by train and river barge to North Bend, Ohio, where he was interred on July 7 at the summit of Mt. Nebo, now the William Henry Harrison Tomb State Memorial.

Harrison's death brought attention to the vagueness in Article II, Section 1, Clause 6 of the Constitution regarding succession to the presidency. The Constitution allowed the vice president to take over the "Powers and Duties of the said Office" in case of a president's removal, death, resignation, or inability. Still, it was unclear whether the vice president formally became president of the U.S. or simply only temporarily accepted the powers and duties of that office in a case of succession.

Harrison's cabinet felt Tyler was "Vice President acting as President." Tyler felt that he was indeed president. The cabinet consulted the Chief Justice, who ruled that if Tyler took the presidential oath of office, he would be president. Tyler agreed and was sworn into office on April 6, 1841. Congress was summoned, and on May 31, 1841, after a short debate in both houses, passed a joint resolution confirming

Tyler as president. The precedent that Congress created in 1841 was followed on seven more occasions when a president died, and it was put into the Constitution in 1967 through Section One of the Twenty-fifth Amendment.

APRIL 5
1968

On this day in history, a day after the assassination of civil rights leader Martin Luther King Jr. in Memphis, Tennessee, singer James Brown gave a free citywide televised concert at the Boston Garden to sustain public order and calm for concerned Boston residents (over the objections of the Boston police chief, who wanted to call off the concert, which he thought would incite violence).

On the morning after the death of Dr. King, municipal officials in Boston, Massachusetts, were clambering to prepare for an anticipated straight night of hostility. Similar arrangements were being made in cities across America, including the nation's capital, where armed units of the regular Army guarded outside the White House and the U.S. Capitol after President Johnson's state-of-emergency speech. But Boston would be alone among the United States' major cities in staying quiet and calm that tumultuous Friday night, thanks largely to one of the most boisterous entertainers of all time. On the evening of April 5, 1968, James Brown kept the peace in Boston with the utter power of his music and his personality.

Brown's concert that night at the Boston Garden had been arranged for months, but it almost did not take place. After a night of disturbances and fires in the primarily black neighborhoods of Roxbury and South End sections of Boston, the city's mayor, Kevin White, had given considerable thought to stop an event that some dreaded would produce a lot of violence in the center of Boston. Fears of racial violence were very much on the surface in a city in which school integration and mandatory busing had played a significant role in the recently held mayoral election. Mayor White found himself in a catch-22 situation – provoke Black Bostonians by canceling Brown's concert over blatantly racial fears or alienate the rest of the population by merely disregarding those fears. The proposal that fixed the mayor's predicament came from a young, African American city councilman named Tom Atkins, who put forward the idea of going on with the concert but looking for a way to present a free, live broadcast of the show in the hopes that most Bostonians would stay at home in front of their TV sets rather than create problems on the streets of the city.

White and Atkins persuaded public television station WGBH to televise the concert on little notice, but persuading James Brown was another matter. Brown at first balked at the idea because he had a non-compete clause relating to an upcoming televised concert, and Brown would lose $60,000 if the Boston concert were televised. Always the astute businessman, Brown made his financial proposal to Mayor White that the city of Boston reimburses him for his loss. After some thought, White astutely decided to agree to Brown's terms.

The white mayor stood in front of a predominantly black audience. Dozens of police stood at attention. The band members, afraid they would be shot on the way to the venue, sat quietly at their instruments.

"We're here to pay tribute to one of the greatest Americans, Dr. Martin Luther King," Mayor White said. "Twenty-four hours ago, Dr. King died for all of us, black and white." The applause drowned out a few catcalls.

"We in Boston will honor Dr. King in peace," White ended with a flourish. At James Brown's behest, the audience gave the white politician a round of applause.

Brown launched into his show, starting with a magnificent soul version of the Frank Sinatra hit, "My Way." Brown later recalled:

"Throughout the show, between songs, I talked about Dr. King and urged the people to stay calm. I announced a song title and tried to work the title into a little rap about Dr. King and the whole situation. I talked about my own life and where I'd come from. At one point, when I was reminiscing about Martin, I started to cry – a few tears rolling out, you know, nothing anybody could really see – but it was like it was all starting to really sink in what we lost. I pulled myself together – I thought that would do the most good – and went on with the show."

The televising of Brown's concert had the desired effect it was supposed to, as Boston had less crime than on a regular Friday night, let alone one after much of the nation had gone up in flames over the death of Martin Luther King Jr. However, at one time in the evening, it seemed like the whole idea might go wrong. A group of young male concertgoers began to climb onto the stage in the middle of the concert. At that point, the white Boston police officers forcefully pushed the youth back off the stage. Sensing the volatility of the situation, that white police were aggressively challenging young black people on television could start the violence in Boston that raged across America. Brown urged the police to leave the young men alone. "Move on back. I'll be all right. I'll be fine," he told the police on stage. He then spoke to the youths and stated, "Wait a minute, wait a minute, now, Wait! Step down, now, be a gentleman…. You make me look very bad 'cause I asked the po-lice to step back, and you wouldn't go down. Now that's wrong, that's wrong. You're not being fair to yourself and me and all your race…I think I can get some respect from my own people."

The show was then rebroadcast repeatedly, and tens of thousands of aggrieved young people stayed home.

The following day the local news media praised James Brown for keeping the peace. It was one of the things that meant the most to him.

Later in 1968, Brown electrified the nation with his record, *Say it Loud – I'm Black and I'm Proud*, which would become an unofficial anthem for the Black Power Movement. It was one of the many records that helped Brown cement his legacy as one of America's greatest entertainers. As Reverend Al Sharpton once said of the singer and civil rights leader, "America produced a Dr. King, but it also produced a James Brown...they were the same effect, and in many ways, they articulated what a whole nation needed to hear."

APRIL 6
1895

On this day in history, writer Oscar Wilde is arrested for committing criminal sodomy and "gross indecency" (a crime only capable of being executed by two men, which might include sexual acts other than sodomy) after losing a libel case against the Marquess of Queensbury.

Wilde was an Anglo-Irish playwright and bon vivant known for his caustic wit and acclaimed works, including *Lady Windermere's Fan, A Woman of No Importance, The Picture of Dorian Gray,* and *The Importance of Being Earnest.* In early 1895, the husband and father of two were at the height of his fame and success; his play, *Earnest,* had arrived in the public realm to great acclaim in February of that year, making him the talk of London.

Oscar Fingal O'Flahertie Wills Wilde was born in Dublin, Ireland, on October 16, 1854. His father, William Wilde, was a respected doctor knighted for his efforts as a medical advisor for the Irish censuses. William later established St. Mark's Ophthalmic Hospital, entirely at his own expense, to tend to the city's poor and disadvantaged. Wilde's mother, Jane Francesca Elgee, was a poet strongly associated with the Young Irelander Rebellion of 1848. She had a tremendous impact on her son's writing.

Wilde went to the Portora Royal School at Enniskillen, where he excelled at Greek and Roman studies. After graduating in 1871, he attended Trinity College in Dublin and placed first in the classic's examination. After graduating in 1874, Wilde was celebrated as the best student in Greek and received a scholarship to study at Oxford University. After Oxford, he moved to London and, in 1881, published his first collection, Poems. The following year, in 1882, Wilde traveled to New York City to start an American lecture tour, for which he gave an amazing 140 lectures in just nine months.

On May 29, 1884, Wilde married Constance Lloyd, a wealthy Englishwoman. They had two sons: Cyril, born in 1885, and Vyvyan, born in 1886. A year later, he became editor of *Lady's World*, a once-popular English magazine that had of late fallen out of fashion. During his years at the magazine, Wilde revitalized it by lengthening its reporting to "deal not merely with what women wear, but with what they think and what they feel."

Wilde met Lord Alfred "Bosie" Douglas in 1891, and the two soon became lovers. This affair would last years, ultimately leading to Wilde's public downfall. Douglas, the third son of the Marquess of Queensberry, was 16 years younger than Wilde. Reportedly a dissolute, extravagant dandy, he was practically inseparable from Wilde until the latter's arrest four years later.

Douglas' father's reaction to the affair prompted the fateful court proceedings. By early 1894, Queensberry was certain the flamboyant Wilde was a homosexual and demanded his son cut off contact with the writer. (The Victorian era was known for its culture of sexual repression, and sexual activity between men was a criminal offense in Britain until the late 1960s.)

"Your intimacy with this man Wilde must either cease or I will disown you and stop all money supplies," Queensberry wrote to his son in April 1894. Douglas refused his father's warnings, incensing Queensberry and fueling his hostility toward his son's alleged lover.

First, Queensberry tried to interrupt the launching of *The Importance of Being Earnest*, where he planned to give the playwright a bouquet of rotten vegetables and inform theatergoers of Wilde's alleged shameful lifestyle. Foiled, he then visited London's Albemarle Club, of which Wilde and his wife were members. Queensberry left a card with the porter of the club for Wilde, which read, "For Oscar Wilde, posing somdomite (sic)." Outraged and humiliated, Wilde informed Douglas that he would criminally prosecute his father for libel. "My whole life seems ruined by this man," he wrote to Douglas. "The tower of ivory is assailed by the foul thing."

Amid a hysteria of newspaper coverage, the libel case against the Marquess of Queensberry began on April 3, 1895, at Old Bailey. The trial went poorly for Wilde. His main problem was that Queensberry's accusations about his homosexuality were true and consequently could not be judged libelous.

Wilde was accused of soliciting 12 other young men to commit sodomy. The defense also asked Wilde about the premise of his 1890 novel The Picture of Dorian Gray, where Wilde used the novel's homoerotic themes to seduce Lord Alfred.

After three days of legal action, Wilde's lawyer terminated the lawsuit. The authorities viewed this as a sign of guilt and issued a subpoena for Wilde's arrest on indecency charges enforced on April 6, 1895.

Friends urged Wilde to flee to France, but he decided to stay and stand trial. The court case against Wilde started on April 26. He pleads not guilty to 25 counts of gross indecency. At a preliminary hearing, hotel chambermaids and a housekeeper had testified that they had witnessed numerous men in Wilde's bed and saw fecal stains on his bedsheets. During the trial, Wilde was questioned substantially about "the love that dare not speak its name," a phrase from Lord Alfred Douglas' poem "Two Loves," published in 1894, that many felt was another way of talking about homosexuality.

The trial concluded with a hung jury. Three weeks later, Wilde was retried. This time, he was convicted of gross indecency and received a sentence of two years of hard labor, the maximum punishment allowable.

On May 25, 1895, Oscar Wilde was escorted to prison. After suffering greatly at the hands of his jailers, Wilde was released from prison in 1897. His health had suffered dramatically while incarcerated, and he continued declining after being released.

He spent the last three years of his life in exile in France, where Wilde wrote his last work, *The Ballad of Reading Gaol*, about an execution in jail he witnessed while imprisoned there.

Oscar Wilde died of meningitis on November 30, 1900, at 46. He was buried in Paris.

APRIL 7
1945

On this day in history, *Sonderkommando Elbe*, a special Luftwaffe unit created to destroy Allied B-17s and B-24s by ramming them in mid-air, is sent on their first and only mission during the dying days of World War II. The tactic was aimed to cause losses sufficient to halt or at least reduce the Allied bombing of Germany long enough to allow the Germans to produce a significant number of Messerschmitt Me 262 jet fighters to turn the tide of the air war.

The pilots were expected to parachute out just before or after colliding with their target. A *Sonderkommando Elbe* pilot's chances of surviving such an event were meager at a time when the Luftwaffe needed more well-trained pilots.

By April 1945, Nazi Germany was in its death throes. The Allied and Soviet armies were approaching Berlin rapidly. Allied bombers, primarily American, were wreaking havoc on Berlin, Dresden, and other German cities with a daily strategic bombing offensive. By late 1944, the Luftwaffe was reduced to mere recruits, many of their commanders and skilled aces having been killed, shot down, or captured. Most of the Luftwaffe force comprised young, enlisted pilots by this time. Oberst Hago Hermann devised a plan to have German pilots ram the American bombers out of the sky instead of trying to shoot them down. The Germans hoped the rammings would cause American bomber pilots to refuse to bomb German cities out of fear of the seemingly suicidal German pilots. The Luftwaffe predicted that the Allies would suspend bombings for at least 4 to 6 weeks. This would allow the German factories to produce enough Messerschmitt Me 262 jet fighters to turn the tide in the air war in Germany's favor.

The *Sonderkommando Elbe* pilots were not like the Japanese *kamikaze* pilots. The Japanese pilots had loaded their planes with explosives on board and crashed their planes completely into American ships, ending their lives. The Elbe pilots were expected to take down American bombers, bailout, and report to the base for more ramming missions.

The aircraft of choice for this mission was a later G-version (Gustav) of the Messerschmitt Bf 109, stripped of armor and armament. The heavily stripped-down planes had one machine gun instead of the four automatic weapons on fully equipped Bf109G interceptors. They were only allotted 60 rounds each, a normally insufficient amount for bomber-interception missions. To accomplish their task, Sonderkommando Elbe pilots would typically try to hit one of three sensitive areas on the bombers: the empennage with its delicate control surfaces, the engine enclosures connected to the extremely explosive fuel system, or the cockpit itself.

On March 7, 1945, a call for volunteers was sent out. Out of 2,000 volunteers, 300 were selected for training for the mission by the Elbe River. Most pilots' training was limited to taking off and flying to the target. The date of the attack was selected for April 7, 1945.

Against 14,000 American bombers and 800 P-51 escort fighters, 180 German fighters were mobilized.

On April 7, 1945, the pilots were launched. Out of 180 fighters mobilized, 60 returned to base with engine problems, and another 47 were shot down by American P-51 fighter planes before they could reach their targets. However, some pilots did take down some bombers. The Luftwaffe documented that they had destroyed 24 heavy bombers on that day. Allied sources state that 15 bombers were smashed into, and eight bombers fell from the sky.

Heinrich Rosner was the most successful German pilot in the

mission, who destroyed two B-24s in one ramming attack. Having been separated from his unit by poor flight coordination, he spotted bombers of the 389th Bomb Group. Diving from the clouds, he missed his target as he pulled up. The B-24 gunners could not fire on the German pilot as he moved through the formation. Picking a new target, Rosner pulled out in front of the formation and then turned to ram the lead aircraft, the *Palace of Dallas*. Rosner's right-wing sliced through the B-24s cockpit, severing it from the fuselage, then the plane careened into the deputy lead bomber, piloted by Walter Kunkel. Both bombers broke up in mid-air with few survivors. Rosner bailed out of his aircraft and survived.

Another B-24, called *Sacktime*, was rammed by Heinrich Henkel. As the gunner ignited the Bf 109s fuel tank, Henkel hit the B-24s tail section, severing the right vertical stabilizer. The Bf 109 also cut a hole in the fuselage and cartwheeled out before the bomber. Though violently slammed by the collision, Henkel managed to bail out just before his plane exploded. *Sacktime* flew towards Allied Belgium for almost an hour before the crew bailed out.

This was the only major attack taken on by the *Sonderkommando Elbe*, a distinct unit whose mission showed the total despair that had befallen the Luftwaffe during the last months of the war. Ten days later, the *Leonidas Squadron* launched another kamikaze-like attack – this time, the pilots dove into Soviet troops crossing bridges over the Oder River, east of Berlin. Similarly, stories are told of a special unit with the same mission known by the name *Leonidas Squadron*, a unit put together to fly the manned version of the V-1 flying bomb. It was canceled because it was considered a waste of personnel and resources.

The result of the *Sonderkommando Elbe* was considered a failure, so the ramming attacks were halted to protect the lives of the remaining trained pilots. The outcome would have made no difference. By April 7, Hitler was mere weeks from defeat and ending his own life.

APRIL 8
1974

On this day in history, Hank Aaron of the Atlanta Braves hit his 715th career home run, breaking Babe Ruth's outstanding record of 714 homers. A record-setting crowd of 53,775 people gathered at the Fulton County Stadium to cheer Aaron on in his pursuit of the all-time home run record. Aaron would achieve his goal from a pitch by Los Angeles Dodger pitcher Al Downing in the fourth inning of the game. However, as Aaron was an African American who had received multiple death threats and racist hate mail during his quest for one of baseball's most prominent records, the accomplishment was bittersweet.

Henry Louis Aaron was born in Mobile, Alabama, on February 5, 1934. He was born to Estella and Herbert Aaron, who made a living as a drydock boilermaker's assistant and a tavern owner.

Aaron developed a strong affinity for baseball at a very young age and played all through school. In late 1951, an 18-year-old Aaron quit school to play full-time for the Negro American League Indianapolis Clowns. He did not stay long in this league, but the talented teenager left his mark by hitting .366 and leading his club to victory in the 1952 World Series. Additionally, he would become the last player to play in both the Negro Leagues and the Major Leagues.

In 1952 he signed with the Milwaukee Braves for $10,000 and was assigned to the team's farm club, Class C Eau Claire Bears. He tore up the league, winning Northern League Rookie of the Year. In 1953 he moved up to Class A and continued his winning ways. Aaron debuted in the Major League in 1954, at age 20, with the Milwaukee Braves. Aaron continued to shine throughout his career. For a decade and a half, he averaged 30 to 40 homers a year and was consistently at the top of every other metric through that time. In 1973, at 39, Aaron was still a force, hitting 40 home runs to finish the season with a career total of 713, just one shy of Babe Ruth's record.

Ruth became baseball's all-time home run leader in 1921 when he hit his 139th homer of his career. Baseball fans had long thought Ruth's record of 714 was unassailable, and as Aaron inched closer to baseball's legendary icon, a vocal minority began to speak up. They sent Aaron threatening letters stating that Ruth would always be the greatest home run hitter who ever lived, beseeching the Atlanta slugger not to go past the Babe. "When my son turns the page in a record book and looks for home runs and sees your name at the top of that list, he's not going to care one bit about Babe Ruth," one fan bemoaned.

Worse, however, were the racist hate mail and death threats Aaron received. Daily he received letters from fans who did not want to see baseball's most storied record in African American hands. He read the vile letters – at least the one the FBI had not confiscated – addressed to "Black Boy." "Jungle Bunny" and worse. "Dear Brother Hank Aaron, I hope you join Brother Dr. Martin Luther King in that heaven he spoke of," read one letter. "Will I sneak a rifle into the upper deck or a .45 in the bleachers? I don't know yet. But you know you will die unless you don't!" threatened one person, while another stated, "My gun is watching your every Black move. This is no joke."

Aaron and his family received around-the-clock protection from the police and the FBI. Aaron wrote in his autobiography, "It should have been the most enjoyable time in my life, and instead, it was hell." Although most of the mail sent to him was well-meaning, he used the terrible ones to stoke his fire. He wrote that he was motivated by "the sense of doing something for my race." He believed the best way to honor Jackie Robinson's legacy as the first black in the Major Leagues "was to become the all-time home run champion in the history of the game that had kept out Black people for more than sixty years."

As the 1974 season began, Aaron was close to Ruth's record. On his first swing on Opening Day, he sent a ball over the wall at Cincinnati's Riverfront Stadium to tie Ruth at 714. He was back in Atlanta four days later for the team's home opener. Aaron walked in his first at-bat in the second inning and broke Willie Mays' National League record for runs when he came around to score. This type of occasion would generally have been meaningful, but compared to the home run chase, it was merely a footnote for the record books.

Aaron was ready to end the suspense when he came to the plate in the fourth inning. Aaron swung and sent the ball into the left field bullpen on a curve ball that did not curve from pitcher Al Downing of the Los Angeles Dodgers. Aaron floated around the bases. "Hammerin' Hank" rarely smiled when he hit a home run, but he did this time. When he rounded second, he found that he had an escort. Teenagers Britt Gaston and Cliff Courtney had jumped onto the field and ran alongside the new home run king to shake his hand and pat him on the back before he got to third base.

Aaron's teammates mobbed him as he reached home plate. One of his teammates brought his home run ball from the bullpen to give it to him. His parents met him and congratulated him at home plate. Aaron said in a ceremony, "I'd just like to say to all the fans here this evening that I just thank God it's all over with."

Hank Aaron ended his baseball career in 1976 with 755 home runs, a record that lasted until 2007 when Barry Bonds, dogged by accusations of using performance-enhancing drugs, broke it. Still, much like baseball fans in the 1970s who consider Ruth the greatest home run hitter who ever existed, many present-day fans feel the same way about Aaron. Reggie Jackson stated that Aaron remains "the people's home run champion." On January 22, 2021, Hank Aaron died at age 86.

APRIL 9
1881

On this day in history, after a one-day trial, Henry McCarty, aka "Billy the Kid," or William H. Bonney, was found guilty of murdering the Lincoln County, New Mexico, sheriff and was sentenced to hang. There is little doubt that Henry McCarty, in fact, shot the sheriff, even though he did so in the context of the very violent and bloody Lincoln County War; it was a clash between two powerful groups of ranchers and businessmen struggling for financial control of Lincoln County. When his boss, rancher John Tunstall, was slain before him in February 1878, the mercurial young McCarty promised revenge. Regrettably, the crew leader who killed Tunstall was the Sheriff William Brady of Lincoln County. When McCarty and his partners killed the sheriff several months later, they became outlaws, irrespective of how crooked Brady may have been.

Henry McCarty's parents were of Irish descent from New York City, and he was born on September 17, 1859. In 1863 the McCarty's had a second son, Joseph, who was born in 1863. After the death of her husband, Catherine and the two boys moved to Indianapolis. There she met William Antrim, and in 1870 they all moved to Wichita, Kansas. After moving again two years later, Catherine married Antrim in Santa Fe, New Mexico Territory. On September 16, 1874, McCarty's mother, Catherine, died of Tuberculosis. William Antrim then abandoned the boys, leaving them orphans. McCarty was then 15 years old.

McCarty had a slim build, sandy blond hair, and blue eyes and wore a signature sugar-loaf sombrero hat with a wide ornamental band. He could be charming and polite one moment, then angry and violent the next, a quixotic nature he used significantly in his dealings with people. In 1876 he apparently killed his first group of men, a group of Apache Indians, in the Guadalupe Mountains. McCarty began committing petty crimes and working as a ranch hand until 1877 when he killed another person – a man named "Windy" Cahill, a blacksmith, with whom he got into an argument within a saloon in the village of Bonita. As people began calling him, Billy the Kid found work as a rancher and bodyguard for John Tunstall, an English-born rancher who lived in Lincoln, New Mexico. When members of a rival cattle gang murdered Tunstall in 1878, McCarty became involved in the Lincoln County War.

Infuriated at Tunstall's murder, McCarty became the leader of a vigilante group of "regulators" sent to apprehend the killers. No arrests were made, however. The regulators shot two of the killers dead, and a deteriorating blood feud soon intensified into all-out warfare. After McCarty's gang shot dead Lincoln Sheriff William Brady, who had authorized Tunstall's murder, McCarty's enemies colluded with the territorial authorities to eliminate the regulators.

In July 1878, the rival gang encircled the place where McCarty and his crew stayed just outside town. The siege lasted five days, and a U.S. Army squadron from Fort Stanton was summoned to help. Still, McCarty and his regulators refused to give up. Suddenly, the regulators attempted a mass escape, and McCarty and several other regulators miraculously managed to shoot their way out of town.

After over two years on the run, McCarty was detained by Lincoln Sheriff Pat Garrett, a man McCarty had befriended before Garrett became a lawman. On April 13, 1881, McCarty was found guilty of murdering Sheriff Brady and was condemned to hang. Upon sentencing, the judge told McCarty he would hang until he was "dead, dead, dead"; McCarty replied, "You can go to hell, hell, hell."

Following his sentencing, McCarty was taken to Lincoln, where he was placed under guard on the top floor of the town courthouse. On the evening of April 28, 1881, two weeks before his scheduled execution, McCarty wrested a gun away from one of his guards and shot him and another deputy dead in an escape. He grabbed a horse and rode out of town; according to some stories, he sang as he left Lincoln. His escape received widespread national scrutiny.

On July 14, 1881, Garrett and two deputies went to a ranch owned by an Acquaintance of McCarty's named Pete Maxwell. Leaving the two deputies on the porch, Garrett went into the dark house, found Maxwell's bedroom, and began questioning him. Maxwell admitted that McCarty had been around, though he was unsure where he was at that moment. Just then, someone appeared at the door, holding a gun and a butcher knife, and asked in Spanish who was there.

"Who is it, Pete?" Garrett whispered to Maxwell.

"That's him," Maxwell responded.

McCarty soon realized that someone besides Maxwell was in the room and raised his pistol within a foot of Garrett's chest. "Who's that?" he asked in Spanish.

Garrett quickly drew his pistol and fired two shots. The first shot hit McCarty in the chest. "He never spoke," Garrett recalled. "A struggle or two, a little strangling sound as he gasped for breath, and the Kid was with his many victims." McCarty was dead at age 21.

When Garrett and his deputies examined McCarty's revolver, they found that he had five cartridges and one shell on the chamber, with the hammer resting on it. If he had not hesitated, Garrett might have been the one lying dead on the floor. "It was the first time, during all his life of peril, that he ever lost his presence of mind or failed to shoot first," Garrett wrote.

The next day, according to Garrett, a Coroner's jury held an inquest, determined that the dead man was Billy the Kid, and ruled that Garrett's killing of him had been justifiable homicide. The outlaw's body was buried the same day. Garrett noted that the corpse went into the ground fully intact to discredit opportunists exhibiting skulls, fingers, and other body parts that they claimed had belonged to Billy the Kid.

APRIL 10
1919

On this day in history, Mexican revolutionary Emiliano Zapata, a leader of indigenous people and peasants during the Mexican Revolution, was ambushed and murdered in Morelos, Mexico, by government forces. Zapata advocated agrarianism and fought in guerrilla conflicts during the Mexican Revolution. He founded and led the Liberation Army of the South, an influential revolutionary group, and his followers were known as Zapatistas.

Born to Cleofas Jertrudiz Salazar and Gabriel Zapata in Anenecuilco, Morelos, Mexico, on August 8, 1879, Emiliano Zapata was the ninth of ten children. The Zapata's were a well-known local family and reasonably well-off. By the time Emiliano was 17, he was an orphan. A revolutionary from an early age, in 1897, he was arrested for participating in a peasant protest with people from his village against the hacienda (plantation) that had appropriated their lands. Afterward, he was pardoned and continued to cause problems among the peasants, so much so that he was drafted into the Mexican army. After serving six months, he was released to a landowner to train horses in Mexico City. In 1909 his leadership skills were already becoming known, and he was called to his village, Anenecuilco, where he was elected as the village's council board president.

Seen as a man of the people, Zapata became a leading person in his village and became involved in the struggles of the local farmers. The continued theft of village land caused many troubles between the villagers and the landowners. Zapata oversaw the land's return from some haciendas peacefully, but it was a continuing battle. Then, after some unsuccessful discussions, Zapata and a group of peasants seized by force the land that had been taken by the haciendas and dispersed it amongst themselves.

For many years to come, Zapata continued to fight for the rights of the peasants, using ancient title deeds to institute their claims to disputed lands and then pressuring the governor of Morelos to act. Finally, because of the government's slow response and apparent bias towards the landowners, Zapata decided that force was the better solution to the problem. So, they took the contested lands and dispersed them as they saw fit.

Zapata's forces contributed to the fall of dictator Porfirio Diaz (President from 1877 to 1880 and 1884 to 1911), defeating the Federal Army in the Battle of Cuautla in May 1911, yet when the revolutionary leader Francisco I. Madero became president with Zapata's help; he denied the role of the Zapatistas, denouncing them as bandits.

In November 1911, Zapata announced the Plan de Ayala, which called for substantial land reforms, and the redistribution of lands to the peasants. Madero sent the Federal Army to eliminate the Zapatistas in Morelos. Madero's forces were ruthless – they burnt villages. They forcibly removed the villagers and drafted many males into the army, with the rest of the people being sent to forced-labor camps in southern Mexico. These actions only strengthened Zapata's standing amongst the people, so Madero's forces ran out of the area. Victoriano Huerta led a coup against Madero in February 1913, yet a coalition of Constitutionalist forces in Northern Mexico ousted Huerta in July 1914 with the help of Zapata's forces. The alliance was led by Venustiano Carranza, Alvaro Obregon, and Pancho Villa. Zapata did not recognize the authority of Carranza when he asserted himself into a leadership role, continuing his observance of the Plan de Ayala.

In 1914 Mexico descended into civil war. Zapata focused on

rebuilding Morelos, instituting the land reforms of the Plan de Ayala. As Carranza consolidated power and defeated Villa in 1915, Zapata began guerrilla warfare against the Carrancistas, who invaded Morelos, again using a scorched-earth policy to eliminate the Zapatistas. Zapata re-took Morelos in 1917 and held it until he died in 1919.

Removing Zapata from the picture was now the focus of President Carranza. In mid-March 1919, General Pablo Gonzalez ordered his inferior officer Jesus Guajardo to begin attacks against the Zapatistas in the mountains around Huautla. But Gonzalez found Guajardo drinking in a cantina and had him arrested, and a public scandal began. On March 21, Zapata tried to sneak in a note inviting Guajardo to join his forces. The message, however, only reached Gonzalez, who planned to use this note to his advantage. After telling Guajardo that his only path to salvation was if he pretended to defect to Zapata's side, Gonzalez put the plan in motion. Guajardo wrote to Zapata that he would bring his men and supplies over if certain circumstances were met. Zapata replied on April 1, 1919, agreeing to Guajardo's terms. After some debate, the men decided that April 10 would be the day for the mutiny. Zapata instructed Guajardo to attack the Federal garrison at Jonacatepec because the garrison consisted of troops who had defected from Zapata. Gonzalez and Guajardo pre-warned the Jonacatepec garrison ahead of time, and a simulated battle was staged on April 9. At the end of the simulated battle, the former Zapatistas were arrested and gunned down. Believing that Guajardo was sincere, Zapata agreed to a final meeting where Guajardo would defect.

On April 10, 1919, Guajardo asked Zapata to attend a meeting, indicating that he intended to defect to the Zapatistas. However, when Zapata approached the Hacienda de San Juan in Chinameca, Ayala municipality, Guajardo's men ambushed him.

Zapata's dead body was photographed, displayed for 24 hours, and then buried in Cuautla. Pablo Gonzalez wanted the body photographed to prove that Zapata was finally dead: "it was an actual fact that the famous *jefe* of the southern region had died."

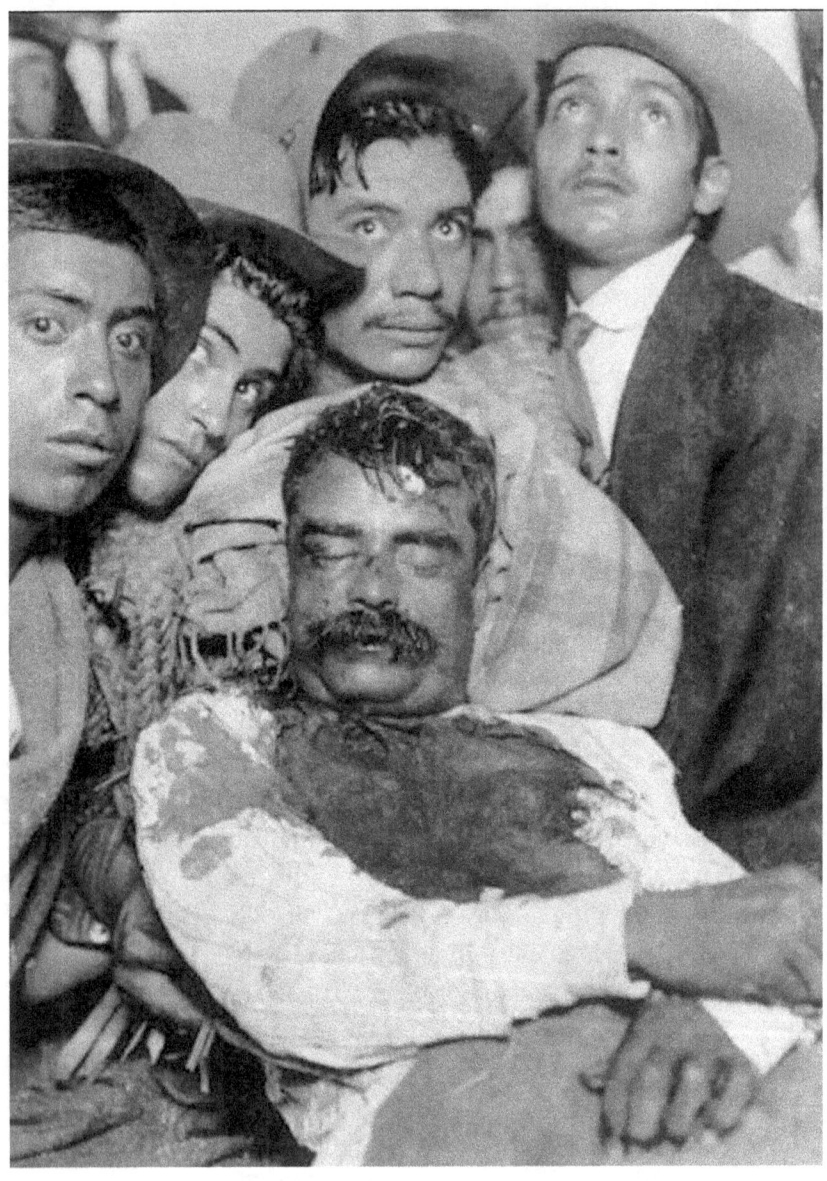

(Photo: Rebel Emiliano Zapata surrounded by his comrades after being killed by Mexican government agents in the town of Cuautla, Morelos, Mexico. April 10, 1919. Wikimedia Commons.)

APRIL 11
1945

On this day in history, the American Third Army liberated the Buchenwald concentration camp. This facility will be deemed second only to Auschwitz in the terrors it inflicted on its prisoners. Between 1933 and 1945, Nazi Germany established more than 44,000 camps and other imprisonment sites (including ghettos). The perpetrators used these locations for various purposes, including forced labor, detention of people deemed "enemies of the state," and mass murder. Millions of people died or were killed. One of these sites was the Buchenwald camp near Weimar, Germany.

The Buchenwald concentration camp was built in 1937, five miles from Weimar in East Germany. It was situated on the northern slopes of the Ettersberg, a hill located north of the city. With its numerous satellite camps, Buchenwald was amongst the largest concentration camps established in Germany in 1937. Along with its usual array of buildings expected in such a site (i.e., barracks, infirmary, kitchen, etc.), Buchenwald also contained 136 subcamps and eventually included a brothel, railway station, and crematorium. SS guard barracks and the camp administration building were in the southern part of the camp.

The camp was open to male prisoners only. Females were not part of the Buchenwald camp system until 1943. In 1944, Buchenwald took over subcamps from the Ravensbruck concentration camp, which primarily imprisoned women. Most of the early prisoners at Buchenwald were political prisoners arrested for political opposition to the Nazi regime. In 1938, in the aftermath of Kristallnacht, the German SS and police ordered almost 10,000 Jews to Buchenwald. They were treated extremely poor when they first arrived, with over 250 dying from injuries incurred during their arrest. Once the war began, large numbers of Polish and Soviet POWs and resistance fighters from many parts of Europe swelled the ranks of Buchenwald.

Beginning in 1941, several physicians and scientists carried out a program of medical experimentation on inmates at the camp. Medical tests assessed the success of treatments and vaccines against contagious diseases, such as typhus, typhoid, cholera, and diphtheria. They resulted in hundreds of deaths. Many prisoners were used as slave laborers for both state-owned and private companies. They were distributed through the system of subcamps as needed. Periodically, the SS physicians conducted selections throughout the Buchenwald camp system and dispatched those too weak or disabled to work to so-called euthanasia facilities such as Sonnenstein. At these facilities, euthanasia workers gassed them as part of Operation 14f13, the extension of euthanasia killing procedures to ill and exhausted prisoners. SS doctors or orderlies used phenol injections to kill other inmates unable to work.

A colossal evacuation endeavor by the SS preceded the arrival of the Americans on April 11, 1945. It is reported that upwards of 28,000 inmates were taken by train from Buchenwald to Flossenburg, Dachau, and Theresienstadt. They left behind 21,000 prisoners. Listening to covert radio reports, the inmates knew the Americans were close. When the last SS left on the morning of the 11th, the prisoners issued weapons long concealed from the Germans (including rifles, machine guns, and hand grenades) and took command of the watchtowers. A white flag was hoisted. In the neighboring woods, inmates, now armed, seized more than 70 SS men.

As American forces closed in on Buchenwald, Gestapo headquarters in Weimar telephoned the camp administration to declare that it was sending explosives to blow up any indication of the camp – including the prisoners. The Gestapo was unaware that the SS had already fled in fear of the Americans. A prisoner answered the telephone and notified the Germans that explosives would not be needed, as the camp had already been blown up, which was not true.

The Allies liberated Buchenwald on April 11, 1945, one day before the death of American President Franklin Roosevelt. When they secured the camp, the Americans could see and understand the extreme horrors the Nazis had perpetrated at this place. They found the block for medical experiments in all its gory detail. From the inmates, they pinpointed the scattered sites for execution and photographed the six ovens in the camp's crematorium, with human remains still present. The enormous tasks of detailing and conveying the horrors of Buchenwald had only just begun for American investigators. General Dwight D. Eisenhower stated, after he inspected the camp, "We are told that the American soldier does not know what he is fighting for. Now, at least, he will know what he is fighting against."

Acclaimed CBS journalist Edward R. Murrow was one of those who visited the camp directly after its emancipation, arriving on April 12. Three days later, in a broadcast to American audiences, he described what he saw and warned those listening about the graphic content he was about to relate to them. Once he entered Buchenwald, the former prisoners crowded around him and praised President Franklin Roosevelt. Murrow told them that this touched him greatly since, unknown to those liberated, the president had died that very day. Murrow walked into a barracks, once a stable, filled with men. They wanted to lift him onto their shoulders to show their gratitude, but they were too weak to do so. Many remained bedridden. Before leaving, he counted the names of 242 men who had died in the barracks in the previous month.

In the yard, Murrow saw weak men crawling to the lavatory and children displaying the numbers tattooed on their arms. In the infirmary, he learned that more than 200 had died from illness or starvation the day before. The most significant shock he experienced was the confrontation with "two rows of bodies stacked like cordwood." Murrow estimated there were 500 corpses piled there. Murrow begged his listeners: "I pray you to believe what I have said about Buchenwald. I have reported what I saw and heard but only part of it. For most of it, I have no words."

APRIL 12
1917

On this day in history, after three days of fierce combat and over 10,600 casualties, the Canadian Corps seized the previously German-held Vimy Ridge during the Nivelle Offensive in Northern France on April 12, 1917.

The Battle of Vimy Ridge was fought from April 9 to 12. It is Canada's most famous military victory – an often-mythologized symbol of the birth of Canadian national pride and recognition. The battle happened on the Western Front in northern France. The four divisions of the Canadian Corps, battling together for the first time, attacked the ridge and wrested it away from the German army. It was the most significant territorial progress of any Allied force to that point in the war – but it would mean little to the outcome of the offensive or the conflict. Many historians and writers have pointed to the victory at Vimy Ridge as a moment of excellence for Canada when it arose from Britain's shadow to achieve its own measure of military accomplishment. As a result of the victory, earned despite the larger Allied offensive's failure, Canadian forces earned a reputation for effectiveness and strength on the battlefield.

The Allied offensive – the brainchild of French commander-in-chief

Robert Nivelle – began Easter Monday, April 9, 1917, as the British and Canadian armies launched concurrent attacks on German locations at Arras and Vimy Ridge, a strongly fortified, seven-kilometer-long raised piece of land with a sweeping view of the Allied lines. The Allies' first day was highly successful, as the British punched through the Hindenburg Line – the defensive positions to which Germany had withdrawn in February 1917 – and overran sections of two German trench lines within a couple of hours, taking 5,600 prisoners.

The Canadians, attacking throughout land scattered with the corpses of 100,000 dead French soldiers from earlier assaults on the same location, also moved rapidly in the first hours of the attack, as four Canadian divisions attacked the ridge at 5:30 a.m. on April 9, moving ahead under the protection of a severe artillery bombardment that forced the Germans to hide in a place in their trenches and away from their machine guns. Over 15,000 Canadian infantry soldiers attacked Vimy Ridge that day, invading the German positions and taking 4,000 prisoners.

Three more days of brutal struggle ended in triumph on April 12, when control of Vimy Ridge belonged to Canadians. Though the Nivelle Offensive failed wretchedly, the Canadian operation had proved a success, although a costly one: 3,598 Canadian soldiers were killed, and over 7,000 were wounded.

Vimy Ridge became a magnificent example of Canada's effort in the Great War and symbolized the sacrifice Canadians had made for the Allied war effort. As Brigadier-General A.E. Ross stated after the war, in those few minutes, "I witnessed the birth of a nation."

In recent years, a new group of historians has begun to examine the revered stature of the battle, telling Canadians that Vimy's reputation has been mainly the result of nationalistic mythmaking.

Vimy was a gratifying moment for Canada and a remarkable military accomplishment. Yet the battle was tactically inconsequential to the outcome of the war. The French offensive of 1917 (which Vimy was intended as a strategic distraction) failed. No sustained Allied breakthrough also followed either the assault on the ridge or the broader Battle of Arras, of which Vimy was a part. As historian Andrew Godefroy writes in Vimy Ridge, a Canadian Reassessment: "To the German army, the loss of a few kilometers of vital ground meant little in the grand scheme of things."

The Great War would continue for another 19 months after Vimy Ridge, taking the lives of many Canadians who had endured and succeeded there. Other Canadian battles, such as Hill 70 in August 1917, were equally astonishing displays of courage and strength. Meanwhile, Canada's victories in 1918 at Amiens and Cambrai had far more impact on the war's course. But these events are less well known than Vimy Ridge or celebrated with as much passion.

Most notably, Vimy was more than just a Canadian achievement. General Julian Byng was a British officer, as were numerous other officers in the Corps. And while a significant portion of the infantry that attacked the ridge was Canadian, they could do so with the British artillery, engineers, and supply units that aided them. Britain and Canada fought together at Vimy Ridge – yet somehow, Vimy gained a reputation as the place where Canadians began standing apart from the British Empire.

In 1922, the French government relinquished to Canada in perpetuity Vimy Ridge and the surrounding land. The sparkling white marble and poignant sculptures of the Vimy Memorial unveiled in 1936, stand as a horrific and emotional reminder of the 11,285 Canadian soldiers killed in France with no known graves.

(Photo: The Vimy Memorial overlooks the Douai Plain from the highest point of Vimy Ridge, about eight kilometres northeast of Arras on the N17 towards Lens. The memorial was designed by W.S. Allward. It was unveiled by King Edward VIII on 26 July 1936. Wikimedia Commons.

APRIL 13
1861

On this day in history, after a 34-hour barrage by Confederate cannons, Union forces relinquish Fort Sumter in South Carolina's Charleston Harbor. The first engagement of the war was over, and the only casualty had been a rebel horse. The Union force was allowed to leave for the north; before leaving the fort, the soldiers fired a 100-gun salute. During the salute, two soldiers died, and four were injured when the troops fired a prematurely exploding cartridge. The first battle of the Civil War ended in a Confederate victory.

During the secession crisis that followed President Abraham Lincoln's election in November 1860, many threats were made against Federal troops occupying forts in the American South. Major Robert Anderson, in command of Fort Moultrie in Charleston Harbor, began asking the War Department for reinforcements and supplies and permission to move to one of the more defensible forts in the harbor – either Castle Pinckney or Fort Sumter.

After South Carolina's secession on December 20, 1860, Governor Francis Pickens was compelled to do something about Major Anderson and his force since many assumed they would not stay at Fort Moultrie. Pickens sent an envoy to Washington on December 24, intending to have Anderson stay put. However, on December 26, Anderson and his men moved by boat to Fort Sumter. A siege of Fort Sumter resulted, with supplies and communication controlled by Pickens.

On January 9, 1861, supplies and 200 soldiers were dispatched from New York to help relieve the force at Fort Sumter. Confederate defenses in the harbor fired upon the American ship, thus preventing the aid from getting to Anderson and his men. Anderson was under direct orders to only fire in defense, so he could only watch as the ship was turned back.

Shortly after, on January 11, Pickens demanded the surrender of Fort Sumter. Anderson refused. By January 20, the food shortage at Fort Sumter was such that moderates in Charleston forced Governor Pickens to supply food to Anderson. Shortly after, Pickens allowed the evacuation of 45 women and children to provide some relief.

On March 1, Jefferson Davis appointed Brigadier General P.G.T. Beauregard to head the military situation for the Confederacy in the Charleston area. He immediately started to strengthen harbor defenses and gun emplacements facing Fort Sumter.

After his inauguration on March 4, 1861, Lincoln dispatched unofficial emissaries to observe the situation in Charleston and to report back to him while he negotiated with Confederate officials in Washington. Lincoln knew that Anderson was low on supplies and informed him on April 3 of a relief expedition coming his way shortly. The Lincoln administration had decided to let the Southerners decide whether to start the war by firing on the relief ship or Fort Sumter because they had no intention of relinquishing the fort.

Beauregard was aware of the relief expedition and was ordered to fire upon it. He was also instructed to demand the fort's surrender and to fire upon it should they refuse. Beauregard started to move men and artillery into place, and he sent an envoy to the fort on April 11 to demand surrender. Anderson polled his men, and they once again refused to surrender. After the refusal, Beauregard was asked to assess how long it would be before the Fort would run out of food and be forced to surrender, so just after midnight on April 12, the envoys arrived back at the fort. Hoping the relief expedition would come before then, Anderson said he would surrender on April 15. He was told that this was unacceptable and that the Confederates would begin to fire at 4:30 a.m.

To reduce his casualties and conserve ammunition, Anderson returned fire at 7:00 a.m. Anderson also tried to minimize losses by only using the guns from his lower casemates, where his men would be less exposed. Later that morning, the barracks caught fire, and many of his men had to be used as a fire crew. In the afternoon, they spotted three vessels flying the U.S. flag just outside the harbor, and they thought that they would be resupplied that night, not realizing that those ships were on their way to Fort Pickens in Pensacola, Florida.

As night fell, Anderson ceased firing, and the Confederates reduced their fire but resumed it the following day. On April 13, the barracks again caught fire and threatened the ammunition store, despite it being a rainy day. At about 1 p.m., the flagstaff was shot down, and the flag was raised on the ramparts on a makeshift staff. On seeing the flag shot away, Colonel Louis Wigfall – aide to Beauregard, fire-eater, and former U.S. senator - rowed out to Fort Sumter on his initiative, without knowledge or approval of Beauregard, amid the continuing barrage to see if Anderson was attempting to surrender. Although initially told that he was not surrendering, Wigfall was able to negotiate a surrender. At 1:30 p.m., the flag was replaced with a white sheet. On seeing the flag of surrender, Beauregard stopped firing and sent his representatives to the fort, where they learned of Wigfall's unofficial mission. After further negotiation, the same terms were agreed to; surrender would occur on April 14 at noon.

The people of Charleston came out in boats on April 14 to watch the surrender and evacuation. As part of the surrender terms, Anderson had received permission to fire a 100-gun salute while lowering the American flag before leaving. Halfway through, one of the guns discharged prematurely, killing two soldiers and wounding four others. The remaining American soldiers were taken by boat to the relief ships outside the harbor. On April 15, 1861, President Abraham Lincoln requested 75,000 volunteers to suppress the Southern rebellion. The Civil War had begun.

APRIL 14
1936

On this day in history, French singer Edith Piaf is questioned by Paris police in the mob death of nightclub owner and her patron Louis Leplee. In 1935, Piaf was noticed in the Pigalle area of Paris by Louis Leplee, whose club *Le Gerny's* off the Champs-Elysees was frequented by the upper and lower classes alike. He persuaded Edith to sing despite her substantial nervousness, which, in combination with her height of only 142 centimeters (4 ft 8 in), inspired him to give her the nickname *La Mome Piaf* or "The Little Sparrow," which would also serve as her stage name and remain with her the rest of her life.

Edith Piaf was born Edith Giovanna Gassion on December 19, 1915, in Belleville, Paris, France. Much of her past is unknown and may have been exaggerated during her time as a celebrity. She is believed to have been named after the British nurse and spy Edith Cavell, who was executed for helping Belgian soldiers escape their German captors. Her mother, Annetta Giovanna Maillard, was a café singer of Moroccan Berber descent who appeared on stage under the name "Line Marsa." Piaf's father, Louis-Alphonse Gassion, was an immensely proficient street acrobat.

Annetta had deserted Piaf and was sent to reside with her maternal grandmother, where she grew malnourished. She was taken from that situation by her father and placed with her paternal grandmother, who ran a brothel. Piaf suffered considerably from impaired vision due to meningitis until she was seven years old. Even at this young age, she became known for her vocal talents. At this age, she joined her father and a circus caravan traveling Belgium, in time, joining street performances all over France.

Piaf later left her father, who was often a temperamental and abusive taskmaster, and she set out on her own as a street singer in and around Paris. At the age of 17, she and a young man named Louis Dupont gave birth to a daughter, Marcelle, who would die of meningitis at 2 years old.

As the story goes, Louis Leplee discovered Piaf on a Paris street corner in 1935. He instantly recognized her soul-baring brilliance, signed her up, and prepared for her unveiling to the luminous Parisian underworld. Leplee was considered the prince of the Montmartre homosexual subculture of the 1930s. His cabaret Le Gerny's in Pigalle was a renowned hotbed of gay prostitution, blackmail, and bribery. Piaf received advice in the Literary arts from French poet/historian Jacques Bourgeat. Leplee ran an effective publicity campaign advertising Piaf's opening night, which was patronized by the likes of Maurice Chevalier. The bandleader that evening was Django Reinhardt, with his pianist, Norbert Glanzberg. She was popular enough to record two albums that same year, with one penned by Marguerite Monnot, a collaborator throughout Piaf's life and one of her favorite composers.

On the morning of April 6, 1936, Leplee was murdered in his apartment. Official dossiers from the time describe a statement from his housekeeper who claimed that in the middle of the night, four men forced their way into the apartment by sheer force and shot Leplee while he slept. The men then ransacked the apartment, apparently looking for the 20,000 francs that were supposed to be there but failed to find them.

In the following days, the police scoured Le Genry's, looking for clues, and in the meantime, they arrested Piaf. The press was close by at the time, and they photographed her seizure. Piaf had ascended to lofty heights of fame in a mere year, but it was now in jeopardy of disappearing all because of her arrest.

Edith Piaf was endlessly questioned by the police and accused of being an accessory to murder. Leplee had been killed by mobsters with ties to Piaf, and the police believed they had acted under her command. There was no evidence to support this theory, and the star was acquitted, but not before her name had been drawn through the mud. One Parisian publication, Police Magazine, issue #282, published on April 19, 1936, ran the sarcastically scathing headline, "The little sparrow, in her repertoire of street songs with her gestures of a little girl beaten, a pale kid who rose up from the cobblestones," along with a picture of her being marched along by the police. The scuff-kneed sincerity of her dignified performance was now publicly being jeered as an ironic act.

With her career in disarray, she recruited the famed French lyricist Raymond Asso to help restore her image. He changed her stage name to "Edith Piaf," barred undesirable acquaintances from seeing her. He commissioned Marguerite Monnot to write songs that reflected or alluded to Piaf's previous life on the streets in a proclamation of defiance.

Edith Piaf may have had no part in the regrettable murder of Louis Leplee, which remains unsolved to this day, but it proved to be a pivotal moment in her career. Her life was continually met with suffering and hardship, which she bore with a shrug of hard-fought resilience and used the power of performance to transfigure into the absolved beauty of music.

Piaf's career and fame gained momentum during the German conquest of France during World War II. She sang concerts for Germans in Paris and Berlin, and she could afford a luxury flat in a house in the fancy 16th arrondissement of Paris. After the Liberation, she was deemed to be a traitor and collaborator. Had it not been for her secretary, Andree Bigard, a member of the Resistance, who spoke up on her behalf, her life, and career would have ended there. Bigard related how Piaf sang for Allied POWS during the war and helped various Jews to hide and escape. Because of this, Piaf's career could continue to climb.

In April 1963, Piaf recorded her last song. With a bevy of health concerns over the years, Edith Piaf died of liver failure on October 10, 1963. She was 47. She is buried in Pere Lachaise Cemetery in Paris beside her daughter Marcelle.

APRIL 15
1947

On this day in history, Jackie Robinson, at the age of 28, became the first African American player during Major League Baseball's modern era when he strides onto Ebbets Field in Brooklyn, New York, to play for the Brooklyn Dodgers. Robinson shattered the color barrier in baseball, which was segregated for over 60 years. Fifty years later, on April 15, 1997, Robinson's innovative career was revered, and his jersey number, 42, was retired from use in Major League Baseball by the Commissioner of the league during a ceremony watched by over 50,000 fans in New York City's Shea Stadium. Robinson's was the first number retired by all teams in the league.

Jackie Robinson was born on January 31, 1919, in Cairo, Georgia, as the youngest of five children to two sharecroppers. His parents had a terrible marriage that ended when his father deserted the family for another woman when Jackie was still only a baby. This left his mother, Mallie, to raise the five children independently. So, the following year, she moved the family by train to Pasadena, California, where her brother lived, and she could work as a maid. Despite her hard work and even taking on various side gigs, the family still lived in poverty.

There were no other black families living in their relatively wealthy neighborhood, and, as a result, Jackie experienced racism early in his life. Both because of the color of his skin and because the family did not have much money, he often did not fit in with many of the other kids in his school and was often excluded from activities with his fellow students.

That would change when Jackie registered at John Muir High School in 1935. His older brother Mack, a silver medallist in track and field at the 1936 Berlin Olympic Games, motivated him to chase his interest in sports. Jackie eventually received varsity letters in baseball, basketball, football, and track and field while at Muir.

After the death of another older brother, Frank, in a motorcycle accident, Jackie decided to honor his memory by enrolling at UCLA in 1939. Once again, he earned four varsity letters and was victorious in the NCAA long jump championship in 1940. Jackie also met his future wife, Rachel, while at UCLA. Due to financial distress, Jackie eventually had to leave UCLA in his senior year. He would spend two years playing semi-pro football for integrated teams in leagues in Hawaii and Los Angeles before being drafted into the U.S. Army in 1942, during World War II.

He entered the army as a lieutenant in a segregated unit, first in Kansas and then in Texas. He never served overseas. In 1944, while at Fort Hood in Texas, he was nearly court-martialled when he refused instructions by an army bus driver to get to the back of the bus due to his color. He was acquitted of the charges, but the whole affair had a profound and lasting effect on Jackie, and the proceedings likely shaped his response to the racist taunts he received a few years later from fans and fellow players at the beginning of his professional baseball career. Jackie was honorably discharged from the Army in November 1944.

In early 1945, Jackie was signed by the Negro Leagues team, the Kansas City Monarchs, where he starred for one season, hitting .387. At the time, Brooklyn Dodgers executive Branch Rickey was scouting the Negro Leagues, looking for players who not only had the talent but the disposition to withstand the pressures associated with integrating Major League Baseball. Robinson was one of several players Rickey interviewed in August for assignment to the Dodgers' farm team in Montreal, the Royals.

Once Robinson agreed to "turn the other cheek" to racial abuse, he was assigned to the Royals for the 1946 season. During that season, he was embraced by the Montreal fans, and he batted an impressive .349. His performance on and off the field earned him a call-up to Brooklyn the following season.

His debut with the Dodgers in 1947 garnered a great deal of attention – both good and bad. Robinson promptly showed that he deserved to be there as a player; the color of his skin was an issue for opposing teams and fans.

It was his play in the field that ultimately silenced his critics. In 1947, his first year with the Dodgers, he earned the "Rookie of the Year" award. Despite being signed to the team at 28, Robinson would bat .311 over a 10-year career. He became the first Black player to win the National League Most Valuable Player Award in 1949, when he outclassed the rest of the league in hitting with a .342 average, most stolen bases (37), and achieving a career-high 124 RBI. Robinson was an All-Star every year from 1949-1954. He led Brooklyn to a World Series championship over the rival Yankees in 1955.

Robinson retired after that season and did not follow the Dodgers when the club moved to Los Angeles following the 1957 campaign.

After retiring from the Dodgers, Jackie acted as a sportscaster, worked as a business executive at Chock Full o'Nuts, and was active in the NAACP and other civil rights groups.

Weakened by heart disease and diabetes, Robinson died in 1972 at 53 from a heart attack suffered at his home in Stamford, Connecticut. Thousands of people attended his funeral, including former teammates and other professional athletes. His eulogy was delivered by the Reverend Jesse Jackson, who declared, "When Jackie took the field, something reminded us of our birthright to be free."

APRIL 16
1457 BCE

On this day in history, Egyptian forces under the command of Pharaoh Thutmose III defeated a large, fractious alliance of Canaanite vassal states led by the King of Kadesh at the Battle of Megiddo. It is the first battle for which we have a clear historical record in relatively reliable detail. The Battle of Megiddo is also where the first recorded use of composite bows and the first body count is noted. All facts of the battle derive from Egyptian sources – principally the hieroglyphic texts on the Hall of Annals in the Temple of Amum-Re at Karnak, Thebes (now Luxor), by the military scribe Tjaneni.

The Egyptians trounced the Canaanite forces, which escaped to shelter in the city of Megiddo. Their action caused the seven-month prolonged Siege of Megiddo. By re-establishing Egyptian supremacy in the Levant – the area of the eastern Mediterranean and the Northern Middle East, including present-day Israel, Jordan, Lebanon, Palestine, Syria, and most of Turkey southwest of the middle Euphrates – Thutmose III began a reign in which the Egyptian Empire touched its most significant area.

Thutmose III ascended to the throne at a time when Egypt had authority over vast areas of the Levant. Early in his reign, he faced a revolt in this area, based around Modern Syria. The King of Kadesh led the rebellion, whose home city possessed a strong fortress that gave him a protected base. The Canaanites, Mitanni, and Amurru joined his renegade coalition, as did the King of Megiddo, another ruler with a strong fortress base. Megiddo was tactically crucial. It controlled the main trade route between Mesopotamia and Egypt, now known as the Via Maris. The renegade armies assembled there.

Like most ancient rulers, Thutmose III took personal control of his army. He assembled forces of between ten and twenty thousand men, comprising infantry and charioteers, at the border fortress of Tjaru. At the center of Pharaoh's army were the most lethal weapons of their day. This was the heyday of chariot warfare. Horses had yet to be bred strong enough to transport an armed soldier, making chariots the only way to move around the battlefield. The recently created composite bow gave chariot riders a lethal weapon to attack the enemy before escaping. Iron weapons, which would negate the chariot's use, had yet to be developed.

The Pharaoh decided not to wait for the King of Kadesh and his army to advance towards Egypt but to leave Tjaru and attack them on their own ground, besieging Megiddo 300 kilometers away. To get there meant crossing the deserts of Sinai and Gaza, so it was necessary to carry sufficient supplies and water to provision his army. Within three weeks, Thutmose and his army traveled over 250 kilometers and reached Yehem, the last stop before Megiddo.

There are three possible routes to Megiddo. The north and south route allow easy access but are longer, while the third through the narrow confines of the Aruna Mountain pass (Wadi Ara), shorter and faster than the others but far more dangerous, as they would have to cross a narrow pass where his army would be forced to walk single file and would be easy prey for an ambush from the heights. Of course, he would have to dismount the wagons and carry them on the backs of the horses.

Against the opinion of his officers, Thutmose III decides on the Aruna Mountain pass route since he intends to reach Megiddo as soon as possible and take the enemy by surprise. The Egyptian army successfully gets through the mountain pass and camps south of

Megiddo. The next day, Thutmose III and his army cross the Kina River and deploy in a concave fashion in three groups west of the city.

The two armies go into battle, the Egyptians with their young Pharaoh at the front, aboard their golden chariot that leads the central part of the front of his army. At the same time, the rest of his force takes on a concave shape that extends along the sides towards the enemy threatening to surround them. The strategy of the Pharaoh and the thrust of the Egyptians driven by their leader overcome the resistance of the men from Kadesh, who break formation and retreat in disorder towards Megiddo. If Thutmose's men had continued the attack, the battle would have ended with the city's capture. Still, instead, they stopped to plunder the rebel camp and the rebel bodies since it was the only way for an ordinary soldier to get rich, losing the opportunity to take advantage of the disorder of the rebels to capture them, giving them time to retreat towards the city, climbing up ropes of made of clothing lowered by people inside the walls. Those who made it to safety comprised the kings of Megiddo and Kadesh. The Pharaoh was enraged at the sight of this scene, but nothing could be done except to berate his generals, who had been unable to control their men.

A siege immediately followed the Battle of Megiddo. Pharaoh and his army excavated a moat and constructed their own defensive wall around the city. After seven months of slow starvation, the city eventually surrendered. The King of Kadesh escaped, but the rest of those in the city were captured and spared by a merciful Pharaoh.

As well as 200 suits of armor and 924 chariots, the victors took home over 2,000 horses, 340 prisoners, nearly 25,000 cattle and sheep, and the royal war gear of the King of Megiddo.

More importantly, the victory at Megiddo enabled the Egyptians to conquer other cities in the region, securing them once more for the Egyptian Empire.

APRIL 17
1942

On this day in history, 61-year-old French General Henri Giraud, who was captured by the Nazis in 1940, escapes from a castle prison at Konigstein, near Dresden, Germany, by lowering himself 150 feet using a makeshift rope down the castle wall. He met up with an agent of the British Special Operations Executive, who furnished him with Id papers, currency, and a map, and he then headed by train to Switzerland with the Germans hot on his trail.

Enraged by such a deed, Hitler decreed that Giraud be assassinated upon being captured. Still, the French general eventually reached North Africa via a British submarine. He joined the French Free Forces under General Charles De Gaulle and ultimately helped to rebuild the French Army.

Giraud made a habit of escaping German captivity in war. During World War I, Giraud was critically wounded while leading a bayonet charge by his unit, the 4th Zouaves, during the Battle of St. Quentin on August 30, 1914, and was left for dead on the field. He was imprisoned by the Germans and put in a pow camp in Belgium. He escaped two months later by feigning to be a roustabout with a traveling circus. He then requested that nurse Edith Cavell help him, and ultimately, he could return to France via the Netherlands with the aid of Cavell's team. His effort earned him an appointment as a knight of the Legion of Honor on April 10, 1915. The result was that from February 26, 1915, he was reappointed as a staff officer. Afterward, Giraud served with French soldiers in Istanbul under General Franchet d'Esperey.

When World War II started, Giraud was a member of the Superior War Council and argued with Charles De Gaulle about using armored soldiers. He subsequently became the commander of the 7th Army when it was ordered to the Netherlands on May 10, 1940, and was able to delay German troops at Breda on May 13. Then the diminished 7th Army was combined with the 9th Army. While trying to prevent a German attack through the Ardennes Forest, he was at the front with a reconnaissance patrol when German soldiers apprehended him at Wassigny on May 19. A court-martial tried Giraud for ordering the killing of two German saboteurs wearing civilian clothes. Still, he was acquitted and taken to Konigstein Castle near the Czech border, which was used as a high-security POW prison.

General Giraud's escape during World War I had not been overlooked by the Germans. Due to his elevated rank, he was to be treated with the utmost respect, but they prioritized putting him in a high-security, "escape-proof" location. Konigstein was the perfect location to stop an escape; it was located beside a 150-foot-high cliff, and every exit was guarded. Regular inside inspections were made; if someone were missing, the Gestapo would be on the case instantly.

Of course, Giraud began to plot his escape as soon as he arrived at the castle. At the age of 61, he was not a spry young man anymore, and the injuries he sustained in World War I left him with a permanent limp. Despite this, Giraud refused to guarantee the Germans that he would not try to escape. He learned to speak German fluently, memorized the map of the surrounding area, and even set up communication with friends back in France, from which he obtained copper materials for a rope.

Giraud was ready on the morning of April 17, 1942, after two years of incarceration in the castle. He shaved off his mustache and readied himself for descending the 150-foot cliff with the rope he had fashioned out of copper, rope, and clothing. When he reached the bottom of the cliff, he got rid of his general's coat, put on a rain jacket, and put on a Tyrolean hat. He met a British agent of the Special Operations Executive who gave him a map, an Id, and some local currency and pointed him toward the local train station.

Giraud had a few close calls after riding the train rails in Germany. On one train, Giraud was sitting across from a German lieutenant who had served in the Afrika Korps; he struck up a friendly conversation. A Gestapo soldier came around and asked for the men's ID. The lieutenant upset at the intrusion, shouted, "How dare you interrupt us!" and told the man to leave. The Gestapo security was particularly tight at one train station, and they were thoroughly searching every passenger. He could not risk it. So, Giraud waited until the train began to leave the station. With a briefcase in his hand and his hat on his head, Giraud started running towards the train without limping. The pain was horrible, but he was not about to give himself away. A Gestapo soldier, fooled completely into thinking he was simply an irritated businessman in a hurry, helped him aboard.

Giraud tried to reach France, but the security was too tight. He then decided to go to Switzerland, where he got off the train near the border and walked across. There he was captured. But luckily for him, they were Swiss soldiers. The Germans were angry to hear that the Swiss had taken him in, but their demands that he be turned over were ignored.

Finally, Giraud made one last great attempt to get back to France. This time he went by road, and after changing vehicles a few times while driving through Switzerland, he managed to throw off the Germans. Giraud had successfully managed to pull off a second escape from the Germans.

Henri Giraud's escape inspired France to make it through one of the darkest periods in its history. Such was the effect that the Germans even tried to assassinate Giraud, forcing him into hiding.

When Giraud returned to France, he telegraphed his wife: "Business concluded excellent health affectionately, Henri." It was an exact replica, word for word, of the telegram he had sent her after his escape during World War I.

APRIL 18
1906

On this day in history, at 5:12 a.m., an earthquake estimated at close to 8.0 on the Richter scale hits San Francisco, California, killing nearly 3,000 people as it destroys over 28,000 structures – with 500 city blocks demolished. The quake fractured the San Andreas fault to the north and south of the city for 296 miles and could be felt from Oregon to Los Angeles and inland to Nevada. The earthquake, with its epicenter offshore of San Francisco, which then had a population of 400,000, lasted only 42 seconds, but the damage was apparent almost immediately. Buildings had crumbled, gas mains had ruptured, and severe road cracks had appeared. But the devastation was far from over. Shortly after the ground stopped shaking, many fires started throughout the city – destroying many structures that had survived the earthquake.

One survivor recalled, "There were a lot of people praying on the street… thinking that the end of the world was here." Another remembered, "I asked a man standing next to me what happened. Before he could answer, a thousand bricks fell on him, and he was killed."

While there's no question that the earthquake itself caused massive damage, it's believed that the fires that came afterward caused the worst damage. Many of the early flames sprang up from the ruptured gas lines during the earthquake. But since many water pipes had also broken, firefighters struggled to extinguish flames. Telephone and telegraph communication was severed, and a frightened herd of cattle stampeded through the streets. Steel-framed buildings withstood the earthquake reasonably well, but with most of the city's structures made of wood or brick, they crumbled with relative ease, particularly in low-lying coastal areas. Even the newly constructed City Hall's majestic bronze dome came tumbling down. "The noise and the dust, and the feeling of destruction, all combined to daze a man," a policeman would later remember. "All about us, houses were tumbling and falling walls and chimneys and cornices were crushing men and horses in the street."

Meanwhile, in California, Santa Rosa's downtown and Stanford University suffered near-complete destruction; a train rolled over in Point Reyes, a lighthouse in Point Arena was critically damaged beyond repair, and over 100 patients died when an insane asylum disintegrated near San Jose.

The earthquake, regrettably, was only the start. Fallen wood, coal stoves, and damaged gas lines and chimneys started fires throughout the city. At around 10:30 a.m., for example, a woman on Hayes Street attempted to cook breakfast but did not realize that her flue had been disabled. Her wall quickly set fire, and the flames spread to other structures. Eventually, this so-called ham-and-eggs fire would consume City Hall, including most civic records, tens of thousands of books, and a large stadium that had become a temporary hospital. Numerous fires, some set by arsonists hoping to collect insurance money, destroyed newspaper row, the Grand Opera House, libraries, art galleries, hotels, banks, religious institutions, and department stores. Most suburban neighborhoods burnt to the ground, from the stately mansions on Nob Hill to the tenements south of Market Street. Firefighters did the best they could with no water. Instead, they tried to create firewalls by blowing up houses with dynamite, starting more fires than they stopped. To make things even worse, the city's fire chief, whose previous pleas to enhance the city's firefighting capabilities fell on deaf ears, was mortally wounded early in the day, leaving the department leaderless.

San Francisco's Mayor Eugene Schmitz, a former musician who would soon be charged with corruption, only created more chaos when he proclaimed that all looters would be shot on sight. Eventually, federal troops put the city on a lockdown like martial law. Reports of their conduct vary. Though many soldiers helped wonderfully with relief and firefighting efforts, others went on a killing spree, driven in part by liquor stolen from saloons they were supposed to be closing. Their supposed victims included a Red Cross official, an old woman who refused to turn down a lamp, and a deaf fireman who unintentionally disobeyed a directive. Despite their orders, the soldiers additionally disregarded looting in Chinatown – and at times joined in the looting themselves – provoking the Chinese consul general in San Francisco to criticize that "the National Guard was stripping everything of value."

When the fires were finally put out four days after the earthquake, 28,000 buildings had been destroyed, and over half the city's population was homeless. "Not in history has a modern imperial city been so completely destroyed," author Jack London wrote in the aftermath of the disaster. "San Francisco is gone. Nothing remains of it but memories and a fringe of dwelling houses on its outskirts. Its industrial section is wiped out. Its business section is wiped out. Its social and residential section is wiped out." City officials initially estimated the death toll at 664. But researchers later stated that the death toll was 3,000. Of U.S. natural disasters, only the 1900 Galveston, Texas, hurricane, and the 1928 Okeechobee hurricane in Florida are thought to have taken more lives than the San Francisco earthquake.

(Photo: San Francisco Earthquake of 1906: Ruins in vicinity of Post and Grant Avenue. Looking northeast. Wikimedia Commons.)

APRIL 19
1993

On this day in history, at Mount Carmel in Waco, Texas, the Federal Bureau of Investigation (FBI) unleashed a tear-gas assault on founder and leader David Koresh and the Branch Davidian compound, ending a stressful 51-day stalemate between the federal government and an armed religious cult. By the end of the day, the compound was razed to the ground, and some 80 Branch Davidians, including David Koresh and 22 children, had died in the blaze.

David Koresh was born Vernon Wayne Howell in Houston, Texas, in 1959. In 1981, he attached himself to the Branch Davidians, a derivative of the Seventh Day Adventist Church founded in 1934 by Bulgarian immigrant Victor Houteff. Koresh, who had acquired extensive command of the Bible, quickly rose in the chain of command of the small religious community, ultimately entering a power struggle with the Davidian's leader, George Roden.

For a brief time, Koresh withdrew with his devotees to eastern Texas, but in late 1987, he returned to Mount Carmel with seven armed supporters and stormed the compound, severely injuring Roden. Koresh was tried for attempted murder, but the charge was eventually dropped after his case was declared a mistrial. By 1990, he oversaw the Branch Davidians, and he legally changed his name to David Koresh, with David representing his standing as head of the biblical House of David, and Koresh meaning Cyrus in Hebrew, who was the Persian king who allowed the Jews being held captive in Babylon to go back to Israel.

Koresh took numerous wives at Mount Carmel and fathered at least twelve children from these women, some of whom were as young as 12 or 13 when they became impregnated. There is also evidence to support the belief that Koresh may have physically abused some of the 100 or so followers living within the compound, particularly his children. One of the central tenants of Koresh's religious teachings was his contention that the events predicted in the Bible's book of Revelation were fast approaching, making it essential, he felt, for the Branch Davidians to amass weapons and explosives in planning for the end times.

On February 28, 1993, the ATF raided the Branch Davidian compound at Mount Carmel. The day before, the ATF received word that Koresh was physically abusing children, engaging in polygamy, and stockpiling illegal weapons and explosives inside the compound. There had been reports of automatic gunfire coming from Mount Carmel and unsubstantiated reports that a methamphetamine lab was being run on the premises.

Koresh's brother-in-law, a local postal worker, had tipped Koresh off about the raid after a journalist asked him for directions to Mount Carmel while he was en route. Koresh was able to prepare – not much, but a little. He asked the men to arm themselves and the women and children to take shelter.

As the agents tried to infiltrate the compound, gunfire exploded, beginning a lengthy gun battle that left four ATF agents dead and fifteen wounded. Six Branch Davidians were killed, and several more were injured, including Koresh. After 45 minutes of gunfire, the ATF agents retreated, and a cease-fire was agreed to over the telephone. The action, which involved more than 100 ATF agents, was one of the largest ever undertaken by the bureau and resulted in the most significant number of casualties of any ATF operation.

During his negotiations with the FBI, who had since taken over the operation from the ATF during the siege, Koresh claimed that he was a messianic figure prophesied in the Bible and that God had graced him with his surname. He threatened violence against those who would attack him and his family but stressed that the Branch Davidians were not planning a mass suicide.

As the siege wore on, the negotiators and the Hostage Rescue Team, which managed all the tactical maneuvers, clashed on overseeing the blockade. The latter team, disappointed by the slow pace of discussions, employed hard-line tactics like playing ear-splitting music or crushing the Davidians' cars - often upsetting fragile negotiation endeavors.

In mid-April, after religious scholars reached out to Koresh through a radio show on the teachings of Revelation, Koresh sent a message through his lawyer announcing that he had received word from God and was writing his statement on the Seven Seals; he would come out with his followers when his work was completed.

The FBI, unconvinced, decided to act to end the siege. Though initially reluctant, Attorney General Janet Reno finally approved a plan to fire CS gas (a form of tear gas) into the Mount Carmel compound to try and force out the Branch Davidians. Just after 6 a.m. on April 19, 1993, FBI agents used two specially equipped tanks to penetrate the compound and deposit 400 gas canisters inside.

Soon after the attack ended, around noon, several fires simultaneously broke out around the compound, and gunfire was heard inside. Safety concerns prevented firefighters from entering Mount Carmel immediately, and the flames spread quickly and engulfed the property.

Though nine Davidians escaped, investigators later found 76 bodies inside the compound, including 25 children. Some of them, including Koresh, had fatal gunshot wounds, suggesting suicide or murder-suicide.

The government's handling of the Waco siege (which played out in the national and international media) was heavily criticized. Reno took responsibility for the botched raid, later admitting there was no evidence of ongoing child abuse within the compound (which had been one of the justifications for ordering the gas attack).

Though the government had always maintained that its actions played no role in starting the fires in Waco, in 1999, it was revealed that some of the gas the FBI used was flammable under certain conditions. Reno subsequently appointed lawyer and former senator John Danforth to lead an investigation into the siege's end. In 2000, he concluded that government agents did not start the fires or shoot at the compound.

APRIL 20
1898

On this day in history, United States President William McKinley requested that Congress declare war on Spain. The U.S. Congress also passed a joint resolution acknowledging Cuban independence on this date. They demanded that the Spanish government give up their control of the Island, foreswear any intent by America to take over Cuba, and allow McKinley to use whatever military means necessary to guarantee Cuba's independence.

The Spanish-American War of 1898 finished Spain's colonial empire in the Western Hemisphere and ensured the status of the United States as a Pacific power. U.S. success in the war created a peace treaty that forced the Spanish to surrender claims in Cuba and relinquish authority over Puerto Rico, the Philippines, and Guam, to the United States. The United States also appropriated the independent state of Hawaii during the conflict. Thus, the war allowed the U.S. to establish its superiority in the Caribbean region and to follow its tactical and economic pursuits in Asia.

The war started as the Cuban struggle for independence from Spain in February 1895. Cuba, situated less than 100 miles south of the United States, struggled to defeat Spanish colonial rule. The insurgents received financial support from private American interests and used the U.S. as a center of operations from which to strike. The Spanish military reacted ruthlessly; approximately 100,000 Cuban civilians died in miserable circumstances within Spanish concentration camps between 1895 and 1898. McKinley initially tried to prevent a war with Spain. Still, the American media, led by newspaper baron Randolph Hearst, castigated McKinley as weak and stirred up widespread opinion for a war to allow Cubans to attain their freedom.

On February 17, 1898, the battleship USS Maine, anchored in Havana's harbor, sank after being shaken by two blasts; 252 men on the ship were killed. Warmongers in the media and inside the government automatically blamed Spain, and President McKinley, foregoing any hopes for neutrality in the Cuban-Spanish conflict, succumbed to Congressional calls for war. (It was later discovered that the cause of the explosion on the Maine was caused by the spontaneous detonation of defective ammunition onboard.)

On April 11, 1898, President McKinley asked Congress for authorization to put an end to the hostilities in Cuba between the rebels and Spanish forces and to create a "stable government" that would "maintain order" and ensure the "peace and tranquility and the security" of Cuban and American citizens of Cuba. As mentioned earlier, on April 20, the U.S. Congress passed a joint resolution to acknowledge Cuban independence. It demanded that the Spaniards give up control of the island and foreswear that the United States would not annex Cuba. They also authorized McKinley to use necessary force to guarantee Cuba's independence.

The Spanish government rebuffed the American provocation and instantly broke diplomatic relations with the U.S. McKinley countered by employing a naval blockade of Cuba on April 22, and he announced a request for 125,000 military volunteers the next day. Spain declared war on the United States the same day, and the U.S. Congress voted for war against Spain on April 25, retroactive to April 21, 1898.

Secretary of State John Hay referred to the conflict as that "splendid little war." The first battle of the war was fought on May 1 in Manila Bay, where the American Asiatic Squadron, under Commodore George Dewey, conquered the Spanish naval force protecting the Philippines. On June 10, American soldiers arrived at Guantanamo Bay in Cuba, and additional troops landed close to the harbor city of Santiago on June 22 and 24. After isolating and conquering the Spanish Army garrisons in Cuba, the U.S. Navy defeated Spain's Caribbean Squadron on July 3 as it tried to escape the American naval blockade of Santiago.

On July 26, at the request of the Spanish government, the French ambassador in Washington contacted the McKinley administration to talk over peace terms, and a cease-fire was agreed to on August 12. The war formally ended four months later when the American and Spanish governments signed the Treaty of Paris on December 10, 1898. In addition to guaranteeing the independence of Cuba, the treaty also compelled Spain to relinquish Guam and Puerto Rico to the United States. America also agreed to purchase the Philippines from Spain for $20 million. The U.S. Senate endorsed the treaty on February 6, 1899, by just one vote.

The defeat and loss of the final vestiges of the Spanish Empire profoundly shocked Spain's national psyche and prompted a comprehensive philosophical and artistic reassessment of Spanish society known as the Generation of '98. The United States, meanwhile, not only became a significant power but also gained several island possessions covering the globe, which incited acrimonious debate over the wisdom of colonialism.

The McKinley Administration also used the war as a pretense to take control of the independent state of Hawaii. In 1893, a faction of Hawaii-based planters and businessmen led a revolt against Queen Liliuokalani and established a new government. They quickly requested annexation by the United States, but President Grover Cleveland rejected this. In 1898, however, President McKinley and the American public were more positively inclined toward obtaining the islands. Supporters of acquiring Hawaii argued that it was vital to the American economy and that it would serve as a strategic base that would help protect American interests in Asia, and that other nations were eager to take over the islands if the United States failed to do so. At McKinley's plea, a joint resolution of Congress brought about Hawaii being made a U.S. territory on August 12, 1898.

APRIL 21
1865

On this day in history, a train transporting the coffin of assassinated President Abraham Lincoln departs Washington, D.C., on its way to Springfield, Illinois, where he would be interred on May 4. The funeral train transported Lincoln's remains 1,654 miles (2,662 km) through seven states on its journey to Springfield. The train, dubbed "The Lincoln Special," never exceeded 20 mph, passed 444 communities, and made numerous stops in key cities and state capitals for processions, speeches, and added lying in state. Millions of Americans viewed the train along the route and participated in related ceremonies.

Mary Lincoln wanted her husband's body to take the most direct route home to Springfield, Illinois, for burial, but Secretary of War Edwin Stanton persuaded her to agree to a more meandering railroad trip that repeated the whistle stops Lincoln had made from the Illinois capitol to the national capitol four years earlier, just before his inauguration.

In the early hours of April 21, the president's black mahogany casket is taken from the U.S. Capitol, where it had spent the previous two nights lying in state, to the neighboring Baltimore & Ohio Railroad station. Soldiers laid Lincoln's body onto the presidential railroad car.

Preoccupied with war, Lincoln never had an opportunity to view the newly built and luxuriously detailed railcar, let alone ride in it.

The presidential coffin would be joined by another one that held the body of his son, Willie, who had died of typhoid fever three years before at the age of 11. Willie's coffin had been kept in a vault in a Georgetown cemetery awaiting interment in Springfield at the end of Lincoln's presidency, which nobody guessed would happen so early.

Mary Lincoln, the president's widow, was too distraught to leave the White House for five weeks and was not amongst the funeral train's 150 passengers, which included a funeral director and an embalmer. The government's wish was to allow Americans to see their stricken president face-to-face one last time. Stanton had secured Mary Lincoln's permission to allow the lifting of the upper half of the coffin lid for public viewings in 10 cities along the route.

With the last vestiges of the Civil War yet to be put out and Lincoln's assassin still at large, people were on edge as the funeral train made its first stop in John Wilkes Booth's hometown of Baltimore, Maryland. The city had previously been very hostile to Lincoln, so as president-elect, he had to travel through the city incognito for fear of his life. No animosity was found four years later as a quartet of horses hauling a rosewood hearse through the streets for three hours before public viewing. The mourners included approximately 30,000 Black marchers and spectators. A *New York Tribune* reporter was struck by the sight of "white and black side by side in the rain and the mud" and the lack of "consciousness of any difference of color."

In Philadelphia, tens of thousands of mourners escorted the presidential casket to Independence Hall, where in 1861, Lincoln stated that he "would rather be assassinated on this spot than to surrender" the principles of the Declaration of Independence. During a 20-hour public viewing, over 150,000 people filed past Lincoln's body as he lay near the Liberty Bell. Similar-sized crowds were witnessed in Manhattan, where a six-year-old Theodore Roosevelt witnessed the funeral procession from the second floor of his family's mansion.

The limits of embalming in an age before refrigeration were becoming clear by the time Lincoln's body left New York. Newspapers reported that Lincoln's eyes were sunken, his visage sallow and withered. "It is not the genial, kindly face of Abraham Lincoln," one newspaper reported. "It is but a ghastly shadow." Yet, the public showings went on. Civic pride encouraged building more elaborate hearses, catafalques, and memorial arches at each consecutive stop as if cities were trying to outdo each other in their manifestations of grief.

The number of people increased along the rails as the funeral train moved into the Midwest. "As the president's remains went farther westward, where the people more especially claimed him as their own, the intensity of feeling seemed, if possible, to grow deeper," stated Brigadier General Edward Townsend. Even at 3 A.M., 12,000 people gathered in Richmond, Indiana, as the funeral train passed under a 25-foot-high arch built by its residents. One woman dressed as the Genius of Liberty wept over a fake casket while a group of ladies boarded the train to give a pair of floral wreaths.

After a public viewing in Chicago, where the line of mourners stretched more than a mile, the funeral train finally reached Springfield, Illinois, on May 3. After a 1,654-mile excursion, Lincoln was home. The funeral train had passed through 444 cities and towns. One million Americans viewed Lincoln's corpse, and millions more saw the train as the North united to bid Lincoln farewell.

"By and large, the funeral train experience – and Lincoln's posthumous image – knitted northern white Democrats and Republicans together and even offered northern African Americans some protected access to public life at a time of great danger for them," stated historian Richard Wightman Fox, author of *Lincoln's Body: A Cultural History*.

After a 24-hour viewing in the Illinois state capitol, Lincoln's casket was finally closed on May 4. Following the burial ceremony at Oak Ridge Cemetery, which included an hour-long eulogy, the coffins of father and son were placed inside a vault, and the doors and iron grating shuttered. Nearly three weeks after he breathed his last, Lincoln was finally laid to rest.

APRIL 22
1954

On this day in history, Senator Joseph McCarthy commences hearings examining the United States Army, which he accuses of being "soft" on communism. These televised hearings gave the American people their first view of McCarty in action, and his carelessness, angry bravado, and harassing methods swiftly caused his fall from grace.

McCarthy was born in 1908 in Grand Chute, Wisconsin, the fifth of nine children. He was the son of Bridget and Timothy McCarthy, and he graduated from Law school in 1935. He then ran for the judgeship in Wisconsin's Tenth Judicial Circuit, a race he worked at persistently and won, becoming the state's youngest circuit judge ever elected at the age of 30. McCarthy joined World War II as a first lieutenant in the Marines. (He would later lie about being wounded in combat.) He was still on active duty when he embarked on his next political campaign: for the Republican nomination to the U.S. Senate. He was defeated but soon began preparing for the 1946 Senate race.

McCarthy successfully ran for the U.S. Senate in 1946. After three mainly unremarkable years as a senator, McCarthy quickly soared to national fame in February 1950 when he declared in a speech that he possessed a list of "members of the Communist Party and members of a spy ring" working at the State Department. In future years after his

1950 speech, McCarthy made further accusations of Communist infiltration into the administration of Harry S. Truman, the State Department, the Voice of America, and the U.S. Army. He also used various charges of communism, communist sympathies, disloyalty, or sex crimes to attack several politicians and other people inside and outside of the government. This includes a simultaneous "Lavender Scare" against alleged homosexuals; as homosexuality was forbidden by law at the time, it was also understood to boost a person's risk for extortion. Despite a lack of proof of treason, more than 2,000 government employees lost their jobs due to McCarthy's investigations.

To bolster his dwindling popularity, McCarthy made a sensational allegation that was a critical blunder: in early 1954, he alleged that the United States Army was "soft" on communism. McCarthy was outraged because David Schine, one of his former investigators, had been drafted, and the Army, much to McCarthy's disbelief, denied the special treatment he fully expected for his one-time aide. In April 1954, McCarthy, chairman of the Government Operations Committee in the Senate, launched televised hearings into his accusations against the Army.

The hearings lasted for 36 days and were televised on live tv by ABC and DuMont, with a projected 20 million people tuning in. After listening to 32 witnesses and over two million words of testimony, the committee concluded that McCarthy did not try to affect the Army on Schine's behalf but that McCarthy's lawyer, Roy Cohn, had participated in "unduly persistent or aggressive efforts" on the same matter. Of greater significance to McCarthy was the adverse effect of widespread publicity on his reputation. Many in the audience viewed him as bullying, reckless, and dishonest, and the daily newspaper reviews of the hearings were also quite often damaging. Late in the hearings, Senator Stuart Symington made an angry and foretelling remark to McCarthy. Upon being told by McCarthy, "You're not fooling anyone," Symington replied: "Senator, the American people have looked at you now for six weeks; you're not fooling anyone, either."

The hearings were a fiasco for McCarthy. He constantly interrupted with irrelevant questions and asides: yelled "point of order" whenever testimony was not to his liking, and verbally attacked witnesses, attorneys for the Army, and his fellow senators. The climax came when McCarthy slandered an associate of the Army's chief counsel, Joseph Welch. Welch fixed McCarthy with a steady glare and declared evenly, "Until this moment, Senator, I think I never really gauged your cruelty or your recklessness.... Have you no sense of decency, sir, at long last?" A stunned McCarthy listened as the packed audience exploded into cheers and applause. McCarthy's days as a political power were effectively over. A few weeks later, the Army hearings dribbled to a close with little fanfare, and no charges were upheld against the Army by the committee.

Even before McCarthy was humiliated by Joseph Welch, broadcast journalist Edward R. Murrow had seriously damaged McCarthy's sway. In a pivotal broadcast on March 9, 1954, Murrow showed clips that demonstrated McCarthy's unfair and unethical practices. In his conclusion, Murrow said of McCarthy: "The actions of the junior Senator from Wisconsin have caused alarm and dismay amongst our allies abroad and given considerable comfort to our enemies. And whose fault is that? Not his. He didn't create this situation of fear; he merely exploited it – and rather successfully. Cassius was right: "The fault, dear Brutus, is not in our stars, but in ourselves."

With McCarthy diminished, a special Senate committee was created to seek a resolution to condemn McCarthy. On December 2, 1954, the vote in the Senate formally reprimanded McCarthy for his "inexcusable," "reprehensible," "vulgar and insulting" conduct "unbecoming a senator." Following the official vote of censure in the Senate, McCarthy's reckless crusade was all but over.

McCarthy stayed in the Senate, but he was a broken man. He drank excessively and was eventually placed in hospital. On May 2, 1957, he died in Bethesda Naval Hospital. His official cause of death is given as hepatitis, but it is believed he died of cirrhosis of the liver due to alcoholism. He was 48 years of age.

APRIL 23
1564

On this day in history, according to belief, actor, playwright, poet, and theatre entrepreneur, William Shakespeare is born in Stratford-upon-Avon, England. It is difficult to ascertain the precise day on which he was born, but church records indicate he was baptized on April 26, and three days was the usual amount of time to wait before baptizing a newborn. Shakespeare's died on April 23, 1616. He was 52 years old and had been retired in Stratford for three years.

William was the son of John Shakespeare, who experimented in wood trading, money lending, farming, tanning, leatherwork, and other occupations; he also held a succession of municipal positions before plunging into debt in the late 1580s. John, the motivated son of a tenant farmer, enhanced his social standing by getting married to Mary Arden, the offspring of a wealthy landowner. Like John, she may have been a practicing Catholic at a time when those who rebuffed the newly formed Church of England faced harassment.

William was the third of eight children, of whom three died in childhood. No records exist of Shakespeare's youth and practically none concerning his education. Academics have speculated that he probably went to the King's New School in Stratford, which instructed students in reading, writing, and the classics. Shakespeare would unquestionably have been eligible for free schooling as a public official's child. But this ambiguity concerning his education has led some to doubt the provenance of his works (and even about whether Shakespeare existed).

Shakespeare married on November 28, 1582, to Anne Hathaway, in Worcester, in Canterbury Province. Hathaway was originally from Shottery, a small village west of Stratford. Shakespeare was 18, and Anne was 26, and, as it happens, pregnant. Their first child, a daughter named Susanna, was born on May 26, 1583. On February 2, 1585, twins Hamnet and Judith were born. Hamnet died of unknown causes at age 11.

There are seven years of Shakespeare's life where records do not exist after the birth of his twins in 1585. Historians call this period the "lost years," and there is wide speculation on what he was up to during this time. One theory is that he may have had to go into hiding for poaching game from the local landlord, Sir Thomas Lucy. Another view is that he might have been working as an assistant schoolmaster in Lancashire, studying law, traveling across continental Europe, or joining an acting troupe passing through Stratford. It is thought that he eventually arrived in London in the mid-to-late 1580s and may have found work as a horse attendant at one of London's theaters.

Whatever the reason, by 1592, Shakespeare had begun working as an actor, written numerous plays, and spent ample time in London to write about its geography, culture, and diverse personalities with sufficient knowledge. Even his earliest works demonstrate an understanding of European affairs and foreign countries, experience with the royal court, and general knowledge that might seem inaccessible to a young man growing up in the provinces by parents who were most likely illiterate. For this reason, some academics have suggested that one or several authors wishing to hide their identity used the person of William Shakespeare as a facade. (Most historians dismiss this premise, although many believe Shakespeare sometimes joined forces with other playwrights.)

Shakespeare's first plays, thought to have been written before or around 1592, include all three of the leading theatrical genres in the bard's works: tragedy ("Titus Andronicus"), history (the Henry VI trilogy and Richard III"), and comedy ("The Taming of the Shrew," "The Two Gentlemen of Verona," and "The Comedy of Errors"). Shakespeare was likely associated with various theater companies when these early works were first performed in London. In 1594 he began writing and acting for a theater company called the Lord Chamberlain's Men, eventually becoming its house playwright and uniting with other members to establish the celebrated Globe Theater in 1599.

Shakespeare wrote the most famous of his 37-plus plays between the mid-1590s and his retirement around 1612, including "Hamlet," "Romeo and Juliet," "A Midsummer Night's Dream," "King Lear," "Macbeth" and "The Tempest." As a playwright, he is known for his continual use of iambic pentameter, meditative soliloquies (such as Hamlet's omnipresent "To be, or not to be" speech), and clever banter. His works knit together and reinvent theatrical principles dating back to ancient Greece, presenting diverse casts of characters with intricate personalities and intensely human interpersonal tensions. Some of his plays – notably "All's Well That Ends Well," "Troilus and Cressida," and "Measure for Measure" – are distinguished by moral vagueness and conflicting shifts in tone, defying, much like life itself, categorization as purely tragic or comic.

He is also recalled for his non-dramatic contributions, Shakespeare published his first narrative poem – the erotic "Venus and Adonis," while London theaters were closed due to a plague epidemic in 1593. The piece was reprinted numerous times, and a second poem, "The Rape of Lucrece," indicate that during his lifetime, the bard was mainly celebrated for his poetry. Shakespeare's famed collection of sonnets was printed in 1609, possibly without its author's permission. (It has been proposed that he planned them for close friends only, not the public.) Maybe because of their explicit sexual innuendos or dark emotional moments, the sonnets did not enjoy the same favorable results as Shakespeare's earlier works.

Shakespeare died at 52 of undetermined causes on April 23, 1616, and left the bulk of his estate to his daughter, Susanna. (Anne Hathaway, who survived her husband by seven years, notoriously received his "second-best bed.") The slab stone over his tomb, located inside a Stratford church, bears an epitaph – written, some say, by the bard himself – warding off body snatchers with a malediction: "Blessed be the man that spares these stones, / And cursed be he that moves my bones." Despite archeologists' requests to reveal what killed him, his remains have yet to be disturbed.

APRIL 24
1916

On this day in history, on Easter Monday in Dublin, the Irish Republican Brotherhood, a clandestine group of Irish separatists led by Patrick Pearse, launches the so-called Easter Rebellion, an armed insurrection against British rule. Aided by radical Irish socialists under James Connolly, Pearse and his fellow Republicans rampaged and assaulted British provincial government headquarters across Dublin and captured the Irish capital's, General Post Office.

After these successes, they declared the liberation of Ireland, which had been under the oppressive hand of Great Britain for centuries, and by the following day, were in command of a large portion of the city. Later that same day, however, British authorities began a counterattack, and by April 29, the insurrection had been put down. After the rebellion had been suppressed, more than 2,000 people were dead or injured. The ringleaders of the insurrection were soon put to death. Initially, there was very little support from the Irish people for the Easter Rebellion; however, public opinion soon changed, and the executed leaders were seen as martyrs. However, the Easter Rebellion is viewed as a substantial step forward to forming an autonomous Irish republic.

With the Acts of Union in 1800, Ireland (which had been subject to some type of English power since the 12th century) combined with Great Britain to give rise to the United Kingdom of Great Britain and Ireland. As a result, Ireland lost its parliament in Dublin and was controlled by a united parliament from Westminster in London. Throughout the 19th century, groups of Irish separatists resisted this plan in differing degrees.

Some moderate separatists supported home rule, under which Ireland would continue to be part of the United Kingdom but also have some form of self-government. Several pieces of home rule legislation were defeated in Parliament in the late 1800s before one was finally approved in 1914. However, the execution of the home rule legislation was suspended due to the outbreak of World War I.

In the meantime, supporters of a clandestine revolutionary group called the Irish Republican Brotherhood (IRB), who felt that home rule would not go far enough and instead pursued total independence for Ireland, began preparing the Easter Rebellion. They hoped their insurrection would be assisted by military support from Germany, which was battling the British in World War I. Roger Casement, an Irish separatist, organized a shipment of German arms and ammunition for the revolutionaries; however, just before the beginning of the rebellion, the British spotted the ship, and its captain scuttled it to avoid capture. Casement was charged with treason and executed in London in August 1916.

The Easter Rebellion was supposed to occur all across Ireland, yet several conditions resulted in it being carried out mainly in Dublin. On April 24, 1916, the rebellious leaders, and their followers (whose numbers would reach some 1,600 people throughout the rebellion, many of whom were followers of a separatist organization called the Irish Volunteers or a small radical militia group, the Irish Citizen Army), seized the city's general post office and other tactical locations. Early that afternoon, from the front of the post office, Patrick Pearse, one of the leaders of the uprising, read a declaration proclaiming Ireland an independent republic and telling those assembled that a provisional government (comprised of IRB members) had been chosen.

Despite the rebels' expectations, the public did not stand up to assist them. The British government quickly declared martial law in

Ireland, and the Army destroyed the rebels in less than a week. Of the nearly 500 people killed, 260 were civilians, 82 were Irish rebels, and 143 were British military and police personnel, including 16 insurgents executed for their roles in the rebellion. More than 2,600 people were wounded. British artillery fire killed or wounded many civilians, or they were mistaken for rebels. Others were caught in the crossfire between the British and the rebels during firefights. The bombing and resulting fires left parts of central Dublin in ruins.

In the beginning, many Irish people disliked the rebels for the destruction and death caused by the rebellion. However, when 15 rebellion leaders were executed by firing squad in May, things began to change. Further, more than 3,000 people alleged to have supported the rebellion, directly or indirectly, were arrested, and upwards of 1,800 people were sent to concentration camps in Wales and imprisoned there without trial. The quick executions, large-scale arrests, and martial law (which remained in effect through the fall of 1916) stoked public hatred toward the British. They were among the reasons that helped construct support for the rebels and the drive for Irish independence.

In the 1918 general election to the parliament of the United Kingdom, the Sinn Fein political party (whose goal was to establish a republic) won the lion's share of the Irish seats. The Sinn Fein members then refused to sit in the UK Parliament, and in January 1919, met in Dublin to assemble a single chamber parliament and declare Ireland's sovereignty. The Irish Republican Army then initiated a guerrilla war against the British government and its forces in Ireland. Following a July 1921 cease-fire, the two sides agreed to a treaty in December that called for the creation of the Irish Free State, a self-governing nation of the British Commonwealth, the following year. Ireland's six northern counties opted out of the Free State and remained with the United Kingdom. The fully independent Republic of Ireland (consisting of the 26 counties in the southern and western parts of the island) was formally declared on Easter Monday, April 18, 1949.

APRIL 25
1917

On this day in history, jazz legend Ella Fitzgerald was born in Newport News, Virginia. Selling over 40 million albums during her lifetime, she gained a devout audience across race, gender, and class lines for over six decades. What is often neglected about her legacy as a celebrated jazz singer, however, is her problematic childhood, years living on the street, and the painful rejection she got from forging beyond racial barriers. Ella Fitzgerald quietly rose from the streets of New York to become the beloved American icon with a glass-shattering voice.

Ella Fitzgerald was the creation of a common-law bond between William Fitzgerald and Temperance "Tempie" Williams Fitzgerald. Ella suffered a difficult upbringing that began with her parents splitting up when she was two and a half years old. With her mother, she proceeded to Yonkers, New York. They lived there with her mother's new boyfriend, Joseph Da Silva. The family grew in 1923 with the birth of Fitzgerald's half-sister Frances. Her first career ambitions were to become a dancer.

As a girl, Ella was shy but still incredibly ambitious. She told neighborhood kids, "Someday, you're going to see me in the headlines. I'm going to be famous." She learned to emulate her favorite singers on the radio and phonograph and would venture to the city to see the latest steps at dance halls. Tragically, in 1932, Temperance died in an automobile accident, causing the 15-year-old Ella to become an orphan during the Great Depression. After her mother's passing, it's alleged that Ella's stepfather mistreated her.

By 1933, she had fled to her aunt's home in Harlem to escape. However, Ella's aunt struggled to support her. She began skipping school and working as a courier, "running numbers" and acting as a lookout for a brothel. With her truancy and connection to criminal enterprises, Fitzgerald was shuffled off to the overcrowded Colored Orphan Asylum in Riverdale. After that, she was banished to a state reformatory school in Albany, infamous for its terrible conditions. Ella was believed to have been kept in the basement of one of the cottages, where she was repeatedly beaten and given only bread and water to eat. When she tried to join the reformatory school choir, she was banned because of her race. Fitzgerald, underage in a racist world, was defenseless within the legal system. She ran away from the reformatory school, living hand-to-mouth and dancing for tips on 125th Street in New York. Fitzgerald slept wherever she could, essentially homeless.

By 1934, Fitzgerald was still trying to make it alone and living on the streets. Still harboring dreams of becoming a dancer, she entered an amateur talent contest at Harlem's Apollo Theater. At the competition, just prior to her going onstage, there was an outstanding dance troupe that did an excellent routine. It was now Ella's turn, and she stood on stage, unsure what to do. She decided at the last moment to sing "The Object of My Affection." The first few notes came out terribly. The MC for the evening rushed onstage and quieted things down and set Ella up to do her routine. She wowed the crowd. She went on to do a second number, "Judy," and she subsequently won the $25 first-place prize in the contest.

That surprising performance at the Apollo helped set Fitzgerald's career in motion. She soon met bandleader Chick Webb and eventually joined his band as a singer. Fitzgerald then recorded "Love and Kisses" with Webb in 1935 and sang regularly at Harlem's hottest club, the Savoy. Fitzgerald then recorded her first No. 1 hit, 1938's "A-Tisket, A-Tasket," which she co-wrote. Later that year, Fitzgerald released her second hit, "I Found My Yellow Basket." In addition to her work with Webb, Ella also performed with the Benny Goodman Orchestra. She also had her own side project - Ella Fitzgerald and Her Savoy Eight.

Webb died in 1939, and Fitzgerald became the head of the band, which was renamed Ella Fitzgerald and Her Famous Orchestra. At this time, Ella was married to Ben Kornegay for a short time. He was a convicted drug dealer and hustler. They married in 1941, but she soon had their marriage annulled.

Going out on her own, Fitzgerald got a deal with Decca Records. She recorded several hit songs with Louis Jordan and the Ink Spots in the early 1940s. Fitzgerald also made her movie debut in 1942's western comedy *Ride 'Em Cowboy* with Bud Abbott and Lou Costello. Her career began to soar in 1946 when she started working with Norman Granz, the upcoming founder of Verve Records.

The 1950s and 1960s proved to be a time of fantastic critical and profitable success for Fitzgerald, and she earned the nickname "First Lady of Song" for her mainstream popularity and incomparable vocal talents. Her exceptional skill in imitating instrumental sounds assisted in popularizing her vocal improvisation of scatting, which became her signature technique.

During this period, she would record the Great American Songbook. She would devote each collection to a particular songwriter like Cole Porter, Duke Ellington, and Irving Berlin. They would be defining recordings of Fitzgerald's and be her most lasting and popular recordings.

In 1960, Fitzgerald made it to the pop charts with her interpretation of "Mack the Knife." She was still a force well into the 1970s, playing concerts across the globe. One especially noteworthy concert series from this time was a two-week concert series in New York City in 1974 with Sinatra and Basie.

By the 1980s, Fitzgerald suffered serious health concerns. She had heart surgery in 1986 and suffered from diabetes. The disease left her blind, and her legs were amputated in 1994.

She made her final recording in 1989 and her closing performance in 1991 at New York's Carnegie Hall. Fitzgerald died on June 15, 1996, in Beverly Hills.

Fitzgerald recorded more than 200 albums and over 2,000 songs in her lifetime. Her total record sales surpassed 40 million records. Her many honors comprised 13 Grammy Awards, the NAACP Image Award for Lifetime Achievement, and the Presidential Medal of Freedom.

APRIL 26
1798

On this day in history, fur trapper, explorer, mountain man, guide, innkeeper, scout, and avid storyteller James Pierson Beckwourth was born. Originating from Fredericksburg, Virginia, this enigmatic and notorious storyteller was born into slavery, the offspring of a white plantation owner and a Black woman, known only as "Miss Kill," who was most likely enslaved. The third of ten children, Beckwourth, was acknowledged by Sir Jennings Beckwith, a descendant of English nobility, as his son (no one knows why James Beckwourth changed the spelling of his last name). Although Beckwourth often embellished his adventures, enough facts remain to herald him as an important personality in the history of the West. And during a time when many African Americans were overlooked, Beckwourth was the exception.

During his childhood, it is most likely that Beckwourth was enslaved. The family was moved to St. Louis, Missouri, in 1809, where Beckwourth was eventually apprenticed to a blacksmith, who abused him by his own account. In 1822, Beckwourth told his father that he wanted to go west. Beckwourth's father then filed a Deed of Emancipation with the court, officially giving his son freedom.

When he first headed west, Beckwourth joined Colonel Richard

Johnson's expedition to the Mississippi River, hoping to negotiate a treaty with the Sac Indians to access some lead mines on their territory. Beckwourth remained with the Johnson expedition for about eighteen months, working in the mines and learning the ways of the Sac and Fox tribes. In 1824, Beckwourth saw an advertisement for the Rocky Mountain Fur Company, which wanted "One Hundred Enterprising Young Men...to ascend the river Missouri to its source." Beckwourth answered the ad and soon headed westward, purchasing horses from the Pawnees, and honing his fur-trapping skills.

Trapping in the Powder River region of Wyoming, Beckwourth began to build a close coalition with the Crow Indians. Sometime between 1826-1828, he deserted American society entirely and merged with the Crow people. The Crow had long been genial with trappers, and they seemingly embraced Beckwourth into their culture. Beckwourth stated that the Crow had captured him before being "mistaken" for the lost son of leader Big Bowl. As Beckwourth related it, he was escorted to Big Bowl's lodge, where someone remembered, "That is the lost Crow, the great brave who has killed so many of our enemies. He is our brother."

Now greeted as family, Beckwourth began living with the tribe and remained among the Crows for twelve years. Beckwourth learned the Crow customs, language, and ways of living, and he married two Crow women and was the father of several children. Beckwourth later maintained that he became a powerful chief among the Crow and fought alongside the Crow against the Blackfoot.

In the late 1830s, Beckwourth left his home with the Crow and began working as a scout with the Missouri volunteer military force. He fought in the Seminole War in Florida, serving under General Zachary Taylor. Beckwourth quit the army in 1840 and spent the next decade wandering around the West, sometimes making quick cash stealing horses. Eventually settling down near Denver, Colorado, Beckwourth would work periodically as a civilian scout for the military. In this capacity, Beckwourth participated in the infamous Sand Creek Massacre of 1864, where 150 Cheyenne were butchered. However, how much Beckwourth knew about or participated in that inexcusable massacre is still disputed. For Beckwourth, who had perpetuated a relationship with the Cheyenne for decades, this event must have been devastating. Afterward, outraged by his association with the massacre, the Cheyenne declined to trade with him any longer. After two more years, Beckwourth left Colorado forever.

Well into his 60s by now, Beckwourth returned to trapping. In 1866, during Red Cloud's War, the U.S. Army employed him as a scout at Fort Laramie and Fort Phil Kearny. Beckwourth was hired to guide military soldiers from Montana to a Crow settlement in Wyoming. This would explain why he was at a Crow village in Albany County, Wyoming, on October 29, 1866. It is surmised that Beckwourth may have been poisoned after refusing to go into battle with the Crows, and they felt that they could no longer trust him. Beckwith became sick shortly after leaving Fort Smith in Montana and "commenced bleeding." He managed to make it to the Crow village, where he died and was laid "on a platform in a tree" in the traditional funerary custom of the Crow Tribe. Beckwourth's body still resides at the Crow Indian Settlement Cemetery, Laramie, Albany County, Wyoming, to this day.

Not long after he died in 1866, the perception of Beckwourth began to shift. By this point, his memoirs, *The Life and Adventures of James P. Beckwourth* (1856), had been widely read for a decade, and they quickly came under attack by historians of the time. By the 1870s, less than ten years after Beckwourth's death, historians called his memoirs "little more than campfire stories" and used his penchant for exaggeration to dismiss his claims and even what he had achieved.

By the time the "Wild West" had become cemented in the minds of the American population, Beckwourth had faded from memory, whiter heroes with equally outlandish tales: Hugh Glass, who fought a grizzly bear and came back from the dead; "Buffalo" Bill Cody, who killed five thousand bison in less than a year, and Davy Crockett, who died fighting at the Alamo and took sixteen Mexican soldiers with him, despite eyewitness accounts to the contrary.

Beckwourth's story was sidelined and dismissed like that of so many other people of color. While it is true that many of the tales in his memoirs were almost undoubtedly exaggerated for entertainment value, there remains a core of truth to them – and there is no excuse for completely dismissing Beckwourth's genuine accomplishments. He achieved as much as, if not more than, his most famous white counterparts. And his contemporaries, the mountain men who traveled and worked with him, greatly respected him for it.

APRIL 27
1865

On this day in history, the steamboat *Sultana* exploded on the Mississippi River near Memphis, Tennessee, killing 1,800 passengers, including newly released Union POWs from the hellholes of Andersonville, Georgia, and Cahaba, Alabama. Although constructed with a maximum capacity of only 376 passengers, the *Sultana* was carrying 2,300 when three of the boat's four boilers exploded and caused it to catch fire and sink. The disaster was surpassed in the press by events surrounding the end of the Civil War, including the slaying of President Lincoln's assassin John Wilkes Booth just the day before. No one was ever held responsible for the disaster.

On April 23, 1865, the *Sultana* left New Orleans with 100 passengers. It stopped at Vicksburg, Mississippi, for a leaky boiler. R.G. Taylor, the boilermaker on the ship, advised Captain J. Cass Mason that two sheets on the boiler had to be replaced, a three-day job. Mason ordered his boilermaker to patch the plates until the ship reached St. Louis, Missouri. This was because these newly released prisoners needed to be moved up the Mississippi, and the government was paying handsomely for it - $5 for an enlisted man and $10 for an officer. Captain Mason had made a deal with the Union quartermaster in

Vicksburg, Captain Reuben Hatch, to pay him a kickback as one of the government-appointed vessels to move the prisoners. He could not possibly wait three days to effect repairs to his vessel because the prisoners would all be gone on other ships, thus losing out on this lucrative opportunity.

Just after 9 p.m., April 24, the *Sultana* left Vicksburg, carrying over 2300 people on her decks. Also on board were 100 mules and horses, 300,000 pounds of sugar, and 90 cases of wine. The first leg of the journey was trouble-free. After 30 hours of travel, the ship stopped briefly in Helena, Arkansas, where an enterprising local photographer took an image of the crowded vessel. Things got scary when so many soldiers swarmed to one side to wave at the cameraman that the ship threatened to capsize. At about 6:30 p.m. on April 26, the boat stopped in Memphis to discharge sugar, wine, and a few paying passengers. The Sultana continued northward, following a short coaling stop in nearby Hopefield, Arkansas. (At least one soldier who had slipped ashore at Memphis and missed the departure could hitch a ride out to the steamboat and rejoin his comrades. He would not survive.)

By 2 a.m. on April 27, the *Sultana* had eased past a collection of islands known as Paddy's Hen and Chickens when, with no warning, first one, then two more of her boilers exploded with a thunderous clap that could be heard seven miles away in Memphis. The force of the blast tore a 45-degree hole from the boat's bowels to her stern. In an instant, shards of the shattered boilers ripped through the passenger throng like shrapnel while white-hot coal and burning cordwood sprayed across beams and planks that had been shattered into ready kindling.

Scores died in an instant. Others found themselves buried under flaming debris blown overboard into the cold dark river. Most of the pilot house was gone; the smokestacks shuddered and then toppled, one forward, the other backward. The entire midsection was a mass of flames driven by a stiff wind toward the stern.

More died within minutes of the explosion. Those not fighting to survive in the water now faced life-or-death decisions. Weakened deck sections collapsed, crushing, or trapping victims. If they were intact, the side paddlewheels acted as jib sails, keeping the stern pointed downwind. But once the fittings burned loose and the wheels broke away, the hapless steamboat pivoted around 180 degrees. Now the blaze reversed course, relentlessly burning towards the bow, where perhaps as many as 500 people huddled. Within minutes all were either burned to death or cast into the water.

The swollen river current scattered the survivors along both sides of the Mississippi and downstream. Some held on to bits of debris until they grounded on dry land or were snagged by trees and clambered into the branches. Alerted by the screaming of victims being carried past, boats put out from nearby Mound City, Memphis, and small settlements in between. Some of the rescuers were able to haul in gasping survivors suffering from various stages of hypothermia; others spent frantic, futile minutes trying to locate voices calling for help that grew fainter and then fell silent.

At approximately 9 a.m., the *Sultana* sank near Mound City. All those who would survive the ordeal were located within 12 hours of the explosion. Body recovery would stretch into late May, some discovered as far as 120 miles below Memphis. Many were never found, including the steamboat's captain, J. Cass Mason.

Three different military commissions would be ordered to investigate the disaster. Each tended to limit its area of authority, and none probed too deeply into the affair; in fact, one commission even appropriated testimony given to another. Just a single officer was brought to trial – Captain Frederick Speed, charged with neglect of duty leading to the overcrowding of the *Sultana*.

Speed plead not guilty. The court-martial that followed was notable for those who did not testify. Several significant witnesses, including Colonel Hatch, had resigned their commissions by this time and, as civilians, could ignore military subpoenas. Speed was found guilty, but his verdict was overturned by the U.S. Army's judge advocate general. Ironically, the reverse decision made a point of the fact that while the *Sultana* might have been overcrowded, she was not overloaded. The number of passengers carried did not cause the vessel to founder; she died when her boilers exploded.

The most likely cause of the disaster is that the ship careened greatly. With the engine requiring maximum steam pressure to maintain its headway against the heavy flood current, keeping sufficient water levels in the boilers was especially critical. It would not have taken too many cycles of red-hot piping suddenly flushed by cold river water to cause a fatigue rupture in one boiler, which would set off two more.

APRIL 28
1945

On this day in history, Benito Mussolini and his mistress, Clara Petacci, were murdered by Italian partisans who had apprehended the couple as they tried to flee to Switzerland.

The 61-year-old Italian dictator, who aspired to become a modern-day Julius Caesar, had first climbed to power more than twenty years earlier when he became prime minister of Italy in 1922. "Il Duce" allied himself with fellow fascist Adolf Hitler and the Nazis during World War II, but his obsolete Italian military was seriously outgunned. By July 1943, with the Allied invasion of Sicily and the bombing of Rome, the Italian military and King Victor Emmanuel III decided to dislodge Mussolini from power and put him under house arrest.

In September 1943, German paratroopers snatched Mussolini from his Apennine Mountain lodge, where he had been imprisoned. Hitler made Mussolini the figurehead of the Social Republic of Italy (the Republic of Salo), a Nazi puppet state in German-occupied northern Italy.

However, by April 25, 1945, Hitler's Nazi empire rapidly lost its hold on northern Italy. Mussolini agreed to meet with a group of partisans at Cardinal Alfredo Schuster's palace with his bastion of Milan wobbling on the edge. There, an angry Mussolini found out that, unknown to him, the Germans had begun negotiating an unconditional surrender to the Allies.

Mussolini angrily left the palace and fled Milan with his mistress, Clara Petacci. The next day, the couple joined a convoy of other fascists and German soldiers heading north towards Lake Como and the border with Switzerland. Mussolini began wearing a German Luftwaffe helmet and overcoat, but his distinct features gave him away when the partisans stopped the convoy outside the town of Dongo on April 27. For 20 years, Mussolini had constructed a cult of personality with his picture displayed on newspapers and posters.

The partisans arrested Mussolini and Petacci. Ever mindful that the Germans would try to free the couple again, the partisans hid the duo in an isolated farmhouse overnight. The next day, the couple was taken to the village of Giuliano di Mezzegra on Lake Como. They were instructed to stand before a stone wall and executed by machine gun fire. The gunman's identity remains a point of contention, but the most agreed upon person is communist partisan commander Walter Audisio.

In the early hours of April 29, the corpses of Mussolini and Petacci and 14 fellow fascists were put in a truck and taken to Milan's Piazzale Loreto and dumped like garbage. On the same spot, eight months before, fascists publicly exhibited the bodies of 15 executed partisans under orders from Hitler's SS.

After Mussolini's arrest in July 1943, excited crowds destroyed pictures of the dictator. At the "Square of the Fifteen Martyrs," residents of Milan had the chance to do it this time for real. They threw curses and vegetables at "Il Duce's" body before kicking, urinating, beating, and spitting upon it. One woman, who decided that Mussolini was not dead enough for her, fired five shots into his head and exclaimed, "Five shots for my five assassinated sons!" The crowds then hung the bodies of Mussolini, Petacci, and other fascists up by their feet from the rafters of a gasoline station in the corner of the square.

In the early afternoon, American soldiers ordered that the bodies be taken down and transported to the city morgue for autopsy. By this time, Mussolini's body was unrecognizable, but a U.S. Army photographer managed to stage the bodies of the couple in each others' arms in a ghoulish pose.

Hitler learned of Mussolini's fate as the Allies closed in on Berlin. Resolved not to be dealt a similar outcome, Hitler killed himself on April 30 and had his body burned by loyal followers. Mussolini's body, however, was buried in an unmarked grave in a Milan cemetery. Its location was not a secret, however, and anti-fascists made regular visits to the graveyard to defile his grave until Mussolini's body was disinterred on Easter Sunday, 1946, by Domenico Leccisi and some other fascist sympathizers. They took the body, cleaned it in a nearby fountain, and pushed it to a waiting getaway car by wheelbarrow. The note they left behind was signed by the "Democratic Fascist Party," and it stated that they would never bear "the cannibal slurs made by human dregs organized in the Communist Party." The corpse remained missing for four months in a monastery outside Milan before it was found in August 1946.

Once the Italian government recovered Mussolini's corpse, they kept its whereabouts a secret for more than ten years. In 1957, newly elected prime minister Adone Zoli needed the support of a far-right wing party. In return for their votes, he delivered the bones of Mussolini to the family for inclusion in the family crypt. After spending eleven years in the closet of a monastery, Mussolini's body finally received a burial in his birthplace of Predappio, which has since become a pilgrimage site for neo-fascists. In 1966, the final piece of Mussolini's body was returned to his widow as the Americans handed over a sample of "Il Duce's" brain that was taken at autopsy and tested inconclusively for syphilis.

APRIL 29
1429

On this day in history, during the Hundred Years' War, 17-year-old peasant Joan of Arc led a French military force in relieving the city of Orleans, beleaguered by the English since October of the previous year. Joan of Arc was a pious country dweller in medieval France who thought God had selected her to lead France to victory in its decades-long war with England. With no military education, Joan persuaded crown prince Charles of Valois to permit her to spearhead a French army to the besieged city of Orleans, where they attained a spectacular triumph. After witnessing the coronation of King Charles VII, Joan was apprehended by rival forces, tried for witchcraft, and burned at the stake at 19. By the time she was canonized by Pope Benedict XV in 1920, Joan of Arc was seen as one of history's ultimate martyrs and the patron saint of France.

Born in 1412, Joan d'Arc (or, in English, Joan of Arc) was the child of a farmer, Jacques d'Arc, from the village of Domremy in northeastern France. She was never taught to read or write, but her pious mother, Isabelle Romee, infused a deep-rooted love for the Catholic Church into her.

At the time, France had long been torn apart by a vicious conflict with England (later known as the Hundred Years' War), in which

England had achieved the upper hand. A peace treaty in 1420 disowned the French crown prince, Charles of Valois, accompanied by assertions that he was illegitimate, King Henry V was made the sovereign of France and England.

His son, Henry VI, acceded to the throne in 1422. Along with their French supporters (led by Philip the Good, Duke of Burgundy), England dominated most of northern France, and most in Joan's village were forced to leave their homes at risk of invasion.

When she was about 16 years old, Joan heard the "voices" of Christian saints telling her to aid Charles in securing the French throne and ousting the English from France. In May 1428, she journeyed to Vaucouleurs, a stronghold of Charles, and told the captain of the garrison of her dreams. Doubting the young peasant girl, he sent her on her way. In January 1429, she returned, and the captain, amazed by her devotion and fortitude, agreed to allow her to see the dauphin at Chinon.

Dressed in men's clothing, with hair cut short, and escorted by a small entourage of soldiers, she arrived at the dauphin's castle at Chinon in February 1429 and was accorded an audience. Charles hid among his courtiers, but Joan instantly picked him out and notified him of her divine mission. For several weeks, Charles had Joan quizzed by theologians at Poitiers, who determined that, given his dire straits, the dauphin would be well-advised to use this strange and enigmatic girl.

Charles provided Joan with a small army and dressed her in white armor, and provided a white horse, on April 27, 1429, she began traveling to Orleans, besieged by the English since October 1428. On April 29, as a French attack distracted the English soldiers on the west side of Orleans, Joan entered unchallenged through its eastern gate. She brought significantly needed supplies and reinforcements, motivating the French to a zealous resistance. She led the charge in numerous battles and, on May 7, was hit by an arrow. After dressing her wound, she returned to the battle, and the French were victorious. On May 8, the English retreated from Orleans.

During the next five weeks, Joan led the French army to several extraordinary victories over the English, and Reims, the long-established city of coronation, was seized in July. Later in the month, Charles VII was crowned king of France, with Joan of Arc present at the coronation. (Despite being remembered as a courageous warrior, Joan never fought in battle or killed an adversary. Instead, she would go along with her men as an inspirational mascot, waving her banner in place of a weapon. She was also in charge of defining military tactics, supervising soldiers, and recommending diplomatic resolutions to the English.)

Joan reasoned that the French should press their advantage with an endeavor to retake Paris. Still, Charles faltered as his favorite at court, Georges de La Tremoille, cautioned him that Joan was becoming too formidable. The Anglo-Burgundians used the extra time to re-fortify their positions in Paris and repelled an attack led by Joan in September.

In May 1430, the king ordered Joan to confront a Burgundian assault on Compiegne. In her effort to defend the town and its people, she was thrown off her horse and subsequently left outside the town's walls. The Burgundians then took her hostage and brought her, amid much commotion, to the castle of Bouvreuil, inhabited by the English commander at Rouen.

In the subsequent trial, Joan was instructed to respond to 70 accusations brought against her, including heresy, witchcraft, and dressing like a man. The Anglo-Burgundians were trying to cleanse themselves of the charismatic French leader and discredit King Charles, who owed his coronation to Joan.

In attempting to distance himself from the accused, Charles made absolutely no attempt to negotiate Joan's release. In May 1431, a year after she was taken into captivity and under the threat of death, Joan capitulated and signed a confession denying that she had ever received heavenly advice.

However, several days later, she defied commands by wearing men's clothing again. As a result, the Anglo-Burgundians declared her death sentence. On the morning of May 30, 1431, at 19, Joan was led to the marketplace in Rouen and burned at the stake.

Twenty years after her death, Charles VII ordered a new trial, and her name was cleared. In 1909 Joan was beatified in Notre Dame

Cathedral in Paris by Pope Pius X. In 1920 Joan was canonized by Pope Benedict XV. A statue in the Notre Dame cathedral of Jeanne d'Arc, who would eventually become the patron saint of France, continues to pay tribute to her legacy.

(Photo: Joan of Arc enters Orléans by Jean-Jacques Scherrer (1887) Wikimedia Commons.)

APRIL 30
1945

On this day in history, hiding in a bunker under his command center in Berlin, Adolf Hitler commits suicide by shooting himself in the head. Eva Braun, his wife of 36 hours, swallowed a cyanide capsule to end her life simultaneously. Germany unconditionally surrendered to the Allied forces eight days later, ending Hitler's visions of a "1,000-year" Reich.

Since 1943, it was becoming more apparent that Germany would capitulate to the force of the Allied armies. In February 1943, the German 6th Army, trapped deep in the Soviet Union, was conquered at the Battle of Stalingrad, and German desires for a prolonged assault on both fronts dissolved. Then, on June 6, 1944, the Allied armies landed at Normandy, France, and began to push the Germans back toward Berlin methodically. By July 1944, several German military commanders recognized their impending defeat and conspired to eliminate Hitler from power to negotiate a more advantageous peace. However, their efforts to assassinate Hitler failed, and in his reprisals, he executed over 4,000 fellow citizens.

In January 1945, facing a blockade of Berlin by the Soviets, Hitler retreated to his bunker to live out his remaining days. Situated 55 feet under the Chancellery, the shelter was made up of 18 rooms and was fully self-reliant, with its own water and electrical supply. Though he grew progressively more unstable, Hitler continued to issue orders and meet with subordinates such as Hermann Goering, Josef Goebbels, and Heinrich Himmler. He also married his long-time mistress Eva Braun one day before his death.

By 1 a.m. on April 30, Field Marshal Wilhelm Keitel had reported that all the forces that Hitler had depended on to rescue Berlin had either been surrounded or driven onto the defensive. At around 2:30 a.m., Hitler emerged in the hallway where about twenty people, mostly women, were gathered to say goodbyes. He went down the line, shaking hands and speaking with each of them, before withdrawing to his rooms. Late in the morning, with the Soviets less than 500 meters (1600 ft) from the *Fuhrerbunker*, Hitler met with General Helmuth Weidling, the commander of the Berlin Defense Area. Weidling told Hitler that the battalion would probably run out of ammunition that night and that the Berlin combat would predictably end within the next 24 hours. Weidling requested authorization for a break-out, which he had vainly made before. Hitler did not answer, and Weidling returned to his Bendlerblock headquarters. At about 1 p.m., he received Hitler's approval to attempt a break-out that evening. Hitler, two secretaries, and his personal cook then ate lunch, after which Hitler and Braun said goodbye to the members of the bunker staff and other occupants, including Bormann, Goebbels, the secretaries, and several military officers. At around 2:30 p.m., Adolf Hitler and Eva Braun went into his study. Hitler's adjutant SS-*Sturmbannfuhrer* Otto Gunsche stood guard outside the study door.

After some time, Hitler's valet, Heinz Linge, entered the lobby to Hitler's quarters, where he found the door closed and could smell gunpowder smoke. Linge returned to the hallway where Bormann was standing, and the two entered the study together. Linge later stated that while in the room, he instantly noted a scent of burnt almonds, indicating hydrogen cyanide. Linge viewed the bodies of Hitler and Braun sitting upright on the sofa, with Hitler on Braun's right. His head was slanted to his right. Gunsche entered the study shortly after that. He described Braun's body as situated on Hitler's left, with her legs drawn up and leaning away from him. Gunsche stated that Hitler "sat...sunken over, with blood dripping from his right temple. He had shot himself with his pistol, a Walther PPK 7.65." The gun lay at his feet. Hitler's dripping blood had made a significant stain on the right arm of the sofa and was accumulating on the rug. According to witnesses, Braun's body had no visible wounds, and it was apparent that she had died from the effects of cyanide poisoning. Gunsche and SS-*Brigadefuhrer* Wilhelm Mihne stated "unequivocally" that all strangers and those working in the bunker "did not have any access" to Hitler's private quarters during the period when they died (between 3 p.m. and 4 p.m.).

Gunsche left the study and told the group, including Goebbels, Krebs, General Wilhelm Burgdorf, and Hitler Youth leader Artur Axmann, that Hitler and Braun were dead, and all viewed the bodies. Linge and another man rolled Hitler's body up in a rug. Then, following Hitler's prior written and spoken directives, his and Braun's bodies were taken up the stairs and through the emergency exit to the garden behind the Chancellery, where they were to be incinerated with gasoline. Although the rug partially covered Hitler's corpse, several witnesses stated that they recognized him, as the top of his head was not covered, nor were his lower legs and feet. Hitler was dead.

After the first attempts to ignite the gasoline did not work, Linge returned inside the bunker with a thick roll of papers. Bormann lit the papers and threw them on the bodies. As the two corpses caught fire, a group, including Goebbels, Bormann, Gunsche, Linge, Erich Kempka, Peter Hogl, Ewald Lindloff, and Hans Reisser, saluted as they stood inside the bunker doorway.

When the Soviets reached the Chancellery, they took Hitler's ashes, continually changing their location to prevent Hitler devotees from building a memorial at his final resting place. Eight days later, on May 8, 1945, the German Army agreed to an unconditional surrender, leaving Germany to be sliced up by the four Allied powers.

MAY 1

1963

On this day in history, after surviving a brief but arduous stretch as a Bunny in Manhattan's Playboy Club, journalist and social-political activist Gloria Steinem published the first half of her groundbreaking report, "A Bunny's Tale," in SHOW magazine. Steinem's covert coverage heightened her profile and laid bare the glitzy façade of Hugh Hefner's empire to expose a world of misogyny and exploitation.

Steinem, a freelance reporter, was hired by SHOW magazine to apply for a job at the Playboy Club under a false name and write about her ordeal. Ads for jobs as servers in the club, whose female employees were all called Bunnies, described the work as being close to paid involvement in a party straight from Playboy Magazine. As Steinem promptly discovered, the truth was far uglier. Bunnies were paid less than publicized and subject to a system of demerits, which could be given for sins such as declining to go out with a customer in a rude way (even though Bunnies were rigidly prohibited from going out with most customers) or letting the cotton tail on the back of their uniforms to get dirty.

Responding to an ad looking for girls who were "pretty and

personable, between 21 and 24," Steinem headed to the garish venue during an open application session with the requisite "swimsuit or leotard" in hand.

Taking on the name of Marie Catherine Ochs, Steinem created a whole new identity, cutting years off her actual age of 28, and she created a resume filled with waitressing jobs in

London and working as a dancer-hostess in Paris. The objectification began as soon as she walked into the building when a guard summoned her with, "Here bunny, bunny, bunny," and the job interviewer demanded – more than once – that she "take off her coat." She was criticized for her age and forced to stuff her costume for extra cleavage. Eventually, she learned that popular items with which to stuff her outfit included: Kleenex, foam rubber, lamb's wools, gym socks, silk scarves, Kotex halves, and, of course, cut-up Bunny tails.

Steinem documented every step of the superficial scrutiny she was put through during the application process, which started with her being told that her fake age of 24 was "awfully old." Throughout the process, she was surrounded by girls "wearing nothing but bikini-style panties" and "lavender satin high heels," forced to wait hours and have Polaroids taken. Finally, she made it into a bright satin blue Bunny costume. "It was so tight that the zipper caught my skin as she fastened the back," Steinem wrote. "She told me to inhale as she zipped again, this time without mishap and stood back to look at me critically. The bottom was cut up so high that it left my hip bone exposed as well as a good five inches of my untanned derriere."

Steinem fit the bunny mold, and no actual interviews were held. She fit the look and was hired. "Hippety-hop, I'm a Bunny!" she wrote.

While some formalities were still being worked out (like being able to produce a copy of a birth certificate and social security number card belonging to "Marie" – which she was able to successfully stall), she had to undergo a medical exam that included an "internal physical." When she inquired why, she was told, "It's free and it's for everybody's good." The medical was with a Playboy-sanctioned doctor. She was also required to get a chest x-ray at the Department of Health.

Steinem now entered Bunny Training, which included make-up

guidance as well as Bunny Bible study, Bunny Mother Lecture, Bunny Father Lecture, Bunny School, floor training, and a written test (which she purposefully messed up to make it look more authentic, and she still received the highest score in her class).

Fully dressed in her Bunny costume, Steinem could enter the inner world as no one had ever done. She quickly learned that behind the joyful appearance ("Bunnies must always appear gay and cheerful") was a system of fear with constant threats of being docked demerits and exposed by secret shoppers. A Bunny's pay was also nowhere near the promised $200 to $300 a week, which would be about $1,700 to $2,600 today.

They were only paid $50 a week (about $430) because of New York City's minimum wage laws at the time – much of their tips were taken away. Steinem wrote in *SHOW*: "The Club takes 50 percent of the first $30 worth of those that are charged, 25 percent of amounts up to $60 and 5 percent after that," for drink orders. "We may keep all cash tips that are given to us in case, but if we indicate any preference for cash tips, we will be fired." And certain positions, like working hat check, did not get tips at all.

The low pay made the embarrassment worse, as did being stared at by men offering their hotel room keys during their alcohol-fueled outings. But no matter what happened, the Bunnies had to stay on script. They were required to use the Bunny Stance, "a model's pose with one hip jutted out," and the Bunny Dip, a "back-leaning way of placing drinks on low tables without falling out of their costumes." ("I felt like an idiot," she wrote when she put the Dip into action.)

Steinem also had to spend numerous hours confined in that unpleasant costume. "My feet were still so swollen from the night before that I could barely get my regulation three-inch heels on, and I had gauze wrapped around my middle where the costume had dug in," she wrote.

While Steinem continually feared getting caught for not having proper credentials – or for being identified by people she knew – she endured about a month as a Bunny unnoticed.

Her two-part story was very well received, and it was seen as part of a revolution – both as a first-person account by a journalist and a report of how Hugh Hefner's empire looked from the inside. The story was converted into a TV movie in 1985, with Kirstie Alley in the title role, and Steinem herself has republished the piece under the name "I Was a Playboy Bunny."

MAY 2
1972

On this day in history, after forty-eight years as director of the Federal Bureau of Investigation (FBI), J. Edgar Hoover died, leaving behind a formidable government organization without the director who had been wholly accountable for its existence and structure.

John Edgar Hoover was born to Dickerson Naylor Hoover and Annie Scheitlin Hoover on January 1, 1895, in Washington, D.C. The Hoover home was located on Capitol Hill, within blocks of the Library of Congress. Those who lived in the neighborhood known as Seward Square were primarily white, middle-class Protestants with government jobs. Hoover's father worked as a printer with the U.S. Coast and Geodetic Survey.

Hoover was a frail child, so his mother paid particular attention to him. She was his moral guide and disciplinarian. Hoover remained very close to his mother, living with her in the house where he was born for forty-three years until she died in 1938.

Hoover was an intelligent youth who graduated at the top of his class from the esteemed Central High School in 1913. After high school, Hoover worked as a file clerk at the Library of Congress and attended National University Law School night classes, which later became part of George Washington University. He obtained his law degree in 1916 and a graduate degree in law in 1917. That same year, the United States entered World War I (1914-1918). The Alien Enemy Bureau in the Department of Justice hired twenty-two-year-old Hoover to process newly arrived German and Austro-Hungarian immigrants; his job was to ascertain whether any of them might present a danger to America.

Within two years of joining the Department of Justice, Hoover had become special assistant to Attorney General A. Mitchell Palmer. Intensely anti-radical in his philosophy, Hoover quickly jumped the queue of federal law enforcement during the Red Scare of 1919 to 1920. The former librarian, Hoover, created a card index system cataloging every radical leader, organization, and publication in America, and by 1921, he had gathered an amazing 450,000 files. More than 10,000 alleged communists were apprehended as well during this time, yet most of these people were only briefly interrogated and freed. Even though the attorney general was decried for misusing his power during the Palmer Raids, Hoover survived untouched, and on May 10, 1924, he was promoted to Acting Director of the Bureau of Investigation, a division of the Justice Department created in 1909.

During the 1920s, with Congress' consent, Director Hoover significantly reorganized and enlarged the Bureau of Investigation. He developed the corruption-ridden Bureau into a professional crime-fighting organization, creating a crime laboratory, a centralized fingerprint file, and a training school for agents. In the 1930s, the Bureau of Investigation initiated a massive campaign against the scourge of organized crime created when Prohibition was brought into being. Infamous criminals like George "Machine Gun" Kelly and John Dillinger both died at the hands of the Bureau. In contrast, others, like Louis "Lepke" Buchalter, the mysterious head of Murder, Incorporated, were effectively investigated and prosecuted by Hoover's "G-men." Hoover, who had a sharp eye for public relations, took part in several of these extensively advertised arrests, and the Federal Bureau of Investigations, as it became known after 1935, became highly regarded by Congress and the American public.

With the beginning of World War II, Hoover revitalized the anti-espionage practices he had created during the first Red Scare in 1919, and domestic wiretaps and other electronic surveillance increased exponentially. After World War II, Hoover concentrated on the danger of extremists, especially communist sedition. The FBI gathered files on millions of Americans believed guilty of dissenting activity. Hoover labored directly with the House Un-American Activities Committee (HUAC) and Senator Joseph McCarthy, the United States' second Red Scare creator.

In 1956, Hoover created Cointelpro, a covert counterintelligence program that initially pursued the U.S. Communist Party but later was enlarged to penetrate and interrupt any militant group in the United States. During the 1960s, the enormous assets of Cointelpro were used against threatening factions like the Ku Klux Klan, but also it was used against African American civil rights movement and liberal anti-war coalitions. One person specifically under attack was civil rights leader Martin Luther King, Jr., who suffered organized persecution from the FBI.

By the time Hoover started working for his eighth president in 1969, the media, the public, and Congress had grown distrustful that the FBI may be misusing its authority. For the first time in his governmental career, Hoover sustained extensive condemnation, and Congress countered by passing laws necessitating Senate approval of future FBI directors and restricting their term to 10 years. On May 2, 1972, with the Watergate affair about to burst onto the national stage, J. Edgar Hoover died of heart disease at 77. The Watergate affair afterward showed that the FBI had unlawfully guarded President Richard Nixon from scrutiny, and Congress systematically scrutinized the agency. Disclosures of the FBI's abuses of power and unlawful surveillance prompted Congress and the media to become more wary of future supervision of the FBI.

Throughout his career as head of the FBI, Hoover diligently worked hard to maintain a clean public image. However, casting a shadow of suspicion over his activities, Hoover instructed his personal secretary to destroy all his personal files upon his death. His tactics of surveillance, wiretapping, and keeping detailed files on innocent citizens he deemed suspicious violated the civil liberties of many Americans.

After his death, Hoover became the subject of a Senate investigative committee in 1975 and 1976. The Select Committee to Study Governmental Operations with Respect to Intelligence Activities concluded that Hoover had significantly misused his governmental power and had infringed the First Amendment rights of free speech and free assembly by bullying those he regarded as a menace. Yet Hoover's constructive contributions could not be ignored. He coordinated and led an efficient, elite federal law enforcement agency through nearly half a century of American history.

MAY 3
1945

On this day in history, an estimated 7500 survivors of the concentration camps at Neuengamme, Stutthof, and Mittelbau-Dora and Soviet POWs in Germany were killed when a squadron of RAF Typhoons attacked and sunk two of the three ships that they had been placed on by the German SS. It was one of the most significant maritime losses of life in a single event ever. None of the ships were marked as Red Cross vessels, and intelligence reporting the status of the prisoners on those vessels was received by the British but not disseminated to the RAF squadron involved. Information about the raid remained classified until the 1970s.

During March and April 1945, concentration camp prisoners originating from Scandinavian countries were brought from camps all over Germany to the Neuengamme concentration camp near Hamburg, in the White Buses program coordinated through the Swedish Red Cross. (White Buses was a Swedish humanitarian operation to free Scandinavians in German concentration camps in Nazi Germany during the end stages of World War II. Although the White Buses program was created to rescue Scandinavians, fifty percent of those taken from the camps to Sweden were from other nations.) Eventually, Heinrich

Himmler agreed that Scandinavians, and selected others regarded as less dangerous to Germany, could be moved through Denmark to liberation in Sweden. Then between 16 and 28 April 1945, it was decided to empty Neuengamme of its remaining prisoners, along with other concentration camp inmates and Soviet POWs, to relocate them to a secret camp, either at Mysen in Norway or on the Baltic Island of Fehmarn where preparations were begun to house them under the authority of concentration camp guards evacuated from Sachsenhausen.

In the interim, they would be concealed from the advancing British and Canadian forces. The SS assembled a fleet of decommissioned ships in the Bay of Lubeck to accomplish this task, consisting of the liners *Cap Arcona* and *Deutschland*, the motor launch *Athen*, and the freighter Thielbek. The ship *Athen* was used to transfer prisoners to and fro, and once on their assigned ships, the inmates would be secured below decks and, in the holds, and not given food or medical attention.

On the evening of May 2, 1945, additional prisoners, primarily women and children from the Stutthof and Mittelbau-Dora concentration camps, were put onto barges and brought out to the anchored vessels. However, the *Cap Arcona* refused to accept any more prisoners, and over eight hundred were returned to the beach at Neustadt on the morning of May 3, where about five hundred were murdered in their barges by machine-gunning or savagely beaten to death while on the beach, their SS guards then looked to escape unencumbered.

By early May, any relocation plans that had been made were ruined by the quick British military proceeded to the Baltic, so the SS leadership, now located at Flensburg, discussed scuttling the ships with the prisoners still aboard. Later, at a war crimes tribunal, it was maintained that the prisoners were supposed to be moved to Sweden although, as none of the ships was Red Cross hospital marked, nor were they seaworthy, this was hardly credible. One SS leader also proclaimed that the prisoners would be killed "in compliance with Himmler's orders."

On May 3, British forces advanced on Lubeck and Wismar and

were informed by the Red Cross that there were 7000-8000 prisoners aboard ships in the Bay of Lubeck. The British also found the bodies of those killed that morning on the beach.

On May 3, 1945, the *Cap Arcona*, *Thielbek*, and the passenger liner *Deutschland* were attacked in the Bay of Lubeck by Hawker Typhoons of the Royal Air Force (RAF). Through Ultra Intelligence, the Western Allies found that most SS leaders and former concentration camp commandants had relocated with Heinrich Himmler in Flensburg, hoping to orchestrate a way to flee to Norway. The Western allies had seized intelligence from the rump Donitz government, also at Flensburg, that the SS leaders were to be helped in their escape to freedom from the Allies. They were issued with false naval uniforms to conceal their identities. Donitz tried to maintain the fiction that his administration had been free from involvement with the camps or in Hitler's policies of genocide.

The Swedish and Swiss Red Cross officials had informed British intelligence on May 2, 1945, of the large numbers of prisoners interned on ships at anchor in Lubeck Bay; this vital information was not passed on. The RAF commanders that ordered the strike believed that the flotilla of vessels being prepared in Lubeck Bay to accommodate leading SS personnel fleeing to German-controlled Norway under Donitz's orders.

Provided with lifejackets from locked storage compartments, most SS guards jumped overboard from *Cap Arcona*. German trawlers were sent to rescue *Cap Arcona's* crew members and guards, and they saved 400 SS men, 16 sailors, and 20 SS women. Three Hundred fifty of the 5,000 former concentration camp inmates aboard *Cap Arcona* survived. Of the 2,800 POWs on board the *Thielbek*, only 50 managed to be saved, whereas all 2,000 prisoners on the *Deutschland* were taken off onto the *Athen* before the *Deutschland* capsized.

On May 4, 1945, a British reconnaissance plane photographed the two wrecks, *Thielbek* and *Cap Arcona*, the Bay of Lubeck being shallow. The capsized wreck of *Cap Arcona* later drifted ashore, and the beached wreck finally broke up in 1949. For weeks after the attack, victims' bodies washed ashore, where they were buried in mass graves at

Neustadt in Holstein, Scharbeutz, and Timmendorfer Strand—parts of skeletons washed ashore over the following 30 years, with the last find in 1971.

MAY 4
1946

On this day in history, five deaths (three inmates and two guards) and fourteen prison guards were injured when a two-day violent escape attempt ended with the help of the marine corps at Alcatraz prison, located in San Francisco Bay. During Alcatraz's 29-year history, there were 14 escape attempts, but the "Battle of Alcatraz" ranks as the most violent in the prison's history.

Alcatraz Federal Penitentiary sits on its own island in San Francisco Bay, off the California coast. A maximum-security prison that operated as a civilian prison between 1934 and 1963, it became notorious for housing high-profile prisoners such as gangster Al Capone and convicted murderer Robert Stroud. Its island location, combined with the cold water and strong currents of San Francisco Bay, meant that it was widely believed to be impossible to escape from. The more than a mile swim was no easy task, let alone for unfit prisoners.

Prisoner Bernard Coy planned the 1946 escape – he had arrived in Alcatraz in 1938 after being sentenced to 25 years for a bank robbery. He was joined in the attempt by fellow prisoners Marvin Hubbard, Joseph Cretzer, Sam Shockley, Miran Thompson, and Clarence Carnes, the latter holding the dubious title of Alcatraz's youngest prisoner, convicted at eighteen and serving a 99-year-sentence for kidnapping and a life sentence for murder. Cretzer and three others had already attempted to break out from Alcatraz in 1941, which landed him in the high-security unit, D Block, for five years.

Coy – a cell-house orderly, a job that allowed him more freedom to move around the prison's main cellblock – first came up with his escape plan after watching the guards, noting weaknesses in their routine and the prison's security. He spotted that the gun gallery was only protected by bars, without any mesh or additional obstacles in front of it. The guards had a routine, so observing when the gallery would not be watched was easy. Coy began deliberately losing weight so that he could squeeze through the bars.

At around 1:30 p.m. on May 2, Hubbard set about distracting prison guard Bill Miller, allowing Coy to attack him from behind. Coy and Hubbard beat Miller unconscious and stole his keys. After releasing Carnes, Thompson, and Cretzer from their cells, Coy used pliers, and pipes to spread the bars of the gun gallery until they were wide enough for him to squeeze through.

By now, the armed gun gallery guard had returned, and he was strangled with his necktie until he was unconscious. The prisoners then raided the gallery for weapons and ammunition before moving on to the second stage of their plan – using hostages to commandeer the prison boat to get off the island.

The group soon had nine guards as hostages and locked them in cells. The only problem was that none of the prison guards Miller's keys seemed to open the door to the recreation yard, which led to the boat – he had hidden the correct key in the cell he was being held in.

By now, the breakout attempt had been discovered, and residents of San Francisco could hear the prison's sirens sounding out from across the bay. People gathered along the waterfront to catch a glimpse of the commotion, and members of the coastguard and Marines were mobilized to assist the prison guards.

Now realizing that their initial plan would not succeed, the prisoners decided to shoot their way out, and Coy began firing on guards in nearby watchtowers. Egged on by some others, Cretzer began firing into the cell where the guards were being held, and he fatally wounded Miller.

Meanwhile, work was underway on the outside to control the situation. A group of military, police, and prison guards began to attack the cellblock with grenades, causing the island to light up from afar. Fourteen guards were wounded in the gunfire that followed, and Officer Harold Stites – who had previously stopped an Alcatraz escape attempt in 1938 – was killed trying to regain control of the cellblock and rescue the guards. Explosives rained down on D Block, and it began to flood as the plumbing was damaged.

By the morning of May 4, 1946, after a nearly 48-hour siege, the cellblock was raided, and the bodies of Coy, Cretzer, and Hubbard were found – full of bullets and shrapnel. The three surviving escapees, realizing they had no choice but to surrender, had returned to their cells.

Thompson and Shockley were later executed in the gas chamber at San Quentin Prison for the murder of Miller. Carnes, who was believed to have attempted to stop the guards' killing, escaped the death penalty but had 99 more years added to his sentence.

Although the most violent in the prison's history, the "Battle of Alcatraz" was just one of fourteen escape attempts from Alcatraz during its twenty-nine years in operation. In June 1962, three men managed to escape the island – brothers Clarence and John Anglin and Frank Morris floated away on a raft. Their fate is still unknown. Of the thirty-six inmates who attempted to escape from the island, twenty-three were recaptured, six were shot and killed, two drowned, and five have been listed as 'missing, presumed drowned.'

MAY 5
1877

On this day in history, nearly a year following the massacre at the Battle of Little Bighorn, Sitting Bull, and a band of 5000 Sioux followers cross into Canada, hoping to find a safe haven away from the United States Army.

On June 25, 1876, Sitting Bull's warriors allied with other Native peoples in the Battle of Little Big Horn in Montana, which destroyed George Custer and over 200 soldiers of the 7th Cavalry. Concerned that their big victory would incite a colossal retribution by the American military, the Native Americans dispersed into smaller groups. During the subsequent year, the U.S. Army chased down and confronted several groups, pressing them to admit defeat and relocate to reservations.

Nevertheless, Sitting Bull and his supporters avoided a significant clash with the United States Army. They devoted the summer and winter after Little Bighorn to hunting buffalo in Montana and fighting small battles with American troops. Colonel Nelson A. Miles met with Sitting Bull in the fall of 1876 at a neutral site and attempted to entice him into surrendering and moving to a reservation. Although eager for peace, Sitting Bull declined. As the winner of the Battle of Little

Bighorn, Sitting Bull felt he should be imposing conditions on Miles, not the other way around.

Infuriated by what he saw as Sitting Bull's stubbornness, Miles moved up his campaign of provocation against the chief and his people. Sitting Bull's group wandered around Montana in search of gradually more scarce buffalo, but the relentless moving, scarcity of food, and military pressure began to take a toll. On this day in 1877, Sitting Bull deserted his ancestral homeland in Montana and led his people north across the border into Canada.

The group settled in the Wood Mountain area in what is now southern Saskatchewan. Inspector James Morrow Walsh of the North-West Mounted Police, traveling with half a dozen men, rode into the camp, which contained 5,000 Sioux. He and his entourage met with Sitting Bull, and they guaranteed him protection from pursuit by the U.S. Army if they obeyed the laws of Canada and did not raid across the U.S.-Canada border. Sitting Bull agreed to these terms, denounced the Americans, and claimed to be a "British Indian."

During the summer of 1877, the air was tense as incidents and disagreements flared-up and threatened to turn into war. Three American emissaries who tried to convince Sitting Bull to return to the U.S. were detained by the Sioux and were released only by the intercession of Walsh and Acheson Gosford Irvine, the assistant commissioner of the NWMP. In another incident, Walsh arrested three Indians for horse stealing in the middle of the Sioux camp. The Canadians wondered if Sitting Bull, despite his promise, would launch forays across the border, perhaps provoking the U.S. Army into chasing him onto Canadian territory. Would the presence of the Sioux on Blackfoot hunting grounds start a war between the two fierce prairie tribes? Were rumors of an alliance between Sitting Bull and Louis Riel, then in Montana, correct in 1878?

The U.S. government wanted Sitting Bull and his Sioux to either return to American territory, where it could control them, or settle for good in Canada. Canadian officials, who did not want the Sioux on Canadian soil, wanted them to recross the border to America but did not dare risk war with the Indians using force. A meeting was held with American officials, and once again, Sitting Bull refused to return to the U.S. Walsh continued to urge Sitting Bull to return as they would never be given a reserve, food, or Canadian status, plus the buffalo would be gone within a few years. The latter prediction came true very quickly. In 1879 American hunters and traders set fires across the border to keep the buffalo south, and the end of the buffalo hunt on the Canadian prairies was within sight.

During the winter of 1880-81, Sitting Bull, thinking about his own return, made inquiries about the reception of those who had previously left and surrendered. Canadian officials, including Walsh, continued to push Sitting Bull to return to his homeland. Finally, in July, a local trader, Jean-Louis Legare, led Sitting Bull and his 187 remaining Sioux back to the United States, where they surrendered at Fort Buford, North Dakota, on July 19, 1881.

Sitting Bull was imprisoned for two years and then allowed to settle in the Standing Rock Agency, where he would remain. He briefly toured with Buffalo Bill's Wild West Show, visiting Toronto and Montreal in August 1885. In the late 1880s, a movement that foretold the return of a Messiah who would wipe out the whites and return the buffalo swept across the American West. This new religion and its Ghost Dance were soon outlawed. Sitting Bull, recognizing a chance to recover his lost status and power, became a leader of the Messiah "craze." The authorities still feared Sitting Bull's influence and announced a warrant for his arrest in December 1890. The Indian police who tried to enforce the warrant at the reserve enraged Sitting Bull's followers, and in the trading of gunfire, Sitting Bull was killed.

The most enigmatic Indian of the era, perhaps of all time, Sitting Bull was seen as a hero by some and a savage murderer by others. On hearing of his friend's death, Major Walsh said: "He was not the bloodthirsty man reports from the prairies made him out to be. He asked for nothing but justice.... He was not a cruel man, he was kind of heart; he was not dishonest, he was truthful."

(Photo: Sitting Bull, 1883. Wikimedia Commons)

MAY 6
1937

On this day in history, the airship *Hindenburg*, the largest Zeppelin ever built and the pride of Nazi Germany, bursts into flames upon landing in Lakehurst, New Jersey, killing 35 passengers and crewmembers.

The *Hindenburg* was built in Germany in 1935, and at 804 feet long, it was considered by its customers as beyond compare. It may have only traveled at 80 mph, yet it still provided the quickest way of crossing the Atlantic Ocean – twice as fast as the swiftest ship. It was like being on a luxury liner and having already made dozens of voyages across the Atlantic from Germany to Brazil or America and back. Of course, it was not cheap – a one-way ticket across the Atlantic cost about US$400 (about US$7,500 in 2022).

With the Nazi swastika on its fins, it was named after the last president of Germany's Weimar Republic, Paul von Hindenburg, who had chosen Hitler as Chancellor in January 1933 and died in August 1934. Joseph Goebbels had wanted the airship to be known as *Adolf Hitler*, but the owner of the Zeppelin Company, Hugo Eckener, a well-known anti-Nazi, refused.

Before it became a transatlantic airship, the *Hindenburg* began its life as an instrument of the Nazi propaganda ministry run by Joseph Goebbels. In March 1936, ahead of a German vote to rally support for ratifying the re-occupation of the Rhineland, the *Hindenburg* was used to drop propaganda flyers while blasting out noisy patriotic music and slogans from massive loudspeakers broadcasting governmental speeches from a temporary onboard radio studio. (The poll returned a 99.8 percent vote in favor). On August 1, 1936, the *Hindenburg* made an extraordinary appearance sailing above the Olympic Stadium during the opening ceremony of the Berlin Olympics, pulling an Olympic flag in its wake.

On its 63rd and last, final journey, the *Hindenburg* departed from Frankfurt on May 3, 1937, and was scheduled to land at Lakehurst, New Jersey, on the morning of May 6. But poor weather had postponed its landing by nearly twelve hours. The captain, Max Pruss, amused his passengers by flying over New York City. (Pruss survived the catastrophe, dying aged 69 in 1960). The *Hindenburg* had a capacity for about 70 travelers, but there were only 36 travelers plus 61 crew on this trip.

At 7:25 p.m., the *Hindenburg* attempted to land by docking onto a 270-foot-high mooring mast, from where it could be winched down to the ground. The flight was the first North Transatlantic trip of the year, and TV and radio crews had assembled to record its appearance.

Radio reporter, Herbert Morrison, was explaining the events when mysteriously, the airship burst into flames. The ship's tail was soon consumed, but the *Hindenburg* stayed level for a few more seconds before the tail began to drop. As the ship slanted, passengers, crew, and bits of furniture were thrown against the walls; one passenger recalled being thrown 15 to 20 feet against a dining room wall and trapped there by several others.

The *Hindenburg* continued to lurch as the flames spread at almost 50 feet per second. Many on board were able to jump for their lives. "Oh, the humanity," wailed Morrison, a phrase that has entered the lexicon of American culture. Within just 32 seconds, the *Hindenburg* had been destroyed. "Approaching Lakehurst," reported British Pathe News in a bit of poetic reportage, "the *Hindenburg* appeared a conquering giant of the skies. But she proved a puny plaything in the mighty grip of fate. It almost seemed fate had set the stage for the horrible tragedy. A graceful craft sailing serenely to her doom."

Of the 97 people on the ship, 35 died: 13 passengers and 22 crew, plus one ground crew member. But 62 did live by jumping at the right time and running for safety. It was not the first or worst airship catastrophe, but the *Hindenburg* tragedy essentially brought the brief age of the airship to an immediate end. Despite many theories, the precise cause of the fire remains a mystery. Still, it is commonly believed to have been initiated by an electrostatic discharge – in simpler terms, a spark that ignited leaking hydrogen.

Radio announcer Herb Morrison, who came to Lakehurst to record a routine voice-over for an NBC newsreel, immortalized the *Hindenburg* disaster in a famous on-the-scene description in which he emotionally declared, "Oh, the humanity!" The recording of Morrison's commentary was immediately flown to New York, where it was aired as part of America's first coast-to-coast radio news broadcast.

Morrison's commentary was synced to the film footage and shown across the globe. The two mediums ran at slightly different speeds, so Morrison's voice had to be speeded up to match the film, adding to its emotional intensity.

Here is Herb Morrison's commentary, with the accompanying footage on YouTube:

https://www.youtube.com/watch?v=jH-mhZLuGRk

And, here, the text:

"It's burst into flames! It burst into flames, and it's falling, it's crashing! Watch it! Get out of the way! Get out of the way! Get this, Charlie; get this, Charlie! It's fire…and it's crashing! It's crashing terrible! Oh, my! Get out of the way, please! It's burning and bursting into flames and the… and it's falling on the mooring mast. And all the folks agree that this is terrible; this is one of the worst catastrophes in the world. Its flames…. Crashing, oh! Four- or five-hundred feet into the sky and it…it's a terrific crash, ladies and gentlemen. It's smoke, and it's in flames now; and the frame is crashing to the ground, not quite to the mooring mast. Oh, the humanity! And all the passengers screaming around here. I told you; it – I can't even talk to people; their friends are out there! Ah! It's…it…it's a…ah! I… I can't talk, ladies and gentlemen. Honest: It's just laying there, mass of smoking wreckage. Ah! And everybody can hardly breathe and talk and the screaming. Lady, I...I... I'm sorry. Honest: I...I can hardly breathe. I... I'm going to step inside, where I cannot see it. Charlie, that's terrible. Ah, oh... I can't. Listen folks; I... I'm going to have to stop for a minute because I've lost my voice. This is the worst thing I've ever witnessed."

(Photo: Zeppelin the Hindenburg on fire at the mooring mast of Lakehurst (United States of America) 6 May 1937. Wikimedia Commons)

MAY 7
1896

On this day in history, H.H. Holmes, one of America's first serial killers, is hanged in Philadelphia, Pennsylvania, for the murder of his one-time partner-in-crime Ben Pitezel. Despite Holmes's admission that he killed 27 other people (some were later found to be alive and well), he was formally connected to nine murders. Some estimates have his murder tally at 200 people, but these claims are most assuredly overstated. In addition to being a serial killer, he was a con artist who also involved himself in insurance fraud, swindling, check forging, three to four bigamous illegal marriages, and horse theft.

H.H. Holmes was born Herman Webster Mudgett in Gilmanton, New Hampshire, on May 16, 1861, to Levi Horton Mudgett and Theodate Page Price. Holmes's father was a farmer, trader, and house painter; his parents were devout Methodists. On July 4, 1878, at 17, he married Clara Lovering, and they had a son born on February 3, 1880. Holmes graduated from the University of Michigan's Department of Medicine and Surgery in 1884. Due to his violence towards her, Clara moved back to New Hampshire and had nothing more to do with him. In 1886, while still married to Clara, Holmes married Myrta Belknap in Minneapolis, Minnesota. He later filed for divorce from Clara, but the divorce was never finalized.

When Holmes appeared in Chicago in 1886, he was wanted by the law. As a con artist and bigamist, he went from one town to the next, evading prison time for different cons, including insurance fraud of a gruesome sort: Holmes was robbing and disfiguring medical corpses and imagining they were victims of accidents to collect insurance money.

Soon after landing in Chicago, Holmes got a job as a pharmacist, and he immediately made plans to build a "murder castle," a three-story structure that took up an entire city block at 63rd and Wallace streets. Holmes would call it the World's Fair Hotel, whose goal was to have room for tourists arriving by the thousands in Chicago for the 1893 Columbian Exposition. He would prey mostly on beautiful young females searching for a new and exhilarating life in the big city.

The *Chicago Tribune* published an article in 1937 that described Holmes' "Murder Castle": "O, what a queer house it was! In all America, there was none other like it. Its chimneys stuck out where chimneys should never stick out. Its stairways ended nowhere in particular. Winding passages brought the uninitiated with a frightful jerk back to where they had started. There were rooms that had no doors. There were doors that had no rooms. It was A mysterious house – a crooked house, a reflex of the builder's distorted mind. In that house occurred dark and eerie deeds."

The Pitezel family were the known victims of H.H. Holmes: Father Ben and his three children, daughters Alice and Nellie, and son Howard. The family was killed in late 1894. Instead of using a random corpse, Holmes used former business partner Ben as a segment of his insurance fraud scheme. Holmes knocked Ben unconscious and killed him by setting fire to his body. On July 15, 1895, Alice and Nellie's remains were located in a Toronto basement. Later, police found teeth and pieces of bone among the charred remains that belonged to Howard in an Indianapolis home that Holmes had leased.

Of Holmes' presumed casualties were Julia and her daughter Pearl Connor (1891), Emeline Cigrand (1892), and sisters Nannie and Minnie Williams (1893). (Minnie had married Holmes, who stole her inheritance.) The bodies of Julia, Emeline, Minnie, and Nannie were never found. Still, speculation was that Holmes most likely sold their bodies to medical schools. He had regularly stated that Julia and Emeline died while experiencing illegal abortions. Julia purportedly was Holmes' lover, and Emeline was Holmes' former secretary to whom he was rumored to have proposed marriage.

While exploring Holmes's hotel, police retrieved Nannie's garter buckle and Minnie's watch chain in one of the ovens. Although forensic evidence was undeveloped then, bones located in the basement probably belonged to 12-year-old Pearl Connor, whom he supposedly poisoned. As for Emeline, the authorities assumed they had come upon her hair and bones. One story alleges that an eyewitness saw Holmes and his janitor carry out a large trunk the day after her vanishing.

Although there is a long list of other prospective victims that Holmes may have murdered, these nine victims have been conceivably ascribed to the serial killer's killing spree.

While in prison awaiting his execution, Holmes wrote his autobiography. In it, he stated that "I was born with the very devil in me. I could not help the fact that I was a murderer, no more than a poet can help the inspiration to song, nor the ambition of an intellectual man to be great. The inclination to murder came to me as naturally as the inspiration to do right comes to the majority of persons."

Just before his execution, Holmes was said to be agreeable and peaceful. His only wish was that his body be buried 10 feet deep with his coffin covered in cement. (He did not want grave robbers to exhume his body and use it for medical experiments.)

When Holmes was finally put to death on the gallows, it was said his neck did not break. Instead, he slowly strangled to death, his body convulsing until he was finally pronounced dead 15 minutes later.

In 2017, amidst allegations Holmes had, in fact, evaded execution, his body was disinterred for testing. Due to his coffin being enclosed in cement, his body did not decompose normally. His clothes were almost completely preserved, and his mustache was found to be undamaged. The body was positively identified as Holmes' by his teeth. Holmes was then reburied.

MAY 8
1947

On this day in history, Polish resistance fighter Witold Pilecki, who had volunteered to be incarcerated in Auschwitz to gain information about the Holocaust during World War II, was arrested by Polish communist police. In September 1940, Witold Pilecki voluntarily surrendered to the Germans during a street raid in Warsaw. He did this to penetrate one of the worst places in Europe – the Auschwitz death camp. At Auschwitz, Pilecki assisted prisoners, wrote about the atrocities of the SS, and had the desire to release all prisoners. However, after the end of the war, the communist government condemned the Polish hero and sentenced him to death.

Witold Pilecki was born on May 13, 1901, in the city of Olonets, the Russian Empire. His family belonged to the aristocracy and had participated in the Polish uprising of 1863-1864. Witold inherited the desire to fight for Poland's independence, so he joined an underground organization called the Harcerstwo, modeled on British scouting.

Pilecki joined the Polish Army in 1920, during the Polish-Soviet War (1919-1921). As part of the 211 Uhlan regiment, Pilecki took part in the Battle of Warsaw, the battle in Rudniki Forest, and the liberation of Wilno. After the war, he restored the family estate, got married, and became a father. However, the quiet life was short.

On September 1, 1939, soldiers from Nazi Germany invaded Poland from the west, and on September 17, the Soviet Union invaded the country from the east. Pilecki was drafted into the Polish Army, and until October 17, 1939, he fought against the German forces as a platoon commander in the 19th Infantry Division.

Shortly after that, he made his way to Warsaw to take part in the creation of the underground Resistance organization called the Secret Polish Army (Tajna Armia Polska, or TAP). It was established on November 9, 1939.

In 1940, Pilecki developed a plan for penetrating the Auschwitz concentration camp. Until then, Auschwitz was considered a large prison, and although it was known for harsh conditions, it was not widely known that a death camp had been established there. Pilecki planned to study the situation at Auschwitz and see if it was possible to start an uprising and free the prisoners. The command approved the plan and gave him false papers.

German soldiers regularly organized raids and searches on the streets of Polish cities to find Jews and Poles involved in the resistance. On September 19, 1940, Pilecki voluntarily surrendered as "Tomasz Serafinski" to the Germans during one of these raids. He and about 2,000 other people were taken to Auschwitz two days later.

In the camp, Pilecki was assigned prisoner number 4859. He became the organizer of an underground network called the Union of Military Organizations (ZOW).

He wrote reports about the camp's structure and the prisoners' condition, and Resistance agents were able to get these reports to the Polish government-in-exile in London. Thanks to Pilecki's work, the world learned that a system of extermination of Jews had been created at Auschwitz.

The camp's SS security teams began to cause trouble for Pilecki and his agents. He proposed holding an armed uprising with the help of the Polish Home Army. The chances for success were slim, at best.

In April 1943, Pilecki was able to escape. When he went to work outside of the camp, he and two other Poles neutralized the guards, took away their weapons, cut the phone line, and got away in the night. After his escape, he prepared a report on the situation in Auschwitz called "Witold's Report."

Later, he was able to join the Home Army. In 1944 Pilecki took part in the Warsaw Uprising, after which he was captured by the Germans and put in a pow camp until the end of the war when the Americans freed him.

In 1945 he wrote a detailed version of "Witold's Report" about Auschwitz, which was not released until 2000. In this report, he described every crime that he witnessed. He testified that the Soviet prisoners of war were exterminated as quickly as the Poles and Jews.

After WWII ended, Pilecki remained among those Poles who wanted to regain Poland's independence. He joined the Polish II Corps, created in 1943 and led by General Wladyslaw Anders. In the autumn of 1945, Pilecki began conducting intelligence activities for Anders in Poland. (He had briefly been in Italy but was ordered back to Poland.) He organized a network of agents and began collecting information on the activities of the new pro-Soviet authorities and Home Army soldiers who were prisoners in the NKVD camps in the country.

Despite the threat of exposure and the order of General Anders, Pilecki did not leave Poland, despite being warned to leave. On May 8, 1947, he was captured. After brutal torture carried out in the Polish Ministry of Public Security, comparable to the NKVD, Pilecki was accused of espionage, illegal possession of weapons, illegal border crossings, using forged documents, and plotting the assassination of officials in the Ministry of Public Security.

Pilecki refused to admit guilt in the assassination charge but did not conceal that he was carrying out intelligence activities for the 2nd Corps. The investigation and the trial were carried out with numerous violations.

On May 15, 1948, Witold Pilecki was sentenced to death. After announcing the death sentence, Pilecki responded, "I've been trying to live my life so that in the hour of my death, I would rather feel joy than fear."

On May 25, the sentence was carried out in the Mokotow Prison in Warsaw. Pilecki was executed with a shot to the back of his head.

Pilecki left behind a wife, son, and daughter. The name of the hero who revealed to the world the truth of what was happening in the Auschwitz death camp was banned in Poland until the Polish People's Republic collapsed in 1990.

MAY 9
1671

On this day in history, Thomas Blood, an Irish soldier of fortune better known as "Colonel Blood," is caught endeavoring to steal the English Crown Jewels from the Tower of London. Masquerading as a clergyman, Blood and his crew snatched the royal regalia from under the nose of their keeper. Still, they were apprehended as they attempted to escape through the capitol. Blood was inexplicably pardoned by the King, and the regalia, although looking a little worse for wear, was given a much more secure home.

Blood was born in 1618 in County Clare in the Kingdom of Ireland. He first rose to distinction during the English Civil War when he left the Royalist cause and joined Oliver Cromwell's Parliamentary Roundheads. The treachery earned him a profitable estate in Ireland, but he lost it following King Charles II's 1660 restoration to the throne. From then on, the slick Irishman became an intriguer, plotter, and conspirator extraordinaire. He participated in numerous Republican schemes to murder the king and even attacked Ireland's Dublin Castle during a failed 1663 coup. In 1670, he masterminded an attempted abduction and killing of the Duke of Ormond, former lord lieutenant of Ireland. Blood – who called himself "Colonel" even though he never achieved that rank in the military – soon had a bounty of 1,000 pounds on his head, causing him to live in hiding under false names.

In 1671, Blood resurfaced and began to plan the theft of England's Crown Jewels. Britain's inaugural royal regalia had been melted down years before. They were disposed of in 1649 during Cromwell's rule, but with the resurgence of the monarchy, Charles II had spent a large sum to acquire substitutes. They encompassed a crown embellished with diamonds and other rare stones, a golden orb, and a gold scepter. The treasures were secured in a basement room in the Tower of London. Their keeper was Talbot Edwards, a 77-year-old ex-soldier who could supplement his income by exhibiting the jewels to tourists in exchange for a small stipend.

Colonel Blood's scheme was a long con. In 1671, he disguised himself as a clergyman and enlisted the help of an actress to play his wife. The two imposters then went to the Tower, met with Edwards, and viewed the Crown Jewels, secured behind a metal grate in a room protected by a reinforced door. At one point, Mrs. Blood faked a severe stomach ailment, prompting Edwards to invite her into his upstairs apartment to recover. "Parson," Blood thanked Edwards for his hospitality. A few days later, he returned with a gift for Edward's wife.

In the following weeks, the Colonel spun a complex web of deceit. He even claimed to have a rich nephew who would be a perfect match for Edward's single daughter. Edward was more than delighted, and it was agreed that a meeting between the two would be set up.

At 7 a.m. on May 9, 1671, Blood arrived at the Tower with four acquaintances: his son Thomas, who was to pose as an eligible bachelor, and Robert Perrot, Richard Halliwell, and William Smith. Each man was armed with hidden pistols and daggers. Blood – still dressed as a clergyman – also had a wooden mallet concealed in his robes.

The gang met with the unsuspecting Edwards. The two young people went upstairs to Edward's living quarters, and the rest of Blood's gang asked to see the Crown Jewels. No sooner had he unlocked the door that he was ambushed by Blood and his men, who overpowered him. When Edwards fought back, Blood hit him in the head with the mallet and stabbed him in the stomach.

With Edwards out of commission, the gang began to prepare the regalia for travel. The Colonel flattened the crown, and another began sawing the four-foot plus state scepter in half to make it easier for travel. Perrot, meanwhile, merely stuffed the golden royal orb down the front of his pants. At that moment, Halliwell, who was the lookout, rushed in and proclaimed that Edwards' son Wythe, a soldier, had come home unexpectedly and was upstairs trying to find his father. The thieves were forced to gather up their bounty and flee. When they left the Jewel House, Talbot Edwards managed to slip off his gag and raise the alarm by yelling, "Treason! The crown is stolen!"

Alerted to the danger, Wythe and a Swedish military engineer named Martin Beckman managed to apprehend Blood and his accomplices despite the thieves taking a few shots. The thieves were in chains, and the Crown Jewels were safe.

Blood, upon capture, defied his jailers and refused to talk to anyone but the king. Surprisingly, he was given an audience with the sovereign. Little is known about what was said, but apparently, Blood confessed to his crimes and gave the king a long-winded account of his exploits. He even admitted that he once planned to assassinate Charles with a musket while the king was bathing in the Thames River. He lost his nerve, he stated, after finding himself "in awe of His Majesty." Asked what he would do if allowed to have his freedom, he replied that he "would endeavor to deserve it." Blood's crimes should have gotten him a traitor's death, but Charles II shocked everyone and issued a full pardon to Blood and his gang. He also granted him land in Ireland worth 500 pounds a year.

Whatever Charles intended to exonerate Blood; he no doubt understood the outlaw's prospective effectiveness as a political operative. After obtaining the King's grace, the Colonel spent his final years as England's most renowned tough guy, working diversely as an informant, spy, and enforcer for the crown. However, he could not give up his propensity for trouble and later involved himself in courtly machinations and independent undercover activities. By the time he died in 1680, sick and deeply in debt, his reputation for deception was so well established that the authorities disinterred his corpse to ensure he did not fake his own death. The famed rogue was then reinterred under a headstone that read: "Here lies the man who boldly hath run through more villainies than England ever knew."

MAY 10
1865

On this day in history, Jefferson Davis, president of the defeated Confederate government, is captured with his wife and staff near Irwinville, Georgia, by a detachment of soldiers from the Union's 4th Michigan Cavalry regiment.

On April 2, 1865, with the Confederate loss at Petersburg, Virginia, on the horizon, General Robert E. Lee advised President Davis that he could no longer safeguard Richmond and recommended the Confederate government abandon its capital. Davis and his cabinet escaped to Danville, Virginia, with Robert E. Lee's surrender on April 9, deep into the South. Lee's defeat of his large Army of Northern Virginia essentially finished the Civil War, and throughout the next few weeks, the remaining Confederate armies conceded one by one. The collapse of the Confederacy shattered Davis. Declining to admit losing the war, he wanted to flee to a friendly foreign country such as Britain or France. He contemplated the advantages of establishing a government in exile when a unit of the 4th Michigan Cavalry arrested him.

A particular measure of debate encompasses his capture, as Davis was dressed in his wife's black shawl when the Union soldiers apprehended him. The Northern press mocked him as a coward, contending that he had concealed himself as a woman in an unfortunate effort to evade capture and that he donned a petticoat to avoid capture. However, Davis, and particularly his wife, Varina, insisted that he was in poor health and that his wife had lent him her shawl to keep him warm during their challenging trip.

The narrative of Jefferson Davis's seizure in a dress took on a life of its own, as one Northern cartoonist after another used his creativity to portray the event. Printmakers published over 20 distinct lithographs of unforgiving sketches depicting Davis in a frilly bonnet and large skirt, holding a knife and bags of gold as he escaped Union soldiers. These sketches were supplemented with derisive descriptions, many of them savoring in sexual jokes and intimations and many placing disgraceful words in Davis's mouth. Over the years, fact and fiction have combined with concern about the specifics of Davis's final arrest. Had he used his wife's dress to escape the Union cavalry? How much of the unfavorable post-capture caricatures, news reports, and song lyrics leaped from Northerners' deep resentment toward the man who epitomized the Confederacy?

After Lee's capitulation, Davis would be on the run for six weeks, an epic trek through four states by railroad, horse, ferry boat, cart, and wagon. By May 10, he would become a prisoner. Others, including his aides, would wonder for years why Davis had not fled to Texas, Cuba, Mexico, or Europe. The Confederate Secretary of War John C. Breckinridge and Secretary of State Judah Benjamin had absconded overseas.

On May 9, Davis made camp for the evening with Varina's wagon train near Irwinville, Georgia. President Davis's escort did not circle their wagons. It would be hard for Davis to take advantage of the confusion and escape. Instead, Davis's party made camp with an open plan and scattered the tents and wagons over a 100 yards radius.

For unknown reasons, the camp posted no guards that night, even though they faced a real threat of attack from ex-Confederate soldiers – ruthless, war-weary bandits bent on plunder – or Union cavalry on the hunt for Davis. It was no secret that criminals had been following Varina Davis's wagon train for several days and could strike anytime without warning. That was why Davis had reunited with Varina instead of pushing on alone.

Davis had put himself into a no-win situation. Union soldiers were flooding into Georgia on the hunt for Davis. They had even enlisted the help of local Blacks in scouring the various back roads. Davis had told his men that he would leave the camp that night. He has dressed for the road: a dark, wide-brimmed felt hat; a signature wool frock coat of Confederate gray; gray trousers; high black leather riding boots and spurs. His horse, tied near Varina's tent, was already saddled and ready to ride. Unknown to the camp, a detachment of the 4th Michigan Cavalry Regiment was approaching Irwinville.

Soldiers of the 1st Wisconsin Cavalry had descended upon Davis's camp at the same time as the 4th Michigan Cavalry had. There had been rumors that Davis was transporting a large amount of Confederate gold in his bid to escape capture. During the confusion, the two cavalry units began firing upon each other. Only after the deadly skirmish that the 4th Michigan realize they had captured Jefferson Davis. One Davis party member later described the captive's rough treatment: "A private stepped up to him rudely and said, 'Well, Jeffy, how do you feel now?' I was so exasperated that I threatened to kill the fellow, and I called upon the officers to protect their prisoner from insult."

The image of the Confederate president posing as a woman stimulated Northerners but angered Southerners. A wave of sheet music artwork and satiric lyrics followed the parodies in newspapers and prints. Davis would spend two years incarcerated at Fort Monroe in Hampton, Virginia, before his release on bail. The federal authorities would never prosecute him for fear he may win, thus giving legitimacy to the secessionists and their cause. He outlived Lincoln by 24 years, wrote his memoirs, and became the South's most beloved living icon of the Civil War. Although he dedicated the rest of his life to upholding the memory of the Confederacy, its honored dead, and the Lost Cause, Jefferson Davis could never disperse the legend of his capture dressed as a Southern belle. The legend has survived to this day.

MAY 11
1891

On this day in history, the Otsu incident occurred, which was an unsuccessful assassination attempt on the Russian Prince Nicholas (future Czar Nicholas II) during his visit to Japan while en route to Vladivostok to mark the beginning of the construction of the Trans-Siberian Railway.

Prince Nicholas was scheduled to attend ceremonies marking the beginning of the building of the Trans-Siberian Railroad. On his way there by sea, he officially visited Japan. The Russian Pacific Fleet with the Prince stopped in Kagoshima, Nagasaki, and Kobe. From Kobe, Nicholas traveled by land to Kyoto, where he was met by a delegation led by Prince Arisugawa Taruhito. This was the first visit by a foreign dignitary since Prince Heinrich of Prussia in 1880 and two British princes in 1881, and the military influence of the Russian Empire was increasing in the Far East. Therefore, the Japanese government placed much weight on using this visit to foster better Russo-Japanese relations. Nicholas showed interest in traditional Japanese crafts, got a dragon tattoo on his right arm, and bought an ornamental hairpin for a Japanese girl who happened to be near him.

On May 11, he was seated in new jinrikishas (rickshaws) sent down by Emperor Meiji, Nicholas and his distant cousin, Prince George of

Greece, who had been accompanying Nicholas on his trek to Vladivostok – and escorted by Prince Arisugawa Takehito – headed out for a day near Lake Biwa in Otsu, Shiga Prefecture. It was a relaxing day with scenic views, shopping (George bought a bamboo cane), and good conversation. However, as the long line of rickshaws made its way out of Otsu, one of the policemen lining the narrow road harbored a boiling animosity toward the young and wealthy Russian royal. Even worse, he had been assigned to protect Nicholas from anyone hostile – a duty he wanted no part of.

According to one eyewitness account, the policeman, Tsuda Sanzo, "drew his sword and struck at the prince's neck. His Royal Highness – riding at the head of a long line of jinrikishas, with two coolies drawing him – jumped back as (Sando) cut at him, and the force of the blow was broken by his cap. However, he was cut on the head, and it is said that a small piece of skull was chipped off." Seeing the attack from afar, Prince George jumped out of his jinrikisha and ran after Sando, striking him with the bamboo cane. It did not bring him down, but fortunately, two rickshaw drivers (Mukaihata Jizaburo and Kitagaichi Ichitaro) abandoned their strollers and ran towards Sando, one tackling the officer and the other disarming him. They were handsomely rewarded for their quick action and bravery – the Japanese government gave them a yearly stipend of 36 yen, while Nicholas gave them 2,500 yen plus an annual amount of 1,000 yen. Later, when Jizaburo and Ichitaro were given the cash amounts on Nicholas' ship, the prince "told them to stop pulling jinrikishas, and settle down to something better."

The attack, which occurred in "only a few seconds," rippled across the two competing nations. Nicholas "suffered all his life from headaches" and had been traumatized enough to ask, every May 11, that the Russian public pray for his well-being. The "9-centimeter wound" would be a lifelong reminder of how close to death he had been.

As for Sando, two weeks after his attack, he was tried and sentenced to life imprisonment in Hokkaido. Several months into his life sentence, Sando died of pneumonia while in jail, although others say he starved himself to death.

Japan, and Emperor Meiji, stood embarrassed and angered by the attack. To his credit, Meiji attempted to smooth over the feelings of the future Russian Emperor by traveling to see Nicholas on his ship while he nursed his wound. Some members of the Japanese government did not want Meiji to visit Nicholas on board the vessel for fear that the Russians would abduct him. Meiji would not be swayed, and the two had a lovely visit that Nicholas appreciated.

Nicholas stated in his diary that "(I) am not so very angry at the good Japanese for the repulsive act of one fanatic. As before, their model order and cleanliness is a pleasure, and I must confess I keep on watching... whom I see on the street from afar." One moment continued to bother him, though, and it stemmed from the passivity of the surrounding Japanese bystanders, who'd only been happy to see him just before. "What I couldn't understand was how Georgie, that fanatic, and I ended up alone, in the middle of the street, why no one from the crowd rushed to my aid."

The "Otsu incident" is sometimes credited as an event that raised tensions to a war-like level between the two countries. Still, thanks largely to Emperor Meiji's in-person visit and a few "private" moments, it appears that Nicholas did not leave Japan with any deep-rooted hostility, nor did many of his close associates believe he longed for war. On January 26, 1904, less than 13 years after Sando's attack, Nicholas wrote in his diary: "...received a telegram... with the news that... Japanese torpedo boats had carried out an attack against the Tsesarevich, Pallada, etc., which were at anchor, and put holes in them. Is this an undeclared war? Then may God help us!" Shortly after that, the Russo-Japanese War began, and Korea, Manchuria, and even a portion of Sakhalin Island were soon brought under Japanese control.

As for the rest of Nicholas's life, a far grizzlier fate awaited than being sword-struck by a Japanese madman. On July 17, 1918, Bolshevik assassins gathered the entire Romanov family (Nicholas, his wife, and their five children) and brought them into a basement. A massacre ensued, and within an hour, the 300-year Romanov dynasty was over, their bodies burnt with acid. Nicholas was 50 years old.

MAY 12
1932

On this day in history, the body of aviation hero Charles Lindbergh's baby is found more than two months after he was abducted from his family's Hopewell, New Jersey, estate.

Lindbergh, who became the first global superstar five years before when he piloted *The Spirit of St. Louis* across the Atlantic, and his spouse Anne Morrow Lindbergh found a ransom note in their 20-month-old child's vacant room on March 1, 1932. The abductor had used a ladder to climb up to the open second-floor window, leaving muddy footprints in the room. In barely readable English, the ransom note demanded $50,000.

Even though there were traces of forced access, including a broken ladder and footprints on the ground underneath the nursery window, there was nothing directly useful to law enforcement. By the next day, the national press had gotten hold of the story and sent teams of journalists to Lindbergh's estate. In addition, many well-wishers and uninvited volunteers showed up as well, and with all these people tramping around, they had rendered the crime scene and the retrieval of further evidence impossible.

The next day J. Edgar Hoover and the FBI offered their aid to the New Jersey State Police. Early on, however, it was Lindbergh himself that was largely supervising the process, which put him in a spot to accept help from colleagues with connections to the mob – they suspected an organized crime extortion plot – and a retired school principal from the Bronx named Dr. John F. Condon who decided to get involved in the high-stakes negotiations to come.

Lindbergh continued to receive ransom letters from the kidnapper. Five days after the original abduction, a letter from Brooklyn upped the stake to $70,000, while a third demanded that Lindbergh use no middlemen. Condon, however, chose to put an ad in *The Bronx Home News*, offering the kidnapper an extra $1,000 if he used him as a go-between.

The kidnapper was okay with using Condon as an intermediary. The communications soon became a grueling wild-goose chase, with more letters indicating where to find other notes, and, at one point, the kidnapper produced a piece of young Charlie's clothing to demonstrate that they were not just unscrupulous fraudsters. Finally, after a series of in-person meetings at an upper Manhattan cemetery and letter swaps that brought them to the twelfth ransom note and took the price down to $50,000, Condon gave the cash to the kidnappers and was told that the infant could be found in Martha's Vineyard on a vessel called the "Nellie."

Charlie Jr. was nowhere to be found.

On May 12, a little over a month after the letdown in Massachusetts and 72 days after the child first went missing, Charlie Jr.'s brutalized body was found alongside a road near the Lindbergh estate. The body was burned, partly decomposed, with missing limbs and a hole drilled into his crushed skull.

The enormous nationwide appeal of the case and urgency put on it by first Hoover and then President Roosevelt led to hundreds of tips from well-meaning (and some not-so-well-meaning) people. Over 200 individuals even "confessed" to the crime, but none of their stories were true.

The kidnapping appeared as if it would remain unresolved until September 1934, when a marked bill from the ransom surfaced. The gas station worker who had accepted the money was suspicious of the driver who had given it to him and written down the license plate number. It was traced back to Bruno Hauptmann, a German immigrant. Investigators found $13,000 of Lindbergh's ransom money when his home was examined. Hauptmann argued that a friend had given him the money to hold and that he had no relationship to the offense.

An astounding 700 reporters went to Flemington, New Jersey, at the beginning of 1935, ready for what was to be a sensational trial. It had all the ingredients necessary for a considerable amount of press-feeding hysteria: An American hero pitted against a German, a strange vanishing, a dead child, and plenty of lingering uncertainty.

The trial continued for six weeks and hung on circumstantial evidence, including a wooden board from a broken ladder that the kidnapper used to sneak into the Lindbergh child's bedroom nearly three years before. Lindbergh and his wife, who had moved out of their house after the kidnapping and killing and donated it to charity, testified about the night their son was kidnapped and likely killed; Anne's testimony was so emotional that the defense chose not to cross-examine her.

Condon, who met the kidnapper twice, also testified in the trial, asserting that Hauptmann had joined him that night for the money transfer, even though he did not indicate that during an earlier police line-up before Hauptmann was charged.

Hauptmann declined to confess. He was found guilty and sentenced to death, conducted by the State of New Jersey via electric chair in 1936. Questions about whether he kidnapped and murdered the Lindbergh baby remain to this day, with some experts indicating that, at the very least, he did not act alone in perpetrating the crime.

MAY 13
1958

On this day in history, an attack on United States Vice President Richard Nixon's motorcade in Caracas, Venezuela, occurred during his goodwill tour of South America. The assault on Nixon's car was called, at the time, the "most violent attack ever perpetrated on a high American official while on foreign soil." Close to being slain while a couple of his aides were wounded in the skirmish, Nixon ended up unscathed, and his group managed to reach the American embassy.

By 1958, relations between America and Latin America had reached a low point. Latin Americans protested that the U.S. attention on the Cold War and anticommunism failed to address many Latin American countries' pressing economic and political needs. They reasoned that their nations needed more basic financial assistance, not more arms, to repel communism. They also questioned the United States' support of dictatorial regimes in Latin America only because those governments claimed to be anti-Communist. Nixon's visit took place only a few months after the January toppling of Venezuelan dictator Marcos Perez Jimenez, who in 1954 had been given the Legion of Merit and was later granted sanctuary in the United States.

This was the atmosphere Vice President Nixon arrived in during his friendship trip through Latin America in April and May 1958. The journey began with controversy, as Nixon participated in loud and bitter debates with student groups during his movements through Peru and Uruguay. In Caracas, Venezuela, however, things took a menacing turn.

Before Nixon arrived in Caracas, it was reported in the media that an attempt had been planned on the vice president's life during his visit. The Caracas municipal government even passed a resolution declaring Nixon *persona non grata*. Meanwhile, the CIA station chief in Venezuela urged that this portion of the South American trip be canceled.

Robert Anderson, retired press attaché to the United States Embassy in Venezuela, claimed that the demonstrators who disrupted the Venezuela portion of the tour "had been bused down by the professional agitators and organizers" associated with Venezuela's Communist Party. At the time, it was considered "another of the well-planned campaigns of harassment" and a "communist-sparked onslaught."

Nixon arrived, by airplane, in Caracas on May 13, 1958. A large group of activists at the airport "purposely disrupted…(the) welcoming ceremony by shouting, blowing whistles, waving derogatory placards, throwing stones, and showering the Nixons with human spittle and chewing tobacco." An American newspaper wrote that "Venezuelan troops and police seemed to evaporate. The vice-president and the whole official party had to struggle to get to their cars behind a thin but sturdy phalanx of U.S. Secret Service agents."

For the first time on the South American tour, the Nixons traveled in closed-top cars instead of convertibles, a decision later credited with saving their lives. As they traveled by motorcade through Caracas, the vehicles slowed to a crawl by heavy traffic. The crowd began stoning the vice president's car and banging the windows with fists. Nixon was protected by twelve Secret Service agents, some of whom were injured in the encounter. Venezuelan police never intervened during the whole trip. When the mob began rocking the car back and forth to overturn it, Secret Service agents drew their firearms and prepared to shoot into the crowd because they felt that the vice president's life was in danger.

Secret Service agent-in-charge Jack Sherwood was ordered by Nixon to hold his fire and shoot only on his orders; no shots were ultimately fired.

Venezuelan Foreign Minister Oscar Garcia Velutini, traveling with Nixon in the motorcade, was "close to hysterics" and kept repeating, "This is terrible, this is terrible." Several people in the limousine were hurt when shattered glass hit them. The vehicle supposedly had "shatter-proof" glass. Nixon's car could finally escape the mob because the U.S. press corps' flatbed truck had cleared a path through the crowd.

Shortly afterward, the Nixons arrived at the embassy, and the Venezuelan army surrounded and fortified the building, reinforcing the small American Marine guard force. That afternoon, the ruling military government members came to the embassy and lunched with Nixon. The following day, representatives of the country's major labor unions went to the embassy and requested an audience with Nixon, which he granted. The union leaders apologized for the previous day's events. They disavowed their involvement, although it was felt by officials that "they probably were the instigators or at least encouraged the actions."

The Americans began mobilizing a Marine Division and the 101st Airborne Division to a staging area in Puerto Rico. They also sent an aircraft carrier, eight destroyers, and two amphibious assault ships toward Venezuela. President Eisenhower was said to be preparing to "invade Venezuela" should Nixon suffer further indignity. Privately, Eisenhower was said to have been very angry about the attack on Nixon and, at one point, told aides, "I am about ready to go put my uniform on."

In response to the movement of American military forces into the area, the leader of the ruling military junta assured the U.S. government that the Nixon party would be "protected fully" after that.

The Nixon group left Venezuela early the next day, cutting its visit short by seven hours. The Venezuelan army protected the motorcade the entire way to the airport.

Eisenhower ordered that Nixon receive a "hero's welcome" upon his return; all American government employees in Washington, D.C., were given the day off work to turn out for the vice president's arrival.

Nixon disembarked the aircraft before "a cheering crowd of 10,000," including congressional leaders and ambassadors from many Latin American nations.

Eisenhower personally greeted Nixon, and the two journeyed to the White House along a route lined by 100,000 people.

MAY 14

1610

On this day in history, Catholic zealot, and delusional fanatic Francois Ravaillac stabs France's first Bourbon king, Henry IV, in a crowded street in Paris one day after the coronation of his wife, Queen Marie de Medici.

Henry IV was the son of Jeanne III of Navarre and Antoine de Bourbon, Duke of Vendome. He was baptized a Catholic but raised in the Protestant faith by his mother. He became heir to the throne of Navarre in 1572 when his mother's died. As a Huguenot, Henry participated in the French Wars of Religion, scarcely avoiding assassination in the St. Bartholomew's Day carnage. He would later lead Protestant armies against the French royal military.

Henry would become King of France in 1589 upon the death of Henry III, his brother-in-law and distant cousin. Henry initially kept the Protestant religion (the only French king to do so), and he had to fight against the Catholic League, which denied that he could be France's king while a Protestant. After a four-year deadlock, he converted to Catholicism to achieve control over his nation. As a practical political figure, he proclaimed the Edict of Nantes (1598), which assured religious freedoms to Protestants, thus essentially putting an end to the French Wars of Religion.

An excellent king, Henry acted to standardize state finance, encourage agriculture, eradicate corruption, and promote education. During his rule, the French colonization of the Americas genuinely began with establishing the colonies of Acadia and Canada at Port-Royal and Quebec separately. He is commemorated in the popular tune "Vive le roi Henri" (which later became a sacred song for the French monarchy during the reigns of his successors) and in Voltaire's *Henriade*.

Considered a usurper by Catholics and a traitor by Protestants, his charm and genuine care for the people's needs could not mollify his enemies. Despite his accomplishments, Henry IV was subject to at least 20 unsuccessful assassination attempts until May 14, 1610. On that morning, Henry seemed anxious. The day before, he had participated in the coronation of his wife, Marie de Medici, as Queen of France. It had been postponed from their wedding due to financial reasons. He took the Dauphin in his arms during the ceremony and exclaimed: "Gentlemen, here is the king." On the 14th, shortly before four o'clock in the afternoon, he decided to go to the Arsenal, east of Paris, to talk with his adviser, the Duke of Sully, Superintendent of Finance, bedridden by a bout of the flu.

Since Sully's home was close, the king decided that he did not need to be escorted by a full complement of his guards. He decided to travel the short distance with four of his officers, along with the Duke of Epernon and the Duke of Montbazon. Henry agreed only at the last moment what route his group would take, and he also raised the curtains on his carriage.

Francois Ravaillac follows the royal carriage as soon as it leaves the Louvre. A fervent Catholic victim of often violent hallucinations, he has been tormented for several years by the idea of killing the king. Obsessed by religion, at one point, he had sought admission to the ascetic Feuillants order, but after a short probation, he was dismissed as being "prey to visions." An application in 1606 for access to the Society of Jesus (Jesuits) was also unsuccessful. In recent months, he has tried several times to meet Henry to convince him to fight the Huguenots. Unable to meet the king, Ravaillac viewed Henry's decision to invade the Spanish Netherlands as starting a war against the pope. Resolved to stop him, he decided to kill the king. Having stolen a knife from an inn, he was ready to commit regicide.

Ravaillac waited in the Rue de la Ferronnerie in Paris (currently south of the Forum des Halles); when the king went by, his carriage halted by a blockage in the street. Henry's guards, who were riding on the sideboard of the king's carriage, left to try and clear the roadblock. It was at this point that Ravaillac made his move. He then stabbed the king to death. Pierre l'Estoile, the chronicler, stated of the king:

His coach, entering from St. Honore to Ferronnerie Street, was obstructed on one side by a cart full of wine and on the other by a cart filled with hay. Ravaillac climbed on the coach's wheel named above and, with a knife, stabbed him between the second and third ribs.

The Duke of Montbazon, who was riding with Henry, was injured in the attack. Ravaillac was immediately arrested by police and taken to the Hotel de Retz to avoid a mob lynching. He was transferred to the *Conciergerie*.

During interrogation, Ravaillac was frequently tortured to make him identify any accomplices, but he denied that he had any and insisted that he had acted alone. His knowledge of the king's route and traffic blockage made people wonder about a conspiracy. The purpose of the king's visit to the Duke of Sully was to make final preparations for imminent military intervention in the disputed succession to Julich-Cleves-Berg after the death of Duke John William. Intervention on behalf of a Calvinist candidate would have brought France into conflict with the Catholic Habsburg dynasty. Ravaillac seems to have learned of the plans; in his tortured mind, "he had seen that the king wanted to make war on the pope to transfer the Holy See to Paris.

On May 27, 1610, he was taken to the Place de Greve in Paris and was tortured one final time before being torn apart by four horses, a method of execution earmarked for regicides. During the process, he exclaimed that "I was deceived when they persuaded me that my deed would be well received by the people." Who were the persons who so "persuaded" Ravaillac? Before he was drawn and quartered, he was scalded with burning sulfur, molten lead, and boiling oil and resin, his flesh being torn by pincers. After his execution, Ravaillac's parents were sent into exile, and the rest of his family was commanded never to use the name "Ravaillac" again.

MAY 15
1800

On this day in history, England's King George III survives two failed assassination attempts on his life just hours apart at different locations.

On the afternoon of May 15, 1800, George III ventured to Hyde Park to review the 1st Foot Guards. A shot was fired during the review, which almost hit the Sovereign. Mr. Ongley, a Navy Office clerk standing nearby, was struck, and it was remarked that "had the wound been two inches higher, it must have been mortal."

Untroubled, the King went to the Theatre Royal, Drury Lane, that evening with the Queen and other royal family members.

The musical director of the theatre, Michael Kelly, stated that

"When the arrival of the King was announced, the band, as usual, played 'God Save the King.' I was standing at the stage-door, opposite the royal box, to see His Majesty. The moment he entered the box, a man in the pit, next to the orchestra, on the right hand, stood up on the bench, and discharged a pistol at our august Monarch, as he came to the front of the box."

"Never shall I forget His Majesty's coolness – the whole audience was in an uproar. The King, on hearing the report of the pistol, retired a pace or two, stopped, and stood firmly for an instant; then came forward to the very front of the box, put his opera-glass to his eye, and looked round the house, without the smallest appearance of alarm or discomposure."

Members of the orchestra grabbed the perpetrator – an ex-soldier named James Hadfield and hauled him into the music room beneath the stage, where he was scrutinized by the Duke of York; Richard Brinsley Sheridan, the theatre's manager; and Sir William Addington, a Bow Street magistrate. The audience insisted that Hadfield be brought on the stage, but Kelly managed to calm them down with the assurance that he was in safe custody and might have a chance to escape if he were brought forward.

Despite the Lord Chamberlain urging him to leave, George III was determined to remain at the theatre and watch the performance. Some suggested that the bullet was "only a squib," but it seems unlikely after the narrow miss earlier in the day.

Michael Kelly wrote: "'God Save the King' was then called for, and received with shouts of applause, waving of hats, &, etc. During the play, the Queen and the Princesses were absorbed in tears; - it was a sight never to be forgotten by those present." The play was a comedy by Colley Cibber, *She Would, and She Would Not*. Kelly stated, "Never was a piece so hurried over, for the performers were all in the greatest agitation and confusion."

At the end of the play, the audience demanded that 'God Save the King' be sung again. Kelly sang an extra verse written "on the spur of the Moment" by Mr. Sheridan, greeted with "the most rapturous approbation."

The man who attempted to kill George III was James Hadfield. Little is known of his early years, but it is known that he was brutally wounded at the Battle of Tourcoing in 1794. Before being caught by the French, he was assaulted eight times on the head with a sword, the injuries affecting him significantly for the rest of his life. After returning to England, he became engaged in a millennialist organization. He considered that the Second Coming of Jesus Christ would be enhanced if the British government killed him. In conjunction with Bannister Truelock, he decided to try to assassinate the King and bring about his own judicial execution.

Hadfield was charged and tried with high treason, and he was represented by Thomas Erskine, the most prominent lawyer of that period. Hadfield pleaded insanity, but the day's requirement for a compelling plea was that the offender must be "lost to all sense... incapable of forming a judgment upon the consequences of the act which he is about to do." Hadfield's preparation for the shooting seemed to undermine such a contention. Due to the 1795 Treason Act, there was little difference between plotting and committing treason. Thus, Erskine chose to contest the insanity test, instead arguing that delusion "unaccompanied by frenzy or raving madness (was) the true character of insanity." Two surgeons and a physician attested that the delusions resulted from his earlier head wounds. At this point, the judge, Lloyd Kenyon, 1st Baron Kenyon, stopped the trial stating that the judgment "was clearly an acquittal" but "the prisoner, for his own sake, and for the sake of society at large, must not be discharged."

Until then, defendants found not guilty because of insanity had faced no inevitable fate and had often been released back to the care of their families. Parliament quickly approved the Criminal Lunatics Act of 1800 to allow for the indeterminate detention of insane accused (and the Treason Act of 1800 made it effortless to prosecute people for attempts on the life of the King). Hadfield would later call for further use of pleading insanity several years in the future during the case of Colonel Edward Despard. Hadfield was incarcerated in Bethlem Royal Hospital for the remainder of his life, save for a short period when he escaped custody. He was retaken at Dover, trying to flee to France. He was temporarily held at Newgate Prison before being assigned to the newly opened criminal hospital at Bethlem (or Bedlam, as it was better known). He died there of tuberculosis in 1841.

MAY 16
1943

On this day in history in Poland, the Warsaw Ghetto Uprising ended as Nazi soldiers gained control over Warsaw's Jewish ghetto, blowing up the last remaining synagogue and starting the mass deportation of the ghetto's remaining inhabitants to the Treblinka concentration camp.

Directly after the German occupation of Poland began, the Nazis compelled the city's Jewish citizens to move into a "ghetto" encircled by barbed wire and armed SS guards. The Warsaw Ghetto was only 840 square acres but soon held almost 500,000 Jews in horrendous conditions. Disease and starvation would kill thousands every month, and starting in July 1942, 6,000 Jews a day were transported to the Treblinka concentration camp. During what was described as the "Great Action" (from July until September 12, 1942), the Germans deported about 265,000 Jews from Warsaw to Treblinka. They killed approximately 35,000 Jews inside the ghetto during this operation. Although the Nazis declared that the remaining Jews, their relatives, and friends were being moved to work camps, news soon reached the ghetto that extradition to the camp meant extermination. By early 1943, the surviving Jews in the Warsaw ghetto numbered approximately 70,000 to 80,000 individuals.

The "Great Action" had been dressed up to look like a "resettlement operation." However, by the late summer of 1942, it was clear to many ghetto inhabitants that deportations from the ghetto meant almost certain death.

In response to these deportations, several Jewish underground organizations joined on July 28, 1942. They created an armed self-defence unit called the Jewish Combat Organization (ZOB). There was also a second force organized by the right-wing Revisionist Zionist movement, especially its youth group, Betar. This second force was called the Jewish Military Union (ZZW). Although there was tension between the ZOB and the ZZW initially, both groups worked together to fight German attempts to demolish the ghetto. When the uprising occurred, the ZOB had about 500 fighters, and the ZZW had about 250.

In January 1943, German SS and police units returned to the Warsaw ghetto to resume mass deportations. They planned to send thousands of the ghetto's remaining Jews to forced-labor camps in the Lublin District of the General Government.

A small group of Jewish fighters armed with pistols infiltrated a column of Jews being forced to a transfer point. This group broke ranks and fought their German escorts at a predestined time. Most of the Jewish fighters died in the battle. However, the attack disoriented the Germans. As a result, the Jews who were arranged in lines at the transfer point had a chance to scatter. Jewish resistance leaders also encouraged fellow ghetto inhabitants to defy deportation orders and hide from German authorities. Seizing only 5,000 – 6,500 ghetto residents, the Germans suspended further deportations on January 21, 1943.

Encouraged by the success of the resistance, people in the ghetto began constructing underground bunkers and shelters. They were preparing for an uprising should the Germans attempt a final deportation of the remaining Jews from the ghetto.

The Jewish Combat Organization (ZOB) had received advanced warning of a final deportation action planned by the Germans. In response, the ZOB warned residents of the ghetto to retreat to their hiding places or bunkers.

Based on their experience in January, German authorities knew the ghetto's defense organization structure. On the eve of the action, they replaced the chief of the SS and Police in Warsaw, Obergruppenfuher Ferdinand von Sammern-Frankenegg, with SS and Police Leader (SS- und Polizeifuher) Jurgen Stroop. Stroop had considerable experience in partisan warfare. He also had significant forces at his disposal. These forces included around 2,000 soldiers and police, reinforced with artillery and tanks.

Twenty-four-year-old ZOB commander Mordecai Anielewicz commanded the Jewish insurgents. The ZOB fighters were armed with only pistols, grenades (many homemade), and a few automatic weapons and rifles. Nonetheless, they stunned the Germans and their auxiliaries on the first day of fighting. They forced the German soldiers to retreat outside of the ghetto wall. Stroop reported losing 12 men during the first assault on the ghetto.

About 750 young Jewish fighters clashed with German forces, sometimes in hand-to-hand combat. These fighters were poorly equipped and lacked military training and experience. The ZOB did have the advantage of waging a guerilla war. They would strike and then retreat to the safety of ghetto buildings, bunkers, and underground tunnels. The general ghetto population likewise thwarted German deportation efforts, refusing to assemble at collection points and burrowing in underground bunkers.

In the end, the Germans razed the ghetto to the ground. They burned and demolished this part of Warsaw, block by block, to smoke out their prey.

The ghetto fighters and the civilian population who supported them held the Germans at bay for nearly a month. On May 8, 1943, German forces succeeded in seizing ZOB headquarters at 18 Mila Street. Anielewicz and many of his staff commanders are thought to have committed suicide to avoid capture.

On May 16, Stroop announced in his daily report to Berlin that "The former Jewish Quarter in Warsaw is no more." Stroop commanded the destruction of the Great Synagogue on Tlomackie Street to symbolize the German victory on May 16, 1943. The ghetto itself lay in ruins.

The SS and police deported approximately 42,000 Warsaw ghetto survivors captured during the uprising. These people were sent to the forced-labor camps at Poniatowa and Trwniki. And to the Lublin/Majdanek concentration camp. Most would be murdered at these camps in November 1943 in a two-day shooting operation known as Operation Harvest Festival.

At least 7,000 Jews died fighting or in hiding in the ghetto. Approximately 7,000 Jews were captured by the SS and police at the end of the fighting. These Jews were deported to the Treblinka killing center, where they were murdered.

For months after the liquidation of the Warsaw ghetto, individual Jews continued to hide in the ruins of the ghetto. On occasion, they attacked German police officials on patrol. After the ghetto was liquidated, perhaps as many as 20,000 Warsaw Jews lived in hiding on the so-called Aryan side of Warsaw.

MAY 17
1974

On this day in history, in Los Angeles, California, police encircle a house in Compton where members of the terrorist group known as the Symbionese Liberation Army (SLA) have taken shelter. The SLA had kidnapped Patty Hearst, of the immensely wealthy Hearst family publishing empire, months earlier, creating headlines across America. Police found the house in Compton when a local mother reported to authorities that her children had seen a group of people working with an arsenal of automatic weapons in the home's living room.

The LAPD's 500-man siege of the Compton house was only the latest event in a short but increasingly bizarre chapter in American history. The SLA was a small but violent group of radicals who quickly came to national prominence, far outstripping their actual influence. They started by killing Oakland's superintendent of schools in late 1973, but they burst onto the scene when they kidnapped Hearst the following February.

Months later, the SLA released a tape in which Hearst stated that she was changing her name to Tania and joining the SLA. Shortly afterward, a surveillance camera in a bank caught Hearst carrying an assault rifle during an SLA robbery. Although police began referring to the SLA as a well-established underground terrorist organization, the SLA had only a few members, most of whom were disaffected middle-class youths.

The SLA felt that they needed to recruit new members, and they realized that they had alienated the radical community in the San Francisco area, where they were based, by assassinating Marcus Foster. SLA leader, Donald DeFreeze, suggested they move to the Los Angeles area, where he had friends they might recruit, but things did not go well. They seemed to be alienating people at every turn. Jailed SLA member Russell Little felt the group had lost sight of its goals. He believed they all wanted a confrontation with the Los Angeles Police Department.

On May 16, 1974, Emily and William Harris went into a sporting goods store in the Los Angeles suburb of Inglewood to shop for supplies. While Emily did the shopping, William decided to shoplift a bandolier. When a security guard confronted him, William took out his pistol. The guard disarmed William and placed a set of handcuffs on his left wrist. Hearst, the armed lookout from the group's van in the parking lot, began shooting at the store's overhead sign. Everyone in the store except the Harrises took cover, and the couple escaped and then jumped in the van and left with Hearst.

The group abandoned the van, but because of the incident, the police inspected the vehicle and found a parking citation with their new safe house address. The rest of the SLA quickly left that house after viewing news coverage of the shooting at the sports shop. They moved to a house at 1466 East 54th Street.

The next day the police were told that the group was in the house on 54th Street. That afternoon, more than 400 LAPD officers, along with FBI agents, California Highway Patrol (CHP), Los Angeles County Sheriff's Department (LASD), and Los Angeles Fire Department (LAFD), surrounded the area. The leader of a SWAT team demanded that the residents of the home come out and give themselves up.

A young child and an older man exited the house. The man said no one was inside, but the child stated that a group of people had lots of guns and ammunition inside. After trying to coerce the group to come out, the Swat team fired tear gas projectiles into the home. SLA members responded with automatic gunfire, and a violent gun battle began. The SLA members were armed with homemade grenades from 35mm film canisters and had thrown them at police.

During the shootout, police fired dozens of tear gas grenades into the house, trying to force the SLA members out. After two hours, the house caught fire, most likely due to an exploding tear gas canister. As the house started to burn, two women escaped from the rear, and one came out the front (she had come home drunk the previous night, passed out, and woke up in the middle of the firefight); all were arrested, but were determined not to be SLA members.

Automatic weapons fire continued to come from the house. Nancy Ling Perry and Camilla Hall then exited the house. Police later said they critically wounded Hall after she pointed a weapon at them; Perry was firing at them, and they shot her twice. After Hall fell, Atwood pulled her body back into the house. Perry's body remained outside.

The rest died inside from gunshot wounds, smoke inhalation, and burns. The coroner's report stated that Donald DeFreeze committed suicide by shooting himself in the head. Patricia Soltysik, Atwood, and Willie Wolfe died of smoke inhalation and burns. After the shooting stopped and the fire extinguished, police gathered 19 firearms – including shotguns, rifles, and pistols. It was one of the largest police shootouts in American history, with over 9,000 rounds fired (5,000 by police and 4,000 by the SLA). There were no casualties among first responders outside of the house.

The SLA leadership was decimated: DeFreeze, Soltysik, and Perry died. The other dead were founding members: Atwood, Hall, and Wolfe were all deceased. Perry's body was outside, but the others were all found in a space under the house, which had burned down around them.

Area TV stations covered the shootout and ensuing fire. Locked up in a hotel in Anaheim, Hearst and the Harrises watched the siege and destruction live from their room.

Patty Hearst would later be put on trial and convicted of armed robbery, despite her claim that she had been kidnapped and forced to comply, through repeated rape, isolation, and brainwashing, into joining the SLA. Prosecutors believed she had orchestrated her own abduction because of her previous involvement with one of the SLA members. Despite no proof of this theory, she was convicted and sentenced to prison. President Carter commuted Hearst's prison term after she had spent almost two years behind bars. President Clinton pardoned Hearst in January 2001.

MAY 18
1926

On this day in history, Aimee Semple McPherson, a nationally renowned evangelist, disappeared from Venice Beach in Los Angeles, California. Police sent out planes and ships to find her, yet she was nowhere to be found. Authorities later learned that radio engineer Kenneth Ormiston, a friend of McPherson's, had also vanished.

McPherson was the Billy Graham of her time. In 1923, she opened Angelus Temple in Los Angeles, where she consistently amassed overflowing crowds. McPherson claimed faith-healing abilities and put on wonderfully elaborate and entertaining shows for the public. Because of her religious nature, McPherson's relationship with Ormiston created a scandal in 1925, and their disappearance in 1926 made headlines nationwide.

On May 18, 1926, Aimee Semple McPherson went to Venice Beach, Los Angeles, to take a swim and write a sermon. The female assistant who had gone with her had to leave to make a short telephone call from a nearby hotel. When she returned, she could not find the evangelist anywhere.

As evening fell, McPherson was still missing, and her followers rushed to the beach to join the search. One young man drowned as he swam out towards two dead seals which he had mistaken for her body.

One local newspaper even speculated that there had been a sea monster in the area and that it had swallowed McPherson whole. Others thought that McPherson would be miraculously resurrected. National newspapers carried rival theories about what had happened to her for five weeks.

Had she drowned? Had she staged the ultimate theatrical stunt? Had the weight of her own fame just become too much? Then one day in June, she re-emerged in the small town of Agua Prieta on the Mexico-Arizona border.

McPherson had claimed that she had been kidnapped – but had she?

Her story to that date had already been quite extraordinary. She was born Aimee Elizabeth Kennedy on a farm in Salford, Ontario, Canada, on October 9, 1890, to James and Minnie Kennedy. As a teenager, she had gone to listen to an Irish Pentecostal preacher, Robert Semple, speak in her town. Before long, she had married him and joined his life on the road. But a trip they took to Hong Kong as missionaries ended in disaster. Both she and her husband fell ill with malaria. He died, but she survived, pregnant with her first child.

When McPherson returned to America, she felt the call to travel and preach. She had learned how to use dramatic tricks to draw audiences, so she became enormously popular. What made her so famous was her ability to lay hands on the sick and heal them. Soon McPherson, known as Sister Aimee to her followers, had become a preaching sensation touring across America during the early 1920s.

In 1923, she built a permanent base for her religious movement – a white-domed church called Angelus Temple in the Echo Park district of Los Angeles. She put on intricate services for the public and purchased a radio station to broadcast to listeners at home.

When McPherson showed up in the dusty border town of Agua Prieta, she went to a family's home and knocked on the door. She told the people inside that she had been walking for hours and hours, having escaped from a little shack where she had been held captive by three people. She stated that she had been persuaded by the three strangers to leave the beach on that fateful afternoon in May to pray for a sick child lying in the back of a vehicle. As she bent into the backseat of the car, she was shoved inside and chloroformed; the next thing she knew, she was imprisoned.

When McPherson returned to Los Angeles, a crowd of more than 50,000 people welcomed her at the train station. The evangelist made a grand re-entrance in a vast parade featuring airplanes that dropped roses from the skies. Despite the presence of Los Angeles officials and dignitaries, not everyone was happy. The Chamber of Commerce saw the event as a "gaudy display," Los Angeles District Attorney Asa Keyes demanded an investigation into the evangelist's account of the abduction.

Within two weeks, McPherson willingly appeared before a grand jury as newspapers continued trumpeting fraud accusations, accompanied by witness "spottings" in Northern California. Gaining the most traction was a story based on the evidence that Kenneth Ormiston, a married employee at the Christian radio station KFSG (owned by McPherson's church), went missing at the same time McPherson did. The two worked together on her regular broadcasts. Police were sent to a cottage in Carmel-by-the-Sea, where Ormiston had been witnessed with an unknown woman during McPherson's vanishing. (Ormiston acknowledged having an adulterous affair at the time of the disappearance but denied that the stranger known as "Mrs. X" was McPherson.) After dusting the cottage for fingerprints, police determined that none matched McPherson's.

The headlines and gossip continued throughout the fall until a judge decided there was enough evidence to proceed with conspiracy charges and obstruction of justice against McPherson. A jury trial was slated for January the following year. However, Keyes had begun to discover that some of his witnesses were unreliable, so he decided to forego the charges.

The kidnapping remained unsolved, and the question of a possible hoax went unsettled. Critics and supporters felt McPherson should have demanded a trial to clear her name; instead, she detailed her abduction story in her 1927 book, *In the Service of the King: The Story of My Life*. She would be ridiculed for years, but the disgrace did not lessen her prominence.

McPherson continued to build her church right up until her death.

On September 27, 1944, Aimee Semple McPherson was found dead in a hotel room in Oakland, California. A lifelong insomniac, the 53-year-old had taken too many sedatives – but her followers insist it was not suicide.

Her body was flown back to Los Angeles, where she lay in state for three days and three nights at the temple she had built for her groundbreaking movement.

Her Foursquare Church still exists to this day and claims a membership of 9 million. You can still visit Angelus Temple on a Sunday for service.

MAY 19
1536

On this day in history, Anne Boleyn, the second wife of England's King Henry VIII, is executed by beheading on charges that include adultery, incest, and conspiracy against the king.

Anne was the daughter of Thomas Boleyn, 1st Earl of Wiltshire, and his wife, Lady Elizabeth Howard, and was tutored in France and the Netherlands, mainly as a maid of honor to Queen Claude of France. Anne returned to England in 1522 to marry James Butler, 9th Earl of Ormond, her Irish cousin; the wedding proposal was scrapped, and instead, she secured a post at court as maid of honor to Henry VIII's wife, Catherine of Aragon.

In early 1526 Henry VIII began pursuing Anne. She repelled his attempts to seduce her, unwilling to become his mistress, as her sister Mary had done previously. As Catherine had not produced a male heir, Henry shifted his hopes for the upcoming prolongation of his royal line to Anne and started getting an annulment or divorce so he could get married to her.

For six years, while his ministers worked on "the King's great matter," Henry and Anne began their romance quietly at first, then publicly – infuriating Catherine and her formidable supporters, including her nephew, Emperor Charles V of Spain.

In 1532, the cunning and ruthless Thomas Cromwell gained command of the king's council and masterminded an audacious upheaval – a break with the Catholic Church and Henry's appointment as the ultimate head of the Church of England. Many disappointed Britons accused Anne, whose sympathies were firm with England's Protestant reformers even before the Church's unwavering hostility opposed to it.

Henry and Anne formally married on January 25, 1533. At Anne's coronation in June 1533, she was almost six months pregnant, and in September, a girl, Elizabeth, was born rather than the much-anticipated male heir. She later had two stillborn children and experienced a miscarriage in January 1536; the fetus seemed male.

Anne's relationship with Henry had begun to sour by then, and he now had become obsessed with her lady-in-waiting, the demure Jane Seymour.

After Anne's most recent miscarriage and the demise of Catherine that same month, reports began circulating that Henry needed to get rid of Anne so he could get married to Jane. (If he had tried to annul his second marriage while Catherine was still living, it would have increased speculation that his first marriage was valid.)

Henry had told himself that Anne had seduced him by sorcery and told Cromwell (Anne's former supporter and now her rival for power in Henry's court) that he would like to take steps towards restoring relations with Emperor Charles V.

Because of Anne's weak position, many of her enemies leaped at the opportunity to cause the downfall of "the Concubine" and began an investigation that gathered evidence against her.

After Mark Smeaton, a court musician, acknowledged (quite possibly under duress) that he had committed adultery with the queen, the show began at the May Day celebration at the king's palace at Greenwich. King Henry left unexpectedly at the halfway point of the day's jousting tournament, where Anne's brother George Boleyn, Viscount Rochford, and Sir Henry Norris, one of the king's closest friends and a royal officer in the household, were featured. He gave no reason for leaving to Anne, whom he would never lay eyes upon again.

Norris and Rochford were then charged with adultery with Anne (incest in Rochford's case) and conspiring with her against the king. Sir William Brereton and Sir Frances Weston were detained in the following days on similar allegations, while Anne was taken into custody at Greenwich on May 2. Led before the investigators (chief among them her uncle, the Duke of Norfolk) to face the allegations of "evil behavior" against her, she was then incarcerated in the Tower of London.

The trial of Brereton, Smeaton, Weston, and Norris occurred in Westminster Hall on May 12. All four men were to be hanged after the conclusion of the trial. They were also to be drawn and quartered. Anne and her brother, Lord Rochford, were placed on trial three days later in the Great Hall of the Tower of London. The Duke of Norfolk officiated over the trial as lord high steward on behalf of the king. The most unfavorable testimony against Rochford was the statement of his jealous wife, who claimed "undue familiarity" between him and his sister.

As for Anne, most historians agree that she was almost definitely innocent of the accusations against her. She never conceded to any unlawful activity, the proof against her was weak, and it seems highly doubtful she would have imperiled her status by adultery or scheming to harm the king, whose support she depended upon so considerably.

Nevertheless, Anne and Rochford were found guilty of the charges, and Norfolk declared that both were to be executed as per the king's desire.

On May 17, the five convicted men were executed on Tower Hill, but Henry showed clemency to Anne, summoning the "hangman of Calais" so she could be beheaded with a sword rather than an axe.

On May 19, a small crowd gathered on Tower Green as Anne Boleyn – dressed in a dark grey dress and ermine cloak, her hair covered by a headdress over a white coif – approached her final fate.

After asking to be allowed to address those gathered, Anne stated: "Masters, I here humbly submit me to the law as the law hath judged me, and as for mine offenses, I here accuse no man. God knoweth them; I remit them to God, beseeching Him to have mercy on my soul." Finally, she requested that Jesus Christ "save my sovereign and master the King, the most godly, noble and gentle Prince that is, and long to reign over you."

With a quick strike from the hangman's sword, Anne Boleyn was dead. Within 24 hours, Henry was formally betrothed to Jane Seymour; they married ten days after the execution.

While Queen Jane would finally give Henry his long-awaited son, who would succeed him as King Edward VI at the age of nine, it would end up being his daughter with Anne Boleyn, who would eventually rule England for over forty years as the most acclaimed Tudor monarch.

MAY 20
1845

On this day in history, HMS *Erebus*, and HMS *Terror*, with 134 men aboard, left Greenhithe, Kent, in England, beginning the disastrous Franklin expedition to find the Northwest Passage. All hands are lost.

The ships stopped briefly in Stromness, Orkney Islands, in Northern Scotland, then sailed to Greenland with HMS *Rattler* and a transport ship, *Barretto Junior*; the passage to Greenland took 30 days. Five crewmembers would disembark in Greenland as they were deemed unfit for service. *Erebus* and *Terror* also carried enough provisions for three years – including 60,000 kg of flour; 30,000 kg of salt beef and pork; 8,000 cans of preserved meat, vegetables, and soup; 500 kg of tinned pemmican; 4,000 kg of chocolate; 4,000 kg of lemon juice; 90 kg of pepper; 3,000 kg of tobacco; and thousands of liters of wine and spirits. The ships also brought research instruments for zoology, botany, and geology as well as early photographic equipment, hand organs, and libraries – 2900 books, including technical manuals and works by Charles Dickens. The vessels were altered for sailing in Arctic waters: the bows were strengthened with sheet iron to resist ice, and steam engines were added for emergencies. The ships were also outfitted with desalinators, which could purify drinking water from seawater, and with boilers. In short, it was a very well-provisioned and well-equipped expedition; the general outlook was highly positive, and many believed they would make it through the Northwest Passage within a year. However, after sailing into Baffin Bay, where it was seen by whaling ships on July 26, 1845, the expedition was never heard from again.

Historians have recreated Franklin's route on this fateful voyage based on evidence gathered during rescue missions and archaeological excavations. Entering Lancaster Sound, they spent their first winter at Beechey Island. During the summer of 1846, they sailed south and navigated through Peel Sound and into Victoria Strait, only to get stuck in thick ice off King William Island, where the ice fields did not retreat all summer. Pinned down, they wintered off King William Island, where Franklin died from unknown causes on June 11, 1847, aboard the *Erebus*. Other crewmembers had also perished. Based on written messages, historians know that the survivors abandoned the ships on April 22, 1848, and tried to reach safety overland. Some died on the journey while some reached Adelaide Peninsula, basically completing the final unknown leg of the Northwest Passage.

Between 1847 and 1859, 30 expeditions hunted for the missing ships, most paid for by the Admiralty and Lady Franklin. Search missions continued periodically into the late 19th and early 20th centuries, although any thoughts of rescue had long been forsaken. Rescue expeditions turned up tantalizing clues: A trio of graves at one site. A note at another location, dated April 1848, indicated that Franklin and 23 others were dead, the ships had been trapped in ice for 18 months, and the survivors were abandoning ship and striking out across the land.

Other clues trickled in; an abandoned sled with two skeletons and numerous personal effects. Letters from one of the men, some written phonetically, some backward, and few fully deciphered. Stories from local Inuit spoke of white men who had slowly perished, and ships caught in and disappeared beneath the ice. Slowly, these missions found evidence that pieced much of the voyage together but left the most critical questions undetermined. John Rae's detection of cannibalism on King William Island shocked Victorian England, with Charles Dickens and others rejecting the possibility of such barbaric behavior by Franklin's men. One of the unexpected benefits of these missions was a heightened understanding and mapping of the Arctic and the realization of Franklin's quest for the Northwest Passage.

For 170 years, these snippets were all that existed. And then, in September 2014, a search team found the wreck of *Erebus*, sitting in just 36 feet (11 meters) of water. Two years later, another group saw the almost-pristine wreck of *Terror* in deeper water to its companion's northwest. And three years later, the wreck site's first-ever visitors, passengers from the Adventure Canada-chartered ship *Ocean Endeavour*, watched as archeologists probed the *Erebus* for answers.

One giant mystery remains – the wrecks were in the wrong place. *Terror* was about 60 miles south of where the 1848 note said the ships had been abandoned, and *Erebus* was 30 miles farther south still. Did the crews decide to sail them south? According to Parks Canada, it's possible that the abandoned ships were carried to their final resting places by the same ice that had entombed them.

But it is notable that in the 19th century, Inuit had reported having observed signs of men on or about HMS *Erebus* before its sinking. It should be noted that the *Erebus* wreck site is precisely where oral traditions have long said one of the ships sank. Initially, British officials paid little attention to Inuit testimonies, repulsed by since-confirmed assertions that at least some of the desperate Franklin crewmembers resorted to cannibalism.

We may never know precisely what happened to the crews of *Erebus* and *Terror*. The working theory remains that they died, one by one, succumbing to scurvy and exposure as they trudged vainly over land in search of safety. But given the location of the two ships, the interpretation of the Franklin story and how it unfolded has to be re-examined.

In the summer of 2019, an amazing video of HMS *Terror* showed a wreck that appeared to be frozen in time: intact cabins, an array of neatly stowed artifacts, and closed drawers and cabinets. Perhaps behind those doors or in those drawers lies a crucial clue: a map, a letter, a journal. For almost 200 years, the fate of the *Erebus* and *Terror* has been a mystery; now, finally, maybe the ships themselves will help solve it.

(Photo: Engraving of HMS Erebus *and HMS* Terror *departing for the Arctic in 1845. Wikimedia Commons.)*

MAY 21
1924

On this day in history, fourteen-year-old Bobby Franks is abducted from a Chicago, Illinois neighborhood and murdered in what later proved to be one of the strangest murders in American criminal history. Nathan Leopold and Richard Loeb were rich and intelligent teenagers whose only motive for killing Franks was their desire to perpetrate the "perfect crime."

Leopold graduated from the University of Chicago at 18, spoke nine different languages, and had an IQ of 200 but also had perverse sexual desires. Also unusually gifted, Loeb graduated college at 17 and was fascinated with criminal psychology. The two made an unusual agreement: Loeb, who was gay, agreed to participate in Leopold's strange sexual practices in return for Leopold's collaboration with his criminal ventures.

Both were convinced that they were too intelligent and rich to get caught. In 1924, the pair began to test this theory by planning to commit a perfect murder. They each established false identities and began rehearsing the kidnapping and murder.

On May 21, 1924, Leopold and Loeb leased a car and went to a school in the Kenwood area of Chicago, where they would pick up their intended victim: Robert Franks. Loeb convinced the boy to get into the car with them because Franks was his cousin, and he had often played tennis at the Loeb's house. With the boy inside, the vehicle sped off. The moment the car turned the corner, one of the young men - it could never be established which one – dragged Franks into the backseat and killed him with repeated blows to the head with a chisel. The two young men wrapped the boy's dead body in a robe and drove to the Illinois/Indiana border. They were heading to Wolf Lake, a piece of wide-open industrial land outside Chicago city limits where Leopold frequently went birdwatching. They got rid of the body in a railroad culvert and returned home. That night, Leopold called Bobby Frank's mother to inform her that her son had been kidnapped. The next day, they sent a ransom demand by mail, which had been typed on a stolen typewriter.

However, the body was discovered even before any ransom note could be delivered, and the police began an investigation. Leopold and Loeb abandoned the kidnapping angle, a ruse only intended to distract the police. They destroyed the typewriter and the robe and then continued with their lives, convinced that they would never be fingered for committing the murder.

While searching the area where the body had been found, a detective found a pair of glasses with a unique hinge design. According to research, the detective found out that there were only three pairs of the glasses sold in the Chicago area, one was to Nathan Leopold. When questioned about the glasses, Leopold informed the police that, as an enthusiastic birdwatcher, he often visited the area around Wolf Lake and that he must have lost the glasses in the swamp on one such expedition.

The police were now treating Leopold and Loeb as suspects. When they were brought in for questioning, both men claimed that they had spent the evening in the family car, driving around Chicago, looking for girls. But the Leopold family chauffeur later told the police he had been working on the family car on the night in question. When faced with this irregularity, Leopold caved in and confessed. Loeb also soon admitted to the crime.

The trial that followed garnered headlines across America. Loeb's family, afraid their son would be executed for his crime, hired Clarence

Darrow, the famous defense attorney, and well-known death penalty opponent.

Following Darrow's recommendation, the young men pled guilty to the murder, which meant they would be tried by a judge alone. Darrow felt he could get leniency more easily from a judge than a jury. With the question of guilt resolved, America's newspapers now focused on whether Leopold and Loeb should hang.

As the trial ended, Darrow's final summation lasted for 2 hours. He made the typical argument that capital punishment did not prevent other crimes. Murderers simply did not think about the consequences the moment they killed someone. He asked the judge to consider the defendants' age: Leopold was 19, and Loeb was 18. He added that hanging the young men would also condemn their families to a life-long sentence of mourning.

But in summing up, Darrow addressed the more significant issue of public vengeance and disrespect for life. He said a blood lust had risen in society from time to time. When Americans were filled with a desire to punish others or defend themselves, they "place a cheap value on human life."

Ultimately, the judge sentenced Leopold and Loeb to life imprisonment plus 99 years for kidnapping.

An inmate killed Loeb after being imprisoned for twelve years, but Leopold was paroled and released in 1958, having served 33 years of his sentence. He had stayed busy in prison by teaching classes for other inmates, learning over twenty languages, organizing prison libraries, and participating in medical research.

After his release, he moved to Puerto Rico, where the Church of the Brethren hired him. For the final 11 years of his life, he worked with the poor as a hospital technician. He married a widow in 1961. Nathan Leopold died of a heart attack on August 29, 1971. He was 66 years old.

MAY 22
1781

On this day in history, Major General Nathaniel Greene and 1,000 Patriot soldiers try an assault on the important village of Ninety Six in the South Carolina hinterland. After neglecting to capture the walled settlement, they began besieging it, which lasted until their withdrawal on June 18, making it the lengthiest of the Revolutionary War.

Ninety Six, on the Saluda River, was crucial for protecting the northwest portion of the state and the most tactically significant location in South Carolina after Camden. It was operated by 550 Loyalists commanded by British Lieutenant Colonel John Harris Cruger. The Patriots lay siege to the city starting on May 22, 1781, using siege lines – trenches and structures built for the use of the besieging army and its artillery – which were created by the Continental Army's renowned engineering talent Thaddeus Kosciusko and are thought to be the best example of their kind in America. The 28-day siege centered on an eastern fortification known as Star Fort. Despite having more troops, Greene was forced to remove the blockade when Lord Rawdon approached from Charleston with British soldiers.

The British Army's goal in the southern states for winning the American Revolutionary War, which had been triumphant in taking

Charleston and winning most of South Carolina and Georgia, hit a roadblock in March 1781, after General Lord Cornwallis vanquished Continental Army General Nathaniel Greene at the Battle of Guilford Courthouse in Greensboro, North Carolina. Cornwallis suffered many casualties in the battle, so he decided to move his army to Wilmington, North Carolina. Greene's army was virtually intact despite the loss, and he decided, because of Cornwallis's move northward, to move into South Carolina and begin operations to eliminate the British from that state.

With the help of militia commanders Thomas Sumter, Francis Marion, and Andre Pickens, the Continental Army managed to take several British garrisons in the hinterland of South Carolina; some were deserted and left for them. By mid-May, only the fort of Ninety Six, in the northern portion of the state, and the port of Charleston, close to 200 miles southeast on the Atlantic coast, remained under British control.

The British garrison at Ninety Six, thus named because it was ninety-six miles from the Indian settlement at Keowee, an important trading post, was manned by 550 experienced Loyalist soldiers, such as De Lancey's Brigade, organized into Provincial regiments (regular army troops who had been enlisted from Loyalists in New York, New Jersey, and South Carolina) under the control of Lieutenant Colonel John Cruger. Inhabited by the British since 1780, the fortifications included a palisade wall surrounded by a deep ditch and an abatis, a row of sharpened logs constructed to deflect an attack – the eighteenth-century equivalent to razor wire. To the west, newly erected defenses protected Ninety Six's water supply. To the east was the Star Fort, an impressive works with sharp angles designed to maximize the defenders' line of fire and prevent assault parties from approaching the fort's walls. A trio of three-pound guns was also on hand to shower an attacking Patriot force with lead and iron.

Greene and his fighting force arrived at Ninety Six on May 22. They began siege operations, targeting the Star Fort, under their chief engineer, Colonel Thaddeus Kosciuszko, from Poland. Cruger attempted to disrupt their siege works by sending out squads at night to harass the workers. At one point, they even managed to steal the workers digging tools after they had been driven away.

By early June, the Patriot forces had excavated a trench within 30 yards (27 meters) of the Star Fort. They constructed a Maham Tower, as General Marion had done to capture Fort Watson, about 30 feet (9.1 m) tall, with a sheltered platform at the top. Under this high cover, American sharpshooters would have a clear firing line into the fort. At first, the snipers were able to shoot several British soldiers. Cruger quickly countered that move by using sandbags to heighten the parapet, giving his forces enough cover so his sharpshooters could fire on the tower through slats between the sandbags. He also attempted to set fire to the tower with heated shot but could not get the balls hot enough. The attackers launched flaming arrows into the fort to set fire to anything flammable within the stronghold. Cruger had his men took the roofs off the buildings in the fort to stop them from catching fire.

On June 7, Lord Rawdon vacated Charleston with 2,000 British soldiers meant to relieve the siege. Greene did not learn of this until June 11. Deciding that he was at a critical juncture, Greene attacked the fort. (Cruger would learn of Radon's approach the next day when the messenger, masquerading as a Patriot, got near enough to the fort to race the remaining distance on his horse.)

Green planned to have one group capture the smaller redoubt while a more significant force would attack the Star Fort, where some men would remove the sandbags to uncover the defenders to fire from the tower. When the assault began on June 18, all went well at first – the smaller redoubt was taken, and men successfully entered the abatis and pulled down the sandbags. At this point, Cruger initiated a counterstrike with a pair of attacks to strike at the flanks of the assaulting party. In a vicious battle dominated by bayonets and the use of muskets as clubs, the commanding officers of the attack were killed, and the men were forced to retreat to their trenches. With the attack's failure and Rawdon only 30 miles in front of the fort, Greene called off the assault and ordered a retreat.

The Americans lost 150 men, while the British lost 100 men. Greene retreated to North Carolina, and Rawdon joined Cruger's forces. Eventually, the British abandoned Ninety Six. General Green blamed the collapse of the operations against Ninety Six partly on Sumter and Marion, who failed to support his operations quickly enough. Later, other officers blamed Greene and Lee for failing to restrict the defenders' water supply at the Spring Branch. Greene would engage Rawdon's forces one last time outside Charleston at Eutaw Springs on September 8, 1781, in the final major battle in the South.

MAY 23
1960

On this day in history, Israeli Prime Minister David Ben-Gurion announced that Nazi war criminal Adolf Eichmann had been apprehended and would stand trial in Israel. Eichmann was the Nazi SS officer who methodically executed Adolf Hitler's "final solution of the Jewish question." He was seized by Israeli Mossad agents in Argentina on May 11, 1960, and smuggled to Israel nine days later.

Eichmann was born in Solingen, Germany, in 1906. In November 1932, he enlisted in the Nazi's exclusive SS (Schutzstaffel) organization, whose members came to have broad powers in Germany, including intelligence, policing, and the enforcement of Hitler's antisemitic policies. Eichmann progressively climbed in the SS hierarchy, and with the German occupation of Austria in 1938, he was sent to Vienna to purge the city of Jews. He set up an effective Jewish deportment center and, in 1939, was sent to Prague for a related purpose. That year, Eichmann was assigned to the Jewish unit of the SS central security office in Berlin.

In January 1942, Eichmann met with leading Nazi officials at the Wannsee Conference near Berlin to develop a "final solution of the Jewish question," as Nazi leader Hermann Goring put it. The Nazis opted to eradicate Europe's Jewish inhabitants. Eichmann was assigned to organize the identification, assembly, and movement of millions of Jews from occupied Europe to the Nazi concentration camps, where Jews were gassed or worked to death. He executed this duty with horrendous proficiency, and between three to four million Jews died in the concentration camps before the end of World War II. Close to two million were murdered elsewhere.

After the war, Eichmann was imprisoned by American soldiers, but he absconded in 1946 before facing the Nuremberg International War Crimes Tribunal. Eichmann journeyed under an alias between Europe and the Middle East and, in 1950, landed in Argentina, which retained lenient immigration guidelines and was a country known to allow Nazi war criminals to hide within its borders. In 1957, a German prosecutor clandestinely notified Israel that Eichmann was residing in Argentina. Israel's intelligence service, the Mossad, sent agents to Argentina, and in early 1960 they ultimately found Eichmann. He lived in the San Fernando section of Buenos Aires under the name Ricardo Klement.

In May 1960, Argentina was commemorating the 150th anniversary of its revolt against Spain, and many tourists were going to be in Argentina from around the world to attend the festivities. The Mossad used the occasion to sneak more agents into the country. Knowing that Argentina might never extradite Eichmann for trial, Israel had opted to kidnap him and take him to Israel unlawfully. Israel decided it was preferable to capture Eichmann rather than kill him outright. They planned to bring him to Israel and make him stand trial before the people he tried to exterminate.

On May 11, Mossad operatives were ready to move into action. Set up around the bus stop where Eichmann arrived on his bus each night at approximately 7:40 p.m. On this night, he was late. Eventually, at 8:05 p.m. man got off the bus and began walking towards Garibaldi Street. As he passed their location, the agents pounced on Eichmann, who "let out a terrible yell, like a wild beast caught in a trap..." as he fell to the ground. They wrestled him into their car, gagged him, tied his feet and hands, and put on a pair of goggles that blocked his vision. Within 45 minutes, they were at their safe house. He was kept under wraps for nine days until May 20. On that date, they drugged him just enough to have him appear to be an injured El Al employee with a concussion returning to Israel. They put Eichmann on a plane, and he was soon in Israel.

In April 1961, Eichmann was placed on trial. For 14 weeks, the three judges appointed to hear the case were subjected to over 1600 documents, many with Eichmann's signature and the testimony of 108 witnesses. Placed behind a bullet-proof glass dock in the courtroom, the assembled crowd listened to the recounting of the ghastly crimes the Nazis perpetrated against the Jews. Memories that had been repressed burst forth in the courtroom. People screamed and cried and wanted to attack and kill Eichmann. The whole story of Eichmann's directing the "final solution" came out into the open. He asked for understanding and mercy from the Jewish people – claiming that he had acted "under orders," that he was just a "cog in the machine," and that it was the Nazi government's fault, not his, for what had been perpetrated on the Jewish people.

The prosecution, however, demonstrated that he played a prominent role in the persecution of the Jews and had personal responsibility for the deportation of hundreds of thousands of Jews to Auschwitz and other camps, which he authorized against the wishes of his superiors even after it was clear Germany had lost the war.

On December 11, 1961, Eichmann was convicted of 15 counts of crimes against the Jewish people, crimes against humanity, war crimes, and membership in a criminal organization. Remarkably, the tribunal of judges found him not guilty of ever personally killing anyone. Eichmann was sentenced to hang on June 1, 1962. Eichmann asked for clemency, but President Yitzhak Ben Zvi rejected the plea.

After he was executed, his body was cremated, and a police boat scattered the ashes on the Mediterranean.

MAY 24
1883

On this day in history, after 14 years of construction, the Brooklyn Bridge over the East River opened in 1883, linking the cities of New York and Brooklyn for the first time. Thousands of Brooklyn and Manhattan Island citizens showed up to watch the dedication ceremony, which U.S. President Chester A. Arthur and New York Governor Grover Cleveland officiated. Created by John A. Roebling, the Brooklyn Bridge was the most enormous suspension bridge ever built at that time.

John Roebling was born in Germany in 1806 and was a remarkable developer in designing and creating steel suspension bridges. He studied industrial engineering at university in Berlin and, at 25, immigrated to Pennsylvania, where he tried, disastrously, to make his living as a farmer. He later moved to the state capitol in Harrisburg, where he got a job as a civil engineer. He advocated the use of wire cables and founded a successful wire-cable factory.

Meanwhile, he gained standing as a designer of suspension bridges, which at the time were extensively used but seen to fail under the powerful winds of heavyweights. Roebling is acknowledged with a significant breakthrough in suspension-bridge technology: a web truss attached to either side of the bridge roadway that significantly steadied the structure. Using this model, Roebling managed to successfully bridge the Ohio River at Cincinnati, Ohio, and the Niagara Gorge at Niagara Falls, New York. Because of these significant accomplishments, New York State accepted Roebling's design for a bridge linking Manhattan and Brooklyn – with a span of 1,595 feet – and hired him as chief engineer. It would be the world's first steel suspension bridge.

Just before the start of construction of the Brooklyn Bridge in 1869, Roebling was mortally wounded while taking some final compass readings across the East River. A boat shattered the toes on one of his feet, and they had to be amputated. Within three weeks, Roebling had died of tetanus. He was the first of more than 30 people to die constructing the bridge: his 32-year-old son, Washington A. Roebling took over as chief engineer. Washington had worked with his father on numerous bridges and assisted in the Brooklyn Bridge's design.

Workers dug the riverbed in massive wooden boxes called caissons to achieve a solid foundation for the bridge. Mass granite blocks pressed these airtight compartments to the river's floor; pressurized air was injected into the chambers to keep debris and water out.

Workers referred to as "sandhogs" – many immigrants earning about $2 a day – used shovels and dynamite to remove the mud and boulders at the base of the river. Each week, the caissons moved closer to the bedrock. When they reached a sufficient depth – 44 feet on the Brooklyn side and 78 feet on the New York side – they began backfilling the caisson with concrete and brick piers, working their way back up to the surface.

Underwater, the workers in the caisson were uncomfortable – the hot, dense air gave them blinding headaches, itchy skin, bloody noses, and slowed heartbeats – but relatively safe. However, the journey to and from the depths of the East River could be fatal. To get down into the caissons, the sandhogs rode in iron containers called airlocks. As the airlock went down into the river, it filled with compressed air. This air made breathing possible and kept the water out of the caisson, but it also dissolved a menacing amount of gas into the workers' bloodstreams. When workers resurfaced, the dissolved gases in their blood were quickly released.

This often causes many painful afflictions known as "caisson disease" or "the bends": numbness, speech impediments, excruciating joint pain, paralysis, convulsions, and, in some cases, death. Over 100 workers suffered from the bends, including Washington Roebling himself, who remained partially paralyzed and bedridden for the remainder of his life. He was required to watch with a telescope while his wife, Emily, took control of the construction of the bridge. Over the years, the bends claimed the lives of many sandhogs, while others died due to more traditional construction accidents, such as collapses, explosions, and fires.

By the early 20th century, scientists had figured out that if airlocks traveled to the river's surface more slowly, causing the workers' gradual decompression, the bends could be stopped completely. In 1909, New York passed the nation's first caisson-safety laws to protect sandhogs excavating railway tunnels under the Hudson and East Rivers.

On May 24, 1883, traffic across the Brooklyn Bridge commenced. The bridge joined the cities of New York and Brooklyn. President Arthur and Governor Cleveland presided over the ceremony while thousands of spectators watched. Emily Roebling was given the first ride over the finished bridge, with a rooster, a symbol of victory, in her lap. Within 24 hours, more than 250,000 people walked across the Brooklyn Bridge, using a promenade over the roadway that John Roebling created solely for the pleasure of pedestrians.

With its unheard-of length and two towers, the Brooklyn Bridge was called the "eighth wonder of the world." It remained the tallest structure in North America for several years after its construction. The connection it provided between the large population centers of Brooklyn and Manhattan altered the course of New York City forever. In 1898, Brooklyn formally amalgamated with New York City, Staten Island, and a few farm towns, creating Greater New York.

MAY 25
1787

On this day in history, four years after America was victorious over the British and won their independence, 55 state delegates, including George Washington, Benjamin Franklin, and James Madison, gathered in Philadelphia to draft an innovative United States constitution.

The Articles of Confederation, approved many months before the British capitulation at Yorktown in 1781, allowed for the creation of a loose coalition of American states, which were autonomous in most of their affairs. On paper, Congress—the central power—had the authority to administer foreign affairs, conduct war, and control currency. However, in practical terms, these authorities were harshly limited because Congress could not implement its requirements to the states for money or soldiers. By 1786, it had become clear that the Union would rapidly disintegrate if the Articles of Confederation were not revised or changed. Five states met in Annapolis, Maryland, to deliberate on the problem, and all the states were requested to send delegates to a new constitutional convention to be convened in Philadelphia.

On May 25, 1787, representatives of every state except Rhode Island gathered at Philadelphia's Pennsylvania State House for the Constitutional Convention. The building, now known as Independence Hall, had earlier witnessed the creation of the Declaration of Independence and the signing of the Articles of Confederation. The meeting immediately tossed out the idea of modifying the Articles of Confederation and started drawing up a new government strategy. George Washington, a delegate from Virginia and a Revolutionary War hero, was chosen as conference president.

During a total of three months of talks, the delegates created a unique federal system categorized by an elaborate scheme of checks and balances. The convention was split over the problem of state representation in Congress, as more populated states desired proportional legislation, and smaller states fought for equal representation. The issue was finally settled by the Connecticut Compromise, which recommended a two-chamber legislature with proportional representation in the lower chamber (House of Representatives) and equal representation of the states in the upper chamber (Senate).

On September 17, 1787, the Constitution of the United States of America was agreed to and signed by 38 of the 41 delegates gathered at the finale of the convention. As called for by Article VII, the document would only become binding once it was sanctioned by nine of the thirteen states.

Starting December 7, five states—Delaware, Pennsylvania, New Jersey, Georgia, and Connecticut—ratified it quickly. However, other states, including Massachusetts, did not want to sign the document, as it did not reserve un-delegated powers to the states and failed to provide constitutional safeguards for basic political rights, such as freedom of speech, religion, and the press. In February 1788, an arrangement was reached where Massachusetts and other states would ratify the document, guaranteeing those amendments would be immediately forthcoming. The Constitution was thereby barely confirmed in Massachusetts, followed by South Carolina and Maryland. New Hampshire became the ninth state to approve the document on June 21, 1788, and it was then agreed that government under the United States Constitution would start on March 4, 1789.

On September 25, 1789, the first Congress of the United States implemented 12 amendments to the U.S. Constitution–the Bill of Rights–and delivered them to the states for approval. Ten of these amendments were accepted in 1791. In November 1789, North Carolina was the 12th state to approve the U.S. Constitution. Rhode Island, which opposed federal jurisdiction over currency and disliked compromise on slavery, avoided ratifying the Constitution until the U.S. government promised to sever commercial interactions with the state. On May 29, 1790, Rhode Island approved the document by two votes and was the last original American colony to join the United States. The U.S. Constitution remains the oldest written national constitution operating worldwide.

MAY 26
1637

On this day in history, Puritan colonizers under Captain John Mason and their Mohegan and Narragansett allies set ablaze the Pequot Fort near the Mystic River. They shot anyone who tried to flee the wooden palisade stronghold and massacred most of the community. Between 400 and 700 Pequot non-combatants were slain during the slaughter, which took only one hour, and the only Pequot who survived were the warriors on a raiding party with their sachem Sassacus.

As the Puritans of Massachusetts Bay pushed further into Connecticut, they became increasingly tense with the Pequots, a tribe centered on the Thames River in southeastern Connecticut. By the spring of 1637, the Pequot had slain 13 English colonists and traders, and Massachusetts Bay Governor John Endecott established a large military force to penalize the local tribe. On April 23, two hundred Pequot warriors reacted rebelliously to the colonial deployment by assaulting a Connecticut village, killing six men and three women, and taking two girls away. This was a significant turning point in the Pequot War as it infuriated the settlers that the warriors would kill colonists and led to heightened support for the Pequot War among colonials.

According to historians, the Great Colonial Hurricane of 1635 ravaged that year's corn and other crop harvests, making food supplies scarce and creating competition for winter food supplies. This caused a rise in hostilities between the Pequots and the Colonists, who were unprepared to face a period of famine.

The Connecticut towns established a Puritan militia led by Captain John Mason comprising 90 men, plus 70 Mohegans under sachems Wequash and Uncas. Another twenty men under Captain John Underhill joined Mason from Fort Saybrook. Also concurrently, Pequot sachem Sassacus took a few hundred warriors and made a separate assault on Hartford, Connecticut.

While moving towards the Pequot fort, Captain Mason met with and recruited more than 200 Narragansett and Niantic warriors to join his army. On the night of May 26, 1637, the Colonial and Native soldiers and warriors arrived at the fortified Pequot village, which was located on a low hill near the Mystic River. The large village was surrounded by palisades with only two exits. The Colonial forces first tried a surprise attack but withdrew after stiff resistance from the Pequot defenders.

As a countermeasure, Mason decided the village should be set on fire and its two exits blocked. As the fire raged out of control, many trapped Pequots were shot and killed, attempting to flee by climbing over the palisade; those men, women, and children that did get out were mowed down by the Narragansett warriors and the colonists.

Jubilant Mohegans would collect the heads of the fallen Pequots; scalps were taken as war trophies. Within an hour of the invasion, 400 – 700 members of the Pequot tribe had been massacred – including women and children. Later, the English reported seven of them were captured while seven escaped successfully.

Observing the brutality of the English, some of the Narragansetts could not help but feel sympathy toward the unarmed mothers and children who were also under fire from English guns or even burnt in their sleep. They subsequently returned to their village. Their sachems, however, did not refuse the gift of captives that the English brought home to them; the Pequot prisoners were divided among the sachems of the Narragansett and Mohegan tribes.

Returning Pequot warriors – who had been with their sachem Sassacus at the time of the attack – attempted to engage the colonial forces after discovering the massacre. But the Puritans managed to avoid any Pequot counterattack despite briefly getting lost during their retreat to the Connecticut Colony.

The colonists suffered between 20 and 27 casualties, with two affirmed dead. Forty Narragansett warriors were wounded because the colonials were confused and thought they were Pequots. The massacre effectively destroyed the Pequots and Sassacus, and many of his followers were surrounded by a marsh near a Mattabesset village called Sasqua. The women and children were allowed to surrender. In the battle which followed, known as the "Fairfield Swamp Fight," close to 180 warriors were killed, wounded, or captured. Sassacus escaped with 80 of his men and headed west.

Sassacus and his warriors had hoped to gain a safe haven among the Mohawk in present-day New York. However, the Mohawk murdered him and his bodyguard, sending his head and hands to Hartford as a symbol of friendship. This ended the Pequot War; colonial officials continued to hunt down what remained of the Pequot after the war ended, but they granted asylum to anyone who went to live with the Narragansetts or Mohegans.

In September, the Narragansetts and the Mohegans met at the General Court of Connecticut and decided on the disposal of the Pequot survivors. The agreement was the first Treaty of Hartford signed on September 21, 1638. About 500 – 1000 Pequots survived the war; they finally gave up and surrendered and placed themselves under the authority of the Mohegans or Narragansetts. They could no longer inhabit what was once their lands, nor could they even call themselves Pequots.

A large segment of the rest of the Pequot people were incarcerated and transported to Bermuda or the West Indies or were forced to become domestic enslaved people in English households in Connecticut and Massachusetts Bay. The Colonies effectively proclaimed the Pequots extinct by forbidding them from using the name any longer.

This was the first time the Algonquin peoples of southern New England had to contend with European-style warfare. After the Pequot War, there were no meaningful confrontations between Indians and southern New England colonists for about 38 years. This long phase of peace ended in 1675 with King Philip's War. According to historians, the Pequot War established the tradition of Colonists and Indians taking body parts as battle trophies. Honor and monetary reimbursement were given to those who brought back heads and scalps of Pequots.

MAY 27

1940

On this day in history, the Le Paradis massacre occurred when Germany's SS Death's Head Division savagely murdered 97 members of the Royal Norfolk Regiment after they flew the white flag after running out of ammunition in the village of Le Paradis. This was during the Battle of France when soldiers of the British Expeditionary Force (BEF) attempted to retreat across the Pas-de-Calais region during the Battle of Dunkirk.

After the defenders surrendered, they were led by the Germans to a wall where they were murdered by machine guns. Two members of the regiment survived with injuries and managed to hide until they were captured by German forces days later. One of these men was repatriated to England in 1943 after he had a leg amputated, and he immediately reported the massacre to officials who thought it too fantastic of a story to be true. An investigation started only after the second survivor was released after the war and corroborated the first man's story. The company commander of the German SS unit responsible for the deaths was placed on trial and found guilty and subsequently hanged in 1949.

It began on May 26, 1940. British and Allied forces in France were withdrawing from the German offensive, withdrawing to Dunkirk for evacuation to Britain. The Germans followed, all expecting to be first. Surprisingly, however, the Germans did not push forward. They stopped moving for three days – long enough to allow the evacuation to occur. By the time it was over on June 4, about 330,000 Allied soldiers had escaped to England.

Not all made it, though. Less remembered were those soldiers who fought to buy those evacuees the needed time.

The 8th Lancashire Fusiliers and the 2nd Battalion of the Royal Norfolk Regiment were commanded to hold the Allied line at the French villages of Le Paradis, Riez du Vinage, Le Cornet Malo, and for as long as possible. They would be neither rescued nor evacuated, and they knew it.

At dawn on May 27, the SS Totenkopf Regiment assaulted the British at Le Cornet Malo and lost four German officers in the melee. By the time the British surrendered, over 150 soldiers from both sides lay dead and about 500 wounded. Le Paradis was next.

The 2nd Royal Norfolk's Headquarters were stationed about one mile north of Le Paradis at a farmhouse called Cornet Farm just beside Paradis Road. Across was the 1st Royal Scots HQ, who also buckled down. At 11:30 a.m., both were ordered to do their best – the last orders they received. Against them was the 14th Company, 1st Battalion of the 2nd SS infantry Regiment under SS-Standartenfuhrer (Colonel) Hans Friedemann Gotze. The British held fast until they were forced to leave the ruined farmhouse and took shelter in the nearby cowshed. Gotze was killed, and the British kept fighting until they ran out of ammunition at 5:15 p.m.

By then, only 99 men remained under Major Lisle Ryder's command. Unable to return fire, Ryder instructed his men to surrender, so they stepped out of the shed waving a white flag. The Royal Scots did the same.

SS-Hauptsturmfuhrer (Captain) Fritz Knochlein oversaw Totenkopf 3 Company, Group A, 2nd Regiment. He ordered all weapons be removed from the prisoners and marched toward another barn. Beside it were two machine guns operated by the No. 4 Machinegun Company. Lining the 99 British soldiers against the wall, he had them shot. Then he ordered his men to bayonet and shoot any survivors.

However, not all the British troops were dead. William O'Callaghan had been hit in the arm, the force throwing him to the ground. Seconds later, another soldier fell on him, so he played dead. Once the Germans left, he found Albert Pooley had also withstood the German assault, although with a fractured leg.

O'Callaghan pulled his compatriot out, then half-carried and half-dragged him to what turned out to be a pig sty. The men lived there for three days on potatoes and dirty water they drank from puddles until they were discovered by Madame Duquenne-Creton and her son, Victor. They owned the farm and hid the men despite the risk to themselves. That came to an end when the Wehrmacht's 251 Infantry Division found them, taking the men as POWS. Fortunately, the Duquenne-Cretons were spared.

Pooley's leg was amputated in a Paris hospital, while O'Callaghan would spend the balance of the war in a German Prisoner of war camp. In 1943 Pooley was invalided back to Britain as he was no longer a threat to the Nazis.

He gave an account of what had happened to authorities at the Richmond Convalescent Camp, but nobody believed him. After the war ended, he returned to Le Paradis in September 1946 and was questioned by the local newspaper. They spoke to locals, who confirmed the story, which angered British authorities.

Why had they not heard his story before this? He had told people, but they were incompetent and disbelieving bureaucrats. The War Crimes Investigation Unit found Knoclein, who had returned to civilian life. He was arrested, brought to Britain, and incarcerated at the London District Prisoner of War Cage in Kensington Gardens.

Knochlein denied being at Le Paradis. Then, after residents of the town identified him, he stated that the executions were legitimate because the British had used dum-dum bullets outlawed by the Hague Convention.

He also claimed the British had enticed his men to the farmhouse with a white flag before killing several of them. Finally, he accused his jailers of physical and mental torture.

The court did not believe any of it, and Knochlein was executed by hanging on January 28, 1949, for his part in the massacre – the only one punished.

(Photo: SS-Obersturmbannführer Fritz Knöchlein. Wikimedia Commons)

MAY 28
1754

On this date in history, in the first engagement of the French and Indian War, a company of provincial troops from Virginia under the command of Lieutenant Colonel George Washington, and a small number of Mingo warriors led by Chieftain Tanacharison (also known as the "Half-King"), ambushed a force of 35 Canadiens under the command of Joseph Coulon de Jumonville. In the surprise attack, the Virginians killed 10 French soldiers from Fort Duquesne, including the commander, and wounded 21 others. Only one of Washington's men was killed in the melee.

The French and Indian War was the final and most significant of a succession of colonial wars between the British and the American colonists on one side and the French and their strong group of Native American allies on the other. Combat began in 1754, but France and Britain did not officially declare war against each other until 1756 when the Seven Years' War erupted in continental Europe.

In November 1752, at 20, George Washington was designated adjutant in the Virginia colonial militia, which involved inspecting, mustering, and regulating various militia companies. In November 1753, he first gained notice when he volunteered to relay a message from Virginia Governor Robert Dinwiddie to the French who were expanding into the Ohio

Valley, warning them to leave the territory already claimed by the British government. Washington was successful in his endeavor and returned with a disturbing message: The French had no intention of leaving.

In 1754, Dinwiddie assigned Washington a lieutenant colonel and ordered him to take 160 men to strengthen a colonial post at what is now Pittsburgh, Pennsylvania. Before Washington could get there, however, it was given up peacefully to the French, who rechristened it Fort Duquesne. Washington relocated within 40 miles of the French position and built a new fort at Great Meadows, which he called Fort Necessity.

The conflict began in this area on May 28, 1754, when a group of British soldiers and Mingo warriors approached the encampment of French Ensign Joseph Coulon de Jumonville. Despite being a lieutenant colonel in the Virginia Regiment, Washington had never seen combat. In contrast, the leader of the Mingo (also known as "Ohio Iroquois" or "Ohio Seneca") was Tanacharison, the "Half-King," an experienced warrior and statesman in his mid-50s who provided guidance and wisdom to young Washington.

Given that the Ohio Valley was a contested area between Britain and France and multiple Native nations, Tanacharison may have had a strong motivation for Britain to advance at war. Tanacharison understood what was going on in the Ohio Valley in a way that Washington did not. The Native leader not only provided guidance to Washington but exploited and manipulated the situation and maneuvered Washington into a conflict with the French – a conflict neither wanted nor needed by any.

When Washington and Tanacharison's forces reach Jumonville's camp, they attack, killing Jumonville and several of his soldiers and taking others prisoner. While the question of who fired first remains in dispute – according to one Mingo warrior, it was Washington himself – the skirmish quickly heightened into a larger conflict. After the "Jumonville affair," the French condemned Washington for leading an unprovoked assault against the French during peacetime, claiming that Jumonville and his men had diplomatic, not military, instructions. For his part, Washington argued that the diplomacy claim was just a red-herring and that his attack was legal in order to defend his forces from French aggression.

It is unclear whether Washington had much of a strategy. Looking at the different first-hand accounts of the skirmish, "I frankly see a young man seeing his first command unraveling before his eyes," one historian notes. "This was a disaster, and I think very quickly thereafter, he's kind of trying to cover it up."

Technically, the skirmish was a military victory for Washington – but a diplomatic loss. The fact that he had attacked France, a country with which Britain was not at war, gave France a considerable propaganda advantage. It also angered Jumonville's half-brother, a French military leader named Louis Coulon de Villiers, who, just over a month after his brother was killed, helped lead an attack on Washington's Virginia Regiment at Fort Necessity.

Unlike the Jumonville affair, the Battle of Fort Necessity was a military and diplomatic disaster for Washington. On July 3, a mix of French, Huron, Odawa, and Iroquois fighters overwhelmed Washington's men at their recently built fort. The Virginia Regiment, unable to drum up its own corps of native allies, was outnumbered and underprotected behind the small, flimsy Fort Necessity, which looked like a tall, circular fence and was situated in an open field. Ultimately, Washington surrendered to terms that included – unbeknownst to him, because of a poor French translation – taking responsibility for the assassination of Jumonville.

This gave the French a huge diplomatic and propaganda advantage. The lieutenant governor of Virginia tried to distance himself from Washington's conduct, which received adverse reactions from as far away as London.

In October 1754, Washington resigned his commission to protest the British underpayment of colonial officers and the British policy of making them inferior to all British officers, whatever the rank. In early 1755, British General Edward Braddock and his army arrived in Virginia, and Washington agreed to serve as Braddock's aide-de-camp and, as a gesture of goodwill, gave him the symbolic rank of colonel. The following expedition against Fort Duquesne was a disaster, but

Washington fought bravely and brought the remaining British forces back after Braddock and 1,000 others were killed.

Governor Dinwiddie appointed Washington commander of all Virginia forces in August 1755. During the next three years, Washington labored with the problem of frontier defense. Still, they participated in no significant battles until he was placed in command of a Virginia regiment participating in the large British offensive against Fort Duquesne in 1758. The French destroyed and left the fort before the British and Americans appeared, and Fort Pitt was built on the site. With Virginia's strategic objective realized, Washington relinquished his military commission with the honorary rank of brigadier general. He reverted to a planter's life and sat in Virginia's House of Burgesses.

MAY 29
1979

On this day in history, Judge John Wood, a federal judge better known as "Maximum John," was assassinated outside his home in San Antonio, Texas, as he tried to fix a flat tire on his vehicle. Actor Woody Harrelson's father, Charles Harrelson, was indicted with the murder after it was revealed that drug kingpin Jimmy Chagra, whose case was coming before "Maximum John" that very day, had paid him $250,000 to kill the judge.

Chagra, worried about the considerable sentence he would soon receive from Judge Wood, apparently plotted with his brother and wife to hire Harrelson to carry out the murder-for-hire. Bullet fragments discovered at the scene were traced to a .240 Weatherby Mark V rifle – the same kind recently bought by Harrelson's wife, Jo Ann. Harrelson, who had a previous conviction for murder in 1968, was convicted and condemned to two life sentences in prison. Jo Ann, convicted of perjury and conspiracy to obstruct justice, would eventually be paroled. Woody Harrelson paid for his father's appeals, enlisting the aid of lawyer Alan Dershowitz. Harrelson would spend $2 million on his father's appeals.

Born on July 23, 1938, in Lovelady, Texas, Charles Harrelson was the son of Alma Lee and Voyde Harrelson. He married four times and began his career as an encyclopedia salesman in Los Angeles. After a stint in prison for armed robbery in 1960, he moved back to Texas and became a professional gambler. Harrelson later confessed that he had been involved in dozens of murder-for-hire, beginning in the early 1960s.

Harrelson was tried for the May 28, 1968 murder of carpet salesman Alan Harry Berg. He would be defended by renowned defense attorney Percy Foreman, who, on September 22, 1970, managed to get Harrelson acquitted by a jury in Angleton, Texas. The slaying is recounted in the book *Run Brother Run* by David Berg, the victim's brother.

Charles Harrelson was then tried for the 1968 murder-for-hire slaying of Sam Degelia Jr., a resident of Hearne, Texas. Harrelson was paid $2,000 for the contract killing of Degelia, a grain dealer and father of four. His trial resulted in a hung jury, although Pete Scamardo had been tried in the case, found guilty of being an accomplice to the murder, and sentenced to seven years probation. Harrelson was retried in 1973, found guilty, and sentenced to 15 years. In 1978, after serving just five years, he was released early for good behavior.

Charles Harrelson would probably just be a true crime footnote if he had not killed a federal judge, but he made American history when, on May 29, 1979, he gunned down Judge John H. Wood Jr. outside his San Antonio home. The story begins with the incarceration of Texas drug dealer Jimmy Chagra. The judge's nickname was "Maximum John" because he always gave stiff sentences to drug dealers, so Chagra decided to even his odds a little.

Chagra decided to hire Harrelson for the impressive sum of $250,000. Wood was getting ready to head to work on that May morning in 1979 when Harrelson shot him in the back with a rifle. The judge died on the way to the hospital, and the killing shook the nation. It was the first time a federal judge had been assassinated in America, and President Jimmy Carter condemned the killing as "an assault on our very system of justice." Soon, there was a $200,000 reward, and Harrelson would not last very long with every law enforcement agent in the country on his trail.

Harrelson was nabbed when calls were made to the police that he was firing a gun at imaginary FBI agents while on drugs. During a six-hour stand-off with police, he confessed to the murder of the judge and to killing John F. Kennedy in 1963. Despite the admission to killing the judge while on drugs, the FBI would need more proof to charge Harrelson. During his incarceration, the FBI used a felon to tape Harrelson confessing to the crime as well as a tape recording of a conversation that occurred in prison between Jimmy Chagra and his brother Joe Chagra. Based on the accumulated evidence, Harrelson was booked with Judge Wood's murder. Harrelson maintained at trial that he did not kill the Judge but merely took credit for it to claim a large payment from Chagra.

Harrelson was sentenced to two life terms for murder. Both Harrelson and Chagra were implicated in the assassination. Chagra received a ten-year prison term as part of his plea deal to testify for the prosecution but not against his brother. Without Joe's testimony, Jimmy Chagra was acquitted of the murder. In a plea bargain, Jimmy admitted to his part in the assassination of Judge Wood and the attempted murder of a U.S. attorney. Harrelson's wife, Jo Ann, received a sentence totaling 25 years on numerous convictions of perjury and conspiracy related to the assassination.

In 2003, Chagra rescinded his previous testimony, maintaining that somebody other than Harrelson had shot Judge Wood. However unsuccessful, Harrelson's son, Woody, attempted to have his father's conviction overturned to secure a new trial. Chagra died in July 2008 of cancer.

During the trial for the murder of Judge Wood, Jimmy Chagra testified that Harrelson asserted that he shot Kennedy and drew maps to show where he hid during the assassination. Chagra said that he did not believe Harrelson's assertion, and it had been announced that the FBI "apparently discounted any involvement by Harrelson in the Kennedy assassination." As per Jim Mars' 1989 book *Crossfire*, Harrelson is thought to be the tallest and youngest of the "three tramps" by many conspiracy theorists. Mars stated that Harrelson was connected "with criminals connected to intelligence agencies and the military" and even suggested that he had links to Jack Ruby and Russell Douglas Matthews, a third party who had connections to organized crime who was known to both Harrelson and Ruby. Lois Gibson, a well-known forensic artist, found the photographs of Harrelson compatible with the pictures of the youngest looking of the "three tramps."

Harrelson and two other inmates attempted to escape from the Atlanta Federal Penitentiary on July 4, 1995. Subsequently, he was transferred to the ADX Florence Supermax prison in Colorado, where on March 15, 2007, he died in his cell from a heart attack at age 68.

MAY 30
1942

On this day in history, Fred Toyosaburo Korematsu was arrested in San Leandro, California, for resisting internment under President Franklin Roosevelt's contentious Executive Order 9066, which ordered the imprisonment of nearly all Japanese Americans in the United States in the aftermath of Japan's attack on Pearl Harbor.

The young man and his girlfriend were walking down a street in San Leandro, California when the police stopped them. On May 30, 1942, police inquired why the man had not complied with American military orders that prevented Japanese Americans from the West Coast. The man, who stated his name was Clyde Sarah, maintained that he was Hawaiian, not Japanese.

Skeptical, the police apprehended "Clyde Sarah" – who was really Fred Toyosaburo Korematsu. He had refused to obey the order that had been driving Japanese Americans into incarceration camps, and he had altered his name to avoid discovery. That day, his rebelliousness got him arrested.

Fred Toyosaburo Korematsu was born in Oakland, California, on January 30, 1919. He was the third of four sons born to parents Kakusaburo Korematsu and Kotsui Aoki, who had immigrated to America from Japan in 1905. Korematsu lived continuously in Oakland from his birth until the time of his arrest. He attended public schools, participated in high school tennis and swim teams, and worked with his family in their flower nursery near San Leandro, California. He endured racism in high school when a U.S. Army recruiting officer passed out recruiting flyers to his non-Japanese schoolmates. The officer told Korematsu, "We have orders not to accept you." Even his girlfriend's Italian parents felt that Japanese people were inferior and unfit to mix with white people.

The U.S. Navy formally rejected Korematsu because of stomach ulcers, yet it is believed that he was denied because he was Japanese. Instead, he trained to become a welder to work in the defense industry. First, he worked at a shipyard but was summarily dismissed again because of his ethnicity. He then found another job but was fired after a week when his supervisor returned from a lengthy vacation to see him working there. Because of his Japanese descent, Korematsu lost every job he tried to get following the attack on Pearl Harbor.

On May 3, 1942, General John DeWitt ordered Japanese Americans to appear on May 9 at Assembly Centers as a prelude to being forced into internment camps. Korematsu declined and went into hiding in the Oakland area. Before his arrest on May 30, 1942, as Clyde Sarah, Korematsu even underwent plastic surgery on his eyelids in an unsuccessful effort to pass as a Caucasian, and he claimed to be Spanish and Hawaiian. Shortly after his arrest and placement in a jail cell in San Francisco, he received a visit from Ernest Besig, the director of the American Civil Liberties Union in northern California, who asked him whether or not he would be willing to allow his case to test the legality of the Japanese American internment. They assigned civil rights attorney Wayne Collins to the case, and the national ACLU thought they should not take this case because many high-ranking members of the ACLU were close to President Roosevelt. The ACLU did not want to be viewed negatively during a time of war, but Besig was determined to fight Korematsu's case nonetheless.

On June 12, 1942, Korematsu received his trial date and was given $5,000 bail (equal to 82,922.61 in today's money). After Korematsu's arraignment on June 18, Besig posted his bail, and he and Korematsu attempted to leave. They were met by military police, who were there to detain him, and Besig advised Korematsu to go with them. Korematsu was taken to the Presidio. He was tried and convicted in Federal Court on September 8, 1942, for violating Public Law No. 503, which criminalized any violations of military orders issued under Executive Order 9066. He was placed on five years probation. He was subsequently taken from the courtroom and returned to the Tanforan Assembly Center. After that, he and his family were transferred to the Central Utah War Relocation Center in Topaz, Utah. He could earn $12 per month by working in the camp. He was put in a horse stall with a single light bulb, and he later stated that "jail was better than this."

While some lauded him, he was hated by others, particularly by fellow Japanese, who cooperated with the government internment order, hoping that it would prove their loyalty to the United States. They saw Korematsu as a threat and ostracized him from camp society, and many felt that if they talked to him, they would be seen as troublemakers as well.

Korematsu then appealed his conviction to the U.S. Court of Appeals, which granted a review on March 27, 1943, but they upheld the original verdict on January 7, 1944. He appealed once again and took his case to the United States Supreme Court, which agreed to hear the case on March 27, 1944. On December 18, 1944, in a 6-3 decision written by Justice Hugo Black, the Court stated that compulsory exclusion, though constitutionally suspect, was reasonable during times of "emergency and peril."

In 1983, however, a federal judge reversed Korematsu's conviction for evading internment, ruling a "great wrong" had been done to him. In 1988, President Ronald Reagan issued a public apology on behalf of the government and authorized reparations of $20,000 to each survivor of former Japanese American internees or their descendants.

Scholars and judges have denounced the Korematsu Supreme Court ruling as among the worst in the Court's history.

In 1998, President Bill Clinton awarded Korematsu, a staunch civil rights advocate, the Presidential Medal of Freedom, the nation's highest civilian honor. Fred Korematsu died in 2005 at the age of 86.

In 2011, an acting U.S. solicitor – the federal government's top courtroom attorney – ruled a predecessor deliberately concealed from the Court a report from the Office of Naval Intelligence that asserted that Japanese Americans posed no military threat. In *Trump v. Hawaii* in 2018, the Supreme Court effectively overturned the Korematsu decision, calling it as "gravely wrong the day it was decided."

On January 30, 2011, California celebrated its first "Fred Korematsu Day" – the first day ever named after an Asian American in America.

MAY 31

1889

On this day in history, the Johnstown Flood happened after the devastating collapse of the South Fork Dam, the largest earthen dam in the world at the time, which was near the south fork of the Little Conemaugh River, 14 miles upriver of Johnstown, Pennsylvania. The dam burst after numerous days of severe rainfall, discharging 20 million tons of water. The flood ultimately killed 2209 people and caused $17 million of damage (about 534 million in 2022 dollars).

Located 60 miles east of Pittsburgh, Johnstown was built on a plain between the Little Conemaugh and Stony Creek Rivers, which made the town subject to reasonably frequent flooding. Like many other towns in the Rust Belt, Johnstown was a bustling community in the late 1800s, when the steel industry was at its peak. In the mid-1800s, a dam was constructed on the Little Conemaugh River, 14 miles from Johnstown, to help control these occurrences.

In 1889, thirty thousand people – many steelworkers – called Johnstown, Pennsylvania, home. The town's inhabitants were acclimated to repeated bouts of flooding when it rained intensely or when the snow in the neighboring mountains melted rapidly, but they were not ready for what transpired when the South Fork Dam failed on May 31, 1889.

When the dam was built in the 1840s, it was the largest earth dam in the United States. The structure of dirt and rock that held in the water on man-made Lake Conemaugh stood 72 feet tall and 900 feet long. The dam was an intrinsic part of a canal system used to transport goods along the rivers of Pennsylvania before the Industrial Revolution. However, with the introduction of railroads across America, they eventually replaced canals as the primary means of transporting goods, and the dam fell into disrepair as its maintenance was neglected.

The South Fork Hunting and Fishing Club purchased Lake Conemaugh and the dam to use as an exclusive area for the club's wealthy and influential membership to go sailing, fishing, and relaxing in 1879. Its members included some of the richest men in America, like Andrew Carnegie and Henry Clay Frick.

Despite having plenty of money, the club's members had failed to maintain the dam suitably. They even lowered the structure's height to make it wider so a road could be built on top of the dam. They also attached screens to the spillway to stop the fish from escaping the lake. Both of these "improvements" significantly caused the dam's failure and the ensuing Johnstown Flood.

On May 31, 1889, an engineer at the dam noticed that the spillway screens had become clogged with debris after days of heavy rain. With rising water levels in the lake and sensing a disaster, he rode a horse into the nearby town of South Fork to warn its residents. Unfortunately, the telegraph lines were down. They were unable to contact the town of Johnstown.

The dam collapsed just past 3 p.m. with a loud bang that could be heard from miles away, and the entirety of Lake Conemaugh rushed forward at speeds of up to 40 miles per hour. The residents of Johnstown, just 14 miles downstream, had absolutely no idea what was about to happen.

The cascading water collected trees, buildings, trains, and other objects in its path as it swept through the villages east of Johnstown. When the wave of floodwater and debris reached the ill-fated town around 4 p.m., it was reportedly nearly 40 feet high.

A New York Times article from June 1, 1889, reported that Johnstown had been "practically wiped out of existence" after the flood "swept onward ... like a tidal wave... houses, factories and bridges were overwhelmed in the twinkling of an eye and with their human occupants were carried in a vast chaos down the raging torrent."

As the 20 million tons of water ripped through Johnstown, the flood destroyed everything in its path. Reliance on telegrams at the time made immediate reporting difficult, but one telegraph operator told reporters that he counted 63 bodies floating past his office in just 20 minutes. Some residents clung to trees, furniture, and roofs that had been torn from homes to stay afloat as the running waters carried them away. Eventually, all of the debris piled up downstream at the Pennsylvania Railroad Company's Stone Bridge. The heap of rubble stretched for 30 acres – and then it all caught on fire, killing many who had survived the initial torrent of water.

However, it did not take long for an accurate picture of the devastation to be revealed. Two thousand two hundred nine people were killed in the flood, nearly ten percent of the town of Johnstown, and 770 of those were never identified. The flood claimed 99 entire families as victims, including 396 children. The waters carried some as far afield as Cincinnati – 300 miles away. The last victim was not found until 1911. The flood wiped out four square miles of downtown Johnstown and destroyed 1,600 homes, with flood lines reaching up to 89 feet above the average river level in some places.

Five days after the flood and fire, Clara Barton and the American Red Cross arrived to begin one of their first significant peacetime disaster relief efforts. The group managed to raise $4 million to aid in the reconstruction of Johnstown. It took five years to rebuild the community, but unfortunately, nature proved to be an unstoppable force. Johnstown faced significant, disastrous flooding again in 1936 and later in 1977, though neither event was comparable to the destruction of 1889.

In fact, until the Galveston Hurricane a decade later, the Great Johnstown Flood marked the largest single-day loss of civilian life in American history.

JUNE 1
1871

On this day in history, John Wesley Hardin, one of the deadliest men in the history of the Old West, arrives in Abilene, Kansas, where he briefly becomes friends with Marshal Wild Bill Hickok.

Hardin had a propensity for violent rages from a young age. At 14, Hardin came close to killing a fellow student in a disagreement over a girl. He stabbed the other boy twice with the boy's knife. The following year, in 1868, he shot a Black man named "Maje" to death after a wrestling match turned heated. According to Hardin, Maje called him a coward and started chasing him, waving a stick. Hardin then shot Maje and fled the scene looking for help. When he returned, Maje was dead and, afraid that the Union soldiers would not give him a fair trial, decided to run. By the time Hardin was finally sentenced to prison in 1878, he claimed to have killed 44 men. That may have been an exaggeration, though historians have only been able to confirm 27 of those deaths.

In 1871, When Hardin was but 18 years of age, a Texas rancher hired the young gunman as a trail boss for cattle drives up the Chisholm trail to Abilene, Kansas. Hardin was eager to exit Texas because a few days before, he had murdered a Texas state police guard who was transferring him to Waco for a trial. Hardin needed to lay low and out of law enforcement's gaze, but, as usual, he could not keep his temper in check. During the cattle drive, a Mexican herd had crowded Hardin's animals from behind. Hardin complained to the Mexican in charge of the other herd, and when the exchange grew heated, Hardin shot the man in the head. A firefight opened between the two camps, and, according to Hardin, six vaqueros were shot and killed (five of those by Hardin). On the same cattle drive, Hardin claims to have killed two Indians in separate instances.

When Hardin and his herd arrived in Abilene, Kansas, on June 1, 1871, the town marshal, Wild Bill Hickok, was unconcerned with prosecuting a murder that had taken place outside of his jurisdiction. On the contrary, he took an almost paternalistic interest in the young gunslinger – Hardin was 16 years his junior – and the two men began an uneasy friendship. Like many early Western lawmen, Wild Bill Hickok had won a formidable reputation by committing several killings. He may have seen something of himself in Hardin, believing he was a hot-tempered young man who would eventually become a reasonably useful and law-abiding citizen. For his part, Hardin was simply proud to be associated with the celebrated gunfighter.

On his first night in Abilene, Hardin was approached by Hickok, who declared to him that he was wearing guns in violation of town ordinance and ordered him to surrender his weapons, which he did but in a surprising way: Hardin handed the guns to Wild Bill butts forward, then quickly rolled them over in his hands and suddenly Wild Bill was staring right into their muzzles. However, both men did back down. Hickok did not know that Hardin was a wanted man, and he advised Hardin to avoid problems while in Abilene.

Hardin met up with Hickok again on a cattle drive in August 1871. This time Hickok allowed Hardin to carry his pistols into town – something he had never allowed others to do. For his part, Hardin was captivated by Wild Bill and rejoiced in being seen on personal terms with the famous gunfighter. Hardin contended that when his cousin, Mannen Clements, was incarcerated for the slaying of two cowhands in July 1871, Hickok – at Hardin's request – arranged for his getaway.

Not long afterward, on August 6, 1871, Hardin, his cousin Gip Clements, and a rancher friend named Charles Couger rented rooms at the American House Hotel after an evening of revelry and gambling. Clements and Hardin shared one room while Couger was in another. All three had been drinking heartily all evening long. Sometime during the night, Hardin was awakened by loud snoring from Couger's room. He yelled at the man several times to "roll over" and then, annoyed by the lack of response, drunkenly fired several bullets through the shared wall to awaken the sleeping man. Couger was hit in the chest by one of the bullets as he lay in bed and was killed immediately. Although Hardin did not mean to kill the man, he had violated an ordinance prohibiting gun firing within city limits. Half-dressed and still drunk, he and Clements escaped through a second-story window onto the hotel's roof. He saw Hickok arrive with four policemen. Hardin wrote in his autobiography, "Now, I believed that if Wild Bill found me in a defenseless condition, he would take no explanation but would kill me to add to his reputation."

Hardin leaped from the hotel roof into the street and hid in a haystack until daybreak. He then swiped a horse and rode to a cow camp 35 miles from town. Hardin then claimed that he killed lawman Tom Carson and two deputies. According to Hardin, he did not murder them but forced them to disrobe and walk back to Abilene. Hardin left for Texas the next day, never to return to Abilene.

In 1894 Hardin was released from prison after serving 17 years for murder. After his pardon that same year, he passed the bar exam and became a lawyer. In 1895, while in EL Paso, Texas, Hardin got into a dispute with a lawman after his girlfriend had her gun taken from her. It is said that Hardin pistol-whipped the young deputy. That afternoon, the deputy's lawman father had a heated discussion with Hardin.

That night, Hardin went to a local saloon to play dice. Shortly before midnight, Deputy John Selman Sr. entered the saloon, strolled up to Hardin from behind, and delivered a bullet to the back of his head, killing him immediately. As Hardin lay on the floor, Selman fired three more shots into him.

Selman was detained and arrested for murder and stood trial. He claimed self-defence, stating that Hardin drew his gun when Selman entered the saloon. The trial ended up in a hung jury, and before a retrial could happen, Selman was killed in a shootout with U.S. Marshal George Scarborough on April 6, 1896, during an argument following a card game.

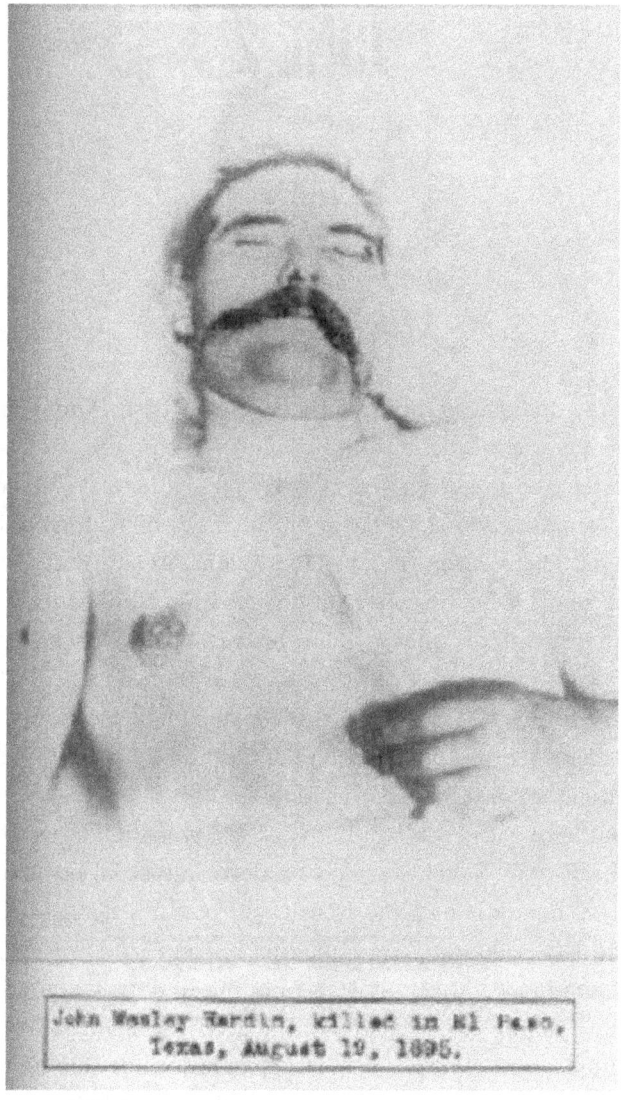

(Photo: John Wesley Hardin's postmortem photograph, 1895. Wikimedia Commons)

JUNE 2
1866

On this day in history, approximately 1,000 Irish American Fenian insurgents invaded Canada from Buffalo, N.Y., and engaged 840 Canadian militia volunteers near Ridgeway, Canada West, currently Ontario, Canada. After a two-hour battle, the Fenians forced the Canadians to retreat towards the Welland Canal. Aware that British and Canadian reinforcements were in the vicinity, the Fenians did not pursue the retreating Canadians but instead headed back toward Fort Erie just across the river from the safety of their base in Buffalo and American territory. At Fort Erie, the Fenians engaged a small 71-man militia force in a small, pitched battle. Outnumbered more than 10-1, the Canadians were ultimately driven off.

The Battle of Ridgeway, on June 2, 1866, was the largest confrontation of the Fenian Raids, the first modern industrial-era battle to be waged by Canadians and the first to be fought strictly by Canadian troops and led exclusively by Canadian officers. The Fenian plan was to seize Canada and hold it hostage, hoping to have Britain relinquish its hold on Ireland in exchange for Canada. The Fenians also mistakenly counted on receiving American recognition for seizing Canadian territory. The Fenians tried this approach five times between 1866 and 1871 in what is collectively known as the Fenian Raids.

The border between the United States and Canada has not always been peaceful. American anger toward Canada increased significantly during the Civil War when Canada became a haven for draft dodgers, escaped prisoners of war, and Confederate agents who plotted hostile covert operations – including raids on border towns, the firebombing of New York City, and the assassination of Abraham Lincoln.

Canada was a natural target to the Irish American members of the Fenian Brotherhood, which sought to end 700 years of colonial rule by England in Ireland. This was mainly because it was the closest British territory to the United States.

Like many Fenians, John O'Neill could never forgive the British for the horrors he had witnessed as a boy during the Great Hunger of the 1840s. Radicalized by this terrible event, a teenaged O'Neill joined hundreds of thousands of Irishmen fleeing to the United States. When Civil War broke out in 1861, he joined the Union Army, sustained severe injuries during the siege of Knoxville, and had a horse shot out from under him during the Peninsular Campaign.

Far from a whiskey-fueled daydream, the Fenian plan to invade Canada was carefully crafted for months by veteran Civil War officers, including the one-armed general Thomas William Sweeny. Although an attack on a foreign country with which America maintained peaceful relations ran afoul of American neutrality laws, the plan also had the implied approval of the White House.

President Andrew Johnson was quite willing to let the Fenians cause problems for the British because he, too, wanted to pressure the British to pay reparations for the damage caused by Confederate warships, such as the CSS Alabama, which had been built in Great Britain. Many Americans also hoped Canada would become the next territory to be absorbed by the United States as it fulfilled its expansionist, Manifest Destiny. The U.S. government sold surplus weapons to the Fenians, and Johnson met personally with their leaders, reportedly giving them his full backing. The Irishmen were free to establish their own state in exile – complete with their own president, constitution, currency, and capital in the heart of New York City.

Summoned to the battlefront in late May 1866, O'Neill left behind his wife, two-month-old son, and business worth $50,000 in Nashville to attack Canada. When the invasion's commanders failed to show in Buffalo, O'Neill was given command of the 800-man force, which called itself the Irish Republican Army.

Early on June 1, 1866, O'Neill fulfilled a lifelong dream by leading his men across the Niagara River and the International border. "The governing passion of my life apart from my duty to my God is to be at the head of an Irish Army battling against England for Ireland's rights," he declared. "For this I live, and for this, if necessary, I am willing to die."

O'Neill proved to be a more than able leader and tactician when he confronted a Canadian force on June 2 outside the village of Ridgeway, 20 miles south of Niagara Falls. The Civil War veteran used his experience to rout a makeshift defense force that included farm boys and the University of Toronto students who had never once fired a rifle. O'Neill followed that up with a victory in the streets of Fort Erie.

This marked the first Irish victory over forces from the British Empire since 1745.

The attack and victory made front-page news nationwide, and Irish Americans poured into Buffalo to join the fight. The American government, however, severed the Fenian supply lines in what the Irishmen saw as a great betrayal by Johnson. Forced to retreat, O'Neill shook hands with nearly two dozen prisoners of war, informed them they were again free men, and vowed to return to Canada soon.

He would be a man of his word. After assuming the leadership of the Fenian Brotherhood, O'Neill launched further attacks on Canada in 1870 and 1871. They failed utterly, and, in one instance, comically, when O'Neill seized two buildings, he thought to be Canadian, they turned out to be in America instead.

However, The Fenian Brotherhood succeeded in forming the creation of a new nation – just not the one he expected. Worried about the failure of the British government to protect its border from attack from the south, Canada achieved the right to self-government in 1867, directing it toward its eventual independence.

JUNE 3
1943

On this day in history, the Zoot Suit Riots, a series of violent confrontations between Latino and Black youths and members of the U.S. military, occurred from June 3 to June 8, 1943, in Los Angeles, California over the wearing of zoot suits – outfits featuring balloon-legged trousers and long coats with wide lapels and over-padded shoulders. While ostensibly blamed on the so-called "zoot-suiters" lack of "patriotism" during World War II, the assaults were more about race than fashion. Racial tensions at the time had been raised by the Sleepy Lagoon murder trial, involving the 1942 murder of a young Latino man in a Los Angeles neighborhood.

After coming from Harlem jazz clubs during the 1930s, the zoot suit style became fashionable with young men in Black and Latino neighborhoods across America. In Los Angeles, which had a large Latino population, many more conservative citizens (including both Mexican Americans and whites) were opposed to the young zoot-suiters who called themselves "pachucos," linking them not only with cultural upheaval but also with lawbreaking and criminal behavior.

These negative views only grew during World War II, when wool rationing in early 1942 caused the manufacturing of zoot suits to be prohibited due to the copious amounts of fabric needed. As well wearing a zoot suit was also seen as unpatriotic. The Los Angeles media, notably, spent much time painting pachucos as dangerous, especially after the so-called Sleepy Lagoon Murder.

Early on the morning of August 2, 1942, 23-year-old Jose Diaz was found unconscious and near death on a dirt road near a reservoir in East Los Angeles. Diaz died without regaining consciousness shortly after being taken to hospital by ambulance. The reservoir, known locally as Sleepy Lagoon, was a popular swimming area mainly used by young Mexican Americans prohibited from using the then-segregated public pools. Sleepy Lagoon was also a favorite gathering place of the 38th Street Gang, a Latino street gang in nearby East Los Angeles.

During the investigation, the police questioned Latinos only and soon arrested seventeen members of the 38th Street Gang. Despite lacking evidence, including the exact cause of death, the men were charged with murder, denied bail, and remanded in prison.

The largest mass trial in California history finished on January 13, 1943, when three of the 17 Sleepy Lagoon perpetrators were found guilty of first-degree murder and condemned to life in prison. Nine others were found guilty of second-degree murder and given five years to life sentences. The other five defendants were convicted of assault.

Later the trial was determined to have been an explicit denial of due process of law, and the defendants were not disallowed from sitting with or talking to their attorneys in the courtroom. At the district attorney's request, the defendants were also forced to wear zoot suits at all times because the jury should see them in clothing "obviously" worn only by "hoodlums."

In 1944, the Second District Court of Appeals overturned the Sleepy Lagoon convictions. All defendants were released from prison with their criminal records wiped clean.

On May 30, 1943, a verbal clash between a group of American sailors and a group of zoot suiters ended in the physical beating of one of the sailors. As an act of revenge, about 50 sailors left the local U.S. Navy Reserve Armory on the evening of June 3, armed with improvised weapons and pursuing zoot suiters (even those as young as twelve or thirteen years of age). On the second night of rampaging, the sailors entered the city's Mexican American neighborhoods, bursting into cafes, bars, and theaters to seek out and attack their victims.

Military personnel and civilians joined in the violence, some traveling to Los Angeles from elsewhere to take part. While news reports treated the rioters as heroes fighting against a supposed Mexican crime wave, many of the attacks were racially motivated, targeting African Americans, Latinos, and other minorities even when they were not wearing zoot suits. Meanwhile, police arrested hundreds of young Latinos – many of whom had been attacked themselves – compared with relatively few sailors or civilians involved in the rioting.

By June 7, the rioting had spread outside downtown Los Angeles to Watts, East Los Angeles, and other neighborhoods. Taxi drivers offered free rides to military personnel going to the rioting areas, and thousands of them and civilians from San Diego and other parts of southern California assembled in Los Angeles to join the riot.

The Mexican American community leaders begged state and local officials to intercede – The Council for Latin American Youth even telegrammed a note to President Roosevelt – but their pleas were disregarded. One eyewitness, writer Carey McWilliams, told a dismal tale:

"On Monday evening, June 7, thousands of Angelenos... turned out for a mass lynching. Marching through the streets of downtown Los Angeles, a mob of several thousand soldiers, sailors, and civilians, proceeded to beat up every zoot-suiter they could find. Street cars were halted while Mexicans, and some Filipinos and Negroes, were jerked out of their seats, pushed into the streets, and beaten with sadistic frenzy."

Some of the most reprehensible violence was clearly racist: According to several reports, a black defense plant worker – still wearing his defense-plant identification badge – was dragged off a streetcar, after which one of his eyes was cut out with a knife.

The Zoot Suit Riots finally calmed down after June 8, when military officials prohibited all military personnel from Los Angeles from leaving their barracks and ordered military police to patrol the city— the L.A. City Council subsequently passed a resolution banning wearing zoot suits on city streets.

No one died during the Zoot Suit Riots, though many were injured.

In the aftermath, Governor Earl Warren tasked an independent citizens' committee with investigating the riots and determining their cause. Though several factors were cited, the committee concluded that racism was the primary cause, made worse by inflammatory, biased media coverage and an uneven response by the Los Angeles Police Department.

JUNE 4
1913

On this day in history, English suffragette Emily Davison dies after throwing herself in front of King George V's horse *Anmer* during the running of the Epsom Derby.

Emily Wilding Davison supported the Women's Social and Political Union (WSPU) and was a radical warrior in the fight for votes for women. She was detained on nine occasions, went on hunger strikes seven times, and was force-fed on forty-nine occasions. She was a steadfast feminist and fervent Christian and regarded socialism as a moral and political force for good. Much of her life has been understood through the manner of her death. She gave no prior notice or reason for what she intended to do at the Derby, and the ambiguity of her motives and intentions has impacted how history has evaluated her. Various theories of the inspiration or rationale for the unpleasant incident at the Derby, including accident, suicide, or an endeavor to pin a suffragette banner to the king's horse.

Davison was born at Roxburgh House, Greenwich, south-east London, on October 11, 1872. Her parents were Charles Davison, a retired merchant, and Margaret nee Caisley, both of Morpeth, Northumberland. By 1868, when he married Margaret, Charles was 45, and Margaret was 19. Emily was the third of four offspring born to the pair. The marriage was Charles' second; his first marriage yielded nine children before the death of his wife in 1866.

She was a bright student at a time when educational prospects were very restricted for women. After attending Kensington Prep School, Davison took classes at Royal Holloway College and Oxford University but could not officially earn a degree from either establishment. Women were forbidden from doing so at that time.

In 1909, Davison quit teaching to commit entirely to the woman's suffrage movement, also known as the suffragette movement. She was unafraid of the consequences of her political actions, willing to be arrested and imprisoned several times for various protest-related offenses.

Davison would spend a month in Manchester's Strangeways Prison in 1909. While incarcerated, she attempted a hunger strike. Many jailed suffragists went on hunger strikes to protest the government's denial to classify them as political prisoners. Davison barricaded herself in a cell for some time. The guards proceeded to flood the cell with water. Later writing about the experience, Davison said, "I had to hold on like grim death. The power of the water seemed terrific, and it was cold as ice."

In 1912, Davison spent six months at Holloway Prison. Suffragists were treated brutally in prison, and those who went on hunger strikes became subject to being force-fed. Davison thought she could end the abuse of her fellow suffragists by jumping off a prison balcony. She later explained her idea: "The idea in my mind was that one big tragedy may save many others." This action showed just how far Davison was willing to go for her friends and her cause.

On June 4, 1913, Davison, with two flags adorned with the suffragette colors of purple, white, and green from the WSPU offices, began her journey to the Derby by train to Epsom, Surrey, England. Once there, she placed herself in the infield at Tattenham Corner, the final turn before the home straight. At this juncture of the race, with some horses having already passed her, she squeezed under the guard rail and bolted onto the course; she may have held one of the suffragette flags in her hands. As she reached up to grab the reins of King George V's horse Anmer, ridden by Herbert Jones, she was struck by the animal, which had been traveling at around 35 miles per hour (56 kph), four seconds after jumping onto the course. Anmer fell because of the collision and partially rolled over his jockey, who had his foot temporarily stuck in the stirrup. Davison was thrown to the ground unconscious; some reports stated that she was kicked in the head by the horse, but the surgeon who operated on Davison reported that "I could find no trace of her having been kicked by the horse." Three news cameras recorded the event.

Spectators rushed onto the track and tried to help Davison and Jones, and both were transported to Epsom Cottage Hospital. Davison was operated on, but she never regained consciousness. While in the hospital, she even received hate mail. One letter, signed "An Englishman," read, "I am glad that you are in hospital. I hope you suffer torture until you die, you idiot.... I should like the opportunity of starving and beating you to a pulp."

Davison died on June 8, aged 40, from a fracture to her skull. Found in her possession were her race card, two suffragette flags, the return stub of her railway ticket to London, a diary with appointments for the following week, and a ticket to a suffragette dance later that day. The King and Queen Mary were present at the race and made inquiries about the health of both Jones and Davison. Jones had a concussion and other injuries; he spent the evening of June 4 in London before returning home the following day. He could not remember the event: "She seemed to clutch at my horse, and I felt it strike her." He recovered sufficiently to race Anmer at Ascot Racecourse two weeks later.

At the coroner's inquest held at Epsom on June 10, the coroner ruled that, because of lack of evidence to the contrary, Davison had not attempted suicide. The coroner also believed that, despite waiting until she could see horses, "from the evidence, it was clear that the woman did not make for His Majesty's horse in particular." The verdict of the court was "death due to misadventure."

Over 5,000 supporters of the Votes for Women campaign turned out for Davison's funeral procession. Over 50,000 spectators lined the procession's route in London. Her body was interred in Morpeth, Northumberland. Her gravestone reads "Deeds not Words," a popular suffragist motto.

Fifteen years after her death, Davison's vision was ultimately achieved. Women achieved the right to vote in England in 1928.

JUNE 5
1967

On this day in history, a brief but bloody conflict known as the Six-Day War began and was fought between Israel and the Arab states of Egypt, Syria, and Jordan. After years of diplomatic tension and clashes between Israel and its neighbors, Israel Defense Forces began preventative air strikes that nullified the air forces of Egypt and its allies. Israel then mounted an effective ground offensive and captured the Sinai Peninsula and the Gaza Strip from Egypt, the West Bank and East Jerusalem from Jordan, and the Golan Heights from Syria. The brief war ended with a U.N.-sponsored ceasefire, but it substantially transformed the map of the Mideast and gave rise to persistent geopolitical tension.

For the Israelis, the six days of the war in June 1967 were a series of spectacular triumphs that doubled the land under their command. Although it instituted Israel's military supremacy over neighboring Arab states, the Six-Day War also intensified belligerency among Palestinian insurgents resolved to find new battlefields.

The Six-Day War began with disagreements between Israel and Egypt over the rights of Israeli shipping to pass through the Suez Canal and the Red Sea. The State of Israel was founded in May 1948.

The borders created by Israel's 1948 war with its Arab neighbors had held awkwardly for a few years when Egypt's ruler Gamal Abel Nasser decided in 1956 to nationalize the Suez Canal and deny passage to Israeli ships both there and in the Straits of Tiran that led to the Red Sea. Israel countered by attacking and occupying the Sinai Peninsula for several months until a United Nations peacekeeping force was established and the right to free shipping was restored. In late May 1967, Nasser told the U.N. force to leave Egypt and closed the Straits of Tiran to Israel again. Egypt also began planning an aborted attack when the Israelis learned of it. On Israel's northern border, the Syrians were intensifying their bombardment of Israeli settlements across the border. Israel struck back by shooting down six Syrian MiG fighters. The United States, which had guaranteed Israel's right to passage through the Straits, asked Israel not to attack while it attempted to find a diplomatic solution. Still, that effort was unsuccessful, and after a May 26 meeting with Israel's foreign minister, President Lyndon Johnson declared, "I've failed. They'll go." On May 30, Jordan signed a mutual-defense treaty with Egypt and Syria, and other Arab states, including Iraq, Kuwait, and Algeria, were sending troop contingents to join the Arab coalition against Israel.

The war began on June 5, 1967, with Israeli preventative air strikes that destroyed 286 of Egypt's 420 combat aircraft. Israeli tanks poured across the Sinai, and its troops took over the Egypt-occupied Gaza Strip. Concentrating on the fight against Egypt, Israel initially did not seek to move against Jordan, which controlled East Jerusalem and the West Bank. Still, the battle plans changed when King Hussein's troops began shelling Israeli positions. Israeli paratroopers captured East Jerusalem on June 7, and the Israeli army stormed across the West Bank, driving opposing forces to the Jordan River.

In the meantime, the United States and the Soviet Union publicly sought a ceasefire while privately warning the other not to intervene in the fighting. (The 1967 war marked the first use of the diplomatic "hotline" between the two countries). While not rebuking Israel for its pre-emptive strike, the Johnson administration did impose an arms embargo on the region. The United States did not retaliate when the Israelis attacked an American intelligence ship, the U.S.S. *Liberty*, on

June 8, accepting the official explanation that the assault had been a tragic accident. Israel later apologized for the attack, which killed 34 Americans and wounded 171 sailors, and offered $6.9 million in compensation, claiming that it had thought the *Liberty* was an Egyptian vessel. However, most involved in the incident believe that the attack was intentional, staged to hide Israel's impending seizure of Syria's Golan Heights, which happened the next day. The ship's listening devices likely overheard Israeli military communications planning this contentious operation. Captain McGonagle was later granted the Medal of Honor for his heroic leadership of the *Liberty* during and after the attack.

The United States became more concerned when Israel did push into the Syrian-held Golan Heights, raising the possibility that the Soviet Union would respond. However, a U.N.-sponsored ceasefire took hold on June 10, and direct confrontation between the superpowers was avoided.

The scale of Israel's military success in the Six Day War was spectacular; its troops captured the Sinai Peninsula, the Gaza Strip, the West Bank, East Jerusalem, and the Golan Heights, doubling the territory under the nation's control. Israel inflicted massive casualties on the Arab states, losing 20,000 soldiers, while Israel lost only 800. Israel captured 6,000 prisoners while giving up only 15. But Israel's military dominance also created problems; roughly 500,000 Palestinians were displaced by the fighting, and a million were now under Israeli control in what became known as the "occupied territories." That November, U.N. Resolution 242 urged withdrawal from these territories in exchange for a permanent end to hostilities; this "land for peace" initiative became the cornerstone of subsequent regional negotiations. But the war had destroyed the dreams many Palestinians had of using Arab armies to defeat Israel and establish an independent state in all of pre-partition Palestine. Despite the defeat, the Palestinian exile leaders were not interested in peace. On the contrary, given the demonstrated military weakness of the Arab states, they were convinced that they had to be more aggressive in opposing Israel and showing that Palestinian nationalism had not died.

The Six-Day War created various militant Palestinian organizations grouped under the loose umbrella of the P.L.O. led by Yasser Arafat. One such group, the Popular Front for the Liberation of Palestine, was formed a few months after the end of the Six-Day War. Within a year, it would stage the first hijacking of an Israeli airplane, ushering in a new phase of the Middle East conflict.

JUNE 6
1865

On this day in history, William Quantrill, the leader of Quantrill's Raiders and one of the American Civil War's most notorious figures, is killed in Kentucky after receiving wounds in a skirmish with federal guerrillas under the command of Captain Edwin Terrell. Since Quantrill's men were guerrillas rather than legitimate soldiers, they were denied the general amnesty given to the Confederate army after the war ended. Some members of Quantrill's Raiders, like Frank and Jesse James, took this as an excuse to become criminals and bank robbers.

Born and raised in Canal Dover, Ohio, in 1837, Quantrill was involved in many illegal enterprises in Utah and Kansas during his teens. In his early 20s, he fled to Missouri after killing a man in a lumber yard where he worked, where he became a staunch supporter of pro-slavery settlers in their sometimes-violent conflict with their antislavery neighbors. When the Civil War began in 1861, the 24-year-old Quantrill became the leader of an irregular force of Confederate soldiers known as Quantrill's Raiders.

By 1862, Union forces had established control over Missouri, but Quantrill's Raiders continued to harass the northern army and unguarded pro-Union towns over the next three years. Quantrill and other guerrilla leaders recruited their soldiers from Confederate sympathizers who resented what they saw as their state's unfairly harsh Union rule. Among those who joined him was a 20-year-old farm kid named Frank James. His younger brother, Jesse, joined an allied guerrilla force a year later.

The vicious guerrilla war happening in Missouri spilled over into Kansas. It precipitated one of the most appalling acts of violence of the whole Civil War when nearly 200 men from the abolitionist town of Lawrence were murdered and the town razed on August 21, 1863, by Quantrill's Raiders.

The Civil War took on a different form in Kansas and Missouri than it did throughout the rest of America. Few regular armies were operating there; instead, partisan bands attacked civilians and each other. The conflict originated in 1854 when the Kansas-Missouri border became the center of tension over slavery. While the people of Kansas attempted to decide the issue of slavery, bands from Missouri, a slave state, began attacking abolitionist towns in the territory. Abolitionists reacted with equal hostility.

In August 1863, the Union commander along the border, General Thomas Ewing, arrested several wives and sisters of members of Quantrill's Raiders. On August 14, the jail in Kansas City, Missouri, where the women were being held, collapsed, killing five and severely injuring three.

Quantrill gathered together 450 men to take revenge. The gang, which included future outlaws like the Younger brothers and Frank and Jesse Kames, headed for Lawrence, Kansas, long known as the center for abolitionism in Kansas. After kidnapping ten farmers to guide them to Lawrence, the gang murdered each of them. Quantrill's men rode into Lawrence, drug nearly 200 men from their homes, many in front of their families, and killed them in cold blood. They burned 185 buildings in Lawrence, then rode back to Missouri with Union cavalry in hot pursuit. This incident incited the North and caused even more killing on both sides along the Kansas-Missouri border.

After the raid on Lawrence, Quantrill's hold over the Raiders began to fade. During the winter of 1863-1864, while in Texas, the group splintered into different bands, each commanded by a "lieutenant" such as George Todd and "Bloody" Bill Anderson. When the bands returned to west-central Missouri in the spring of 1864, the final break occurred with Quantrill taking a small nucleus of forty loyal bushwhackers and heading east towards Kentucky.

Unknown to the 27-year-old leader of Quantrill's Raiders, the final hour was near. Ironically, he would be chased by authentic guerrilla hunters. With the end of the Civil War around the corner, the Union had driven the formal Confederate army presence from Missouri. It was redirecting troops to hunt down the guerrilla bands still operating in the upper South. Pursuit by guerrilla-hunting units became ruthless.

Union Captain Edwin Terrell, a leader of federal guerrillas in Kentucky, was the man chosen to hunt down Quantrill and his raiders. Quantrill was tracked to an area near Taylorville in Spencer County, Kentucky, on May 10, 1865. Headquartered at the James A. Wakefield farm, the gang had sheltered its horses in an adjacent barn. Thinking that Terrell was miles away, the band relaxed. Unfortunately for them, Terrell and his crew were very close by. Terrell's men closed within yards of Quantrill's position and opened fire.

The terrified men scrambled wildly for their horses. Some would flee, but Quantrill, who had been sleeping, had been unable to secure his gun-shy horse, and he pursued his men on foot, looking to be carried away from the melee. Two men heard his pleas to stop and returned to wait for him, guaranteeing their demise from pursuing federal soldiers as bullets mortally struck their leader.

Quantrill was shot by a Union guerilla by the name of John Langford. He stated, "I shot him in the left shoulder – just back of the shoulder blade – the ball ranging downward and lodging in his right groin." Quantrill was reportedly shot a second time as he fell, the bullet cutting off the trigger finger of his right hand. One source states that Captain Terrell fired the second shot.

Quantrill was carried to Wakefield's farmhouse, paralyzed below the arms from gunshot damage to the spine. A doctor examined him and advised him that his days were numbered and he should settle his business affairs. Terrell provided wagon transportation to a military hospital and prison in Louisville. He arrived at the prison hospital on

May 13, 1865. On June 6, 1865, some twenty-seven days after he was wounded, Quantrill died.

Even the remains of the troubled young warrior, William Clarke Quantrill, have found little peace in death. In a twisted set of circumstances, some playing out in recent years, the guerrilla leader's bones have been scattered in restless interment at Dover, Ohio; Louisville, Kentucky; and the old Confederate Soldiers Home Cemetery in Higginsville, Missouri.

JUNE 7
1692

On this day in history, an enormous earthquake leaves desolate the town of Port Royal in Jamaica, killing 3,000 people, with 3,000 more deaths in the weeks following due to sickness and injury. The powerful tremors, soil liquefaction, and a tsunami brought on by the earthquake combined to demolish the town in its entirety.

Port Royal was built on a peninsula off the coast of Jamaica in the harbor across from present-day Kingston. The 6,500 residents lived and worked in many buildings constructed over the water. In the 17th century, Port Royal was known throughout the New World as a headquarters for piracy and smuggling.

Earthquakes in the area were not uncommon but were usually rather small. In 1688, a tremor toppled three homes. But four years later, at 11:43 a.m. on June 7, three powerful quakes struck Jamaica. A giant tsunami hit soon after, putting half of Port Royal under 40 feet of water. The HMS Swan was carried from the harbor and placed on top of a building on the island. It turned out to be a refuge for survivors. Larger houses collapsed almost immediately, and smaller ones slid off the land into the harbor as liquefaction dislocated their sandy foundations. Before the end of the day, most of the city had disappeared beneath the waters of Kingston Harbor. Most of those left standing during all the destruction were swept into the sea by the tsunami. The city's graveyard was a victim of the earthquake, so the survivors had to cope with a frightening scene as they sought to recover some of their possessions. There were coffins and bodies from the graveyard floating around, along with those who had just been killed. As they continued their search, they had to fight against a group of thieves who were taking advantage of the chaotic situation.

Port Royal is the only underwater city in the western hemisphere. Founded soon after the conquest of the island of Jamaica by the Spanish by an English invasion force in 1655, Port Royal went through a spectacular rise in wealth and influence. Before the earthquake, it was the most prominent English town in the New World and the most affluent. Unlike other English colonial towns in the New World, every visitor was impressed with the multistoried brick buildings. It had a population of 6,500 and rivaled Boston in size and economic power, the only other city of comparable importance at that time.

The English turned Port Royal into a strategic military and naval base. Its location in the middle of the Caribbean made it ideal for trade. Trade, as well as loot, dominated the economy in those times. The European powers extracted wealth from their colonies and brought it back to Europe in ships. If a country happened to have a powerful navy, it was considered fair game to raid the ships of other countries and empty their cargoes of gold and other valuables. England was one country engaged in that kind of enterprise.

On the morning of June 7, 1692, the church rector of a Port Royal church was running late for a lunch appointment, but a friend implored him to delay just a while longer. It was a small choice that ultimately saved his life. The ground began to roll and rumble, but the friend waved off the rector's alarm; earthquakes on the island usually passed quickly. But this quaking only increased in intensity, and the two men soon heard the church tower collapse into rubble.

The rector sprinted outside, racing for open ground. By his description, the land split open, swallowing crowds of people and homes in one gulp and then sealing it closed. The sky darkened to red, mountains crumbled in the distance, and water geysers exploded from the seams ripped in the earth. He turned to see a great wall of seawater swelling high above the town. In a letter describing the disaster, the shocked rector wrote, "In the space of three minutes... Port Royal, the fairest town of all the English plantations, the best emporium and mart of this part of the world, exceeding in its riches, plentiful of all good things, was shaken and shattered to pieces."

A tsunami followed the earthquake, which scientists believe measured 7.5 on the Richter scale, making it a "major" event. When the catastrophe ended, most of Port Royal lay beneath watery depths.

Due to its licentious reputation, Port Royal faced what to many people must have looked like Judgement Day. It certainly felt that way to the church rector. In letters, he confessed that he longed to escape the disaster scene. Still, his conscience drove him to stay, venturing into the town daily to pray with survivors in a tent pitched amid their flattened houses, which were looted nightly by "lewd rogues." "I hope by this terrible judgment, God will make them reform their lives, for there was not a more ungodly people on the face of the earth," he wrote.

Nothing like seventeenth-century Port Royal remains in that location today. Visitors see a fishing community of less than 2,000 and an abandoned British Naval Base, now used by the Jamaican Coast Guard. Jamaica is an independent nation now, so the marks of former British activities lie primarily under the sea. The ships and houses that sank in 1692 now form part of a magnificent museum and a unique center for archeological research. On land and sea, above all these, in the years since 1692, Jamaica has experienced many more disasters. A fire in 1703 destroyed all that was left or had been rebuilt of the old city of Port Royal. Hurricanes hit it in 1722 and again in 1744, and on both occasions, everything came down and had to be rebuilt. Two earthquakes came later, one in 1770 and one in 1907. The former destroyed the hospital and the latter a large part of the dockyard. Another fire, in 1815, did extensive damage to all the buildings, and a third earthquake destroyed the old fortifications.

JUNE 8
1758

On this day in history, a British force of 40 warships, 14,000 soldiers, and 12,000 sailors and marines began the siege of Louisbourg, located on the approaches to the St. Lawrence River in what is now Nova Scotia, Canada. The British, who first attempted to seize the fort in 1757, were led by Major General Jeffrey Amherst and Admiral Edward Boscawen, and they landed forces near the town and conducted a siege of its defenses. After several weeks of fighting, Louisbourg fell to Amherst's men, and the path to advancing up the St. Lawrence River towards Quebec had opened up.

Situated on Cape Breton Island, the fortress town of Louisbourg had been captured from the French by American colonial forces in 1745 during the War of the Austrian Succession. With the end of that conflict in 1748, Louisbourg was returned to the French in the Treaty of Aix-la-Chapelle in exchange for Madras, India. This decision proved controversial in England as it had been understood that Louisbourg was critical to defending French possessions in North America as it controlled the approaches to the St. Lawrence River.

Nine years later, with the French and Indian War raging, the English once again needed to capture and subdue Louisbourg as a precursor to a move against Quebec. In 1757, Lord Loudoun, the

British commander in North America, planned to fight on the defensive along the frontier while mounting an expedition against Quebec. A change in government in London, along with delays in receiving orders, ultimately saw the expedition redirected against Louisbourg. In the long run, the campaign failed due to the arrival of French naval reinforcements and terrible weather.

The disaster of the expedition in 1757 led English Prime Minister William Pitt (the elder) to prioritize the seizure of Louisbourg in 1758. To accomplish this, a huge force was assembled under the command of Major General Jeffrey Amherst and Admiral Edward Boscawen. The expedition sailed from Halifax, Nova Scotia, in late May 1758. Moving up the coast, Boscawen's fleet met the ship that carried Amherst. The two met and assessed the overall plans to land an invasion force along the shores of Gabarus Bay, which was 3 miles from Louisbourg.

Aware that the English intended to attack, the French commander at Louisbourg, Chevalier de Drucour, prepared to fend off the English landing and defend against a siege. Entrenchments and gun emplacements were constructed along the shores of Gabarus Bay, while five French ships of the line were positioned to protect the harbor approaches. Arriving off Gabarus Bay, the English were delayed in landing by inclement weather. Finally, on June 8, the landing force set out under the command of Brigadier General James Wolfe and supported by the guns of Boscawen's fleet. This effort was helped by feints against White Point and Flat Point by Brigadier Generals Charles Lawrence and Edward Whitmore.

Meeting heavy resistance from the French defenses near the beach, Wolfe's boats were forced to fall back. As they withdrew, some floated east and found a small landing spot guarded by heavy rocks. Going ashore, English light infantry secured a small beachhead, allowing the remainder of Wolfe's men to land. Attacking, his men struck the French line from the flank and rear, forcing them to retreat to the safety of Louisbourg. Largely in control of the area around the town, Amherst's men endured rough seas and boggy terrain as they landed their supplies and guns. Overcoming these issues, they began to advance against the town.

As the English siege train moved towards Louisbourg and lines were built opposite the defenses, Wolfe was ordered to move around the harbor and capture Lighthouse Point. Marching with 1220 picked men, he succeeded in his objective on June 12. Building a battery on the point, Wolfe was in a prime location to bombard the harbor and the water side of the town. On June 19, English guns started firing on Louisbourg. Pounding the fortress's walls, the bombardment from Amherst's artillery was met by fire from Louisbourg's 218 guns.

As the days passed, French fire slowed as many of their guns malfunctioned, and the fortress's walls were reduced. While Drucour was determined to hold out, their luck quickly ran out on July 21. As the bombardment continued, a mortar shell from the battery on Lighthouse Point struck the ship *Le Celebre* in the harbor, causing an explosion and setting her on fire. Fanned by a strong wind, the fire grew and soon consumed the two adjacent ships, *Le Capicieux* and *L'Entreprenant*. Drucour lost three of his five remaining vessels in a single stroke.

The French position worsened further two days later when heated English shot set the King's Bastion on fire. Situated inside the fortress, the King's Bastion was the fortress headquarters and was the largest building in North America. This loss, quickly followed by the burning of the Queen's Bastion, paralyzed French morale. On July 25, Boscawen dispatched a cutting-out party to capture or destroy the two remaining French warships. Slipping into the harbor, they captured *Bienfaisant* and burned *Prudent*. *Bienfaisant* was sailed out of the port and joined the British fleet. Realizing that the end had come, Drucour surrendered the fortress the following day.

Having fought a spirited defense, the French expected to be granted "honors of war" as given to the surrendering English at the Battle of Minorca. However, Amherst refused, tales of atrocities supposedly committed by France's native allies at the surrender of Fort Oswego and Fort William Henry probably fresh in his mind. The defenders of Louisbourg were ordered to surrender all their arms, equipment, and flags. These actions outraged Drucour, but because the safety of the non-combatant inhabitants of the Fortress depended upon him, he reluctantly accepted the terms of surrender.

The siege of Louisbourg cost the English 172 killed and 355 wounded, while the French suffered 102 killed, 303 wounded, and the remainder, 6,000, were taken prisoner and sent to England. The Louisbourg victory allowed the English to campaign up the St. Lawrence River to take Quebec. Following that city's surrender in 1759, English engineers began systematically reducing Louisbourg's defenses to prevent it from being returned to the French by any future peace treaty.

(Photo: *Burning of the French ship Prudent and capture of Bienfaisant, during the siege of Louisbourg in 1758,* by British marine artist Richard Paton, (1717 – 7 March 1791)

JUNE 9
1534

On this day in history, French explorer and navigator Jacques Cartier becomes the first European to discover the Gulf of St. Lawrence in present-day Canada. He would be the first to see Prince Edward Island, Iles de la Madelaine, and the Bay of Chaleur. In 1535, during his second voyage to the New World, he discovered the St. Lawrence River; he explored a new country with the immediate possibility of penetrating deeper, he allied with natives, and he received the assistance of two Indians who were learning to express themselves in French. He had found no gold or precious metals, nor did he find the Northwest Passage to India, but he did open up a new land to France for exploration and conquest.

Jacques Cartier was born on December 31, 1491, in the port of Saint-Malo, France. He belonged to a family of mariners and became very respectable when he married Mary Catherine des Granches, a member of a family of well-known shipowners. Cartier was among the most frequently chosen as godfather and witness during baptismal celebrations in Saint-Malo.

There was no record of any significant events in his life before 1534, except that he studied navigation in one of France's prominent centers for navigation. After his studies, he became a world-class French navigator and explorer. Historians marked his discovery of the Gulf of St. Lawrence and the St. Lawrence River, as well as the Canadian coast, as his greatest accomplishments.

Before his first voyage to the New World in 1534, it is believed that Cartier traveled to the Americas in 1524. He accompanied Giovanni da Verrazzano, a Florentine explorer, penetrating South Carolina, Nova Scotia, Newfoundland, and Brazil. The expedition was made with a formal commission from the French crown.

In 1534 King Francis I of France decided to send an expedition to explore the so-called "northern lands" of the New World. Francis hoped they would find precious metals, jewels, spices, and a passage to Asia. Cartier was selected for the commission.

With two ships and 61 crewmen, Cartier arrived off the barren shores of Newfoundland just 20 days after leaving France. He wrote, "I am rather inclined to believe that this is the land God gave to Cain." The expedition then entered the Gulf of St. Lawrence by the Strait of Belle Isle, went south to the Magdalen Islands, and reached the provinces of Prince Edward Island and New Brunswick. Going north to the Gaspe peninsula, he met several hundred Iroquois from the village of Stadacona (now Quebec City), who were there to fish and hunt for seals. He planted a cross on the peninsula to claim the area for France, although he told Chief Donnacona that it was just a landmark. During the expedition, Cartier took hostage two of Chief Donnacona's sons, Domagaya and Taignoagny, to return to France. They went through the strait separating Anticosti Island from the north shore but did not discover the St. Lawrence River before returning to France.

Cartier set out on a more extensive expedition with three ships and 110 men the following year. Donnacona's sons had told Cartier about the St. Lawrence River and the "Kingdom of the Saguenay" in an effort, no doubt, to get a trip home, and these became the objectives of the second voyage. The two former captives served as guides for this expedition.

After a 50-day sea crossing, the ships entered the Gulf of St. Lawrence and went up the "Canada River," later named the St. Lawrence River. Guided to Stadacona, the expedition decided to spend the winter there. But before winter set in, they traveled up the river to

Hochelaga, the site of present-day Montreal. Returning to Stadacona, they faced deteriorating relations with the natives and a severe winter. Nearly a quarter of the crew died of scurvy, although Domagaya saved many men with a remedy made from evergreen bark and twigs. Tensions grew by spring, however, and the French feared being attacked. They seized ten hostages, including Donnacona, Domagaya, and Taignoagny, and fled for France.

Because of his quick escape, Cartier could only report to the king that untold riches lay further west and that a great river, said to be 2,000 miles long, possibly led to Asia. These and other reports, including some from the hostages, were so encouraging that King Francis decided to send a sizeable colonizing expedition next. He put military officer Jean-Francois de la Rocque, Sieur de Roberval, in charge of the colonization plans, although the actual exploration was left to Cartier.

War in Europe and the massive logistics of colonization slowed Roberval. Cartier, with 1,500 men, arrived in Canada a year ahead of him. His party settled at the bottom of the cliffs of Cap-Rouge, where they built forts. Cartier started a second trip to Hochelaga, but he turned back when he found the route past the Lachine Rapids too difficult.

On his return, he found the colony under siege from the Stadacona natives. After a brutal winter, Cartier gathered drums filled with what he thought were gold, diamonds, and metal and started to sail for home. But his ships met Roberval's fleet with the colonists, who had just arrived in St. John's, Newfoundland. Roberval ordered Cartier and his men to return to Cap-Rouge, but Cartier ignored the order and sailed for France with his cargo. When he arrived in France, he found that his load was iron pyrite – also known as fool's gold – and quartz. Roberval's settlement efforts lasted a year but ultimately failed. He and the colonists returned to France after experiencing one bitter winter.

While he was credited with exploring the St. Lawrence region, Cartier's reputation was tarnished by his harsh dealings with the Iroquois and his abandoning the incoming colonists as he fled the New World. He returned to Saint-Malo but received no new commission from the king. He died there on September 1, 1557.

Despite his failures, Jacques Cartier is credited as the first European explorer to chart the St. Lawrence River and explore the Gulf of St. Lawrence. He also discovered Prince Edward Island and built a fort at Stadacona, where Quebec City stands today. And in addition to providing the name for a mountain that gave birth to "Montreal," he gave Canada its name when he misunderstood or misused the Iroquois word for village, "Kanata," as the name of a much broader area.

JUNE 10
1968

On this day in history, General William Westmoreland honestly evaluates past and present developments in the Vietnam War during a press conference where he is relieved of his command of the U.S. Military Assistance Command in Vietnam (MACV). Westmoreland stated that it would, in due course, make continued fighting "intolerable to the enemy." He also felt that because it was impossible to "cut a surface line of communication with other than ground operations," Washington's ban on ground attacks to embargo communist penetration through Laos impeded the attainment of military success. Westmoreland disagreed, however, that the military situation was deadlocked.

President Lyndon Johnson chose William Westmoreland, a distinguished veteran of World War II and the Korean War, to command the U.S. MACV in June 1964. Over the next four years, Westmoreland guided much of the American military strategy during the Vietnam War, spearheading the buildup of American troops in the region from 16,000 to more than 535,000. His strategy of attrition intended to wreak heavy losses on North Vietnamese and Viet Cong forces using greater U.S. firepower, yet this caused, for all intents and purposes, a stalemate by late 1967. The enemy's courageous Tet Offensive in early 1968 shed immense doubt on Westmoreland's claims of progress in the war effort, even as he called for 200,000 more troops.

On June 10, President Johnson replaced Westmoreland with General Creighton Abrams as commander of the MACV. Back in the U.S., Westmoreland fought off criticisms of his conduct of the war (including a libel lawsuit against CBS News), and he became a committed supporter of Vietnam veterans.

William Westmoreland was born in 1914 near Spartanburg, South Carolina, into a military family whose ancestors fought in the Revolutionary War and served in the Confederate Army during the Civil War. He earned an appointment to the U.S. Military Academy at West Point and graduated in 1936; his fellow cadets called him "Westy." As a young field officer, Westmoreland met and married Katherine Van Deusen, and the couple went on to have three children.

During World War II, Westmoreland fought in North Africa and Sicily and was chief of staff of the U.S. Army's Ninth Division when it entered Germany in 1944. He also served in the Korean War as the 187th Regimental Combat Team commander. In 1955, the 42-year-old Westmoreland was promoted to major general, becoming the youngest person to achieve that rank in the U.S. Army. He was given command of the 101st Airborne Division in 1958 and became superintendent of West Point two years later. A few months after the Kennedy assassination, newly inaugurated President Lyndon Johnson chose Westmoreland to go to Vietnam as deputy to General Paul Harkins, then head of the U.S. Military Assistance Command in Vietnam (MACV). In June 1964, he became a full four-star general and replaced Harkins in command of U.S. forces in Vietnam.

When Westmoreland first arrived in Vietnam, the total deployment of U.S. troops was 16,000. Immediately, he began to increase the number of soldiers in the area, arguing that escalation was necessary to prevent the weak Saigon government from collapsing because of the threat posed by the Communist North Vietnamese (NVA) and the National Liberation Front (NLF) (also known as the Viet Cong). The military buildup began in earnest after North Vietnamese gunboats attacked American destroyers in the Gulf of Tonkin in August 1964, and the number of American ground troops in Vietnam plateaued at 535,000.

Westmoreland's strategy in Vietnam depended on the superiority of U.S. firepower, including intensive aerial bombardments of regular enemy units. The goal was not to seize and hold territory but to inflict more losses than the Communist forces could sustain. Westmoreland's "war of attrition" overlooked the enemy's skill for irregular or guerrilla warfare and drastically underestimated the nationalist zeal and will to fight that motivated North Vietnamese and Viet Cong forces. Like many American officials, Westmoreland generally failed to see the North Vietnamese war effort for what it was – a passionate nationalist struggle – and viewed Ho Chi Minh and his supporters as mere puppets controlled by Communist giants China and Russia.

In September 1967, North Vietnamese and Viet Cong forces began a series of attacks on American garrisons (notably the Marine base at Khe Sanh). Westmoreland saw this as a positive development, as the enemy finally engaged in open combat. After U.S. and South Vietnamese forces inflicted heavy losses, including some 90,000 killed among NVA and NLF forces, Westmoreland reported to Johnson that the war's end was in sight, as the Communists could not possibly replace the men they had lost. But the ambitious Tet Offensive, a coordinated series of fierce attacks on more than 100 cities and towns in South Vietnam that on January 31, 1968 (the lunar new year) disproved Westmoreland's claim of progress. Though U.S. and South Vietnamese forces managed to repel the Tet attacks, it was clear the war was far from over.

With antiwar sentiment growing on the home front, the Johnson administration lost confidence in Westmoreland's strategy of attrition and its chances for victory in Vietnam. The beleaguered president turned down Westmoreland's request for 200,000 more troops and recalled him to Washington as the U.S. Army's Chief of Staff. General Abrams took over at MACV effective immediately. After four years as chief of staff, Westmoreland retired in 1972. He returned to South Carolina, where he unsuccessfully ran for the Republican nomination for governor in 1974. In 1976 he published his memoir, "A Soldier

Reports." After a CBS News documentary stated that Westmorland lied about enemy troop numbers before the Tet Offensive, he sued CBS for $120 million for libel in 1982. He would ultimately withdraw the lawsuit, with both sides claiming victory.

Westmoreland died in 2005 at the age of 91.

JUNE 11
1979

On this day in history, John Wayne, the iconic American film actor famous for starring in numerous Westerns, dies at 72 after a long battle with cancer.

John Wayne, nicknamed "Duke," began his silent film career in the 1920s. He was a major movie star from the 1940s to the 1970s, mainly for the Westerns he starred in. Of the 180 movies he made over a 50-year career, he also made a surprising variety of other films. Wayne epitomized a certain kind of rugged individualistic masculinity and has become an enduring icon in American culture.

During his career's last couple of decades, Wayne transformed into an American folk hero. While a hero to some, he was a villain to others for his outspoken, politically conservative views. Although he carefully avoided political roles for himself, he was a highly enthusiastic supporter of Richard Nixon, Barry Goldwater, Ronald Reagan, and others who, he felt, represented the best ideals of Americanism and anti-communism.

But for the masses of movie-going fans who idolized him on the big screen, Wayne as an icon of conservatism had little significance compared to Wayne the movie star. Although he did not always play clean-cut "good guys," as other Western heroes such as Gene Autry did, he was a leader in casting the role of the Western hero who fought the conflict between good and evil on the Western Plains. Indeed, it was impossible to mention the word "Western" without thinking of "The Duke."

John Wayne was born Marion Michael Morrison in Winterset, Iowa 1907. His father was Clyde Leonard Morrison, and his mother was Mary Alberta Brown. The family moved to Glendale, California, in 1911. His neighbors in Glendale started calling him "Big Duke" because he never went anywhere without his Airedale terrier dog named "Little Duke." He preferred "Duke" to Marion, and the name stuck for the rest of his life.

John Wayne's early life was marked by poverty. His father was a pharmacist who did not manage money well. As a teen, Wayne worked in an ice cream shop for someone who shoed horses for local Hollywood studios. He played football for the 1924 champion Glendale High School team. Duke was a good student and popular but had a bad reputation as a drinker. Tall from an early age, he was recruited to play football for the University of Southern California (USC). His football career would end after two years due to injury. This caused him to lose his scholarship, forcing him to leave the university.

While at university, Wayne began working at the local film studios. Western star Tom Mix got him a summer job in the props department in exchange for football tickets, and Wayne soon moved on to bit parts in the late 1920s in films by director John Ford, with whom he established a life-long friendship. From 1925 to 1929, Wayne appeared in nine silent films. Wayne's imposing presence and exaggerated mannerisms translated well on the silent screen.

At Ford's recommendation, Wayne's first starring role was in the 1930 epic Western, The Big Trail. The director of the movie, Raoul Walsh, gave him the stage name "John Wayne." His pay was raised from $35 to $75 weekly, and the studio's stuntmen tutored him in riding and other western skills.

During the next nine years, Wayne occupied himself in several B-Westerns and serials. But it was roles that brought out his manliness that was to make Wayne a huge star with men and women alike.

Despite appearing in many war movies and is frequently being called an "American hero," Wayne never served in the armed forces. However, his friend Bob Hope speculated that Wayne did more for the WWII war effort as an actor than he could have done on the battlefield. Between 1940, when the military draft was reinstated, and the end of WWII in 1945, he remained in Hollywood and made 21 movies. He was of draft age (34) at the time of the Pearl Harbor attack in 1941 but requested and received a deferral for family dependency, a classification of 3-A. This was later changed to a deferment in the national interest, 2-A.

Wayne played the male lead in 142 movie appearances, an unsurpassed record. Despite his prolific output, John Wayne only won a single Best Actor Oscar for the 1969 movie *True Grit*. He was nominated for Best Actor in *Sands of Iwo Jima* and another as producer of Best Picture nominee The Alamo, which he also directed. In 1973, he released a best-selling spoken word album titled America, *Why I Love Her*, which was nominated for a Grammy.

Wayne was well known for his pro-American, conservative political views. In 1968, he directed *The Green Berets*, the only feature film of the time to support the Vietnam War openly. It was produced in close cooperation with the armed forces. Surprisingly, he often starred with actresses of a liberal bent, like Bea Arthur, Lauren Bacall, Colleen Dewhurst, and Katharine Hepburn.

Wayne was married three times, always to Spanish-speaking Latina women: Josephine Alicia Saenz, Esperanza Baur, and Pilar Palette. Wayne had seven children from his marriages; two ended in divorce, with more than 15 grandchildren. All but one of his children would go on to have minor Hollywood careers.

John Wayne died of stomach cancer at the UCLA Medical Center on June 11, 1979, at 72. He was interred in the Pacific View Memorial Park cemetery in Corona Del Mar, Orange County, California. Some trace his cancer back to his work on the film, *The Conqueror*, filmed about 100 miles downwind of Nevada nuclear weapons test sites. Nevertheless, it should also be stated that until 1964 Wayne was a heavy smoker, which was more likely to have caused his cancer. Other actors who starred in that movie and later died of cancer were also heavy smokers, including Dick Powell, Susan Hayward, Agnes Moorehead, Pedro Armendariz, and John Hoyt.

JUNE 12
1937

On this day in history, Marshal Mikhail Tukhachevsky and a group of seven other senior officers from the Soviet High Command were found guilty and executed at a show trial of coordinating a German-funded military plot inside the Red Army.

The execution of what became better known as the "military-fascist plotters" sparked a massive military purge and the accompanying arrests as Stalin's paranoid regime sought to cleanse the ranks of anyone associated with the accused conspirators. In reality, the Tukhachevsky group was innocent of all charges of treason. The Soviet secret police had beaten confessions from the accused, yet there was no German-inspired conspiracy in the Soviet military. Nevertheless, the purge continued into 1938, costing the Red Army over 38,000 officers and commissars.

The Red Army had undergone several purges over the years. In the mid-1920s, Leon Trotsky was removed as Commissar of War, and his known supporters were removed from the armed forces. Former tsarist officers had been expelled in the late 1920s and early 1930s. The latter purge had been accompanied by the "exposure" of the "Former Officers Plot." The next surge of arrests of military commanders started in the last half of 1936. It increased in magnitude after the February-March

1937 Plenary Meeting of the Central Committee of the Communist Party of the Soviet Union (CPSU), where Vyacheslav Molotov demanded a more thorough uncovering of "wreckers" within the Red Army because they 'had already been found in all segments of the Soviet economy."

General Mikhail Tukhachevsky, and seven other Red Army commanders, were arrested on May 22, 1937, and charged with the creation of a "right-wing-Trotskyist" military conspiracy and espionage for Nazi Germany, based on confessions from other arrested officers.

Before 1990, it was repeatedly contended that the indictment against the eight generals was founded on falsified texts created by the Abwehr. These documents deceived Stalin into imagining that a conspiracy was being incited by Tukhachevsky and other Red Army officers to overthrow him. However, once Soviet archives were opened to investigators after the collapse of the USSR, it became apparent that Stalin essentially fabricated the false narrative by the most prominent and essential of his Soviet generals to get rid of them in a convincing fashion.

At Stalin's command, the NKVD ordered one of its agents, Nikolai Skoblin, to fabricate evidence indicating a conspiracy by Tukhachevsky and the other Soviet generals against Stalin and give it to Reinhard Heydrich, chief of the German *Sicherheitdienst* intelligence service. Recognizing a chance to direct a setback at both his archenemy Wilhelm Canaris of the German Abwehr and the Soviet Union, Heydrich directly proceeded on the material and commenced to expand on it, falsifying a series of papers incriminating Tukhachevsky and other Red Army commanders, these were later delivered to the Soviets via Edvard Benes and other neutral parties.

While the Germans assumed they had effectively deceived Stalin into executing his best generals, they had acted as helpful and unsuspecting pawns of Stalin. It is important to note that the falsified records were not even utilized by Soviet military prosecutors against the generals in their clandestine trial but, in its place, depending upon fake statements forced or beaten out of the defendants.

Afraid of the reaction of prosecuting popular generals and war heroes in a public setting, Stalin decided that the trial would be kept secret and the defendants to be executed immediately following their trial. Tukhachevsky and the other seven generals were most assuredly tortured into giving confessions for their supposed transgressions.

NKVD Chief Nikolai Yezhov personally directed Tukhachevsky's interrogation and torture. Stalin ordered Yezhov, "See for yourself, but Tukhachevsky should be forced to tell everything.... It's impossible he acted alone."

A few days later, a defeated Tukhachevsky admitted that Avel Yenukidze had enlisted him in 1928 and was a German agent working with Nikolai Bukharin to take power. His confession, which survives in the archives, is sprinkled with a brown spray later found to be blood-spattered by a body in motion.

Stalin commented, "It's incredible, but it's a fact, they admit it."

On June 11, 1937, the Russian Supreme Court assembled a special military court to prosecute Tukhachevsky and the eight generals for treason. The trial was dubbed the Case of Trotskyist Anti-Soviet Military Organization. Upon hearing the accusations, Tukhachevsky was heard to say, "I feel I'm dreaming." Most of the judges were also terrified. One was heard to comment, "Tomorrow, I'll be put in the same place."

At 11:35 p.m. that night, all defendants were declared guilty and condemned to death. In awaiting the verdict with Yezhov, Molotov, and Lazar Kaganovich, Stalin did not even examine the transcripts. He simply said, "Agreed."

At 1:00 a.m. on June 12, 1937, Tukhachevsky was summoned from his cell by NKVD captain Vasily Blokhin. As Yezhov watched, the former Marshal was shot once in the back of the head.

Immediately afterward, Yezhov was summoned to Stalin's office. Stalin asked him, "What were Tukhachevsky's last words?" Yezhov stated, "The snake said he was dedicated to the Motherland and Comrade Stalin. He asked for clemency. But it was obvious that he was not being straight, he hadn't laid down his arms."

On January 31, 1957, all executed generals were rehabilitated for the "absence of essence of an offense." It was concluded that the arrests, along with the investigations and trials, were conducted in contravention of standard practices and based on forced confessions obtained with physical violence.

The execution of Marshal Tukhachevsky and the other seven generals profoundly diminished the Soviet military. This was first witnessed in the Red Army's disastrous execution of the Soviet-Finnish war of 1939-1940, in which the Soviet military experienced more than 100,000 dead or missing against a smaller and inadequately equipped Finnish army. The loss of the eight generals united with the 1941 Red Army Purge, facilitated the early achievements of the German Wehrmacht in the 1941 Invasion of Russia, leading to a severe loss of life and the destruction of most of the European portion of the USSR.

JUNE 13
1807

On this day in history, U.S. President Thomas Jefferson receives a subpoena to testify in the treason trial of his former vice president, Aaron Burr. In the summons, Burr requests that Jefferson produce pertinent documents that might exonerate him from the treason charge.

Burr had previously been politically and socially tarnished by slaying Treasury Secretary and Revolutionary-era hero Alexander Hamilton in a duel in 1804. After killing Hamilton, Burr, still Jefferson's vice president, went underground. Burr then devised a subversive plan to procure the assistance of Britain and Spain to establish an independent nation in the southwestern portion of the American continent, together with parts of Mexico, over which Burr would govern. The shocking proposal failed miserably when one of Burr's co-conspirators, General James Wilkinson, deceived Burr and informed Jefferson of the scheme. Burr was tracked down and detained in 1806 and indicted for treason.

Anthony Merry, the British ambassador to the United States, endorsed Burr's imperial aspirations. Burr had other formidable allies for his scheme. Senator Jonathan Dayton of New Jersey and a wealthy Ohioan named Harman Blennerhassett joined Burr and offered monetary assistance for the proposed insurrection. Finally, Burr had the help of General-in-Chief of the Army James Wilkinson, also one of the joint commissioners for the Territory of Louisiana.

The conspirators' stalling, however, turned out to be their downfall. By the fall of 1806, they had still not moved the scheme forward. England's new foreign minister, Charles James Fox, withdrew Anthony Merry and concluded English support for Burr's plan. Wilkinson grew uneasy and went to President Jefferson about Burr's sedition. When Burr ultimately chose to act in November 1806, he used Blennerhassett's Ohio estates and private island as the center of operations for the insurrection. Jefferson prepared for Ohio Governor Edward Tiffin to send in the local militia, and the plot was crushed. Burr went into hiding but was apprehended within a few months.

On March 26, 1807, Burr was taken to Richmond, Virginia, where he would stand trial before Supreme Court Chief Justice John Marshall. The principal charge against Burr was treason against the United States. The prosecutors also made a related charge of "high misdemeanors" against Burr. George Hay, William Wirt, and Gordon MacRae formed a team of prosecutors for the government. Burr's defense attorneys were Edmund Randolph, John Wickham, Luther Martin, and Benjamin Botts. Their task was much easier than that of the prosecution due to the particular requirements of Article III, Section 3 of the Constitution, which states:

"Treason against the United States, shall consist only in levying war against them, or in adhering to their Enemies, giving them Aid and Comfort. No Person shall be convicted of Treason unless on the Testimony of two Witnesses to the same overt Act, or on Confession in open Court."

Thus, the prosecution not only had to deliver two witnesses, but those witnesses had to have seen some overt act by Burr in "levying war" or leading the proposed insurrection against the United States. Fortunately for Burr, he had not been at hand in Ohio when Governor Tiffin's militia captured Blennerhassett's island compound. As Burr himself stated, Jefferson's prompt action based on General Wilkinson's declaration led to the destruction of the plot before the procrastinating Burr had taken many measures: "Mr. Wilkinson alarmed the President and the President alarmed the people of Ohio."

Marshall's worry over whether the prosecution could carry the substantial burden of proof insisted upon by the Constitution caused the trial to be delayed until August 3, 1807. In the short term, the prosecution submitted several witnesses, including General Wilkinson. These witnesses gave evidence of traitorous declarations by Burr and the military and measures taken on Blennerhassett's island. The evidence persuaded a grand jury that Burr should be tried on the charges filed against him, and Marshall finally opened the trial.

The prosecution argued that Burr's involvement in the conspiracy made him "constructively present" on the island and thus involved in an overt act. Referring to the mercenaries arrested during the Blennerhassett raid, the prosecution stated, "What must be the guilt of (Burr) to that of the poor ignorant man who was enlisted into his services with some prospect of benefiting himself and family?"

Burr's defense counsel countered by focusing on the prosecution's strained interpretation of what constituted an "overt act." After all, the only act of the revolt remotely "overt" had been the preparations at Blennerhassett's island, during which Burr had not been present. Therefore, Botts retorted: "Acts on the island were not acts of war; no war could be found in Mississippi or Kentucky. There was no bloody battle. The energy of... (the) government prevented the tragical consequence."

On August 31, Marshall made an extended judgment on the opinions offered by both sides, later turning the tide in favor of Burr. Marshall held that the actual overt act could have been established if the prosecution had proven with two witnesses that Burr had "procured" or caused the men and material to assemble on the island to initiate a rebellion. The prosecution had yet to do this, however. All they had offered at trial was testimony that would "confirm" or "corroborate" such eyewitnesses, but not any eyewitnesses themselves. Therefore, the prosecution's evidence was inadmissible, and the jury had to ignore it.

Faced with Marshall's ruling, the jury had no choice. On September 1, the jury acquitted Burr when it gave its somewhat left-handed verdict: "We of the jury say that Aaron Burr is not proved to be guilty under this indictment by any evidence submitted to us."

Although he was acquitted, the press and public still deemed Burr a traitor, and his political career was destroyed. Burr went to Europe for several years, staying one step ahead of creditors who bankrolled his lifestyle, and finally returned to the United States in 1812. He lived out the remainder of his life in obscurity, dying a broken man in 1836.

JUNE 14
1789

On this day in history, English Captain William Bligh and 18 others set adrift from the HMS *Bounty* seven weeks before, finally reaching Timor in the East Indies after traveling 4,000 miles (6,500 km) in the ship's open launch. From there, he would return to England and bring the mutineers to justice.

In the late 1780s, it was proposed that breadfruit plants grown on Pacific islands could be brought to and grown in the Caribbean to provide a cheap food source for enslaved people forced to work on British plantations. To aid this endeavor, the Royal Navy bought the collier *Bethia* in May 1787 and renamed it His Majesty's Armed Vessel *Bounty*. The ship was armed, and Lieutenant William Bligh was assigned to command the ship. Bligh was a talented sailor and navigator who had previously sailed with Captain James Cook aboard HMS *Resolution* (1776-1779). Throughout the latter part of 1787, the ship was outfitted for its mission, and by December, Bligh and the HMS *Bounty* set a course for Tahiti.

In the beginning, Bligh tried to enter the Pacific via Cape Horn. After a month of attempting and failing due to unfavorable weather, he turned and sailed east around the Cape of Good Hope. The remainder of the 28,000-mile voyage to Tahiti was uneventful.

Reaching Tahiti on October 26, 1788, Bligh and his men were forced to endure a five-month layover because they had arrived during the rainy season, and the breadfruit plants needed to mature before transporting them to the Caribbean. During this time, Bligh allowed the crew to live amongst the Native Tahitian islanders. Some of the men, including Christian, compelled Tahitian women into marriage. Because of this type of environment, naval discipline began to break down.

Bligh attempted to control the situation, and he was increasingly forced to punish his men, and flogging happened more frequently. Reluctant to submit to this treatment after enjoying the island's warm hospitality, three sailors, John Millward, William Muspratt, and Charles Churchill, deserted. They were quickly tracked down, and even though they were punished, it was more lightly than recommended. During events, searching their belongings produced a list of names, including Christian and Midshipman Peter Heywood. Lacking additional evidence, Bligh could not charge the two men as aiding the desertion plot.

Though unable to act against Christian, Bligh's relationship with him continued deteriorating, and he began to ride his acting lieutenant relentlessly. On April 4, 1789, *Bounty* departed Tahiti, much to the chagrin of most of the crew. On the evening of April 28, Christian and eighteen of the crew surprised and restrained Bligh in his cabin. Dragging him on deck, Christian bloodlessly took control of the ship even though most of the crew (22) sided with the captain. Christian and his cohorts had had enough of Bligh's caustic behavior and yelling and berating, and belittling of the crew to carry on. Bligh and 18 loyalists were forced over the side into *Bounty's* cutter and given a sextant, four cutlasses, and several days of food and water.

As *Bounty* turned to return to Tahiti, Bligh set course for the closest European outpost at Timor. Though perilously overburdened and lacking charts, Bligh managed to sail the cutter first to Tofua for supplies, then on to Timor. After sailing 4,000 miles, Bligh landed at Timor after a 47-day voyage. Only one man was lost during the nightmare when Native people murdered him on Tofua. Moving on to Batavia, Bligh could obtain transportation back to England. In October 1790, Bligh was honorably exonerated for the loss of *Bounty*, and records show him to have been a benevolent captain who repeatedly spared the lash.

Keeping four loyalists aboard, Christian proceeded to Tubuai, where the mutineers tried to settle. After three months of battling with the Native people, the mutineers re-embarked and cruised to Tahiti. Returning to the island, twelve mutineers and the four loyalists were put ashore. Not trusting that they would be safe in Tahiti, the remaining mutineers, including Christian, boarded supplies and enslaved six Tahitian men and eleven women in September 1789. Though they explored the Cook and Fiji Islands, the mutineers did not feel either presented adequate protection from the Royal Navy.

On January 15, 1790, Christian found Pitcairn Island, which had been misplaced on British charts. Landing, the party quickly created a community on the island. To decrease their discovery odds, they destroyed *Bounty* on January 23. Though Christian struggled to preserve goodwill in the small community, dealings between the Britons and the Tahitians soon disintegrated, leading to violence. The community fought for several years until Ned Young and John Adams took control in the mid-1790s. Following Young's death in 1800, Adams persisted in building the society.

While Bligh was exonerated for losing his ship, the Royal Navy aggressively pursued the *Bounty's* mutineers. In November 1790, HMS *Pandora* was sent to search for *Bounty*. Reaching Tahiti on March 23, 1791, Captain Edward Edwards was met by four of *Bounty's* men. A search of the island soon found ten additional *Bounty* crew members. These fourteen men, a blend of mutineers and loyalists, were kept in a cell called the "Pandora's Box." Departing May 8, Edwards searched the adjacent islands for three months before turning for a home. While passing through the Torres Strait on August 29, *Pandora* ran aground and sank the next day. Of those on board, 31 crew and four prisoners were lost. The remainder embarked in *Pandora's* boats and reached Timor in September.

Transported back to England, the ten surviving prisoners were court-martialed. Four of the ten were found guiltless with Bligh's backing, while six were found guilty. Two, Heywood and James Morrison, were pardoned, while another was released on a technicality. The remaining three were hung aboard HMS *Brunswick* on October 29, 1792.

A second breadfruit expedition departed England in August 1791. Again, led by Bligh, this group successfully delivered breadfruit to the Caribbean, but the experiment failed when the enslaved people declined to consume it. On the other side of the world, Royal Navy ships relocated to Pitcairn Island in 1814. Making contact with those ashore, they recounted the final details of *Bounty* to the Admiralty. In 1825, Adams, the sole surviving mutineer, was granted amnesty.

(Photo: The Mutineers turning Bligh and part of the Officers and Crew adrift from His Majesty's Ship the Bounty (29 April 1789) Wikimedia Commons.)

JUNE 15
1904

On this day in history, the *General Slocum*, a sidewheel passenger steamboat, caught on fire and disappeared to the bottom of the East River of New York City. At least 1,021 of the 1,342 people on board died in the ensuing fire and sinking. At the time of the disaster, the *General Slocum* was on a chartered run carrying members of St. Mark's Evangelical Lutheran Church from Little Germany in Manhattan to a church picnic. The *General Slocum* disaster was the New York area's deadliest accident until the September 11 attacks in 2001.

General Slocum worked as a passenger ship, taking people on excursions around New York City. On June 15, 1904, the ship had been chartered for $350 by a church group from Little Germany in Manhattan. This annual event that had been happening for 17 years. The 1342 passengers, mostly women, and children, were to sail up the East River and eastward across Long Island Sound to Locust Grove, a picnic site in Eaton's Neck, Long Island.

Shortly after 9:30 a.m., the crew of the General Slocum cast off, and the ship sailed away from the pier. It steamed northward up the East River, gradually picking up speed. Hundreds of children were on the upper deck, taking in all the sights. Like most mornings, the river was full of boats of all descriptions – barges, lighters, tenders, and tugs. The adults talked and listened to a band play some German songs.

Then catastrophe struck. As the ship passed East 90th Street, smoke started coming out of the forward storage room. A spark, probably from a match or a cigarette, lit a straw pile. Several crew members attempted to extinguish the fire, but as they had never practiced fire drills or undergone any emergency training, they could not extinguish it. To make matters worse, the ship's rotten fire hoses burst when the water was turned on. By the time they notified Captain William Van Scaick of the emergency – fully ten minutes after discovering the fire – the blaze had raged out of control.

The captain looked to the piers along the East River but feared he might cause an explosion among the many oil tanks there. Instead, even as onlookers on the Manhattan shore shouted for him to dock the ship, he proceeded at top speed to North Brother Island a mile ahead. Several small boats followed the floating inferno as it roared upriver.

The increased speed fanned the flames. Panicked passengers ran about the deck, unsure where to take refuge. Mothers screamed for their children, and husbands for their families. The fire, accelerated by a fresh coat of highly flammable paint, rapidly enveloped the ship, and passengers began to jump overboard. Some clung to the rails before jumping into the churning water. A few were rescued by nearby boats, but most did not know how to swim and drowned.

The inexperienced crew was of no help. Nor were the 3,000 life-jackets on board. Rotten and filled with disintegrated cork, they had long since lost their buoyancy. Those who put them on sank as soon as they hit the water. Wired in place, none of the lifeboats could be dislodged. Even if they had, they would never have made it safely into the water with the ship moving along at top speed.

When the ship finally beached at North Brother Island, it was engulfed in fire. Survivors poured over the railings into the water. Some huddled in the few places not yet reached by the flames, too terrified to jump. The *General Slocum* left a grisly wake. The boats that followed, seeking to help, plucked a few survivors from the water. But mostly, they found only the lifeless bodies of the ship's ill-fated passengers. The fact that most were young children only added to the horror.

With more than 1,300 people on the outing, nearly everyone in the neighborhood knew someone on the ship. As word of the fire spread, it caused panic and confusion. Nobody seemed to know what to do or where to go. Thousands gathered at St. Mark's Church awaiting word about survivors. Thousands rushed uptown to the East 23rd Street pier, which had been transformed into a temporary morgue. Many lost hope by mid-afternoon when they were not reunited with family members. Many learned they had lost a wife or child. Dozens learned they had lost their entire families.

City officials vowed to conduct a thorough investigation, and within weeks, Captain Van Schaick, executives of the Knickerbocker Steamboat Co., and the Inspector who certified the *General Slocum* as safe only a month before the fire were indicted. At his trial, Van Schaick offered plausible explanations for his actions, but the jury was unconvinced. A convenient scapegoat, he was convicted of criminal negligence and manslaughter and sentenced to ten years of hard labor in Sing Sing prison. He served three years before receiving a pardon from President William Taft.

In contrast, the officials at the Knickerbocker Steamship Company escaped with only a nominal fine. This is even though the trial revealed the company had illegally falsified records to cover up their lack of attention to passenger safety.

The neighborhood of Little Germany, which had been declining for several years before the disaster, almost disappeared afterward as residents moved uptown. After the tragedy and the loss of many prominent settlers, most Lutheran Germans in the Lower East Side eventually moved uptown. The church whose congregation chartered the ship for the fateful voyage was turned into a synagogue in 1940 after Jewish residents settled there.

The submerged remains of the *General Slocum* were salvaged and converted into a 625-gross register-ton barge named *Maryland*, which sank in the South River in 1909 and again in the Atlantic Ocean off the New Jersey coastline during a storm on December 4, 1911, while transporting a cargo of coal. All four people aboard *Maryland* survived the sinking.

JUNE 16
1822

On this day in history, Denmark Vesey (aka Telemaque), a Black American carpenter, is accused of planning a slave rebellion in Charleston, South Carolina, involving thousands of enslaved Black people and the subsequent murder of antebellum slave owners. He would quickly be tried and convicted, and thirty-five enslaved people would be executed by hanging.

The plot coordinated by Denmark Vesey, a free black carpenter, in Charleston, South Carolina, in 1822 was perhaps the most significant slave plot in North American history. Although brought into the city in 1783 as a slave of Captain Joseph Vesey, Telemaque, as he was then known, acquired his freedom in December 1799 with lottery winnings. For the next twenty-two years, Vesey made his living as a carpenter. According to Caucasian authorities, he was "distinguished for (his) great strength and activity"; the black community "always looked up to (him) with awe and respect." His last (and probably third) wife, Susan Vesey, was born into slavery but became free just before his death. His first wife, Beck, stayed enslaved, as did Vesey's sons, Polydore, Robert, and Sandy, the last of whom was the only one of his children to be incriminated in his 1822 conspiracy.

About 1818, Vesey joined the city's new African Methodist Episcopal congregation. The African Church, as both races called it, quickly became the center of Charleston's enslaved society. Sandy Vesey also joined, as did four of Vesey's closest friends, Peter Poyas, a well-read and highly skilled ship carpenter; Monday Gell, an African-born Ibo who worked as a harness maker; Rolla Bennett, the manservant of Governor Thomas Bennett; and "Gullah" Jack Pritchard, an East African priest purchased in Zinguebar in 1806. City authorities' interim closing of the church in June 1818 and the apprehension of 140 congregants, one of whom was Vesey himself, only strengthened the fortitude of black Carolinians to preserve a place of objective worship and founded the inspiration for his plot.

At age fifty-one, Vesey was determined to choreograph an uprising followed by mass migration from Charleston to Haiti. President Jean-Pierre Boyer had lately urged black Americans to bring their talents and money to his struggling nation. Vesey did not propose to stay around Charleston long enough for white military power to produce a successful counterassault. "As soon as they could get the money from the Banks and the goods from the stores," Rolla Bennett insisted, "they should hoist sail for Saint Doming(ue)" and live as free men. For all of his assimilation into Euro-American society, Vesey, as a native of St. Thomas, remained a man.

Vesey had been organizing the getaway for nearly four years. Although there are no reliable statistics for the number of recruits, Charleston was home to 12,700 enslaved people. Pritchard bragged that he had 6,600 recruits on the plantations across the Cooper and Ashley Rivers. The plan called for Vesey's supporters to rise at midnight on Sunday, July 14 – Bastille Day – murder their masters and sail for Haiti and liberty.

Those enlisted into the plot during the winter of 1822 were instructed to arm themselves from their masters' storerooms. Vesey was mindful that the Charleston Neck militia company stored their three hundred muskets and bayonets in the back room of Benjamin Hammet's King Street store and that Hammet's slave Bacchus had a key. But as few enslaved people were familiar with guns, Vesey persuaded his supporters to arm themselves with swords. Vesey also hired several enslaved blacksmiths to construct "pike heads and bayonets with sockets, to be fixed at the end of long poles."

Vesey and his lieutenants enlisted men out of the African church. Vesey knew each church member well – he knew whom to trust and avoid. As former Charleston slave Archibald Grimke later wrote, Vesey's nightly classes provided him "with a singularly safe medium for conducting his underground agitation."

The scheme fell apart in June 1822 when two enslaved people disclosed the plan to their owners. On June 16, Vesey and the other uprising leaders were accused and arrested for their part in the affair. Mayor James Hamilton instructed the city militia to muster and called for a special court to try the imprisoned rebels. Vesey was hung on the morning of July 2, together with Rolla, Poyas, and three other men. According to Hamilton, the six men jointly "met their fate with the heroic fortitude of Martyrs." In total, thirty-five enslaved people were hanged. Forty-two others, including Sandy Vesey, were sold outside the United States; some, if not all, became enslaved people in Spanish Cuba. Robert Vesey lived to re-establish the African Church in the fall of 1865.

As a result of the scheme, Charleston officials destroyed the African Church. The state assembly afterward passed regulations barring the entry of free blacks into the state, and city officials implemented laws against instructing African Americans to read. The City Council also established a permanent force of 150 guardsmen to patrol the streets around the clock at an annual cost of $24,000. To deal with the problem of black mariners bringing into the state information about outside events, in December 1822, the legislature passed the Negro Seamen Act, which placed a quarantine on any vessel from another "state or foreign port, having on board any free negroes or persons of color." Although U.S. Circuit Court Judge William Johnson struck down the law as unconstitutional, a rebellious legislature reinstated the act in late 1823. Many who abolished federal law in 1832 – including Governor James Hamilton, who stepped down from his office in 1833 to command troops to defend his state's right to resist national tariffs – were veterans of the courts that had prosecuted Vesey and his men a decade previous.

JUNE 17
1928

On this day in history, famed aviatrix Amelia Earhart made her first transatlantic flight as a passenger, not a pilot, thus making her the first female to accomplish that feat.

Amelia already knew how to fly. She had gotten her pilot's license five years previously, but her expertise did not matter; a transatlantic flight was considered too stressful and terrifying for a member of the fairer sex. Earhart had decided to go along with it because she was passionate about flying – and being the first woman, even if she was not in control, was nevertheless a fantastic thing. She was tucked in the back of the airplane Friendship, which was about the size of a Chevrolet Suburban, behind pilot Wilmer "Bill" Stultz and co-pilot Louis "Slim" Gordon. Amelia was in charge of keeping the flight log and enduring the discomfort of the 20-hour, 40-minute flight from Trepassey Harbour, Newfoundland, to Burry Port Wales, nevertheless became an instant celebrity.

When she returned to New York, Earhart was thrown a ticker tape parade. Afterward, a limo had been hired to take her to another appearance. It was a hot day; the traffic was congested. Automotive air-conditioning had yet to be invented. Amelia looked at the car and imagined being stuck in the backseat in a pool of her own sweat. But then she spied an empty sidecar attached to the motorcycle ridden by one of her police escorts. Without a second thought and without asking any of her minders' permission, she hopped in. The police officer turned on his lights and siren and sped away with his passenger.

Amelia Earhart was born on July 24, 1897, in Atchison, Kansas, the daughter of Samuel "Edwin" Stanton Earhart and Amelia "Amy" Otis. She was born in the house of her maternal grandfather, Alfred Gideon Otis, a former federal judge, the president of the Atcheson Savings Bank, and a leading citizen in the town. Amelia was an adventuresome child who liked to careen down hills on her sled in the winter and hunt rats with a rifle. Long considered a tomboy by friends and family, Amelia and her younger sister Grace kept "moths, worms, katydids and a tree toad" in a growing collection. In 1904, with her uncle's aid, Amelia cobbled together a homemade ramp and secured it to the roof of the family toolshed. Earhart's first flight ended spectacularly. She emerged from the crushed wooden box that was her sled with a bruised lip, torn dress, and a "sensation of exhilaration." She exclaimed, "Oh, Pidge, it's just like flying."

In 1920, while on a trip to California with her father, she was at an airshow where she noticed a pilot named Frank Hawks, who was offering a 10-minute flight in his airplane for $10. Amelia, always restless, was eager to go. Her father paid the fee, and up she went, and from there, she was hooked. In the summer of 1921, she bought a used Kinner Airster biplane. In 1923, she became the 16th woman in the world to receive her pilot's license.

Amy Guest, a 55-year-old heiress, wanted to become the first woman to journey across the Atlantic Ocean by air. Yet after pressure from her family, she bowed out but was willing to help another woman worthy of the accolades. She contacted publisher George Putnam and brought him on board as one of the project coordinators. They made a list of potential women who could make the flight. Amelia's reputation as an up-and-coming star of aviation, with more than 500 hours in the air under her belt and no serious accidents, preceded her. Also, and equally important, her daredevil tomboy soul was hidden beneath a soft-spoken, ladylike exterior.

Then came the triumphant flight of Friendship. Amelia was

instantly famous when the plane landed in Wales on June 18, 1928. In New York, the Times banner headline read: "City Greets Miss Earhart; Girl Flier, Shy and Smiling, Shares Praise With Mates."

That summer of 1928, after the flight that made her famous, Amelia moved into George and Dorothy Putnam's home in Rye, New York. The reason was that Amelia and George could work together on her memoir, *20Hrs., 40 Min.: Our Flight in the Friendship*, but there was also a hint of romance in the air. George was falling in love with Amelia, and presumably, she felt the same, even though she was a person who kept her cards close to her chest. Amelia wrote all day, every day, while George focused on promoting her and the forthcoming book. Meanwhile, Dorothy pined for her much younger lover, George Weymouth, a sophomore at Yale. Amelia was commonly believed to have stolen George from under Dorothy's nose, but nothing could be further from the truth. According to George and Dorothy's granddaughter, Sally Putnam Chapman, "Amelia gave (Dorothy) the excuse she needed (to divorce George)."

In December 1929, Dorothy moved to Reno and filed for divorce, and George persuaded Amelia to marry him, and the couple got married on February 7, 1931.

George and Amelia continued "growing the Amelia Earhart brand." Throughout the early 1930s, Amelia devoted herself to advocating for women in aviation, served on committees, gave many speeches, and wrote letters on behalf of many aeronautical issues. Shoe founded the Ninety-Nines, an organization for female pilots, and her clothing line. She was made an honorary major in the U.S. Air Service and given a pair of silver wings, which she often wore with pearls.

On May 20, 1932, five years after Lindbergh made his historic transatlantic flight, Amelia Earhart finally made her solo journey by air across the Atlantic Ocean. Her career could only get more significant from this point onward. Amelia once stated that "Adventure is worthwhile in itself. Men have always done things because it gave them pleasure and a sense of achievement. So why shouldn't women be granted the same privilege?"

(Photo: Amelia Earhart prior to her transatlantic crossing of June 17, 1928. Wikimedia Commons.)

JUNE 18
1945

On this day in history, William Joyce, nicknamed Lord Haw-Haw, a fascist politician and Nazi propaganda broadcaster, is charged with treason by the British government. After moving from New York City to Ireland and then to England, Joyce became a member of Oswald Mosley's British Union of Fascists (BUF) in 1932 before finally moving to Berlin and taking German citizenship in 1940.

At the end of the war, after being captured by the British, Joyce was convicted in Great Britain of high treason in 1945 and condemned to death, with the Court of Appeal and the House of Lords upholding the conviction. He was hanged in Wandsworth Prison on January 3, 1946, making him the last individual to be executed for treason in Great Britain. What led Joyce to become one of World War II's most recognizable German broadcasters? What drove Joyce, a man of Irish-American descent, to become a traitor willing to join forces with the Nazis?

To understand Joyce's choices, we must look at his early life. Joyce was born in New York City on April 26, 1906. His father was Michael Francis Joyce, a naturalized U.S. citizen of Irish origin, and his mother, Gertrude Emily Brooke, was from an Anglo-Irish family. However, Joyce's time in America was short-lived. When William was three, his family moved to Galway, Ireland. In 1921, he was enlisted by the

British Army as a courier during the Irish War of Independence and was almost killed by the IRA on his way home from school. Fearing for his life, the army officer who recruited him, Captain Patrick William Keating, had him sent to Worcestershire, England.

During his time in England, while he continued his education, he became interested in fascism. At one point, he was attacked by communists after a meeting, and he received a razor cut across the right side of his face. The assault left a permanent scar from his ear to his mouth. This event reinforced Joyce's hate of communism and his devotion to fascism.

Following his injury, Joyce climbed the ranks of fascist organizations in England. He joined Oswald Mosley's British Union of Fascists in 1932 and became known for his oratory. Eventually, however, Joyce was thrown out by Mosley after the 1937 London County Council elections. Angry, he split from BUF and created his own political party, the National Socialist League. More wildly antisemitic than the BUF, the NSL aimed to integrate German Nazism into British society to form a new type of British fascism. By 1939 however, the other heads of the NSL had opposed Joyce's movements, opting to model the organization on German Nazism. Embittered, Joyce turned to alcohol and dissolved the NSL, a fateful decision.

Immediately after the dissolution of the NSL, Joyce traveled to Germany in late August 1939. He had obtained a British passport in 1938 by falsely claiming that he was British when he was actually an American citizen. After a brief broadcasting audition, Joyce then traveled to Berlin, where he was recruited by Joseph Goebbels' Reich Ministry of Propaganda and given his own radio show, "Germany Calling." Goebbels needed foreign fascists to spread Nazi propaganda to Allied countries, especially Britain and America.

After he arrived in Germany, Joyce immediately got to work. It was his job to undermine the confidence of his foreign listeners in the validity of their nation's role in the war. In one segment, Joyce states

"The whole system of English so-called democracy is a fraud. It is an elaborate system of make-believe, under which you may have the illusion that you are choosing your own government, but which in reality simply ensures that the same privileged class, the same wealthy people, shall rule England under different names.... Your nation is controlled... by big business,... newspaper proprietors, opportunist statesmen,... men like Churchill,...Camrose and Rothermere."

British audiences found "Germany Calling" quality entertainment thanks to Joyce's harsh rhetoric. Joyce's dramatic, fiery oratory was much more entertaining than the dry, old BBC. The British press called him "Lord Haw-Haw" in 1939 due to the "sneering character of his speech." By 1940, "Germany Calling" had six million regular listeners and 18 million occasional listeners in England. Goebbels was highly pleased with Joyce's broadcasts.

Because of his celebrity status, Joyce was given a pay raise and elevated to Chief Commentator of the English Language Service. While Lord Haw-Haw's broadcasts stressed eroding British faith in their administration during the first year of the war, the dynamics changed when Germany invaded Denmark, Norway, and France in 1940. Joyce's propaganda became more violent. It emphasized Germany's military strength, threatened England with invasion, and urged the country to surrender. Eventually, British citizens saw Joyce's broadcasts not as entertainment but as legitimate threats to Britain and the Allies.

Despite Joyce's best efforts, his incendiary propaganda only had a minimal effect on English morale during the war. Listeners grew tired of Joyce's constant contempt for and sarcasm about Britain and took his propaganda less seriously. Eventually, he moved his broadcast studios to Hamburg because of the Allied bombing, where he remained until May 1945. Joyce was captured by British forces on May 28, 1945, transported to Britain, and put on trial for high treason. Joyce was convicted and condemned to death on September 19, 1945. The court argued that since Joyce possessed a British passport between September 10, 1939, and July 2, 1940, he owed his allegiance to Great Britain. Since Joyce also served Nazi Germany during that time, the court concluded that he had betrayed his country and therefore committed high treason. After being found guilty, Joyce was taken to Wandsworth Prison and hanged on January 3, 1946.

Joyce appealed the verdict, but his conviction was upheld. Remorseless, he uttered, "In death as in life, I defy the Jews who caused this last war, and I defy the power of darkness which they represent. I warn the British people against the crushing imperialism of the Soviet Union. May Britain be great once again, and in the hour of the greatest danger in the West, may the standard be raised from the dust, crowned with the words – "You have conquered nevertheless." I am proud to die for my ideals, and I am sorry for the sons of Britain who have died without knowing why."

JUNE 19
1867

On this day in history, Austrian Archduke Ferdinand Maximilian, installed as Emperor of Mexico by French Emperor Napoleon III in 1864, is executed in Queretaro, Mexico, at 6:40 a.m. by order of Benito Juarez, the president of the Mexican Republic.

Maximilian's involvement in Mexico came about after France, together with Spain and Great Britain, had occupied the port of Veracruz in late 1861 to pressure the Mexican government into paying its debts with the three powers after Mexico had declared that they would be making no further debt payments; the Spanish and British both withdrew the following year after negotiating an agreement with the Mexican government and realizing the true intentions of the French, who were aiming at regime change. Seeking to legitimize French intervention, Emperor Napoleon III invited Maximilian to establish what would come to be known as the Second Mexican Empire, which gained the collaboration of Mexican conservatives and certain moderate liberals. With a vow of French military support and at the invitation of a Mexican delegation, Maximilian accepted the crown on April 10, 1864.

After the British and the Spanish parted ways with France after the initial showdown in Veracruz, by 1862, the French were moving inland, intending to occupy Mexico City. Benito Juarez's liberal government was fighting an immense, formidable European power, and they would not win a long war against a France that meant business. So it came as a complete surprise to everyone – even the Mexicans – when on May 5, 1862, a Liberal Mexican army of 2,000 men defeated a French force of 6,000 at the Battle of Pueblo. The victory is celebrated every year as "Cinco de Mayo," as an emblem of Mexican patriotism and remembrance. The French retreated to the east coast of Mexico and spent the rest of 1862 building up their forces.

Maximilian was the brother of Austrian Emperor Franz Josef, a genial and mild nobleman with a desire for adventure. He was a Habsburg, so he had connections with virtually every royal family in Europe, and Napoleon III wanted to patch up ties with Austria after a recent war. So he offered Maximilian the option to become Emperor of Mexico, with French backing, but only if he gave up all claims to his Austrian titles. Maximilian agreed and sailed for Mexico; by 1864, he had assumed the role of Emperor of Mexico.

Juarez and his Liberal government refused all offers of peace from Maximilian – especially since they still controlled most of the country. They began to fight a guerrilla war of resistance against the French, and even though the French won some significant battles in 1864 and 1865, they never managed to pin down and destroy Juarez's armies. Mexico is a large country that proved too large for 40,000 Frenchmen to hold down.

As for Maximilian, he quickly became unpopular. The Conservatives, who had invited the French in the first place, were disappointed to find that Maximilian was a mild liberal who left most of Juarez's democratizing reforms in place. He respected freedom of religion, tried to introduce modern legal practice, and in general, wanted to bring Mexico into the modern age and turn it into a liberal, enlightened monarchy like Napoleon III's France. This was precisely what the Conservatives had NOT wanted a monarch for, and soon they were souring on Maximilian. And, of course, the Liberals hated him. The only thing keeping Maximilian on the throne at this point was the French Army.

As the guerilla war dragged on, Maximilian grew more frustrated.

Out of that frustration grew Maximilian's "Black Decree" policy, issued on October 3, 1865. It declared that any Mexican caught bearing arms against the Empire would be immediately executed; almost 11,000 Liberal fighters were killed under the Black Decree. It was one of Maximilian's worst decisions and among the most self-destructive. It only made the Mexican resistance more bitter and dedicated, and this decision would come back to bite its creator less than two years later.

On May 31, 1866, Napoleon III announced the beginning of French withdrawal from Mexico. With the completion of the American Civil War in 1865, America could now pay attention to matters below its southern Border. They sold many weapons to Juarez's army, which helped turn the tide in the resistance. America had never been happy with France's intervention in its sphere of influence but could never do anything until 1865. And now the French were leaving Mexico.

Maximilian's empire was crumbling; by 1867, the last French troops were preparing to leave Mexico. Napoleon III had recommended to Maximilian that he leave the country. The Emperor, though, chose to stay. He believed the Mexicans loved him and wanted to honor his duties to "his" empire. Even as the French withdrew, Maximilian rallied his small core of loyalists and led them to fight to the bitter end.

In February 1867, Juarez's army surrounded Maximilian forces in Queretaro. Maximilian changed his mind and tried to escape but was captured. Juarez had not forgotten the Black Decree, and Maximilian was subsequently put on trial, found guilty, and sentenced to death. Despite pleas from European monarchs and people like Victor Hugo and Guiseppe Garibaldi urging that Maximilian be spared, Juarez felt he needed to send a strong signal against any future thoughts of intervention in Mexican affairs.

At 6:40 a.m. on June 19, 1867, Maximilian was led in front of a firing squad. He spoke only in Spanish and gave each of his executioners a gold coin not to shoot him in the face so that his mother could look upon him at his funeral. His last words were, "I forgive everyone, and I ask everyone to forgive me. May my blood, which is about to be shed, be for the good of the country. Viva Mexico, viva la independencia!"

Maximilian, the last Emperor of Mexico, was laid to rest in Vienna on January 18, 1868, where his bier can still be seen today.

JUNE 20
1947

On this day in history, Benjamin "Bugsy" Siegel, the man who introduced organized crime to the West Coast of the United States, was assassinated at his mistress Virginia Hill's home in Beverly Hills, California. Siegel had been talking to Allen Smiley when nine bullets pierced his main window, with two entering his head, killing him instantly.

Siegel's early years had been very comparable to that of other organized crime leaders: Growing up with little money in Brooklyn, he established himself as a teenage hoodlum. With his pal Meyer Lansky, Siegel intimidated local vendors and amassed protection money. Before long, they had a company with gambling and bootlegging all over New York City.

By the late 1930s, Siegel had become a significant player in a powerful crime syndicate, which gave him $500,000 to start a Los Angeles franchise. Bugsy immersed himself in the Hollywood entertainment scene, making friends with some of the era's brightest stars – Cary Grant, Clark Gable, and Jean Harlow. All-night parties at his Beverly Hills mansion became the hot spot in town. He also started a gambling and narcotics operation to keep his bosses back east happy. Just before World War II began, Siegal traveled to Italy to sell explosives to Mussolini, but the deal fizzled when tests of the explosives did too.

In 1946, Siegel found an opportunity to reinvent his image and diversify into a legitimate business with developer William Wilkerson's Flamingo Hotel. Siegel wrestled control of the Flamingo away from Wilkerson under threat of death, and he went into hiding in Paris for a time. From this point, the Flamingo became syndicate-run.

Siegal was spending money on the hotel like it was going out of style. He wanted the finest structure that money could buy at a time when building materials were in short supply due to WWII. By October 1946, the Flamingo's costs were above $4 million. By 1947, the tally was over $6 million (equivalent to $64 million in 2021). By early December of that year, the work on the hotel was nearly done.

Problems with the Outfit's wire service had cleared up in Nevada and Arizona, but Siegel refused to report business in California. He later announced to his colleagues on the East Coast that he was running the California syndicate by himself and would return the loans in his "own good time." Despite his defiance to mob bosses, they were willing to be patient with him because he had always proven to be a great earner for them.

The Flamingo opened on December 26, 1946, when only the casino, lounge, theater, and restaurant were ready. Although local people attended the grand opening, few celebrities attended due to inclement weather that weekend. There was construction noise and a lobby draped with drop cloths. The desert's first air conditioning system only worked periodically. While the gaming tables were operating, the luxury rooms in the hotel that would have served as the enticement for people to stay and gamble were not ready. As he became more aware of the losses that first night, Siegel became increasingly angry and verbally abusive, even throwing at least one family out of the casino. After two weeks, the Flamingo was $275,000 in the red, and by late January 1947, the whole operation was shut down.

After being given a second chance, Siegel finished the hotel and hired a publicist. The Flamingo reopened on March 1, 1947 – with Lansky present – and immediately began making a profit. However, the mob bosses above Siegel had enough of him by this time, and time was running out. By this point, Siegel had made a name for himself in the annals of organized crime and Las Vegas history.

On the evening of June 20, 1947, while Siegel sat in the home of his mistress, Virginia Hill, in Hollywood, reading the newspaper and in the company of Allen Smiley, an unknown attacker shot at him through the window with a .30 caliber military M1 carbine, hitting him multiple times, including twice in the head. Nobody was ever indicted with the Murder of Siegel, and the crime remains formally unsolved.

Some surmise that Siegel's death was due to his excessive spending and possible theft from the syndicate. In 1946, a gathering was held with the "board of directors" of the mob in Havana, Cuba, so that Luciano, exiled in Sicily, could attend and take part. From the meetings came a resolution to put a hit out on Siegel. Lansky grudgingly agreed with the ruling. There is another theory that posits Siegel was murdered by Mathew "Moose" Pandza, the lover of Moe Sedway's (who was a trusted lieutenant of Meyer Lansky) wife Bee, who begged Pandza to help her after she found out that Siegel was planning to kill her husband. At mob behest, Siegel was supposedly progressively angrier about the power Moe Sedway was exercising over Siegel's assets and intended to execute him. Former Philadelphia family boss Ralph Natale alleged that Frankie Carbo, a known mob hitman, was responsible for murdering Siegel at the behest of Lansky. Some believed Virginia Hill's family was involved in the murder. Hill and her military brother were seen before the Flamingo, arguing about Siegel beating her up. Hill's brother stated that he was going to kill Siegel. Virginia Hill boarded a plane a few days before the shooting and inexplicably flew to Paris.

The day after Siegel's death, the *Los Angeles Herald-Express* showed a photograph on its front page from the morgue of Siegel's bare right foot with a toe tag. Even though Siegel was killed in Beverly Hills, his demise put Las Vegas square into the national spotlight as photographs of his dead body were published in newspapers throughout America. The day after Siegel's death, David Berman and his Las Vegas mob associates, Sedway and Gus Greenbaum, walked into the Flamingo and took control of the operation of the hotel and casino.

JUNE 21
1734

On this day in history, Marie-Joseph Angelique, an enslaved Black woman in Montreal, New France (now Quebec), was tortured and hanged after being convicted on circumstantial evidence of arson in a fire that destroyed Montreal's merchants' quarter. It was alleged that Angelique committed the act while attempting to flee her bondage with her white lover. While it is unknown if she set the fire, Angelique's story has come to symbolize Black resistance and freedom.

Angelique was born around 1705 in Madeira, Portugal. She was later sold to a Flemish man named Nichus Block, who brought her to New England. She lived in New England and was sold in 1725 to a French-Canadian businessman from Montreal named Francois Poulin de Francheville. After he died in 1733, she belonged to his wife, Therese de Couagne. Slavery in New France and New England was primarily a domestic affair since, unlike the southern portion of the United States, the economy was not based on large-scale plantation labor. Angelique subsequently worked in the Francheville home in Montreal and occasionally helped on the family's small farm on the island of Montreal.

Angelique had three children while in Montreal: a boy born in 1731 who lived only one month and twins in 1732 who died within five months. The father listed in the baptismal records was Jacques Cesar, an enslaved Black man from Madagascar who was the property of Ignace Gamelin, a friend of Francheville. It is unknown whether Angelique and Cesar were lovers by choice or whether their owners forced them to procreate (the children of enslaved people became enslaved people and the property of the mother's owners).

After the death of her children, she got involved in a romantic relationship with Francois Thibault, a white servant who also worked for the Francheville widow. The Montreal community disapproved of this union between a Black woman and a white man. During the winter of 1734, the pair planned an escape: they fled together, by night, across the frozen St. Lawrence River. They aimed to reach New England, where they would catch a ship back to Europe. However, after a couple of weeks, they were captured by three constables in the town of Chambly and returned to Montreal.

Angelique was immediately returned to the widow Francheville who did not reprimand her. Thibault, though, was sent to prison. Angelique would visit him and bring him food, much to the chagrin of Madame Francheville. Thibault was liberated two months later, on April 8, 1734, two days before the fire of Montreal.

Soon afterward, Angelique was told she was sold to a new owner in Quebec City once the St. Lawrence River thawed, and Thibault was sent back to prison. She threatened to burn Madame Francheville's house, which unnerved the woman. Thibault, who Francheville had fired after the escape attempt, continued to visit Angelique when her owner was not around.

On the night of April 10, 1734, a large portion of Old Montreal was destroyed by fire. At least 46 buildings, mainly homes, were burnt, plus the convent and the Hotel-Dieu de Montreal. Angelique was accused of starting the fire by police the next day. Angelique was charged and tried. French law then allowed a suspect to be arrested based on "public knowledge" when the community agreed the suspect was guilty. The accused was presumed to be guilty, and in New France, trials by jury did not exist, only inquisitorial tribunals where the defendant had to prove their innocence. Lawyers were prohibited from practicing in the colony by Louis XIV.

Angelique's trial lasted an amazing six weeks. Trials usually lasted two or three days. Twenty-two people testified at the trial, and everyone admitted that they never saw Angelique start the fire, but they were unanimously convinced of her guilt. Only her owner, the widow Francheville stood up for Angelique, sure of her innocence. The problem with this trial was that they had no definitive proof that she started the fire. That is, until a surprise witness appeared from thin air after six weeks of trial: Amable Lemoine Moniere, the five-year-old daughter of Alexis Lemoine, a merchant. The young girl swore under oath that she saw Angelique going to the attic of the Francheville house with a shovel full of coals just before the fire.

This testimony sealed her fate. Angelique was found guilty and condemned to death despite her continually pleading her innocence. She was made to endure the torture of the boot – wood planks bound to the prisoner's legs, squeezing them and crushing the bones – before her execution to make her name her accomplices. Under torture, she admitted the crime, but, begging for mercy and quick death, she maintained she was acting alone. Nevertheless, she refused to name Claude Thibault as co-conspirator and co-arsonist. (The judges believed that Thibault and Angelique had set the fire together.)

After the torture, Angelique, dressed in white chemise and holding a lit torch (the symbol of her crime), was put in a garbage cart and taken to the portal of the Notre Dame Basilica, where she confessed to her crime and begged for God's pardon and pardon of the king and from the people. She was then hanged. The hangman and torturer were Mathieu Leveille, an enslaved Black man employed as a royal executioner. Angelique's body was exhibited on a gibbet for a couple of hours. At 7:00 p.m., her body was put on a pyre and burnt, her ashes gathered and then scattered.

The burning of Montreal and the arrest and trial of Angelique reveals much about the nature of enslavement in Canada, a legal institution that existed for over two hundred years. It is possible that Angelique did not cause the fire. But she made the perfect scapegoat for the crime: she was Black, enslaved, poor, a foreigner, and so in every respect, a social outcast. As an enslaved, Angelique had no rights that New France or white society would respect.

On the other hand, Angelique may have set the fire. She had many grievances against white society in Montreal. Caucasians had enslaved her, taken her freedom and human rights, and removed her from her homeland. In Montreal, she had attempted at least one escape but was thwarted. Centuries later, Marie-Joseph Angelique has become a symbol of Black resistance and freedom.

JUNE 22
1813

On this day in history, upon learning of plans by the American Army to execute a surprise attack at Beaver Dams, Upper Canada, Canadian heroine Laura Secord walks 20 miles (32 km) through hostile terrain to warn British soldiers and their native allies, resulting in a surprise British victory at the Battle of Beaver Dams.

Laura Secord (nee Ingersoll) was born on September 13, 1775, in Great Barrington, Massachusetts, the eldest daughter of Thomas Ingersoll and Elizabeth Dewey. When Laura was eight, her mother died, leaving four daughters. Her father married twice more and had a large family with his third wife. During the American Revolutionary War, Ingersoll fought on the rebel side, but in 1795 he moved to Upper Canada, where he was given a grant for settlement. His homestead became the site of the modern town of Ingersoll, Ontario. He ran a tavern at Queenston until his township (Oxford-upon-Thames) was surveyed. Within two years, about 1797, Laura married James Secord, a young merchant from Queenston. He was the son of a loyalist officer of Butler's Rangers, whose family came to Niagara in 1778. James and Laura Secord eventually have six daughters and one son.

They lived first at St. David's but soon moved to Queenston. James, a sergeant serving in the 1st Lincoln Militia, was injured early in the

War of 1812 while fighting in the Battle of Queenston Heights and was extricated from the battlefield by his wife. The following summer, when neither the Americans nor the British had a firm hold of the Niagara peninsula, Laura heard a conversation, on June 21, 1813, between American officers who had been billeting at her home that the Americans intended to surprise the British outpost at Beaver Dams and capture the officer in charge, Lieutenant James Fitzgibbon. Laura and James felt that it was important that someone warn Fitzgibbons, and since James was still suffering the lingering effects of his injury from the Battle of Queenston Heights, Laura would have to be the one to convey the message the next day to the British.

Laura decided to take an indirect route to Beaver Dams, fearing being captured by Americans or Natives. She first went to St.David's, where her niece, Elizabeth Secord, joined her, and then to Shipman's Corner (St. Catharines). Elizabeth became exhausted and had to stop the journey. Laura continued alone, uncertain of the path ahead but she followed the general direction of Twelve Mile Creek through fields and woods. That evening, Laura came unexpectedly upon an Indian camp. She was afraid, but after she explained her mission to the chief, he agreed to escort her to Fitzgibbon. Two days later, on June 24, 1813, an American force led by Colonel Charles Boerstler was ambushed near Beaver Dams by some 400 Indians led by Dominique Ducharme and William Kerr. Fitzgibbon persuaded Boerstler to surrender with 462 men to his own 47. No mention of Laura Secord's contribution is made in the official reports of the victory.

In the post-war years, the Secords lived in poverty until 1828 when James, receiving a small military pension for his war service, was appointed registrar, then judge (1833), of the Niagara Surrogate Court. In 1835, he became a collector of customs at Chippawa. He died in 1841, leaving Laura without means of support. She ran a school for children from her home for a brief period. Petitions to the government for a pension were unsuccessful.

Laura Secord was 85 years old when she finally achieved widespread public recognition for her heroic deed. While visiting Canada in 1860, Edward, the Prince of Wales (the future Edward VII), became aware of Laura's 20-mile walk. She had completed a memorial for the prince describing her wartime service and placed her signature among those War of 1812 veterans who presented an address to him. After the prince returned to England, he sent Laura a reward of 100 pounds. She died in 1868 at 93 and was interred beside her husband in Drummond Hill Cemetery, Niagara Falls.

Laura Secord became remembered as a heroine in Canadian history, poetry, and drama, after 1860. Legends grew, like when she had a cow on her journey to Fitzgibbon as a diversionary tactic. Another was that she had accomplished the trek barefooted. As popular as these tales had become, they simply were not true. Her widespread fame was such that two monuments were erected in her honor, one at Lundy's Lane in 1901, the other at Queenston Heights in 1910. Her portrait was hung in the halls of the parliament buildings in Toronto, and a memorial hall was built in the Laura Secord School at Queenston.

Some 20th-century historians, however, have questioned her place in history; for example, W. Stewart Wallace, in The Story of Laura Secord: a Study in Historical Evidence (1932), concluded from the available documents that Laura Secord had undoubtedly taken a message to Fitzgibbon, probably on June 23, but that she had arrived in time for her information to be of any value. In his official report on the Battle of Beaver Dams, Lieutenant Fitzgibbon said, "At (John) De Cou's this morning, about seven o'clock, I received information that ... the Enemy ... was advancing towards me...." It was stated that this information, brought by Indian scouts, was Fitzgibbon's first warning. Wallace also cited a certificate written by Fitzgibbon in 1837 testifying that Laura Secord had given notice of an American attack; unfortunately, Fitzgibbon gave no specific date, and he wrote, he stated, "in a moment of much hurry and from memory."

The perplexing chronology and Laura's role in the events were solved when two earlier testimonials came to light, both written by Fitzgibbon in 1820 and 1827, to support petitions the Secords had made to the government. In the 1827 certificate, Fitzgibbon said that Laura had come "on June 22, 1813," and that "in consequence of this information," he had put the Indians in a position to stop the Americans. He clarified that Laura's warning had made the victory possible at Beaver Dams. It was a notable victory, and for her part, Laura Secord became rightly became known as the heroine of the War of 1812.

Laura Secord signified your typical settler woman's endurance, courage, and strength in the face of hardship. Fitzgibbon recalled her as a woman of "slender frame and delicate appearance," but underneath was a strong and persistent will.

JUNE 23
1992

On this day in history, Mafia boss John Gotti, who was labeled the "Teflon Don" after evading untouched from multiple prosecutions during the 1980s, was condemned to life in prison after being found guilty on 14 counts of conspiracy to commit murder and racketeering. Minutes after his verdict was pronounced in a federal courthouse in Brooklyn, hundreds of Gotti's supporters stormed the building. They upended and destroyed cars before being driven back by police units.

John Gotti was born in New York City on October 27, 1940. He was the son of Italian immigrant couple John Joseph Gotti Sr. and Philomena "Fannie" DeCarlo. It was a difficult life with Gotti's father earning a meager living as a day laborer. The family moved often before settling in East New York when Gotti was 12.

Gotti was one of five brothers who were made men in the Gambino crime family. In his formative years, Gotti learned a life of crime by running errands for Carmine Fatico, a capo in the early days of the Gambino crime family. During this time, he first met Aniello Dellacroce, who would ultimately become a lifelong member of the future crime boss.

Gotti quit school when he was 16 and led his mafia-related street gang in his Queens, New York neighborhood called the Fulton-Rockaway Boys, which included future Gambino mobster Angelo Ruggiero.

Gotti would rack up arrests for such petty crimes as street fighting and stealing cars, all before his first significant arrest in 1968 when the FBI charged him, his brother Gene and childhood friend Ruggiero with committing three cargo thefts and truck hijacking near JFK international airport. They all pleaded guilty to reduced charges, and Gotti was given a three-year sentence. After his release in 1971, Fatico gave Gotti control of the crew's illegal gambling operations.

In May 1973, Gotti committed his first murder. As a Fatico crew captain, it was Gotti's job to find Jimmy McBratney, a rival gang member who had killed a member of the Gambino family. The hit squad bungled the abduction at a Staten Island bar, and McBratney was shot dead in front of many witnesses. Because Gotti botched the operation, he was arrested and charged with murder in 1974, receiving a four-year sentence for attempted manslaughter.

Gotti, his wife, three sons, and two daughters lived in a modest Howard Beach home. Frank, Gotti's 12-year-old son, was killed in 1980 after being run into by a car while driving his bicycle by neighbor John Favara. Even though it was ruled an accident, four months after the incident, Favara was seen by witnesses being struck over the head and thrown into a van. Gotti and his family were on vacation at the time in Florida. Favara was never seen again, and Gotti denied knowledge of the vanishing.

Underboss Dellacroce died of cancer in 1985. In a move seen as disrespectful by Gotti, then-boss Castellano did not attend Dellacroce's funeral. Two weeks later, Castellano was gunned down at a restaurant in Manhattan. Gotti was made the boss of the Gambino crime family with Salvatore "Sammy the Bull" Gravano – who would later become a government witness against Gotti – as his underboss. Gravano would later testify in court that he and Gotti watched the shooting of Castellano from a parked car, stating that Gotti had orchestrated the murder.

Under Gotti's leadership, the Gambino family was grossing $500 million a year in proceeds from its enterprises. Gotti declared a personal income of $100,000 annually as a plumbing supply salesman and from his work with a garment accessories company. Mafia informants stated that Gotti routinely took home over $10 million yearly from the family's endeavors. Gravano said that Gotti's annual take at over $1 million from construction industry shakedowns alone.

Gotti was a recognizable public figure, and his whereabouts were easily tracked. By the late 1980s, the FBI had installed listening devices in an apartment above the social club Gotti frequented, recording conversations implicating him, Gravano, and family consigliere Frank Locascio.

Gotti was arrested in December 1990. The FBI not only had taped conversations, but they had Gravano, who made the deal to testify against his old boss after hearing disparaging remarks about himself made by Gotti on tape. The trial was a media sensation, with about 1,000 of Gotti's supporters gathered outside the courthouse at various times.

But Gotti would not get off this time. He was convicted on all 14 counts against him, including federal charges of loan sharking, racketeering, multiple murders, jury tampering, and gambling. Gotti was sentenced to life in prison, while Gravano received a five-year sentence.

The self-styled crime boss spent half his seven-year tenure as head of the Gambino family in jail awaiting trial, the rest trying to avoid prosecution. In prison from 1992 to 2000, Gotti was kept in solitary confinement. In 1998, he was operated on for neck and head cancer that would ultimately claim his life.

Gotti died June 10, 2002, at the federal prison hospital in Springfield, Missouri. He was 61.

Like all things associated with John Gotti, his funeral was a big and bold affair. Twenty-two limousines, 19 flower cars, and hundreds of private vehicles drove the streets of Ozone Park, Howard Beach, and sections of Queens. Gotti was laid out beside his son Frank at St. John Cemetery, a graveyard that is the final resting place of many New York mobsters. Though none, perhaps, as famous as the Dapper Don.

JUNE 24
1812

On this day in history, following the Russian Czar's denunciation of the French Continental System, French Emperor Napoleon Bonaparte ordered his *Grande Armee*, the most significant European military force ever assembled to that date, into Russia. This massive army, featuring nearly 600,000 soldiers, included troops from all European countries under the grip of the French Empire. By this point, the French Emperor had won many military victories, giving him control over much of Europe. However, his invasion of Russia would be a disastrous point in the Napoleonic wars and a significant blow to his political and military power across Europe.

Napoleon Bonaparte (1769-1821) was a French military leader and emperor who conquered much of Europe in the early 19th century. Born on the island of Corsica, Napoleon quickly climbed through the military ranks during the French Revolution (1789-1799). After grasping political power in France in a coup d'état, he crowned himself emperor in 1804. The shrewd, ambitious, and skilled military strategist Napoleon successfully waged war against various European coalitions and expanded his empire. However, the disastrous French invasion of Russia in 1812 contributed to Napoleon's downfall.

Napoleon had always viewed Russia as a natural ally due to its lack of territorial conflicts with France. However, this stance promptly changed when the Russian Czar Alexander I moved against Napoleon. In 1810, Alexander I stopped complying with Napoleon's trade embargo against Britain, known as the continental system. This was due to the adverse effects the prohibition had on Russian trade. Added to this was Alexander I's levy of excessive taxes on French luxury items. On top of this, the Czar refused Napoleon's request to marry one of his sisters.

The formation of the Duchy of Warsaw (also known as Napoleonic Poland) in 1807 set the stage for Russian non-compliance. The formation of Napoleonic Poland increased Russia's fear of a French invasion. It also exacerbated the Czar's worries about anti-Russian sentiment in Poland. His fears came true in 1812 when Napoleon moved a massive army to the borders of Russia in Poland. The size of the army was 600,000 me from all over Europe. It has been described as the most diverse European force since the Crusades.

Understanding the dangers of Russian winters, Napoleon knew that his invasion needed to be quick and decisive. However, he was not expecting the refusal of Russian troops to engage his army near the border or the realities of the harsh Russian terrain.

Napoleon and his army crossed the Nieman River from Poland on June 24, 1812. Instead of engaging the enemy, Russia pulled its 200,00 man army back. By June 27, the French military had quickly captured the city of Vilna. A storm swept over the city that night, bringing freezing rain, hail, and sleet, killing several soldiers and horses. Many troops had also begun to desert the French army in search of food. Despite this, Napoleon marched on.

The Russian forces continued to retreat, leaving nothing but devastation in their wake. The scorched earth tactics were even carried out by peasants, who burned their crops to deny them to the French. The lives of the French soldiers only worsened as they became overwhelmed by typhus and dysentery. While many soldiers were lost during minor battles, most died from these diseases and lack of supplies.

Napoleon's army reached the small village of Borodino, 70 miles from Moscow, on September 7. The Imperial Russian Army met them, and the bloodiest battle of the invasion ensued. It is reported that the fight involved over 200,000 troops from both sides and killed over 70,000 men.

Both armies fought with overwhelming firepower for the times. The battle ended the next day as the Russian army retreated again, leaving the road to Moscow open. While this was another victory for Napoleon, the battle exhausted his forces. This battle was also the last offensive action fought by Napoleon in Russia, becoming a pivotal point in the campaign.

The French arrived in Moscow on September 14, but instead of meeting resistance from Russian soldiers, they were faced with a burning city. The citizens of Moscow were ordered to evacuate by their government. They left very little behind as they escaped the conflagration. Napoleon waited for Alexander I to surrender while the French troops pillaged the empty city. Napoleon and his army stayed in Moscow for over a month, but no peace offer was forthcoming. By October 19, the cold had begun, and Napoleon was forced to leave Moscow.

By this point, Napoleon's army only numbered 100,000. Many had died from disease and small battles, many had left of their own accord, and many died due to the harsh Russian winter.

Throughout November, the humiliating realities of Napoleon's losses were exposed to the world. On December 5, amid rumors of a potential coup, Napoleon left his devastated army. Just over a week later, what was left of Napoleon's *Grand Armee* limped back over the Nieman River.

By the end of 1812, Austria, Prussia, and Sweden reformed their coalition to fight a weakened foe. By the following year, most of Europe had risen up against Napoleon.

Napoleon still managed to raise a large army to fight his new enemies. However, his devastating losses in Russia meant he was short of experienced officers, soldiers, and cavalry. Despite this, the War of the Sixth Coalition ensued.

France managed to win a few battles but was ultimately defeated. In October 1813, the Battle of Leipzig resulted in Napoleon's loss, further weakening his withering control. Paris was eventually captured in March 1814, and Napoleon was pushed into exile on the island of Elba off the coast of Italy. He attempted to regain power again a year later, and with the Battle of Waterloo, Napoleon was defeated for the last time.

Napoleon Bonaparte managed to gain control of most of Europe throughout the Napoleonic wars. But his six-month-long invasion of Russia sparked the beginning of the end for his empire. While his attack was well-planned, the harshness of Russia's seasons, terrain, and clever military tactics would prove devastating. Napoleon's failed invasion would encourage mutiny amongst his allies, ultimately resulting in his downfall, exile, and death.

(Photo: Napoleon watching the fire of Moscow in September 1812, by Adam Albrecht (1841). Wikimedia Commons)

JUNE 25

1876

On this day in history, the Battle of Little Bighorn was fought near the Little Bighorn River in Montana Territory, which pitted American troops led by Lieutenant Colonel George Custer against a force of Lakota Sioux and Cheyenne warriors. Tensions between the two groups had risen since the unearthing of gold in the Black Hills, which was part of Native American lands. When several tribes missed a federal deadline to relocate to reservations, the U.S. Army, including Custer and his 7th Cavalry, was sent to confront them. Custer had been oblivious to the size of Indian forces under the command of Sitting Bull and Crazy Horse at Little Bighorn, and his army was outnumbered and quickly overwhelmed in what became known as Custer's Last Stand.

After gold was discovered in the Black Hills and the U.S. government reneged on previous treaties ceding the land to the Native Americans, many Sioux and Cheyenne tribesmen left their reservations to meet Sitting Bull and Crazy Horse in Montana. By the spring of 1876, more than 10,000 Native Americans had assembled along the Little Bighorn River – called Greasy Grass – in defiance of an American War Department order to return to their reservations or risk being attacked.

In mid-June, three columns of U.S. troops prepared to march

against the native camp. A force of 1,200 Native Americans repulsed the first column on June 17. Five days later, General Alfred Terry ordered George Custer's 7th Cavalry to scout ahead for native forces. On the morning of June 25, Custer marched near the camp and decided to move forward rather than wait for reinforcements.

Custer had divided his more than 600 men into four groups. He ordered one small group to stay with the supply train and the other two, led by Captain Frederick Benteen and Major Marcus Reno, to attack from the south and prevent the tribesmen from escaping. Custer would lead the final group – 210 men strong – and planned to attack from the north.

Reno's men attacked first but quickly embarked on a disorganized retreat after realizing they were completely outnumbered. By the time they had regrouped, at least 30 soldiers had been killed.

Benteen's troops came to Reno's aid, and the combined battalions joined forces on what is now known as Reno Hill. They remained there despite Custer's order: "Benteen. Come on. Big village. Be quick. Bring packs. P.S. Bring packs."

The actual events of Custer's Last Stand are unclear. It is known that neither Benteen nor Reno helped Custer despite later admitting they had heard heavy gunfire coming from Custer's position. Custer and his men faced scores of Native American warriors alone. Some historians believe many of Custer's men panicked, dismounted from their horses, and were shot as they fled.

No one knows when Custer realized he was in trouble since no eyewitness from his command lived to tell the tale. The Sioux and Cheyenne warriors led by Crazy Horse attacked with Winchester, Henry, and Spencer, repeating rifles and bows and arrows. Most of Custer's men were armed with Springfield single-shot carbine rifles and Colt .45 revolvers; they were easily outgunned. Custer's line and command structure quickly collapsed, and soon it was every man for himself.

In the end, Custer found himself on the defensive with nowhere to hide or to run to and was killed along with every other man in his battalion. His body was found near Custer Hill, also referred to as Last

Stand Hill, alongside the bodies of 40 of his soldiers, including his brother and nephew, and dozens of dead horses.

Custer had suffered two bullet wounds, one near his heart and one on his forehead. Once news spread of Custer's demise, many Native Americans claimed to be his executioner.

After the battle, Native American warriors stripped, scalped, and dismembered their enemy's corpses on the battlefield, possibly because they believed the souls of disfigured bodies were doomed to walk the earth forever.

The Battle of Little Big Horn did not end with the massacre of Custer and his men. The Native Americans quickly regrouped and pursued Reno's and Benteen's battalions. The troops fought until General Terry's reinforcements finally arrived. Now it was the Native Americans who were outnumbered, so they packed up camp and fled, bringing the most significant defeat of the U.S. Army during the Plains Indian Wars to an end.

The Sioux and Cheyenne reveled in their victory for a time, but their celebration, as was their freedom, was short-lived. When word of Custer's death reached Americans celebrating their nation's centennial on July 4, they demanded retribution.

The U.S. Army intensified its efforts to hunt down all resisting Native Americans and either wipe them out or force them back onto reservations. Within a year, most had been rounded up or killed.

In May 1877, Crazy Horse surrendered at Fort Robinson, Nebraska, where he was later bayoneted and killed after an altercation with an army officer. After fleeing to Canada, Sitting Bull eventually surrendered in 1881. He lived on Standing Rock Reservation until Native American agent policemen killed him during a conflict at his house in 1890.

The Battle of the Little Bighorn is steeped in controversy. Many people still question Custer's actions on that fateful day. He's often accused of arrogance for not following the original battle plan and leading his men to certain death. Yet it's possible Custer believed reinforcements were on the way and wanted to strike before the Sioux and Cheyenne dispersed; it's unlikely he expected such a well-armed attack.

It's also argued that Reno and Benteen were simply cowards who ignored Custer's orders when the fighting got difficult, leaving Custer and his men to fight a losing battle. In their defense, though, they may have thought that following Custer's orders was simply suicide.

The deceased at the Battle of the Little Big Horn was given a rapid burial when they fell by the first soldiers who arrived on the scene. Custer was later exhumed and reburied at West Point. Other troops were also exhumed for private burials.

(Photo: The Battle of Little Bighorn. Artist unknown. Wikimedia Commons.)

JUNE 26
1541

On this day in history, Spanish conquistador and Governor of Peru Francisco Pizarro is assassinated. He was killed by a group of soldiers led by the son of his former collaborator Diego de Almagro, also a Spanish conquistador, who was killed on Pizarro's orders. It was an internal conflict among the conquistadors over who should rule over certain areas in South America. Francisco Pizarro died in Lima, a city he had founded six years earlier and in which he had his headquarters.

Pizarro was the illegitimate son of a Spanish gentleman, and he served under Spanish conquistador Alonso de Ojeda during his expedition to Columbia in 1510 and was with Vasco Nunez de Balboa when he discovered the Pacific Ocean in 1513. He had heard stories of the great wealth of the Incas in South America, so Pizarro formed an alliance with fellow conquistador Diego de Almagro in 1524 and sailed back to the Americas. Their first expedition only penetrated as far as present-day Ecuador, but their second reached farther and discovered evidence of the existence of the Inca kingdom.

Securing aid from Emperor Charles V and a guarantee that he, not Almagro, would receive the majority of the expedition's future profits, Pizarro sailed to Peru and landed at Tumbes in 1532. He led his army up the Andes Mountains to the Inca City of Cajamarca and met with

Atahualpa, the king of the Inca kingdom of Quito. After winning his trust, Pizarro captured Atahualpa, extracted 24 tonnes of gold and silver as a ransom for his life, and then treacherously had him executed. The conquest of Peru came quickly to Pizarro and his army, and in 1533 Inca resistance ended with their defeat at Cuzco.

Pizarro's partnership with Diego de Almagro had been strained for some time. When Pizarro went to Spain in 1528 to secure royal charters for their expedition, he had acquired the governorship of all lands conquered and a royal title: Almagro only received a title and governorship of Tumbez. He was also promised the conquest of Chile as appeasement by Pizarro for claiming most of the Incan gold. Almagro was furious and nearly refused to participate in their third joint expedition: only the promise of the governorship of Chile and any undiscovered lands made him come around. Almagro never shook the feeling that the Pizarro brothers were trying to take his fair share of the riches from him.

In 1535, after the Inca empire was conquered, the crown decided that the northern half would be given to Pizarro and the southern half to Almagro. However, vague wording allowed both conquistadors to argue that the prosperous city of Cuzco was theirs. Groups steadfast to both men nearly began fighting: Pizarro and Almagro conferred and agreed that Almagro would journey to the south (into present-day Chile). He hoped to find great wealth there and drop his claim to Peru.

Between 1535 and 1537, the Pizarro brothers were busy. Manco Inca, the puppet ruler, escaped and openly rebelled, raising a large army and laying siege to Cuzco. Francisco Pizarro was living in the newly created city of Lima a lot of the time, trying to send soldiers to his brothers and fellow conquistadors in Cuzco while arranging shipments of gold to Spain (he was always diligent about setting aside the "royal fifth," a 20% tax gathered by the crown on all treasure compiled). In Lima, Pizarro had to fight off a ferocious attack led by Inca General Quizo Yupanqui in August 1536.

Cuzco, under siege by Manco Inca in early 1537, was saved by the return of Diego de Almagro from Chile with the remainder of his expedition. He relieved the siege and drove Manco away, only to take possession of the city for himself, detaining Gonzalo and Hernando

Pizarro. The Almagro expedition found the conditions rough in Chile and encountered ferocious natives. Afterward, he came back to demand his share of Peru. Almagro had much support amongst Spaniards, primarily those who had come to Peru too late to share in the wealth: they hoped that if the Pizarros were overthrown that Almagro would reward them with lands and gold.

Gonzalo Pizarro escaped, and Almagro released Hernando during the peace negotiations. With his brothers supporting him, Francisco decided to eliminate his old partner once and for all. He sent Hernando into the mountains with a contingent of conquistadors, and they met Almagro and his forces on April 26, 1538, at the Battle of Salinas. Hernando was victorious, while Almagro was captured, tried, and executed on July 8, 1538. Almagro's execution shocked the Spaniards in Peru, as he had been elevated to nobleman status by the king some years before.

Francisco mainly lived in Lima, administrating his empire for the next three years. Although Diego de Almagro had been defeated, there was still much resentment among late-coming conquistadors against the Pizarro brothers and the original conquistadors, who had left slim pickings after the fall of the Incan Empire. These men rallied around Diego de Almagro, the younger son of Diego de Almagro and a woman from Panama.

On June 26, 1541, in Lima, a group of 20 heavily armed supporters of Diego de Almagro the Younger stormed Francisco Pizarro's palace, assassinating him and forcing a terrified city council to appoint Almagro as the new governor of Peru. Most of Pizarro's guests fled, but a few fought the intruders, numbering between seven and twenty-five. While Pizarro struggled to put on his breastplate, his defenders, including his half-brother Martin de Alcantara, were killed. For his part, Pizarro killed two intruders and ran through a third. While trying to pull his sword out of the opponent, he was stabbed in the throat and then dropped to the floor, where he was stabbed many times. He died within minutes. Diego de Almagro, the Younger, was captured and executed the next year after losing the Battle of Chupas.

JUNE 27
1950

On this day in history, two days after the North Korean People's Army invaded South Korea by crossing the 38th parallel, President Harry S. Truman ordered the U.S. Air Force and Navy to assist the South Koreans in repelling the invaders. He initially refrained from committing ground forces after being advised that North Koreans could be stopped solely by America's superior air and naval power. In addition to ordering U.S. forces to Korea, Truman also deployed the U.S. 7th Fleet to Formosa (Taiwan) to guard against invasion by communist China. He called for accelerating military aid to French forces fighting communist guerrillas in Vietnam.

Truman responded after the U.N. Security Council unanimously called for member nations to provide military assistance to the South Korean government headed by Syngman Rhee after the North Koreans invaded on June 25. North Korea's move caught the government of South Korea off-guard and caused them to retreat southward. The North Koreans ignored the U.N. Security Council's resolution for an "immediate cessation of hostilities" and to withdraw to the 38th parallel. (As a permanent member, the Soviet Union could have exercised a veto had it not been boycotting the council's meetings. The Kremlin had been absent since January 1950 because it held that the People's

Republic of China, the communist-led government on the mainland, rather than the Taiwan-based Republic of China, should hold the seat.)

Rhee and other government officials fled the beleaguered South Korean capital on the same day. Rhee put South Korea's forces under U.N. command as the fighting escalated. In all, 21 United Nations members contributed to the force charged with countering the invasion. The United States provided nearly 90 percent of the military personnel and almost all the funding.

The North Korean invasion came as a considerable shock to the Americans. They felt this was more than a border dispute between two unstable dictatorships in Asia. Instead, it was feared that this was the first step in a communist drive to take over the world. For this reason, non-intervention was not considered an option by many top decision-makers. (in April 1950, a National Security Council report known as NSC-68 recommended that America use military force to "contain" communist expansionism anywhere it was happening, "regardless of the intrinsic strategic or economic value of the lands in question.")

On June 27, President Truman told the nation and the world that America would intervene in the Korean conflict to prevent the conquest of an independent country by communism. Truman suggested that the USSR was behind the affair, carried out by Soviet-made tanks and weapons. Truman's decision was met with overwhelming support from legislators and the American public. Truman did not request a declaration of war, but Congress voted to continue the draft and allowed Truman to call up reservists.

On June 28, the Security Council met again and, in the continued absence of the Soviet Union, passed a U.S. resolution approving the use of force against North Korea. On June 30, Truman agreed to send American ground forces to Korea, and on July 7, the Security Council recommended that all U.N. forces sent to Korea be put under U.S. command. The next day, General Douglas MacArthur was named commander of all U.N. forces in Korea.

In the war's opening months, the U.S.-led U.N. forces swiftly advanced against the North Koreans, but Chinese communist troops entered the war in October, throwing the Allies into a quick retreat. In April 1951, Truman relieved MacArthur of his command after he publicly announced that he would bomb China despite Truman's declared war policy. Truman feared an upsurge in fighting with China would entice the Soviet Union to enter the Korean War.

By May 1951, the communists were forced back to the 38th parallel and remained in that area for the remainder of the conflict. After two years of deliberations, an armistice was agreed to on July 27, 1953, ending the war and re-establishing the 1945 division of Korea that still exists today. Approximately 150,000 soldiers from participating U.N. nations were killed during the Korean War, and nearly one million South Korean civilians died. About 800,000 communist soldiers were killed, and more than 200,000 North Korean civilians died.

The original figure of American soldiers lost – 54,246 killed – became controversial when the Pentagon acknowledged in 2000 that all U.S. soldiers killed worldwide during the Korean War were included in that total. For example, a United States soldier killed in a traffic accident anywhere in the world from June 1950 to July 1953 was counted as a casualty of the Korean War. If these deaths are deducted from the 54,000 total, leaving just the Americans who died (from whatever cause) in the Korean theater of operations, the total number of U.S. dead in the Korean War numbers 36,516. Despite two prisoner-of-war exchanges, Operation Little Switch and Operation Big Switch, 7,800 Americans are still missing in action, while South Korea is still searching for over 124,000 service members.

JUNE 28
1778

On this day in history, Revolutionary War heroine Mary Ludwig Hays, aka "Molly Pitcher," carried water to American troops during the Battle of Monmouth before taking over for her husband operating a cannon on the battlefield after her husband collapsed due to heat exhaustion and was carried off the field.

Mary Ludwig Hays was born in Trenton, New Jersey, in 1754. Her father was George Ludwig, a butcher, and her mother was Maria Margaretha Ludwig. Her father passed away in 1769, and her mother married John Hays the following June. In early 1777, Mary married William Hays, a barber in Carlisle, Pennsylvania.

During the Revolutionary War, William was an artilleryman who enlisted in Proctor's 4th Pennsylvania Artillery, which became Proctor's 4th Artillery of the Continental Army. During the winter of 1777, Mary Ludwig Hays gathered with her husband at the Continental Army's winter camp at Valley Forge, Pennsylvania. She was part of a circle of women, along with Martha Washington, who would wash clothes and blankets and care for the sick and dying soldiers in the camp.

In early 1778, Hays trained as an artilleryman under Baron von Steuben. Mary and the other women, known as camp followers, served as water carriers, carrying water to soldiers who were drilling on the field. Artillerymen also needed water to soak the sponge used to clean sparks and gunpowder out of the barrel after each shot. During this time, Mary probably received her nickname, as troops would shout, "Molly! Pitcher!" whenever they needed her to bring fresh water.

In June 1778, at the Battle of Monmouth, Mary Hays continued to bring water to the soldiers. Just before the battle began, Mary found a spring to serve as her supply. She spent much of the early day bringing water to soldiers and artillerymen, often under heavy fire from British forces. It was sweltering and dry that day, and William Hays collapsed during the battle, suffering from heat exhaustion. As he was taken from the battlefield, Mary jumped into action, took over at William's place at the cannon, and continued to "swab and load" the weapon using her husband's ramrod. A British cannonball flew between her legs and tore off the bottom of her skirt. She exclaimed, "Well, that could have been worse," and returned to loading the cannon.

The battle eventually ended for the day due to darkness. George Washington and his commanders fully expected the fight to resume the next day, but instead, the British withdrew during the night and went to Sandy Hook, New Jersey.

After the battle, Washington inquired about the woman he had viewed loading a cannon on the battlefield. As a reward for her service, Washington issued a warrant to Mary as a non-commissioned officer. Subsequently, she was known as "Sergeant Molly" (women named Mary were often called Molly during the Revolutionary period), a moniker she used for the rest of her life.

At the end of the Revolutionary War, Mary and William Hays returned to Carlisle, Pennsylvania. During this period, Mary gave birth to a son named Johannes. In 1786, William Hays died. In 1793, Mary married another Revolutionary War veteran named John McCauley, who was from the same unit as her late husband. He was a stone cutter for the local Carlisle prison. However, the marriage was unhappy, as McCauley was reputed to have had a vicious temper. McCauley caused Mary to sell the 200 acres of land she had inherited from her husband for a mere $30, which he stole. This caused Mary to fall into financial hardship, and McCauley seems to have left the scene around 1807, leaving Mary to her own devices.

Mary McCauley lived in Carlisle for the remainder of her life. She worked as a general servant for hire, cleaning and painting houses, washing windows, and caring for children and sick people. "Sergeant Molly," as she became known, was often seen wearing a striped skirt, wool stockings, and a ruffled cap. She was well-liked by the town's citizens, even though she "often cursed like a soldier."

In February 1822, the Commonwealth of Pennsylvania granted Mary McCauley an annual pension of $40 for her service. Mary died January 22, 1832, in Carlisle, at 87. She was interred in the Old Graveyard in Carlisle under the name "Molly McCauley."

In 1856, when Mary's son John L. Hays died, his obituary stated that he "was a son of the ever-to-be-remembered heroine, the celebrated "Molly Pitcher," whose deeds of daring are recorded in the annals of the Revolution and over whose remains a monument ought to be erected."

In 1876, the centennial of the American Revolution sparked interest in her story, and the town of Carlisle had a statue of Mary McCauley created, with Mary described as "the Heroine of Monmouth." In 1916, Carlisle established a three-dimensional representation of Molly Pitcher loading a cannon.

(Photo: Mary Ludwig Hays, the heroine of the Battle of Monmouth. Wikimedia Commons)

JUNE 29
1914

On this day in history, Russian mystic and self-proclaimed holy man Grigori Rasputin was attacked during an assassination attempt by a peasant woman who was an adherent of defrocked Russian priest Hieromonk Iliodor, in his home village of Pokrovskoye, Western Siberia.

Rasputin's attacker was Jian Guseva, a 33-year-old woman from Tsaritsyn (now Volgograd) with no nose. She testified that she never suffered from syphilis but "was damaged by medicines" since she was 13. She attempted to assassinate Rasputin in his home village on Sunday, June 29, 1914.

Grigori Rasputin, a friend of Czar Nicholas II of Russia and the Czarina, was staying with his family in his village, along the Tura River, in Western Siberia. After having dined on the afternoon of June 29, Rasputin left his house. He had just received a telegram and was on his way to reply when he was attacked by Guseva, who drove a knife into his stomach. After the attack, Guseva screamed, "I have killed the Antichrist!". Not yet deceased, Rasputin was pursued throughout the village by Guseva in order to finish the task. He hit her strongly with a rod, and a crowd gathered, chanting, "Let's kill her!" She turned herself over to the local constabulary and was placed on trial. After seven weeks, Rasputin recovered.

Guseva was a follower of Iliodor, a former priest who had supported Rasputin before denouncing his sexual escapades and self-aggrandizement in December 1911. A radical conservative and anti-semite, Iliodor had been part of a circle of establishment figures who had tried to come between the royal family and Rasputin in 1911. When the effort failed, Iliodor was banished from Saint Petersburg and was ultimately defrocked. Guseva maintained that she had acted alone, having learned about Rasputin in the newspapers and believing he was a "false prophet and even an Antichrist." Both the police and Rasputin, however, thought that Iliodor had instigated the attempt on Rasputin's life. Iliodor fled the country by going to Norway. Guseva was found to be not guilty by reason of insanity and was placed in an asylum in Tomsk until March 15, 1917. Then she was then released by order of Alexander Kerensky. She attempted and failed another assassination attempt, this time on Patriarch Tikhon of Moscow, in 1919. The fate of Guseva after 1919 is unknown, and her date of death is unclear.

Born into a Siberian peasant family in the late 1860s, Rasputin received little schooling and probably never learned to read or write. In his early years, some people in his village said he possessed supernatural powers, while others cited examples of extreme cruelty.

Rasputin entered the Verkhoture Monastery in Russia intending to become a monk, but he left shortly afterward, presumably to get married. At age 19, he wed Proskovia Fyodorovna, and they later had three children. In his early 20s, Rasputin abandoned his family and went to Greece and the Middle East, making several pilgrimages to the Holy Land.

In 1903, his wanderings took him to Saint Petersburg, where he brought a reputation as a mystic and faith healer. Within a couple of years, he was introduced to Czar Nicholas II and his wife, Alexandra Fedorovna, who were seeking help for their son, who was ill with hemophilia. Rasputin rapidly gained their trust by seemingly curing the boy of his illness. This won him the zealous support of the Czarina.

Many of the royal family's opponents used Rasputin's association with them to undercut the Romanov's credibility and push for reforms.

Rasputin aided their cause by declaring he was the Czarina's advisor, and reports of his unrestrained lustful conduct surfaced in the press, deepening disdain among state officials. In truth, however, Rasputin's influence at this time was limited to the health of Alexis.

When Russia entered the Great War, Rasputin foresaw that disaster would happen to the nation. The Czar took command of the Russian Army in 1915, and Alexandra took charge of domestic affairs. Always Rasputin's champion, she sacked ministers who were said to be distrustful of the "mad monk." Government officials attempted to warn her of Rasputin's excessive influence, but she continued to defend him, giving the sense that Rasputin was her strongest counselor.

On December 29, 1916, a group of conspirators, including the Czar's first cousin, Grand Duke Dmitri Pavlovich, and Prince Felix Yusupov, invited Rasputin to Yusupov's palace and gave him wine and cakes laced with cyanide. Though Rasputin ultimately became drunk, the poison appeared to have no impact on him. Perplexed but not discouraged, the collaborators chose to shoot Rasputin numerous times. He was then packaged in a carpet and tossed into the Neva River, where his body was discovered three days later.

Even though Rasputin was dead, his final prophecy was yet to unfold. Just before his death, Rasputin wrote to the Czar to forecast that the Russian people would assassinate the entire royal family if government officials killed him. His prediction came true 15 months later when murderers massacred the Czar, his wife, and all their children during the Russian Revolution.

JUNE 30
1704

On this day in history, six men, including Captain John Quelch from the Brigantine *Charles*, were hanged in the first trial for piracy by the British Admiralty outside of England.

In July 1703, Governor Joseph Dudley of Boston sent Captain Daniel Plowman of the *Charles* with a privateering license to attack French and Spanish ships off the coast of Newfoundland and Acadia. John Quelch was the lieutenant commander of the *Charles*. Captain Plowman had come down with an illness that caused the ship's owners to order him to stand down until a replacement could be found. Plowman and the crew decided to leave Marblehead, Massachusetts, anyway. At this point, for unknown reasons, the crew committed mutiny against Plowman and locked him in his quarters. The uprising was led by John Quelch, whom the crew elected as their new captain. Not long after, former Captain Plowman was thrown overboard, either dead or alive; it is not known which.

Although John Quelch is a famous pirate, his time of piracy was short-lived. Although a treaty alliance was signed between England and Portugal on May 16, 1703, Quelch and his crew captured nine ships under Portugal's rule off the coast of Brazil, and from them, looted goods, guns, money, and at least two enslaved blacks. It is likely that Quelch knew about the treaty but attacked the ships anyway as an act of piracy and defiance. Though capturing nine ships in such a short time is impressive, they were not his most valuable prize. Sometime between November 1703 and May 1704, John Quelch came across a shipwreck in the West Indies where he found what all pirates hoped for – gold. This gold made John Quelch's name go down in history, eventually leading to his trial and death.

In May 1704, John Quelch and his crew anchored the *Charles* back in Marblehead. Soon after, rumors of Captain Quelch's successful adventures spread, and the Boston News-Letter published an article about the gold on May 22. This intrigued the *Charles'* previous owners as it brought up questions about what had happened – the ship left with one captain but returned with another and much illicit loot. On May 24, the Lieutenant-Governor of Boston, who had also caught on, declared that John Quelch and his crew were "violently suspected to have gotten and obtained (the gold) by felony and piracy." This announcement led Quelch's crew to scatter throughout the New England coast.

Quelch claimed that he and his crew had found a treasure during the recovery of a wreck in the West Indies to hide his ransacking of Portuguese ships and account for the bountiful rewards he returned with. But the owners knew this story was false since they had yet to receive notification from any port in the West Indies that their vessel had been seen in the vicinity.

Acting on their intuition, the owners of the Charles complained to the Attorney-General, and a manhunt began to find Quelch and his crew members. Within two days, Quelch and six crew members were arrested, and others were soon to follow. The Governor also sought to confiscate the gold that Quelch brought to Massachusetts and recovered seventy ounces and the same amount of silver. Ultimately, 25 of the 43 pirates were captured with considerable treasure, ensuring that handsome rewards would be handed out to the informers and the officials involved in bringing the pirates before a magistrate.

The captured pirates were rapidly brought before a judge in Boston on June 3, 1704. Quelch was prosecuted for perpetrating murder, piracy, and robbery, and two crew members of the plundered ships testified about how Quelch and the pirates had attacked and killed the captains and crew of the Portuguese vessels.

In the end, Quelch and six other pirates were sentenced to death. The rest were imprisoned for a year until they finally received royal pardons. On June 30, 1704, the seven pirates condemned to hang walked in procession from the prison down to Scarlet's wharf with the Silver Oar carried in front of them. They were loaded on a boat and taken to their place of execution in Boston.

Thousands of people assembled to witness the executions. Quelch climbed up to the scaffold and said to the minister, "I am not afraid of death, I am not afraid of the gallows, but I am afraid of what follows; I am afraid of a great God and a judgment to come." But his fears seemed to disappear once he reached the stage spotlight because he tore off his hat and bowed to the audience. Rather than show remorse when the minister called upon Quelch to address the gathered crowd, he declared, "Gentlemen, but little I have to speak; what I have to say is this, I desire to be informed for what I am here, I am condemned only upon circumstances. I forgive all the world: So the Lord be merciful to my soul." And while one pirate warned the crowd about socializing with lousy company, Quelch said, "They should also take care how they brought money into New England, to be hanged for it."

One of the pirates received a reprieve at the last minute, but the remaining six did not. As was the tradition with pirates after execution, the six corpses were placed in gibbets and stayed in them until they decayed and eventually disappeared.

(Photo: Captain John Quelch from the 1933 World Wide Gum Co. "Sea Raiders" trading card series. Wikimedia Commons.)

THE END

www.ingramcontent.com/pod-product-compliance
Lightning Source LLC
Chambersburg PA
CBHW071732150426
43191CB00010B/1542